Studien zum
Bank-, Börsen- und Kapitalmarktrecht

Herausgegeben von

Prof. Dr. Dr. h.c. Ulrich Immenga
Prof. Dr. Lars Klöhn, LL.M.
Prof. Dr. Daniel Zimmer, LL.M.

Band 75

Konstantin Oppolzer

Ring-Fencing in Europe

The EU's Bank Structural Reform and a Legal Comparative Look at National Legislation in Europe's Three Financial Capitals

Nomos

The prepress was supported by the Swiss National Science Foundation (SNSF).

FNSNF

SCHWEIZERISCHER NATIONALFONDS
ZUR FÖRDERUNG DER WISSENSCHAFTLICHEN FORSCHUNG

This publication is a Ph.D. dissertation accepted by the University of St.Gallen, School of Management, Economics, Law, Social Sciences and International Affairs under the title "Ring-Fencing in Europe – The EU's Rocky Path Towards Bank Structural Reform and a Legal Comparative Look at National Legislation Concerning Structural Reform in Europe's Three Financial Capitals". The public defence of the dissertation took place on September 27, 2018.

The Deutsche Nationalbibliothek lists this publication in the Deutsche Nationalbibliografie; detailed bibliographic data are available on the Internet at http://dnb.d-nb.de

a. t.: St. Gallen, School of Management, Economics, Law, Social Sciences and International Affairs, Diss., 2019

ISBN 978-3-8487-6229-3 (Print)
978-3-7489-0345-1 (ePDF)

British Library Cataloguing-in-Publication Data
A catalogue record for this book is available from the British Library.

ISBN 978-3-8487-6229-3 (Print)
978-3-7489-0345-1 (ePDF)

Library of Congress Cataloging-in-Publication Data
Oppolzer, Konstantin
Ring-Fencing in Europe
The EU's Bank Structural Reform and a Legal Comparative Look at National Legislation in Europe's Three Financial Capitals
Konstantin Oppolzer
342 pp.
Includes bibliographic references.

ISBN 978-3-8487-6229-3 (Print)
978-3-7489-0345-1 (ePDF)

1st Edition 2019

Published by
Nomos Verlagsgesellschaft mbH & Co. KG
Waldseestraße 3-5 | 76530 Baden-Baden
www.nomos.de

Production of the printed version:
Nomos Verlagsgesellschaft mbH & Co. KG

Waldseestraße 3-5 | 76530 Baden-Baden

Printed and bound in Germany.

ISBN 978-3-8487-6229-3 (Print)
978-3-7489-0345-1 (ePDF

DOI: https://doi.org/10.5771/9783748903451

Acknowledgements

I especially wish to thank Prof. Dr. Dr. Peter Sester for his supervision of my thesis, his guidance regarding my research plans, his profound knowledge and for supporting me by making available his extensive network of high-level experts in academia and the industry. I furthermore want to thank Prof. Dr. Brändli for co-supervising the dissertation and for providing valuable inspirations over the course of this project.

In addition, I want to express my gratitude to Prof. Geoffrey P. Miller at NYU Law and to the many experts in academia and the industry who contributed to this dissertation through interviews, background talks and guidance and who have provided phenomenal support to me in writing this dissertation.

I am furthermore very grateful to the *Heinrich Graf Hardegg´sche Stiftung* for its generous funding and to the *Interessengemeinschaft Sanierungsrecht* and *ReTurn Forum für Restrukturierung und Turnaround* for awarding my thesis with the Austrian Award for Reconstruction Management and Insolvency Law. In addition, I want to thank the *Swiss National Fund* for providing generous funding for the publication of this dissertation.

I wish to thank every single one of the friends and colleagues who have consistently encouraged and motivated me and who at the same time always provided welcome distractions, which I will cherish forever. I am furthermore very grateful to my girlfriend Caroline for her love and support and the great time had over the course of this project.

Finally, thanks go to my parents, my brother and to the rest of my family, who have provided unwavering and solid support throughout my life.

Konstantin Oppolzer
Zurich
October 2019

Abstract

This dissertation explores structural reforms for banks that stipulate the separation of deposit-taking and other services considered vital to the real economy from certain investment banking activities deemed particularly risky with the aim of, *inter alia*, mitigating systemic risk and the too-big-to-fail problem. These structural reforms can collectively be referred to as "ring-fencing". The focus of the dissertation is on the legal developments on a European Union level and in the United Kingdom, Germany and Switzerland, which are home to Europe's most important financial centres.

The dissertation is divided into three parts: In its first part, it establishes a concept and a definition of ring-fencing that allow to distinguish it from related bank structural reforms. In its second part, it assesses legislative steps already taken in the European Union and the withdrawal of the file by the European Commission and discusses potential alternatives for installing a union-wide ring-fence. In its third part, a legal comparative analysis is conducted, discussing conceptual differences in national bank structural reform legislation in the United Kingdom, Germany and Switzerland and exploring whether the countries adopted legislation that matches the concept and definition of ring-fencing established in the first part.

Altogether, the dissertation contributes to the terminology and classification of existing and future ring-fencing initiatives and paints a comprehensive picture of current developments and prospects on EU level. It furthermore highlights structural differences of national approaches of Europe's three most important financial centres, and casts light on Switzerland's unique yet barely recognized ring-fencing efforts.

Zusammenfassung

Die vorliegende Dissertation befasst sich mit Bankenstrukturreformen, welche eine Trennung des Einlagengeschäfts und anderer für das Funktionieren der Realwirtschaft unentbehrlicher Dienstleistungen von bestimmten als besonders risikoreich erachteten Aktivitäten des Investmentbanking vorsehen. Sie können zusammenfassend als „Ring-Fencing" bezeichnet werden und bezwecken es unter anderem, systemische Risiken und das Too-Big-to-Fail Problem zu reduzieren. Das Hauptaugenmerk der Dissertation liegt auf den einschlägigen rechtlichen Entwicklungen in der Europäischen Union sowie auf den Regelungen Europas wichtigster Finanzplätze: dem Vereinigten Königreich, Deutschland und der Schweiz.

Die Dissertation ist in drei Teile gegliedert: Im ersten Teil werden ein Konzept und eine Definition von Ring-Fencing erstellt, welche es erlauben, Ring-Fencing von anderen verwandten Bankenstrukturreformen zu unterscheiden. Im zweiten Teil, werden die bereits erfolgten Gesetzgebungsschritte der EU-Bankenstrukturreform sowie ihr Scheitern im europäischen Gesetzgebungsprozess diskutiert und mögliche Alternativen für die Einführung eines unionsweiten Ring-Fencing ausgelotet. Im dritten Teil werden konzeptuelle Unterschiede zwischen nationalen Bankenstrukturreformen im Vereinigten Königreich, Deutschland und der Schweiz aus rechtsvergleichender Perspektive erarbeitet und es wird überprüft, ob die in den Staaten erlassenen Rechtsakte das im ersten Teil erfasste Konzept und die Definition von Ring-Fencing erfüllen.

In Ihrer Gesamtheit trägt die Dissertation zur Abgrenzung der Begrifflichkeiten und der Systematik von bestehenden und zukünftigen Ring-Fencing Regelungen bei und zeichnet ein umfassendes Bild der gegenwärtigen Entwicklungen sowie möglicher Perspektiven auf Ebene des Unionsrechts. Weiters beleuchtet sie strukturelle Unterschiede zwischen bestehenden nationalen Regelungen in Europas drei wichtigsten Finanzplätzen und wirft Licht auf die einzigartigen aber international wenig beachteten Schweizerischen Ring-Fencing-Bestrebungen.

Résumé

Cette dissertation explore les réformes structurelles prisent par les banques prévoyant de séparer la collecte de dépôts et d'autres services considérés essentiels pour l'économie réelle de certaines activités de banque d'investissement considérées particulièrement risquées, avec le but, *inter alia*, de diminuer le risque systématique et le problème corollaire de « too-big-to-fail ». Ces réformes structurelles peuvent être collectivement désignées de « ring-fencing ». Cette dissertation se focalise essentiellement sur les développements légaux au niveau de l'Union Européenne, de l'Allemagne, du Royaume Uni et de la Suisse, où se trouvent les centres financiers les plus importants d'Europe.

La dissertation est divisée en trois parties : Dans la première partie, elle établit un concept et une définition de « ring-fencing », qui permettent de le différencier d'autres réformes structurelles voisines. Dans la seconde partie, elle examine les étapes législatives que l'Union Européenne a déjà entamées ainsi que le retrait du dossier par la Commission Européenne et évalue ensuite des alternatives potentielles pour une réalisation d'une « ring-fence » au sein de l'Union Européenne. Dans la troisième partie, une comparaison juridique est établie permettant de discuter les différences conceptuelles existant dans les législations concernant les réformes structurelles des banques du Royaume Uni, de l'Allemagne et de la Suisse. En outre, elle explore si les pays en question ont adopté une législation se rapprochant du concept et de la définition de « ring-fencing » qui fut établie dans la première partie.

En somme, la dissertation contribue à la terminologie et à la classification des initiatives actuelles et ultérieures de « ring-fencing » et donne une présentation globale des développements présents et futurs au niveau de l'Union Européenne. De plus, elle souligne les différences structurelles existant dans les démarches nationales des trois centres financiers les plus importants d'Europe et met en lumière les uniques, mais à peine reconnus, efforts en matière de « ring-fencing » pris par la Suisse.

Table of Contents

List of Abbreviations

BaFin	German Federal Financial Supervisory Authority
BCBS	Basel Committee on Banking Supervision
BoE	Bank of England
BRRD	Bank Recovery and Resolution Directive
cf.	compare with
CRD	Capital Requirements Directive
CRR	Capital Requirements Regulation
D-SIB	Domestic systemically important bank
e.g.	for example
EBA	European Banking Authority
ECB	European Central Bank
ECJ	European Court of Justice
ECON	European Parliament Committee on Economic and Monetary Affairs
EEA	European Economic Area
EFD	Swiss Federal Department of Finance
et seqq.	et sequentia, and those which follow
EU	European Union
FCA	UK Financial Conduct Authority
Finma	Swiss Financial Market Supervisory Authority
FSB	Financial Stability Board
FSMA 2000	Financial Services Markets Act 2000
G-SIB	Global systemically important bank
GDP	Gross domestic product
GLBA	Gramm-Leach-Bliley Act
GSA	Glass-Steagall Act
GVA	Gross value added
i.e.	id est, that is
OECD	Organisation for Economic Co-operation and Development
PRA	UK Prudential Regulation Authority

RRP	Recovery and resolution plans
SNB	Swiss National Bank
SRB	Single Resolution Board
SRMR	Single Resolution Mechanism Regulation
TBTF	too-big-to-fail
TFEU	Treaty on the Functioning of the European Union
UK	United Kingdom
VR	Volcker Rule

Introduction

I. Overview

After the economic meltdown of 2008 it has been widely recognized that the crisis was not just the effect of greedy bankers, but of an unsound system which now needs to undergo far-reaching changes. The broad consensus in politics and the public was that the conditions leading to the economic crisis had to be revised in order to prevent it from happening again. Among the multitude of reforms aiming to achieve that, one of the most controversial ones is structural reform. Ring-fencing has become a buzzword for certain structural reform measures: in order to protect deposits and services considered vital to the real economy, it has been proposed to separate these services from investment banking and other financially risky activities. Alternatively, it has been proposed to separate certain investment banking activities deemed particularly risky from the rest of the bank. Both concepts aim to mitigate systemic risk and the too-big-to-fail problem and should ultimately lead to more stability, less risk taking and the effect that tax payer bailouts can be avoided.

This dissertation establishes a concept and definition of ring-fencing that allows to distinguish it from related bank structural reforms. While ring-fencing legislation has been implemented in many countries, the focus of this dissertation is on the legal developments on a European Union level and on national structural reform legislation of Europe's three most important financial players: the United Kingdom, Germany and Switzerland. Regarding the European Union, it assesses legislative steps already taken and the withdrawal of the file by the European Commission and discusses potential alternatives for installing a union-wide ring-fence. Regarding the three countries of interest, it conducts a legal comparative analysis, discussing conceptual differences in national bank structural reform legislation and exploring whether the countries adopted legislation that matches the established concept and definition of ring-fencing, which is especially important regarding Switzerland's unique approach.

II. Current State of Scientific Research

Assessing the state of scientific research, one finds many academic articles discussing the various structural reforms. Many of these cover the legislation in the United States in particular. One of the reasons for this may be that in the United States, the discussion about the separation of traditional commercial banking and investment banking is especially fierce due to the country's historical experience with the Glass-Steagall Act.[1] The Volcker Rule of the USA Dodd-Frank Act,[2] which was introduced as part of the post-crisis regulatory framework, is criticised heavily in academic literature. Another reason may be that the United States adopted its structural reform legislation earlier than its European counterparts. In Europe, the so-called Vickers Report[3] concerning structural reform in the United Kingdom was the first to receive worldwide attention. Its ring-fencing proposal was implemented to a large extent by the UK Banking Reform Act 2013,[4] which has remained a topic of discussion up until today. On a European Union level, the so-called Liikanen Report[5] and the draft regulation of the European Commission[6] have been subject of scientific debate. The negoti-

1 "Glass-Steagall Act" is a popular term for certain provisions of the Banking Act of 1933, Public Law 73–66, 73d Congress, H.R. 5661. Most authors consider it to refer to Sects. 16, 20, 21, 32 of the Banking Act of 1933, (e.g. *Masciandaro/Suardi* (2014) Public Interest and Lobbies, 308; *Pace* (2012) Business of Banking, 12; *Manasfi* (2013) Systemic Risk, 185 Fn 9); *Wilmarth* also includes Sec. 5(c) (*Wilmarth* (2005) Universal Banks, 564 Fn 8). This provision extends the securities limitations for national banks on state-chartered banks (see *Carpenter/Murphy* (2010) Permissible Securities Activities, 5 Fn 27).

2 "Volcker Rule" refers to Sec. 619 of the Wall Street Reform and Consumer Protection Act, Public Law 111–203, 111th Congress, H.R. 4173, July 21, 2010, which is commonly known as the Dodd-Frank Act.

3 *ICB* (2011) Vickers Report. While the official title of the report is "Final report of the Independent Commission on Banking", it is usually referred to as the "Vickers Report", named after *John Vickers,* who chaired the *Independent Commission on Banking.*

4 Financial Services (Banking Reform) Act 2013, c. 33.

5 *HLEG* (2012) Liikanen Report. While the official title of the report is "Final report of the High Level Expert Group on reforming the structure of the EU banking sector" it is usually referred to as "Liikanen Report", named after *Erkki Liikanen*, Governor of the Bank of Finland, who chaired the expert group.

6 *European Commission*, Proposal for a Regulation of the European Parliament and of the Council on structural measures improving the resilience of EU credit institutions, COM(2014) 43 final (*European Commission* (2014) Proposal for a Regulation).

ating stance of the Council of the European Union[7] has not attracted comparable attention. The recently announced decision by the European Commission to withdraw the Bank Structural Reform has been discussed sparsely, alternative ways of imposing a ring-fence are expected to become more important in the discussion. In Germany the Trennbankengesetz,[8] which translates a number of recommendations of the EU's Liikanen Report into German Law has been discussed heavily. The exceptional Swiss Too-Big-To-Fail legislation[9] has mainly been discussed within the country and has received little attention abroad.

There are also numerous articles comparing the different approaches. They mostly include a detailed description of the United States' approach and are thus usually restricted by the length of an article. As structural reform legislation is constantly evolving, many articles do not refer to the current legal situation. Especially with regards to national legislation in Germany, the United Kingdom and Switzerland, a methodical legal comparison such as the one described by *Zweigert/Kötz*[10] is missing in the scientific debate.

Despite the importance of the topic, there are few dissertations on the subject, let alone ones taking a comparative view on the different structural reforms in Europe.[11]

7 *Council of the EU,* Proposal for a Regulation of the European Parliament and of the Council on structural measures improving the resilience of EU credit institutions, 10150/15 (*Council of the EU* (2015) Negotiating Stance).

8 Gesetz zur Abschirmung von Risiken und zur Planung der Sanierung und Abwicklung von Kreditinstituten und Finanzgruppen, August 7, 2013, Bundesgesetzblatt Part I, 3090 (German Ring-fencing Act).

9 See, in particular, Art. 8(1), Art. 9(2)(d) Bundesgesetz über Banken und Sparkassen, November 8, 1934, SR 952.0 (Swiss Banking Act); Art. 60 et seqq. Verordnung über die Banken und Sparkassen, April 30, 2014, SR 952.02 (Swiss Banking Ordinance). See also *Expertenkommission* (2010) Schlussbericht.

10 *Zweigert/Kötz* (1996) Rechtsvergleichung, 4, 42; See also *Zweigert/Kötz* (1998) Comparative Law 5, 43–44.

11 An interesting dissertation comparing the Swiss too-big-to-fail regime to the United Kingdom ring-fencing rules is *Hofer* (2014) Structural Reforms. However, since 2013 the situation in both countries has evolved and therefore requires new research. *Hofer* furthermore undertakes a very detailed review of Swiss legislation, whereas the intent of this dissertation is to outline the major differences of the national approaches, allowing to acquire an understanding for each nation's plan for structural reform while ensuring that the reader does not lose perspective of the bigger picture. A dissertation comparing a wide range of structural reforms is *De Vogelaere* (2016) Bank Structure Reforms. Due to the wide scope of the legal comparative analysis (Belgium, Germany, France, U.S., UK, EU and the respec-

Considering the terminology, one finds significant ambiguities. While some authors use the terms "ring-fencing",[12] "ring fencing",[13] "ringfencing",[14] "activities-oriented ring-fencing",[15] or "functional ring-fencing",[16] others describe the concept simply as "structural reform".[17]

From the perspective of economics, there is extensive research on various topics connected to ring-fencing such as on implicit subsidies[18] and on economies of scale and scope for banks.[19]

It can therefore be concluded that there is neither a comparable up-to-date examination of the EU's rocky path towards structural reform, nor a comparable comparative legal analysis of national legislations concerning structural reform in Germany, the United Kingdom and Switzerland.

III. Research Problem

In the years before the global economic crisis, there had been large changes in the realm of international banking. Due to a number of factors, financial institutions had become bigger in size and scope, more complex and more interconnected.[20]

---

tive preparatory works), its findings are limited. It furthermore only takes into account a fraction of the available academic literature on the topic.

12 See e.g. *Schwarcz* (2013) Ring-Fencing; *Hardie/Macartney* (2016) EU Ring-Fencing; *Zaring* (2014) Ring-Fencing.

13 See e.g. *Masciandaro/Suardi* (2014) Public Interest and Lobbies.

14 See e.g. *Brown* (2014) With this Ring, I Thee Fence.

15 See *Binder* (2015) Ring-Fencing; *Binder* (2014) To ring-fence or not, and how?.

16 See e.g. *D'Hulster* (2014) Ring-Fencing, 2 Fn 2.

17 See e.g. *Krahnen/Noth/Schüwer* (2016) Structural Reforms; *Guynn/Kenadjian* (2015) Structural Solutions. This dissertation falls in line with the original use of the word, namely "ring-fencing".

18 For an overview of various studies attempting the difficult quest of assessing implicit subsidies see e.g. *European Commission* (2014) Impact Assessment Part 2, Annex A4.1.

19 For an overview of various studies on the mentioned topics see e.g. *Gambacorta/Van Rixtel* (2013) Structural Bank Regulation Initiatives, 8–9; *HLEG* (2012) Liikanen Report, 130 et seqq.

20 *HLEG* (2012) Liikanen Report, 88; see also e.g. *Blundell-Wignall/Wehinger/Slovik* (2010) The Elephant in the Room, 16–17 (noting that G-SIBs looked more like *"large highly-leveraged hedge funds"* than banks); *Martel/Van Rixtel/Mota* (2012) Business Models of International Banks, 99 (underscoring the intensified *"internationalisation of the banking industry"*); *Laeven/Ratnovski/Tong* (2014) Systemic Risk, 7 et seqq. (discussing bank growth); *Boot/Ratnovski* (2012) Banking and

The economic meltdown of 2008 was followed by an unprecedented wave of bailouts in the United States and Europe. Taxpayer money was used to rescue banks that had run into difficulties due to tremendous losses suffered because of speculation with complex financial products. Often governments felt to have little choice in the matter of bailing out banks to secure the provision of services considered vital to the real economy and to prevent a run on banks' deposits.[21]

The central problem ring-fencing rules are meant to address is therefore the danger that depositors' savings and the provision of services considered vital to the real economy are jeopardized by risky activities.[22]

Ring-fencing aims to insulate these functions from functions deemed riskier and less important.[23] Banks shall be kept from risking their deposits and their ability to provide important services in order to prevent negative consequences for the financial system as a whole and to ensure the continuity of financial services.[24]

Proponents of ring-fencing claim its implementation would tackle various problems in today's financial world: ring-fencing can protect desired

---

Trading, 4 (underscoring that in Europe banks overexposed themselves to trading); *Blundell-Wignall/Atkinson/Roulet* (2013) Bank Business Models, 76–77 (discussing the *"extreme systemic importance"* of G-SIBs); *Boot* (2014) Financial Sector, 131 (describing the *"increased fluid and complex nature of the banking industry"*).

21 See *Lehmann* (2014) Ring-Fencing, 2–3. For Switzerland see e.g. *Schiltknecht* (2010) "Too Big to Fail", 435. History has shown that politicians *"have proven unable to resist the temptation of 'bailouts'"* (*Sester* (2010) Bank Restructuring Law, 515); This willingness to bail out banks has been examined in numerous studies, (for a good overview of factors influencing governments" bailout decision, see Hofer (2014) Structural Reforms, 114 et seqq.). Between 2008 and 2016, the EU Member States alone spent 653.8 billion € on capital-like aid instruments and 1.3 trillion € on liquidity aid instruments. In 2016, state aid was at its lowest since the beginning of the financial crisis. It was also the first year in which no recapitalisations were needed (*European Commission*, State Aid Scoreboard 2017, http://ec.europa.eu/competition/state_aid/scoreboard/index_en.html; see also *European Parliament* (2013) Report on Structural Reform, 4).

22 Cf. *Gambacorta/Van Rixtel* (2013) Structural Bank Regulation Initiatives, 1 (using the term "structural reform"). See also *ICB* (2011) Vickers Report, 11; On European Union level, the protection of the activities mentioned above is not emphasized as the key objective and is mostly noted together with other benefits, presented in the next paragraph (see *European Commission* (2014) Proposal for a Regulation, 15 Sec. 12); The Swiss too-big-to-fail legislation also stresses the importance of the continuation of systemically relevant services (Art. 8(1), Art. 9(2)(d) Swiss Banking Act; see *Bahar/Peyer* (2013) Systemrelevante Banken 409).

23 Cf. *Gambacorta/Van Rixtel* (2013) Structural bank regulation initiatives, 1.

24 *Proctor* (2014) International Banking, 16.

activities from losses incurred in other areas of operation. It can end the subsidisation of risky activities by means meant to support desired activities, such as central bank lending facilities and deposit guarantee schemes. It may readjust costs of risk-taking and decrease moral hazard in other areas of operations. Furthermore, it may reduce the complexity as well as potentially the size of banks, which would improve their manageability, transparency, and resolvability. It may further keep the aggressive risk culture of certain areas of operation away from desired activities. All of these benefits would reduce the probability of future tax payer bailouts.[25] Ring-fencing may therefore tackle systemic risk and the too-big-to-fail problem.[26]

Since the financial crisis, many countries have decided to adopt legislation implementing a ring-fence. Although mostly guided by the same principles, the various approaches differ considerably. While the EU structural reform of banking was recently announced to be withdrawn following failure to reach an agreement in the European Parliament,[27] it has strongly influenced the academic and political discourse and thus developments on a national level. Due to the advanced stage in the legislative process, it will remain a benchmark for future structural reform proposals both in the EU and abroad. Alternative ways of imposing a ring-fence are expected to become more important: certain provisions of the BRRD[28] and the SRMR[29] are considered potential gateways for union-wide ring-fencing,[30] and may approximate the EU solution to the Swiss'.

---

25 *Gambacorta/Van Rixtel* (2013) Structural Bank Regulation Initiatives, 2; See also *Van Kann/Rosak* (2013) Regierungsentwurf des Trennbankengesetzes, 1476; *HLEG* (2012) Liikanen Report, 100, 102; *ICB* (2011) Vickers Report, 35–36; *FSB* (2014) Structural Banking Reforms, 3.

26 See *European Commission* (2014) Impact Assessment Part 1, 26; see also *FSB* (2014) Structural Banking Reforms, 3; *ICB* (2011) Vickers Report, 163; *Expertenkommission* (2010) Schlussbericht, 54.

27 *European Commission* (2017) Commission Work Programme 2018: Annex 4, 2.

28 Directive 2014/59/EU of the European Parliament and the Council of 15 May 2014 establishing a framework for the recovery and resolution of credit institutions and investment firms, L 173/190 (BRRD).

29 Regulation 806/2014 of the European Parliament and the Council of 15 July 2014 establishing uniform rules and a uniform procedure for the resolution of credit institutions and certain investment firms in the framework of a Single Resolution Mechanism and a Single Resolution Fund, L 225/1 (SRMR).

30 In particular Art. 17 BRRD and Art. 10 SRMR. See e.g. *Alexander* (2015) Universal Model Banking, 494–498; *Binder* (2014) Resolution Planning, 16 (noting with regard to the BRRD that *"[o]n the basis of their powers given under this part of the Directive, authorities could go a long way towards implementing fully-fledged structural*

Some European countries have already adopted and some have even made use of their national legislation concerning structural reform. In a time of increased competition between financial centres and their participants, it is crucial to apply a legal comparative view to the instruments already in place. The objective is not just to assess their character and effectiveness and to gain insights for potential future bank structural reform initiatives but also to allow for an evaluation of the competitive position of the locations and their participants.

IV. Research Questions

The main research questions of this dissertation are therefore:

1. What comprehensive concept of ring-fencing as a category of bank structural reform can be established and how can its definition be contributed to?
2. What are the current developments concerning ring-fencing on EU level and in what direction is it expected to evolve?
3. What structural differences can be found in a legal comparative analysis of bank structural reform legislation in the United Kingdom, Germany and Switzerland and do they match the established concept of ring-fencing?

V. Scientific Approach

A. Part I

In the first part of the dissertation, the foundation for the main research questions shall be set. After a short introduction to its economic and political background, a comprehensive concept of ring-fencing as a category of bank structural reform shall be established.[31] It shall then be put into per-

---

reforms of banking in the relevant jurisdictions, even without a more specific formal mandate to do so"); see also *Binder* (2015) Gleichung, 165 (noting that a segregation of commercial and investment banking may be introduced via these provisions).

31 While "structural reform" is an umbrella term, ring-fencing is to be identified as an own concept, as it can be clearly delimited from other structural reforms. Three core characteristics are established that identify ring-fencing as a concept of structural reform on its own, and that are used to delimit it against other struc-

spective by delimiting it from two related structural solutions: full separation[32] and the *activities ban* of full separation.[33] In this context, a digression looking at United States legislation, in particular the Glass Steagall Act and the Volcker Rule of the Dodd-Frank Act is considered useful.[34]

---

tural reforms of banking: (i) the separation of commercial banking activities and certain investment banking activities, (ii) the establishment of a fence, (iii) the full maintenance of universal banking.

32 Full separation is regarded by some as a form of ring-fencing. See e.g. *Brown* (2014) With this Ring, I Thee Fence, 1038–1039; However, in the author's opinion it is rather to be regarded as a related form of structural reform, because, *inter alia*, it is much more far-reaching and invasive and cannot be subsumed under the concept of ring-fencing identified above, in particular because it does not allow for universal banking and because there is no fence.

33 The *activities ban* of full separation can be described as *the prohibition of a limited set of investment banking activities, which are considered high-risk, for the whole banking group, thereby limiting universal banking*. As pointed out by the Vickers Report, it is categorically a a *"form of full separation in that it prevents common ownership of banks and entities which conduct such activities"*. *ICB* (2011) Vickers Report, 45. It is most prominently featured in the Volcker Rule and is sometimes combined with ring-fencing legislation, for example in the European Commission's draft regulation.

34 In the United States, a full separation was in place for most of the 20th century in the form of the Glass-Steagall Act. Adopted in 1933 during the Roosevelt administration's New Deal, the Glass-Steagall Act up until today holds significant appeal for politicians and the public. This is demonstrated by the fact that it was referenced frequently during the 2016 U.S. presidential election. The future of the Volcker Rule has come under considerable pressure by President Trump, (see e.g. *Dexheimer*, Volcker Rule Change Backed in House Panel's Dodd-Frank Remedy, Bloomberg (March 21, 2018); *Buhayar*, Trump May Ax Volcker Rule, Ease Banks' Burden First, Whalen Says, Bloomberg (November 10, 2016); *Jenkins/McLannahan*, Trump's deregulatory stance expected to dilute financial reforms, Financial Times (November 10, 2016)), who has made it a key target of his deregulation efforts (see *U.S. Department of the Treasury* (2017) Treasury Report, 71 et seqq.). The U.S. has taken a pioneering role in both the Glass-Steagall Act and the Volcker Rule and has significantly influenced European ring-fencing legislation. To understand the origins of certain ideas in the European legislation, a short digression to U.S. structural reform is considered beneficial. Furthermore, both structural reforms are sometimes associated with ring-fencing, which is to be opposed; they therefore need to be delimited from the concept.

Subsequently, the basic rationale and goals of ring-fencing shall be set out[35] and different methods of ring-fencing shall be identified.[36] Due to the ambiguity of terminology mentioned above, it is critical to develop a definition that reflects the concept established and helps to differentiate it from other bank structural reforms.[37]

B. Part II

The second part of the dissertation shall examine the European Union approach, discussing the three legislative steps taken before the withdrawal by the European Commission: the recommendations of the Liikanen Report, the European Commission's Draft Regulation and the Negotiating Stance of the Council of the European Union. The dissertation aims at identifying an overall trend, beginning with the relatively stringent recommendations of the Liikanen Report, turning into a quite strict draft regulation and then turning into a rather lenient negotiating stance by the Council of the EU, which preceded the recently announced withdrawal. The events in the European Parliament shall be briefly touched upon, dur-

35 The division between the basic rationale of ring-fencing and other objectives that may also be reached by its implementation is considered useful as it highlights that the protection of systemically important activities is an essential precondition for the achievement of the other objectives.

36 Its variety of forms can be subsumed under two key methods, which are both based on the underlying assumption that the large variety of different services provided by universal banks can be divided into three groups, of which two are highlighted: desired activities, which include deposit-taking and other financial services essential for the real economy; and risky activities, which include trading activities, such as proprietary trading, market making and dealing in derivatives. The (i) *defensive method* protects desired activities by separating them and isolating them within a ring-fence. The (ii) *containment method* protects desired activities by separating risky trading activities. Both methods share the same aim and use similar tools to reach it.

37 The quest for a definition will begin with a literal interpretation of the word "ring-fencing", which will identify two important aspects already inherent in the expression: (i) a defensive element, in that a fence represents a barrier or an obstacle and (ii) a valuing element, in that something precious needs protection. As the term ring-fencing has also been used in contexts other than structural reform, those too will be briefly touched upon. Subsequently, the chapter will narrow down to definitions for bank structural reform. Ultimately, it will try to establish its own definition for bank structural reforms that match the established concept of ring-fencing.

ing which the assembly's Economic and Monetary Affairs Committee vetoed a draft approach of moderate structural banking rules for being too lenient.[38] The European Parliament therefore had to restart its negotiations, something that has not occurred with any other major financial reform package.[39] As no agreement could be reached, the Commission announced its withdrawal recently.[40] Both the withdrawal and potential alternatives for installing a union-wide ring-fencing regime shall be discussed.[41]

C. The Concept of Ring-Fencing II

While the fate of the European Union's regulation had long been uncertain, a number of countries in Europe already adopted structural reform legislation with some of them even having applied it already. The third part of the dissertation shall analyse and comparatively discuss national legislation in Europe's most important financial centres: the United Kingdom, Germany and Switzerland. This shall be achieved by identifying a number of aspects, which will then be used to examine the different approaches allowing an aspect-to-aspect comparative analysis.[42] The intention is to outline the major differences between the national approaches, allowing to acquire an understanding for each nation's plan for structural reform while ensuring that the dissertation does not lose its perspective on the bigger picture. The unique approach of Switzerland comprising of rather scarce legislation and giving lots of power to authorities makes it

38 See further *Moshinski*, EU Bank-Structure Rules Falter with Parliament Divided, Bloomberg, (May 26, 2015).

39 *Hogan*, Bank Ring Fencing Edges Closer in Europe, KPMG Insights, (June 28, 2015), https://home.kpmg.com/xx/en/home/insights/2015/06/bank-ring-fencing-edges-closer.html.

40 *European Commission* (2017) Commission Work Programme 2018: Annex 4, 2.

41 Potential alternatives include (i) existing regimes, such as provisions of the BRRD and SRMR, which can be considered potential gateways for union-wide ring-fencing; and (ii) legislative options. An example for the latter are the amendments proposed by Members of Parliament in February 2019, adding a chapter on bank structural reform to CRDV (*European Parliament Committee on Economic and Monetary Affairs* (2018) Amendments CRDV, 81–89).

42 The aspects used, (e.g. the height of the fence, what activities fall on which side of the fence), are in line with the general practice. See e.g. *ICB* (2011) Vickers Report, 35, 36, 62; *Brown* (2014) With this Ring, I Thee Fence, 1047, 1049, 1053; *Hofer* (2014) Structural Reforms, 477, 479, 488.

necessary for the comparative analysis to refer in some areas to the separation process of its largest banks, *UBS* and *Credit Suisse*. It shall further be explored to what extent the jurisdictions match the concept and definition of ring-fencing established in the first part. This will be particularly interesting in the case of Switzerland, as it originally chose not to implement far-reaching structural reforms.

VI. Methodology

The main research questions of this dissertation shall be addressed in a jurisprudential approach. The relevant norms and proposals adopted by both national legislators as well as actors of the European Union legislative procedure shall be analysed legally. The dissertation shall be based upon a thorough review of jurisprudential literature. Most of the sources are from the United States, Germany, the United Kingdom and Switzerland. It will further be beneficial to include sources from the field of economics and political science as necessary. Particularly the second part of the dissertation, addressing the developments on a European Union level, requires political research.

The legal comparative analysis of structural reforms in Germany, the United Kingdom and Switzerland shall be conducted as a micro-comparison as described by *Zweigert/Kötz*.[43] The author has conducted interviews and background talks with experts who have been involved or worked on the respective structural reform projects, including interest group representatives, specialists at banks (as parties affected) and regulators (as executive authorities); the findings of these are incorporated into the dissertation.

43 *Zweigert/Kötz* (1996) Rechtsvergleichung, 4, 42; See also *Zweigert/Kötz* (1998) Comparative Law, 5, 43–44.

Part I – The Concept of Ring-Fencing

I. Universal Banking Model

This chapter addresses the universal banking model. It examines its definition, taking into account the effect of ring-fencing and its dominance. It then discusses key arguments concerning the benefits and social costs that may result from the combination of both commercial banking and investment banking.

The following discussion of universal banking is considered important because ring-fencing rules structurally interfere with the universal banking model.[44] As discussed in the chapter, they aim at (i) maintaining universal banking, while (ii) averting its potential downsides.

A. Universal banking in Europe

The following paragraphs discuss the role of universal banking in Europe. They will (i) establish a definition, taking into account ring-fencing and (ii) present its dominance in the European banking landscape and within global systemically important banks.

a. Definition

1. "The entire range of financial services"

In continental Europe, the universal banking system has a long history. Banking legislation traditionally does not distinguish between commercial and investment banks, allowing institutions authorized to operate as a bank the provision of a wide selection of financial services.[45] In addition to

---

44 See *Gambacorta/Van Rixtel* (2013) Structural Bank Regulation Initiatives, 1 (noting that bank structural reforms limit the universal banking model by segregating commercial and investment banking).

45 *Rime/Stiroh* (2003) Universal Banks, 2122–2123; see further *European Commission* (2014) Impact Assessment Part 2, 2 et seqq.

commercial banking and investment banking, many banks also provide insurance activities.[46]

Services banks typically provide include deposit-taking, lending, underwriting, brokerage, portfolio management and trading.[47] *Benston* therefore defines universal banks as *"financial institutions that may offer the entire range of financial services"*.[48]

They can also be defined negatively, namely as *institutes that are not restricted to specific banking operations due to internal or external organisational decisions, even when they do not conduct all banking operations.*[49] This definition excludes banks that only conduct certain activities, either due to internal organisational decisions (for instance a business strategy) or due to external organisational decisions (for example a prohibition to conduct proprietary trading).[50]

In Europe, external organisational decisions are uncommon. Universal banks are usually not restricted by law from providing certain financial services. Moreover, European banks traditionally do not have to establish particular legal structures to engage in universal banking.[51]

Universal banking in the United States, in contrast, requires certain legal structures because of historic reasons.[52] Reflecting this, one can define uni-

46 See e.g. *Saunders/Walter* (1994) Universal Banking, 84 (defining universal banking as *"the conduct of a range of financial services comprising deposit-taking and lending, trading of financial instruments and foreign exchange (and their derivatives), underwriting of new debt and equity issues, brokerage, investment management and insurance"*).

47 *Rime/Stiroh* (2003) Universal Banks, 2122–2123; see further *European Commission* (2014) Impact Assessment Part 2, 2 et seqq.

48 *Benston* (1994) Universal Banking, 121.

49 This definition is based on *Grundmann* (2016) Bankvertragsrecht, 14. *Grundmann*'s definition is focused on banks in jurisdictions that do not restrict the universal banking model. The decision to conduct only certain banking operations is thus usually based on internal organisational decisions, e.g. business policy. The author has modified *Grundmann*'s definition to include jurisdictions that stipulate bank separation (see Chapter I.IV.C: Ring-fencing and full separation; Chapter I.IV.D: Ring-fencing and the activities ban) and in which as a result the decision to provide only selective banking operations is external.

50 A restriction to conduct certain activities, e.g. proprietary trading, is a strong interference with the universal banking model. Strictly speaking, banks that are prohibited from certain activities are no longer universal banks. This will be discussed in Chapter I.IV.C: Ring-fencing and full separation; Chapter I.IV.D: Ring-fencing and the activities ban.

51 *Vickers* thus refers to this system as *"[u]nstructured universal banking"*. See *Vickers* (2016) Banking Reform Presentation, 20.

52 See Chapter I.IV.C.a: Digression: The Glass-Steagall Act.

versal banks in the U.S. as *organisations that can engage, directly or indirectly through affiliates, in all respects of the banking, securities and insurance businesses.*[53]

In summary, it can be stated that all definitions of universal banking set out above highlight the ability of a banking group to provide unlimited financial services.[54]

2. Universal banking after ring-fencing

With the adoption of ring-fencing legislation in Europe, universal banking approximates the United States': The provision of unlimited financial services remains allowed, it, however, requires certain legal structures.[55]

Ring-fencing interferes with universal banking in a number of ways: banks may, for example, no longer use the same IT for the retail and the investment banks, they are furthermore limited in their ability to combine the earnings of these businesses segments.[56] By implementing these measures, ring-fencing aims to tackle specific problems associated with universal banking while maintaining its benefits.[57]

It, however, does not limit the freedom of banking groups to engage in all financial services, which has been identified above as the central characteristic of universal banking. In contrast to other structural reforms of banking, ring-fencing therefore does not limit universal banking.[58]

---

53 This definition is based on *Wilmarth* (2002) U.S. Financial Services Industry, 223 Fn 23 (defining universal banks as *"a regime under which a single organization can engage, either directly or indirectly through affiliates, in all aspects of banking, securities, and life insurance business"*) and *Saunders/Walter* (1994) Universal Banking, 84, 128–129, (adopting a similar definition). However, in contrast to *Wilmarth's* definition, and in line with his more recent work, universal banking is not limited to the business of life insurance. See *Wilmarth* (2005) Universal Banks, 559 (describing universal banks as *"diversified conglomerates that offer[] banking, securities and insurance services"*, while still referring in Fn 5 to the definition above).

54 They thereby differentiate it from a full separation, such as the one adopted with the Glass-Steagall Act or (to smaller extent) the Volcker Rule. See Chapter I.IV.C: Ring-fencing and full separation; Chapter I.IV.D: Ring-fencing and the activities ban.

55 *Vickers* therefore refers to it as "structured universal banking". *Vickers* (2016) Banking Reform Presentation, 20.

56 See *ICB* (2011) Vickers Report, 136.

57 See Chapter I.I.B: Benefits and costs of universal banking.

58 See *Vickers* (2016) Banking Reform Presentation, 24 (*"Go for structured universal banking, not ending universal banking -more robust than unstructured universal bank-*

After introducing ring-fencing, universal banks can thus be defined as *financial institutions that can engage, through ring-fenced and non-ring-fenced entities, in all respects of the banking, securities and insurance business.*[59]

b. Dominance

European banks are typically universal banks.[60] According to *Pagano et al.*, there are almost no pure investment banks in the EU and only a small number of banks that provide solely retail banking services. They demonstrate, in a comparison with the U.S., that in the EU most assets are held by universal banks.[61]

Examples for banks that specialize entirely in a certain service are the few special purpose banks in Germany[62] as well as building societies in the UK.[63] As there are no limitations for the business of banking in most European countries, the decision to concentrate on certain services is usually based on internal organisational decisions.[64]

On a global level, *Martel/Van Rixtel/Mota* paint a similar picture: in spite of very different business models between large international banking groups, they divide global systemically relevant banks (G-SIBs) into four groups: first, specialised commercial banks; second, specialised investment banks; third, investment-banking oriented universal banks; and fourth, commercial-banking oriented universal banks. They find that the majority of banks are either investment banking or commercial banking oriented

---

ing"); *HLEG* (2012) Liikanen Report, 102 (*"The proposal addresses the core weaknesses in the banking sector, while retaining the key benefits of the universal banking model and allowing for business model diversity"*); See Chapter III.IV: What Activities Fall on Which Side of the Fence? (setting out that banking groups in the UK, Germany and Switzerland can continue to provide all sorts of banking activities). See also Chapter I.IV.C: Ring-fencing and full separation; Chapter I.IV.D: Ring-fencing and the activities ban.

59 This definition is based on the ones of *Benston* (*Benston* (1994) Universal Banking, 121) and *Wilmarth* (*Wilmarth* (2002) U.S. Financial Services Industry, 223 Fn 23), taking into account the specialties of ring-fencing.

60 *HLEG* (2012) Liikanen Report, 89; See also *Grundmann* (2016) Bankvertragsrecht, 14; *Schoenmaker* (2016) Euro-Area Banks, 4.

61 *Pagano et al.* (2014) Is Europe Overbanked?, 29.

62 See Chapter III.I.B.b: Number of banks and their nature.

63 See Chapter III.I.A.b: Number of banks and their nature.

64 For special purpose banks in Germany, see Chapter III.I.B.b: Number of banks and their nature.

universal banks. Moreover, all European banks listed as G-SIBs are universal banks.[65]

B. Benefits and costs of universal banking

Universal banking has many benefits, but can also result in social costs. The discussion about advantages and disadvantages of universal banking in comparison with a separation of commercial banking and investment banking dates back decades. This dissertation does not aim to answer this question as it would be far beyond its scope.

The following paragraphs, however, outline selected arguments for and against universal banking. This is considered valuable because, as will be discussed, ring-fencing aims at maintaining the advantages of universal banking while reducing its disadvantages. Interestingly, the disadvantages discussed decades ago, for example by *Saunders/Walter* in 1994,[66] are as relevant as can be today and correspond well with the goals of ring-fencing set out below.

a. Benefits

Proponents of universal banking regularly argue that the combination of commercial banking and retail banking allows for informational advantages. Both the bank and the clients can profit from them, e.g. through lower costs of credit or fees for emissions of securities.[67]

Furthermore, it is mostly argued that universal banking can achieve economies of scope, which could lead to cost saving: for example, information only needs to be gathered once and can then be used for various business segments. Operative costs can potentially be reduced, e.g. by a centralised IT. Economies of scope could also increase profits, as universal banks can offer clients a whole range of products and services. Diversified profits can also lead to more stability, so that universal banks may be better

65 See *Martel/Van Rixtel/Mota* (2012) Business Models of International Banks, 102–102, 114, (taking into account G-SIB distribution by end-2010); See also *Gambacorta/Van Rixtel* (2013) Structural Bank Regulation Initiatives, 7.

66 *Saunders/Walter* (1994) Universal Banking, 125.

67 *Dombret/Liebig/Stein* (2014) Trennbankensystem, 53.

equipped to withstand shocks.[68] In the case of large banks, many proponents of universal banking also underscore the importance of economies of scale.[69]

However, as argued by *Gambacorta/Van Rixtel*, and *Dombret/Liebig/Stein*, economic assessments vary a great deal. Empirical academic studies usually have problems demonstrating remarkable economies of scale and particularly of scope.[70]

b. Costs

1. Access to the safety net: explicit and implicit subsidies

Universal banks provide deposit-taking and other services that are important for the real economy. They are therefore protected by having access to the safety net. The safety net for universal banks includes usually: (i) de-

---

68 See *Dombret/Liebig/Stein* (2014) Trennbankensystem, 53; See also *Gambacorta/Van Rixtel* (2013) Structural Bank Regulation Initiatives, 8–9.

69 *Gambacorta/Van Rixtel* (2013) Structural Bank Regulation Initiatives, 8–9. For an overview of studies concerning economies of scale and scope of universal banks, see *Laeven/Ratnovski/Tong* (2014) Systemic Risk, 24–25; *Gambacorta/Van Rixtel* (2013) Structural Bank Regulation Initiatives, 8–9. For an extensive analysis of the advantages and disadvantages of universal banks and specialised banks, see *Canals* (1997) Universal Banking, 83 et seqq.

70 *Gambacorta/Van Rixtel* (2013) Structural Bank Regulation Initiatives, 8–9 (giving an overview of a range of important studies); *Dombret/Liebig/Stein* (2014) Trennbankensystem, 53 (also pointing out that benefits are hard to prove empirically); cf. *Becalli/Anolli/Borello* (2015) Are European Banks too Big?, 234 (noting that a small body of research evidence has in recent years documented economies of scale); see also an article by *John Reid*, former chairman and chief executive of Citigroup, in which he notes: *"One [thing we were wrong about] was the belief that combining all types of finance into one institution would drive costs down — and the larger the institution the more efficient it would be. We now know that there are very few cost efficiencies that come from the merger of functions — indeed, there may be none at all. It is possible that combining so much in a single bank makes services more expensive than if they were instead offered by smaller, specialised players"*. *Reid*, We were wrong about universal banking, Financial Times (November 11, 2015).

posit insurance[71] and (ii) lender of last resort facilities.[72] It also regularly comprises (iii) government bailout guarantees.[73]

While all these functions aim at preventing systemic crisis and contributing to financial stability, they can also have detrimental effects: creditors anticipate public support (through each of the functions above). They consider banks with access to the three functions safer and are therefore willing to lower their requested return. Banks under the public safety net can therefore be regarded as profiting from subsidies.[74]

The subsidies stemming from the public safety net functions are split up in two groups, depending on the way they are communicated: (i) subsidies from deposit insurance and lenders of last resort facilities are referred to as "explicit subsidies"; (ii) government bailout guarantees, which are mostly not communicated directly but rather expected by the market, on the other hand, are referred to as "implicit subsidies".[75]

These subsidies can give universal banks unfair advantages and impede competition.[76] Universal banks may use *"public subsidies notionally attached to their retail bank operations"* for their investment banking, potentially for their trading activity.[77] They furthermore have the potential to create moral hazard, as they may incentivise parties to alter their behaviour because they are not fully exposed to the consequences of its actions.[78]

---

71 Deposit insurance is a foundation of banking in most banking systems. It shields small saver deposits from losses in case of a bank failure and prevents bank runs. (*Lambert/Noth/Schüwer* (2013) Insured Deposits, 1) Banks that accept deposits are by their very nature in danger of bank runs. Reason for that is their combination of illiquid assets and liquid liabilities. As deposits can be withdrawn at any given time, banks that are actually solvent, may need to sell illiquid longterm assets at loss, to match withdrawals (*European Commission* (2014) Impact Assessment Part 2, 56; see also *Diamond/Dybvig* (1983) Bank Runs, 402). Deposit insurance schemes move insolvency risk away from the bank, usually onto taxpayers. *Langfield/Pagano* (2015) Bank Bias, 19. See also *Carnell/Macey/Miller* (2017) Financial Institutions, 222–229.

72 See *Dobler et al.* (2016) Lender of Last Resort, 11–12; see *IMF* (1998) Financial Stability, 27–29; see also *Carnell/Macey/Miller* (2017) Financial Institutions, 220–221.

73 See *European Commission* (2014) Impact Assessment Part 2, 55–56.

74 See *European Commission* (2014) Impact Assessment Part 2, 55–56.

75 See *European Commission* (2014) Impact Assessment Part 2, 55–56. Implicit subsidies will be discussed in Chapter I.III.C: Implicit subsidies.

76 *Saunders/Walter* (1994) Universal Banking, 125.

77 See *Pagano et al.* (2014) Is Europe Overbanked?, 30–31.

78 *ICB* (2011) Vickers Report, 248. The recognition that parties are more diligent when they are exposed to the consequences of their actions is evident and has

2. Risk-taking, trading risks, culture and complexity

Saunders/Walter also list risk-taking as a controversy of universal banks, noting that they "*may use their powers to undertake securities and insurance activities in order to enhance their risk-taking (and thus risk exposure)*".[79]

Social costs arise when universal banks accept large exposures and take excessive risks on securities markets and thereby increase links between asset price shocks and the supply of credit, and ultimately the real economy.[80] This can intensify systemic risk and as a result costs for society – particularly if universal banks are large and are exposed to correlated security risks.[81]

Another concern, often articulated in relation to universal banks is the contagion effect of high-risk investment banking culture on the traditional commercial banking activity[82] as well as conflicts of interest, for example regarding the responsibilities of a bank and its role as investment banker.[83]

---

long been described in the context of personal liability. See e.g. *Eucken* (1990) Wirtschaftspolitik, 279 et seqq. (noting that the diligence in investments increases with personal liability); *Smith* (1976) Wealth of Nations, V.1.107 ("*The directors of such companies, however, being the managers rather of other people's money than their own, it cannot well be expected that they should watch over it with the same anxious vigilance with which the partners of a private copartnery frequently watch over their own*"); *Brändli/Rieder* (2009) Vertrauensbildung, 62–64. In the context above, diligence correlates not (necessarily) with personal liability, but with other factors, for example insolvency (in case of the bank) or job-loss (in the case of employees). The basic idea, however, remains the same: moral hazard can be prevented if parties face the consequences of their actions.

79 *Saunders/Walter* (1994) Universal Banking, 125.

80 When securities prices drop, universal banks may be negatively impacted on both the asset and the liability or funding side: in the case that they hold marketable securities, their own market value and thus the value of their equity is reduced. If they rely on the issuance of these securities to fund their activities, asset price drops increase their cost of capital. Universal banks may therefore have to deleverage and sell assets to comply with capital requirements. By doing so, they contribute to a further decrease of securities prices. *Pagano et al.* (2014) Is Europe Overbanked?, 31.

81 See further *Pagano et al.* (2014) Is Europe Overbanked?, 31.

82 See e.g. *Coates* (2015) Volcker Rule, 16–17; *Reid*, We were wrong about universal banking, Financial Times (November 11, 2015) (in which former chairman and CEO of Citigroup, *John Reid* emphasizes the importance of culture and the dangers of mixing incompatible cultures).

83 *Saunders/Walter* (1994) Universal Banking, 124; Conflicts of interest were one of the main arguments for the introduction of a full separation of commercial and investment banking in the United States in 1933. See Chapter IV.C.a: Digression:

Another controversy listed by *Saunders/Walter* and many others, which is as up-to-date as can be, is that universal banks are regularly complex and heterogeneous and thusly may be more difficult to regulate.[84] This is discussed today by the term "too-complex-to-fail",[85] in reference to the complex resolution of banks, especially when they are large and internationally active.[86]

II. Changes in the Realm of International Banking

This chapter discusses two important developments in the realm of international banking before the global economic crisis. The first one is the substantial change in banks' business models, which took place when banks started focussing on activities new to the banking sector. Special attention will be given to the illustration of proprietary trading and market making. The second one is the transformation of large financial institutions, becoming bigger in size and scope, more complex and more interconnected.[87]

Structural reform measures aim to be a response to the two developments. They all (i) address trading activities in some way, but differ in their strictness and focus depending on the respective jurisdiction. They furthermore (ii) strive to limit the complexity and interconnectedness of financial institutions.

The Glass-Steagall Act; For example, during the financial crisis, *Goldman Sachs* was accused of speculating against their own clients. See e.g. *Macalister*, Revealed: Goldman Sachs 'made fortune betting against clients', The Guardian (April 25, 2010).

84 *Saunders/Walter* (1994) Universal Banking, 125; The complexity may not just be an impediment for regulators but also for the management itself; see *Canals* (1997) Universal Banking, 82 (noting that the *"chief problem is the tremendous complexity that universal banks must deal with"* and that the most important challenge for commercial banks *"is that of increasing management complexity"*); see also *Dombret/Liebig/Stein* (2014) Trennbankensystem, 53 (underscoring that universal banks are typically more complex).

85 See Chapter I.III.B: Bailout decision and too-big-to-fail.

86 See e.g. *Gordon/Ringe* (2015) Bank Resolution, 8–9 (arguing that the complex organizational structure of European banks impedes effective resolution).

87 See *HLEG* (2012) Liikanen Report, 11 et seqq., 88.

A. Change of banks' business models

The following paragraphs discuss changes in the operating environment of banks and set out their adjustment of focus from traditional relationship-based banking to market-based banking.

a. Environment

In the years before the economic crisis, the setting in which financial institutions operated changed substantially. The trend of an increased internalisation of the banking industry persisted, with cross-border capital flows and cross-border entry into banking sectors intensifying.[88] Liberalization, deregulation[89] and advances in information technology[90] reconfigured the financial services sector as they led to increased competition between financial players: banks competed vigorously, not just among themselves but also faced growing rivalry from non-bank financial institutions and the markets.[91]

b. Relationship-based banking

In response to the enhanced competition, banks' activities moved increasingly away from their traditional role,[92] namely commercial banking – accepting deposits and making loans to businesses and individuals – as well

---

88 *Martel/Van Rixtel/Mota* (2012) Business Models of International Banks, 99.

89 A prime example of deregulation is the Gramm-Leach-Bliley Act which repealed the full separation requirement of the Glass-Steagall Act and, therefore, allowed for the return of universal banking in the United States. Similar deregulation efforts also took place in the United Kingdom and the European Union. This can be regarded as a global trend towards deregulation in the mid- and late-1990's. See *Laeven/Ratnovski/Tong* (2014) Systemic Risk, 7.

90 About technological change spurring financial innovations see *Frame/White* (2014) Technological Change. See also *Armour et al.* (2016) Financial Regulation, 5.

91 *Boot* (2011) Banking, 1; Competition increased not only between banks, but also between banks and non-bank financial institutions, and the financial markets. *Boot* (2011) Banking, 1.

92 See *Armour et al.* (2016) Financial Regulation, 6–7; *Brunnermeier/Dong/Palia* (2012) Banks' Non-Interest Income, 1; *Boot* (2011) Banking, 1.

as investment banking – providing underwriting and advisory services.[93] Both traditional activities are characterized by repeated business with long-term clients and can therefore be referred to as "relationship-based banking".[94]

c. Market-based banking

Services new to the banking sector became of increasing interest.[95] These operations include: proprietary trading, market-marking, the origination and/or holding of securitized debt, security dealing and custodian services. They further comprise a variety of financial market services, from advisory to hedging, to customers.[96] These operations are usually attributed to the investment banking side of banks.

93 *HLEG* (2012) Liikanen Report, 13.

94 *Boot/Ratnovski* (2012) Banking and Trading, 4; Traditional investment banking services, such as underwriting and advisory are considered relationship-based banking by *Boot/Ratnovski: "Underwriting, insofar as it requires hard and codified information that is to be transmitted to the markets, may have a lower relationship intensity that commercial bank lending based on soft information. Nevertheless, at its core, underwriting remains a relationship-based activity." Boot/Ratnovski* (2012) Banking and Trading, 4 Fn 2; See also *European Commission* (2014) Impact Assessment Part 1, 46 (emphasizing the relationship-based nature of underwriting).

95 Prior to the crisis, banks earned an increasingly higher proportion of profits from non-interest income, such as trading and securitization, instead of traditional deposit-taking and lending (*Brunnermeier/Dong/Palia* (2012) Banks' Non-Interest Income, 1). *Blundell-Wignall/Wehinger/Slovik,* for example, compare banks at the time to highly-leveraged hedge funds: they note that while some banks may have the *"structure of a "bank" as it is thought of by politicians and the public at large, i.e. an institution that funds itself mainly via deposits and longer-term borrowing and lends to households and to companies for investment and consumption, this is not the case of Citigroup or Deutsche Bank, whose balance sheet structure is similar to that of many large European and UK banks. On a consolidated basis these latter institutions look much more like large highly-leveraged hedge funds – though we can hardly imagine any hedge fund running these sorts of structured products would risk of having a leverage ratio of almost 50 (assets versus equity), as is the case of Deutsche Bank". Blundell-Wignall/Wehinger/Slovik* (2010) The Elephant in the Room, 16–17.

96 *Laeven/Ratnovski/Tong* (2014) Systemic Risk, 8; See also *Martel/Van Rixtel/Mota* (2012) Business Models of International Banks, 101; *Armour et al.* (2016) Financial Regulation, 7 (*Armour et al.* emphasize market making, proprietary trading but also an increase in underwriting).

Boot/Ratnakovski refer to the activities as "trading".[97] *Hardie/Macartney* argue that *"[t]he dichotomy between banking and financial markets was replaced by a system where the two were deeply intertwined"*. In combination with increased financing on the wholesale markets on the funding side, they refer to it as "market-based banking".[98]

"Trading" or "market-based banking" activities are characterised by being short-term, individual and transaction-based. They can be contrasted with the aforementioned relationship-based banking. Unlike the latter, trading activities are capital-constrained, scalable and profit from spare capital available in the bank. Banks that engage in relationship-based banking may therefore expand into trading to make use of their spare capital. They thereby, however, run the risk of overexposing themselves to trading.[99]

B. Proprietary trading and market making

The following paragraphs discuss two of the trading activities mentioned above that are of special relevance regarding structural reform: proprietary trading and market making. The former in particular has attracted a lot of criticism and has been targeted by structural reforms in both Europe and the United States.

a. Proprietary trading

Proprietary trading can best be understood as the *"purchase and sale of financial instruments with the intent to profit from the difference between the purchase price and the sale price"*.[100] This simply means that a bank uses its own money to invest in financial instruments: it puts its own money at risk to profit from its investments.

97 See *Boot/Ratnovski* (2012) Banking and Trading, 3–5.

98 *Hardie/Macartney* (2016) EU Ring-Fencing, 507. See also *Hardie/Howarth* (2013) Market-Based Banking, 25–32; Another expression frequently used is "capital markets banking". See *Blundell-Wignall/Atkinson* (2012) Capital Markets Banking, 41.

99 *Boot/Ratnovski* (2012) Banking and Trading, 3–4.

100 *Duffie* (2012) Market Making, 2; See also, almost identically, *European Commission* (2014) Impact Assessment Part 3, 56.

As shown above, banks started to increasingly engage in proprietary trading before the financial crisis. They did that generally through "Prop Desks", i.e. units of the banks whose only task was proprietary trading; by single traders, who also performed other investment banking activities, such as market making or underwriting, or through their own in-house hedge funds. For long-term speculation in non-listed stock, banks used their own private equity funds.[101]

The description of proprietary trading above already implies its key issue: if a bank puts its own money at stake, it has, on the one hand, the chance of making profits which it does not have to share with anyone. On the other hand, if investments go wrong, it has to bear the losses on its own. In other words, banks engaged in proprietary trading assume the *"full risks and rewards of [...] their speculation"*.[102]

The literature on the risks associated with proprietary trading is controversial. While a causal link to the financial crisis is difficult to establish, many authors are of the opinion that it at least intensified the crisis.[103]

However, there are numerous obvious dangers connected to it: as indicated above, proprietary trading causes large open positions and counterparty risk. If a counterparty to an investment fails, a bank may get into serious trouble. These exposures also add to interconnectedness between financial institutions. Proprietary trading is furthermore a complex activity by itself, as its nature makes it hard for supervisors and even for the bank's management to properly understand the risks. Moreover, it is prone to cause moral hazard as financial institutions profit from their trading operations, while eventual losses may be shifted to the public through government assistance. Proprietary trading may also give rise to conflicts of interest.[104]

---

101 *Elliott/Rauch* (2014) Volcker Rule, 3.

102 *Elliott/Rauch* (2014) Volcker Rule, 3.

103 *Dombalagian* (2013) Proprietary Trading, 392–393; See *Duffie* (2012) Market Making, 25; *Chow/Surti* find that there is a *"[p]ositive association [...] between susceptibility to distress and the importance of trading income as a revenue generator for U.S. and European banks."*. However, they also note that *"[r]isk could emanate from losses attributed to non-proprietary trading activities such as market-making, investment banking and hedging"*. *Chow/Surti* (2011) Making Banks Safer; *Dombalagian* (2013) Proprietary Trading, 393 Fn 37.

104 See *European Commission* (2014) Impact Assessment Part 3, 56–58; see also, extensively, *Dombalagian* (2013) Proprietary Trading, 393–399; see also the critique and the recommendation for a prohibition of proprietary trading of the *Group of Thirty* (2009) Financial Reform, 27–28; *Dombalagian* also portrays in detail the dangers of possible conflicts of interests that only played a minor role

From a legal and in particular from a law-making point of view there is another, very practical problem: proprietary trading has the remarkable characteristic of being easy to explain and easy to understand, even easy to define for purpose of explanation (see above), but also of being very difficult to define for the purpose of regulation. This problem is encountered particularly if the concept has to be distinguished from other related trading activities, such as market making or hedging.[105]

Since the financial crisis, proprietary trading decreased considerably, due to capital requirements, capital pressures and commercial performance. *PwC* found in a study for the interest group *AFME* that almost 90% of studied banks have announced decreases in proprietary trading, with over half completely ceasing the activity.[106]

b. Market making

Market making is a trading activity that can be described as the purchasing and selling of financial instruments by standing ready to trade for own account whenever an order arrives.[107]

A market maker could be characterised as a central counterparty which buys financial instruments for a certain price and sells them for another. A buyer may buy financial instruments at the market makers ask price, while

---

in the European debate, see *Dombalagian* (2013) Proprietary Trading, 395; they were much more emphasized in the U.S. debate, Senator *Volcker*, for example wrote of *"virtually insolvable conflicts of interest with customer relationships"*. *Volcker*, How to Reform Our Financial System, The New York Times (January 30, 2010).

105 This problem pervades all structural reforms that aim for a special treatment of proprietary trading (see Chapter I.IV.D.a: Digression: The Volcker Rule; Chapter II.II.C: Separation of proprietary trading; Chapter II.III.C: Separation of proprietary trading). A good example of how difficult it can be to differentiate proprietary trading from hedging is the famous London whale incident of JP Morgan. See in particular the argumentation of the bank's CEO *Jamie Dimon*, *Fontevecchia*, Dimon's Volcker Rule Contradiction: On Hedging, Prop Trading, And The London Whale, Forbes (June 13, 2012). See also *Baisch* (2014) Risikogewichtete Aktiva, 85–90.

106 *PwC* (2014) AFME: Bank Structural Reform Study, 7.

107 See the description of *O'Hara/Oldfield* (1986) Market Making, 361; See also *Kumpan* (2014) Verbot von Eigengeschäften, 208.

a seller may sell financial instruments at the market makers bid price. Market makers are usually compensated by the bid-ask-spread.[108]

Through this, the market maker provides so-called "immediacy" to clients, i.e. *"the ability to immediately absorb a client's demand or supply of an asset into its own inventory"*:[109] it allows them to buy or sell immediately. If, for example, an investor is concerned about a certain financial instrument such as a bond, and wants to get rid of it, he may turn to a market maker and rely on its ability to buy it for itself immediately. The same goes for an investor wanting to buy that bond immediately.[110]

In contrast to proprietary trading, market making is generally considered beneficial for the market and its functioning.[111] Market making, by providing immediacy, can ensure market liquidity and has the potential to absorb temporary supply or demand shocks.[112] It can, therefore, ensure investor confidence in the functioning of the financial markets.[113]

At the same time however, market making is very similar to proprietary trading. *Duffie* even describes it as *"proprietary trading that is designed to provide immediacy to investors"* and argues that it is *"inherently a form of proprietary trading"*: The goal of a market maker is indeed to "buy low and sell high" and it depends on its expectation of the future development of market prices.[114] Various jurisdictions apply different methods to identify it, including complex metrics and historical data. Differentiations beyond doubt, however, are hard to achieve.[115]

108 See *O'Hara/Oldfield* (1986) Market Making, 361; While voluntary market makers act on own initiative and profit from the bid-ask-spread, designated market makers are contractually required to offer the best bid or ask price for each market order transaction for a specified period of the trading day. They regularly profit from reduced trading fees, monthly payments and a share of net trading revenue by exchanges. See further on the different types of market makers, *European Commission* (2014) Impact Assessment Part 3, 59 Fn 61.

109 *Duffie* (2012) Market Making, 7.

110 See *Duffie* (2012) Market Making, 2.

111 *Kumpan* (2014) Verbot von Eigengeschäften, 208.

112 See *Committee on the Global Financial System* (2014) Market-making, 5.

113 *European Commission* (2014) Impact Assessment Part 3, 59.

114 See further *Duffie* (2012) Market Making, 2, 3–4; see also *Whitehead* (2011) Volcker Rule, 40 Fn 4, regarding market making (among other permitted activities of the Volcker Rule) as a proprietary trading activity; See with regard to the Volcker Rule Chapter I.IV.D.a: Digression: The Volcker Rule.

115 See *Kumpan* (2014) Verbot von Eigengeschäften, 208–209.

According to *PwC*, multiple banks have announced departures from market making since the financial crisis.[116] However, it remains an important business for many banks.[117]

Summarizing, two conclusions can be drawn: (i) On the one hand, market making is generally acknowledged as an important trading activity that is beneficial to society and is, therefore, to be preserved. (ii) On the other hand, it is very difficult to differentiate it from proprietary trading. These two conclusions pervade the chapters presenting various structural reform proposals.

C. Bigger, more complex, more interconnected

Corresponding with the expansion of investment banking activity, in particular with the expansion of market-based banking described in the chapter above, was the transformation of large banks, becoming bigger in size, more complex and more interconnected.[118]

a. Bigger banks

The changes in the financial system, characterised by increased market-based operations, affected all banks. Large banks, however, were particularly prone to this behaviour. Their business models *"became clearly distinct from that of small or medium-sized banks"*. As *Laeven/Ratnovski/Tong* demonstrate, large banks (i) became disproportionately more involved in market-based activities, (ii) held less capital than small banks, (iii) relied on less stable funding than small banks, and (iv) became more organizationally complex.[119]

---

116 *PwC* (2014) AFME: Bank Structural Reform Study, 7.

117 This can be derived from only few banks exiting market making since the financial crisis. That market making remains a profitable business segment is indicated by industry data. *JP Morgan,* for instance, noted an increase of market making revenues of 21% from 2014 to 2016, amounting to 12.0 billion $. *JP Morgan Chase & Co* (2017) Corporate & Investment Bank, 12.

118 *HLEG* (2012) Liikanen Report, 90.

119 See *Laeven/Ratnovski/Tong* (2014) Systemic Risk, 8.

As engaging in market-based activities requires huge inventories of securities that are subject to price volatility and counterparty risk,[120] balance sheets of large banks grew significantly bigger[121] and less stable.

Europe nowadays has by far the world's largest banking system. Total assets of banks in the EU alone[122] amounted to 42 trillion € corresponding to 334 % of EU GDP in 2013. Between 1996 and 2015 its size almost doubled, corresponding solely with the expansion of the 20 largest European banks.[123] Large banks have also increased their market shares within their home markets, with the three largest banks in Germany, Switzerland and the United Kingdom in charge of two-thirds to three-quarters of total deposits from 1990 to 2007.[124]

b. Complexity and interconnectedness

The complexity of large banks also increased considerably. This happened on the one hand through trading and the sheer size and scope of banking activities:[125] financial innovations that augment marketability led to increased interconnectedness between the various market participants and to a much higher speed of transaction;[126] on the other hand, through opaque legal structures with little relation to the actual business:[127] Banks were not required or incentivised to align their structure with the activities they provide.[128]

---

120 See *Blundell-Wignall/Atkinson/Roulet* (2013) Bank Business Models, 76.

121 Cf. *Krahnen/Noth/Schüwer* (2016) Structural Reforms, 6 (noting that the high leverage of *"stock monsters"* is the *"almost accidental by-product of their market making function"* rather than high-risk strategies).

122 A similar situation can be seen in Switzerland, where the balance sheets of the two largest banks, *Credit Suisse* and *UBS*, despite significant deleveraging, amounted in 2014 to about 230% of the countries GDP. See e.g. *IMF* (2014) Switzerland, 6, 13. For an assessment of the current situation regarding bank size in the UK, Germany and Switzerland, see Chapter III.I: Banking Landscape.

123 *Langfield/Pagano* (2015) Bank Bias, 3, 18.

124 *Haldane* (2012) The Right Size, 2.

125 See *Herring/Carmassi* (2014) Complexity, 77–80.

126 See *Boot* (2014) Financial Sector, 131.

127 See *Herring/Carmassi* (2014) Complexity, 77–80.

128 In this regard, considerable efforts have been undertaken. See e.g. *FSB* (2014) Key Attributes, 16; Chapter III.V.C.a.2: Resolvability incentives; Chapter II.IV.C.c: Existing regimes.

Trading activities contributed to the growth of interconnectedness between large banks, as they enhanced links between banks and increased their exposure to counterparty risks.[129] The resulting "*more intertwined nature of banks and financial markets has exposed banks to the boom and bust nature of financial markets and augmented instability*".[130]

Complexity and interconnectedness of large universal banks are an almost insurmountable obstacle in the way of resolution in times of distress, especially at short notice.[131]

c. Post-crisis response

Since the financial crisis, a multitude of reforms have been launched and enormous efforts have been undertaken to revise the regulatory and institutional framework for financial institutions and markets.[132] A thorough reform of the Basel rules for capital adequacy and liquidity standards and regulatory reforms relating to recovery and resolution have had an impact

---

129 *HLEG* (2012) Liikanen Report, 90.

130 See *Boot* (2014) Financial Sector, 131.

131 *Krahnen/Noth/Schüwer* (2016) Structural Reforms, 4. See also *Herring/Carmassi* (2014), Complexity, 3.

132 Among the variety of post-crisis regulatory reforms, there are many whose similarities or overlaps with ring-fencing are interesting to explore. One of them is the regulation of central securities depositories, central counterparties and their participants (mostly internationally active banks) (on central counterparties and their emergence, see Brändli (2011) Zentrale Gegenpartei, 3 et seqq.), in particular with a view to their provisions on "segregation": Such institutions are obliged to separate the accounts comprising their own assets and positions from the ones of their clients (see, inter alia, Art. 54, 59, 69 Bundesgesetz über die Finanzmarktinfrastrukturen und das Marktverhalten im Effekten- und Derivatehandel, June 19, 2015, SR 958.1 (Financial Market Infrastructure Act); Art. 39 Regulation (EU) No 648/2012 of the European Parliament and of the Council of 4 July 2012 on OTC derivatives, central counterparties and trade repositories, L 201/1 (EMIR)), which is meant "*as a means of client asset protection*" (AFME (2016) Client Asset Protection, 2; see Bundesrat (2014) Botschaft Finanzmarktinfrastrukturgesetz, 7544; cf. Chapter I.V: The Basic Rationale and Goals of Ring-fencing). However, given the limitations in scope and the research focus of the dissertation, emphasis is placed on bank structural reforms, in particular those often associated with ring-fencing. See Chapter I.IV: Structural Reform and Ring-fencing.

on banks' business models as well as their size, complexity and interconnectedness.[133]

Many banks have considerably decreased their size since the global financial crisis.[134] This goes hand in hand with the decrease of trading activities and many banks paying more attention to retail services:[135] According to the Bank of England, trading assets of large global banks have halved since the global financial crisis.[136]

III. Bailouts and Too-Big-to-Fail

This chapter enlarges on the too-big-to-fail problem and on governments' decisions to bail out banks in the wake of the global economic crisis. Global systemically important banks and current developments regarding bank size shall be set out.

Structural reforms of banking aim to respond to these problems. Their objectives contribute to a mitigation of the too-big-to-fail problem, for example through enhanced resolvability and a reduction of implicit subsidies.[137]

---

133 *Krahnen/Noth/Schüwer* (2016) Structural Reforms, 2. Since the crisis, capital requirements have been sharpened and increased. Large banks are now required to hold *ten* times more capital than before the crisis. In addition, the introduction of a leverage ratio is regarded as an important backstop against unreliability and riskiness inherent in risk weights and models. *Bank of England* (2017) Financial Crisis 10 Years On, 1.; *IMF* (2017) Global Financial Stability Report, 2 (underscoring that G-SIBs *"have become more resilient since the crisis, with stronger capital and liquidity"*).

134 For example, *UBS* reduced the size of its balance sheet by 35%, Barclays by 27% and Royal Bank of Scotland by 40%, between 2008 and 2010. (*Martel/Van Rixtel/Mota* (2012) Business Models of International Banks, 107); From 2008 to 2014 *UBS* deleveraged by more than 40% and *Credit Suisse* by 21%, however, their balance sheets still amount to about 230% of Switzerland's GDP. *IMF* (2014) Switzerland, 13. See further Chapter III.I: Banking Landscape.

135 *European Central Bank* (2016) Financial Stability Review, 12.

136 *Bank of England* (2017) Financial Crisis 10 Years On, 1; The findings of *PwC's* study for *AFME* regarding proprietary trading and market making point to a similar direction. See *PwC* (2014) AFME: Bank Structural Reform Study, 7; see Chapter I.II.B: Proprietary trading and market making.

137 See Chapter I.V: The Basic Rationale and Goals of Ring-Fencing; *FSB* (2014) Structural Banking Reforms, 3.

A. Bailouts

The global economic crisis was followed by an unprecedented wave of bailouts both in the United States and in Europe. Taxpayer money was used to rescue banks that had run into difficulties due to tremendous losses suffered because of speculation with complex financial products.[138] In particular the U.S., Switzerland, the United Kingdom and Germany had to keep many banks alive through vast packages of aid, including direct capital injections, asset purchases, loans and guarantees.[139]

Between 2008 and 2016, the EU member states alone spent 653.8 billion € on capital-like aid instruments and 1.3 trillion € on liquidity aid instruments. In 2016, state aid was at its lowest since the beginning of the financial crisis. It was also the first year in which no recapitalisations were needed.[140]

B. Bailout decision and too-big-to-fail

Governments that decide to bail out banks typically do not have much choice. Banks play a crucial role in modern day life, in particular by financing the real economy. In Europe, financing of companies and households is traditionally performed by banks rather than by the capital markets. In corporate finance, banks are especially important for small-and-medium enterprises, but thus also for the large corporations contracting with them.[141] Furthermore, banks accept deposits. Letting banks fail al-

---

138 *Lehmann* (2014) Ring-Fencing, 2–3.

139 *Blundell-Wignall/Wehinger/Slovik* (2010) The Elephant in the Room, 15. These four countries are also dominating the world's investment banking landscape. *Blundell-Wignall/Wehinger/Slovik* (2010) The Elephant in the Room, 15.

140 *European Commission*, State Aid Scoreboard 2017, http://ec.europa.eu/competition/state_aid/scoreboard/index_en.html; see also *European Parliament* (2013) Report on Structural Reform, 4.

141 *HLEG* (2012) Liikanen Report, 88.

ways carries the risk of a bank run,[142] which can create a domino effect due to direct contagion or indirect reputational or informational contagion.[143]

When assessing the necessity of a bailout, governments usually consider the costs of a failure. If the failure of a bank would lead to systemic implications, governments will do almost anything to avert it. These systemic implications are given if the failure of the bank would either (i) affect the country by disrupting financial intermediation to a degree that the economy and therefore other financial firms would suffer significantly; or if it would (ii) affect the stability of other financial firms connected in counterparty transactions so that financial intermediation would be impacted.[144]

Banks that have evolved in a manner that their failure would result in such systemic implications are considered "too-big-to-fail" (TBTF).[145] It is, however, important to emphasize that not just size but also other qualities, notably complexity and interconnectedness can lead to systemic implications.[146]

---

142 *Lehmann* (2014) Ring-Fencing, 2; Banks that accept deposits are by their very nature in danger of bank runs. Reason for that is their combination of illiquid assets and liquid liabilities. As deposits can be withdrawn at any given time, banks that are actually solvent may need to sell illiquid longterm assets at loss, to match withdrawals. *European Commission* (2014) Impact Assessment Part 2, 56; See also *Diamond/Dybvig* (1983) Bank Runs, 402; *Carnell/Macey/Miller* (2017) Financial Institutions, 200–203.

143 *European Commission* (2014) Impact Assessment Part 2, 56.

144 *Blundell-Wignall/Wehinger/Slovik* (2010) The Elephant in the Room, 22. Furthermore, as history has shown particularly since the financial crisis, politicians *"have proven unable to resist the temptation of 'bailouts'"*. *Sester* (2010) Bank Restructuring Law, 515; This willingness to bail out banks has been examined in a number of studies, for a good overview of factors influencing government's bailout decision, see Hofer (2014) Structural Reforms, 114 et seqq.

145 *Blundell-Wignall/Wehinger/Slovik* (2010) The Elephant in the Room, 22. For a compact discussion of the too-big-to-fail problem, see e.g. *Morrison* (2011) Systemic Risks, 500–508, *White* (2013) Too-Big-to-Fail, 25–28.

146 "Too-big-to-fail" is a rather imprecise term, as it refers only to the size of a financial institution. As has been set out, size alone is not the only reason for governments to intervene. Other terms in use are, *inter alia*, "too-complex-to-fail" or "too-interconnected-to-fail". See e.g. *Goldstein/Veron* (2011) Too Big To Fail, 2 Fn 1; *Hofer* (2014) Structural Reforms, 113.

C. Implicit subsidies

Banks can arguably have an interest in being considered TBTF,[147] as the qualification entails an important subsidy: market participants anticipate that banks considered TBTF will be bailed out in case of distress and are therefore willing to fund them at lower returns that do not reflect the actual risks. This implicit subsidy[148] stems from the government, hence from taxpayers, and distorts competition.[149]

Moreover, the subsidy creates moral hazard.[150] Moral hazard arises when a party is incentivised to alter its behaviour because it is not fully exposed to the consequences of its actions.[151] The implicit subsidy is an incentive for banks to increasingly engage in risky activities, because funding costs do not correspond with their actual level of risk. Banks that are not considered TBTF may furthermore be tempted to achieve the status via an increase of size or other qualities. Another important aspect is that TBTF subsidies distort competition.[152]

---

147 *Moenninghoff/Ongena/Wieandt, for example,* quote a number of instances in which executives of G-SIBs allegedly underscored the importance of being considered systemically important. See *Moenninghoff/Ongena/Wieandt* (2015) Too-Big-to-Fail, 222 Fn 7.

148 For an explanation of explicit and implicit subsidies, see Chapter I.A.B.b: Costs.

149 *Siegert/Willison* (2015), The "Too Big to Fail" Problem, 4–5.

150 *Siegert/Willison* (2015), The "Too Big to Fail" Problem, 4–5.

151 *ICB* (2011) Vickers Report, 248. The recognition that parties are more diligent when they are exposed to the consequences of their actions is evident and has long been described in the context of personal liability. See e.g. *Eucken* (1990) Wirtschaftspolitik, 279 et seqq. (noting that the diligence in investments increases with personal liability); *Smith* (1976) Wealth of Nations, V.1.107 ("*The directors of such companies, however, being the managers rather of other people's money than their own, it cannot well be expected that they should watch over it with the same anxious vigilance with which the partners of a private copartnery frequently watch over their own*"); *Brändli/Rieder* (2009) Vertrauensbildung, 62–64. In the context above, diligence correlates not (necessarily) with personal liability, but with other factors; for example insolvency (in case of the bank) or job-loss (in the case of employees). The basic idea, however, remains the same: moral hazard can be prevented if parties face the consequences of their actions.

152 *Siegert/Willison* (2015), The "Too Big to Fail" Problem, 4–5; The distortion of competition can materialize between larger and smaller banks, because larger banks have the advantage of low-priced funding. It can also materialize between banks headquartered in different countries depending on the state of their public finances, hence the potential of government support. Furthermore, a distortion can arise between the financial sector and other sectors, making the finan-

Implicit subsidies are difficult to calculate but are likely of material size: according to *Haldane*, implicit subsidies for the 29 largest banks amounted to 70 billion $ per year between 2002 and 2007, equalling *"roughly 50% of the average post-tax profits of these banks over the period"*.[153] The *OECD Survey on Implicit Guarantees* found that annual implicit subsidies range between 0.5 and 12 billion $ in countries with smaller banking sectors to close to even 100 billion $ in countries with large banking sectors.[154]

D. Global systemically important banks (G-SIBs)

After the economic crisis, the Basel Committee on Banking Supervision (BCBS)[155] established criteria to identify "global systemically important banks" (G-SIBs),[156] i.e. global banks that are considered too-systemically-relevant to fail.[157] The BCBS uses an indicator-based measurement approach, taking into account banks' size, interconnectedness, global activity, complexity and the lack of readily available substitutes or financial institution infrastructure that would take on services provided by the bank.[158] The specific identification of the banks is then performed by the FSB:[159] Currently the FSB lists 30 G-SIBs; the list is renewed annually.[160]

---

cial sector more profit-making, therefore drawing away resources from other sectors. *European Commission* (2014) Impact Assessment Part 2, 55, 60.

153 *Haldane* (2012) On Being the Right Size, 3; *Bundesrat* (2015) Bericht Too Big to Fail, 1934.

154 *Schich/Aydin* (2014) OECD Survey Results, 13–14.

155 https://www.bis.org/bcbs/.

156 G-SIBs can be regarded as a subcategory of global systemically important financial institutions (G-SIFIs). The latter also comprise non-bank financial intermediaries, for example insurance companies. *Moenninghoff/Ongena/Wieandt* (2015) Too-Big-to-Fail, 221. SIFIs are defined as *"financial institutions whose distress or disorderly failure [...] would cause significant disruption to the wider financial system and economic activity"*. *FSB* (2011) Systemically Important Financial Institutions, 1.

157 *Moenninghoff/Ongena/Wieandt* (2015) Too-Big-to-Fail, 221.

158 *Basel Committee on Banking Supervision* (2013) Global Systemically Important Banks, 5.

159 http://www.fsb.org/.

160 *FSB* (2017) Global Systemically Important Banks, 1; The list comprising all banks considered G-SIBs was published for the first time in 2011 (see *FSB* (2011) Systemically Important Financial Institutions); Banks listed as G-SIB carry the burden of increased supervision, capital surcharges and the establishment of resolution regimes. However, some authors criticise the official designation of

As there are many banks that are not significant from an international perspective but could, in case of distress or failure, have major adverse effects on their domestic financial system and economy, a category of "domestic systemically important banks" (D-SIBs) was created.[161]

E. Bank Size and TBTF

While many banks considerably deleveraged since the financial crisis, decreased their financial trading activities and increased capital a great deal,[162] the too-big-to-fail problem seems to be far from being solved: The Worldbank recently investigated trends in bank size in its *Global Financial Development Report.* It found a *"dramatic increase in bank size"*: in spite of regulatory efforts to tackle TBTF, total assets of the world's largest banks increased by more than staggering 40% from 2005 to 2014. The largest banks are the ones most active internationally.[163]

IV. Structural Reform and Ring-fencing

Among the post-crisis reform measures, one of the most controversial is structural reform. This chapter defines the term bank structural reform and puts it into relation with ring-fencing. Ring-fencing is then delimited from two important structural reforms that are related to it.

---

banks as being G-SIB, because that may strengthen existing TBTF perceptions and increase moral hazard. *Moenninghoff/Ongena/Wieandt* (2015) Too-Big-to-Fail, 222 et seqq.; See also relating to SIFIs *Elliott/Litan* (2011) Systemically Important Financial Institutions, 10–14.

161 *Basel Committee on Banking Supervision* (2012) Domestic Systemically Important Banks, 1; BCBS only adopted a framework comprising a minimal set of principles, so that local authorities have appropriate discretion. *Basel Committee on Banking Supervision* (2012) Domestic Systemically Important Banks, 1–2.

162 See Chapter I.II.C.c: Post crisis response.

163 See *Worldbank* (2018) Global Financial Developments Report, 10 (This trend has continued since the beginning of the economic crisis and can be observed globally. Only in high-income OECD countries bank size has decreased relatively to GDP since 2008; however, bank size is still exceeding substantially 2005 values); See also with regard to the global increase in bank size, *White/Mehmood* (2017) 10 years on; *Martel/Van Rixtel/Mota* (2012) Business Models of International Banks, 116 (noting a long-term trend towards bigger international banking groups and higher concentration).

A. Structural reform as an umbrella term

Structural reform is a broad term that is applied in many fields of expertise.[164] In banking, it can be understood as an umbrella term for a variety of regulations that intervene with the organisation of banks.[165] As there is no limitation inherent in the term, all substantial requirements for banks to adapt a certain organisation, or to refrain from a certain organisation can be considered "structural reform".

For the purpose of this dissertation, bank structural reform is defined as *any regulatory reform that substantially affects the legal entity structure, the size, the management organization or the ability to provide activities.*[166]

In practice, certain organisational requirements are most prominent and therefore most widely associated with the term: for instance, the FSB conducted a survey in 2014, in which jurisdictions were asked to consider certain structural banking reforms. It included but was not limited, *inter alia,* to ring-fencing, activity restrictions, incentives or requirements for banks to operate in certain structures (e.g. subsidiaries instead of branches).[167]

---

164 The main use of the term "structural reform" outside banking is for changes to a country's economy to enhance *inter alia* growth, competitiveness, productivity and stability. (See e.g. *The Economist,* What structural reform is and why it is important (December 9, 2014) (discussing structural reform for governments); *OECD* (2015) Structural Reforms in Europe, 3–4 (quantifying the impact of structural reforms on Portugal, France and Italy)); The term is furthermore used in other fields such as education (e.g. *Elmore* (1995) Structural Reform and Educational Practice) or law (e.g. *Gilles* (2000) Reinventing Structural Reform Litigation).

165 See e.g. the use of the term "structural reform" in *Gordon/Ringe* (2015) Bank Resolution, 19.

166 This definition is based on *Hofer*'s, but includes activity restrictions, such as the Volcker Rule and full separation (see *Hofer* (2014) Structural Reforms, 218 (defining structural reform as *"any regulatory reform substantially affecting either the legal entity structure, the size or management organization of [large and complex financial institutions]"*). *Hofer* excludes activity restrictions, such as the Volcker Rule from his concept of structural reform but includes full separation (*Hofer* (2014) Structural Reforms, 251–257). This is inconsistent, as activity bans are to be seen as a subcategory of full separation. See Chapter I.IV.D: Ring-fencing and the activities ban. Cf. *Armour et al.* (2016) Financial Regulation, 505 (describing structural reform as *"measures designed to limit the range of activities that may be carried on by a banking firm"*).

167 *FSB* (2014) Structural Banking Reforms, 3 (The fact that there is no specific limitation to the term "structural reform" can be seen in the non-conclusive nature of the request of the FSB to consider certain measures but also others than the ones explicitly asked for).

To illustrate the variety of measures that can be attributed to structural reform, *Hofer's* categorization of bank structural reforms according to their strictness is briefly laid out: *Hofer* distinguishes between soft structural reforms, intermediate structural reforms and strict structural reforms. According to him, soft structural reforms *"do not compellingly force [banks] to restructure"*. They include indirect incentives such as capital surcharges, insurance or tax solutions and rebate systems and recovery and resolution planning.[168] As intermediate structural reforms, he considers requirements that *"aim at some form of corporate separateness, while the different entities are still allowed to be under the same roof"*. He attributes to that group ring-fencing, the requirement to establish a service company, and geographical subsidiarization. Strict structural reforms majorly impact banks' structures. They include the full separation of banks and the introduction of size caps.[169] One could add to the last group the concept of narrow banking.[170]

Hofer's by far non-exhaustive categorisation illustrates how many different structural reforms have been discussed. While his assessment contributes to the categorisation of bank structural reforms, one should keep in mind that it is an isolated consideration of each measure. In practice, these measures often interact and are intertwined. As will be demonstrated in Part III of the dissertation for example, ring-fencing as the functional separation of commercial and investment banking can also be achieved through a combination of incentives and emergency planning.[171]

In summary, one can establish that structural reform in banking is an umbrella term that describes a variety of regulations that substantially in-

---

168 *Hofer* also mentions Swiss emergency planning as a soft, i.e. not compelling, structural reform. See *Hofer* (2014) Structural Reforms, 218.

169 See *Hofer* (2014) Structural Reforms, 214–252. Differentiating between structural reforms by considering their strictness is not unusual. See *Vickers* (2016) Banking Reform Presentation, 17.

170 Narrow banking can be understood as a severe restriction of a bank's business model with regard to deposit-taking. Goal is to reach a total or at least very high matching of maturities between deposits and loans. Expertenkommission (2010) Final Report, 116. For a comprehensive explanation, see e.g. *Chow/Surti* (2011) Making Banks Safer, 9–11; see also *Wilmarth* (2014) Narrow Banking, 7–10; *Alexander/Lorez* (2010) Universal Banks, 465–468. *Carnell/Macey/Miller* (2017) Financial Institutions, 234–235. This structural reform has been overwhelmingly discarded. *Hofer* discusses it as non-structural, but related reform. See *Hofer* (2014) Structural Reforms, 254–257.

171 See Part III: Legal Comparative Analysis. See also the example of the service company in the chapter below, (Chapter I.IV.B: Ring-fencing as a structural reform).

tervene with the organisation of banks. Certain measures are more prominently associated with the term "bank structural reform" than others. Due to the broad scope of the term, it includes measures of very diverse nature, which is reflected by the differences in their strictness.

B. Ring-fencing as a structural reform: the concept of ring-fencing

Ring-fencing constitutes one of the structural reform measures set out above. The line between the terms "ring-fencing" and "structural reform" is somewhat blurred as they are often used synonymously.[172] In the EU for example, the ring-fencing agenda is pursued under the name "bank structural reform".[173]

Ring-fencing should, however, be regarded as its own concept as it can be clearly delimited from other structural reforms. This dissertation establishes three core characteristics that identify ring-fencing as a concept of structural reform on its own, and that are used to delimit it against other structural reforms of banking:

Core characteristics of ring-fencing are (i) the fact that it separates commercial banking activities from investment banking activities: ring-fencing rules all segregate certain activities attributed to commercial banking from certain activities attributed to investment banking.[174] (ii) that it at the same time seeks to maintain universal banking:[175] banking groups must

172 For the use of "structural reform" instead of "ring-fencing", see e.g. *HM Treasury* (2012) Banking Reform, 7; *Gambacorta/Van Rixtel* (2013) Structural Bank Regulation Initiatives.

173 *European Commission* (2014) Proposal for a Regulation, 2.

174 See *ICB* (2011) Vickers Report, 54; *HLEG* (2012) Liikanen Report, 101; See Chapter III.IV: What Activities Fall on Which Side of the Fence? (setting out the separation in the UK, Germany and Switzerland).

175 See *Vickers* (2016) Banking Reform Presentation, 24 ("*Go for structured universal banking, not ending universal banking -more robust than unstructured universal banking*"); See also *HLEG* (2012) Liikanen Report, iii ("*The long-standing universal banking model in Europe would remain, however, untouched, since the separated activities would be carried out in the same banking group. Hence, banks' ability to provide a wide range of financial services to their customers would be maintained*"); *HLEG* (2012) Liikanen Report, 102 ("*The proposal addresses the core weaknesses in the banking sector, while retaining the key benefits of the universal banking model and allowing for business model diversity*"); See Chapter III.IV: What Activities Fall on Which Side of the Fence? (setting out that banking groups in the UK, Germany and Switzerland can continue to provide all sorts of banking activities).

apply a certain structure to continue providing all sorts of activities. There are, however, no limitations for providing activities, whereby the universal banking model remains unimpeded;[176] and (iii) that the separation of activities is protected by a fence, i.e. provisions that aim to ensure that the separated activities can be provided independently from each other.[177]

These three core characteristics of ring-fencing will be an essential part of the following chapters and will be reflected in the established definition of ring-fencing. While there are no objections to the synonymous use of the terms, it should be kept in mind that the term "ring-fencing" is narrower than the term "structural reform".

Ring-fencing selectively makes use of parts of structural reform measures that *Hofer* differentiates from it:[178] For example, ring-fencing rules regularly include the requirement to establish a service company or set down rules how services between the ring-fenced and the non-ring-fenced entities can be provided.[179] Ring-fencing describes a certain structure banking groups have to implement. It does not necessarily need to be stipulated by one law, but can theoretically also be reached by a combination of other structural reforms, for example by combining minimum requirements with additional incentives.[180]

C. Ring-fencing and full separation

Ring-fencing needs to be contrasted against another form of structural reform: the full separation of commercial banking and investment banking. It is most prominently featured by the Glass-Steagall Act (GSA). A short digression on the GSA and a subsequent delimitation of ring-fencing is considered important at this point, because the GSA (i) considerably influenced ring-fencing initiatives and because it (ii) is sometimes associated with ring-fencing.

---

176 See Chapter I.I.A.a.2: Universal banking after ring-fencing.

177 See *ICB* (2011) Vickers Report, 62 et seqq.; *HLEG* (2012) Liikanen Report, 102; See also Chapter III.V: Height of the Fence (setting out provisions governing the strength of separation).

178 See the Chapter above (Chapter I.IV.A: Structural reform as an umbrella term).

179 See Chapter III.V.A.e: Continuity of services (and the respective chapters on Germany and Switzerland).

180 This will be discussed in the context of the Swiss solution. See, *inter alia*, Chapter III.II.b: Policy mix and core measure organization.

a. Digression: The Glass-Steagall Act

1. Reasons for the adoption of the Glass-Steagall Act

The GSA was adopted in 1933 during the Roosevelt administration's New Deal.[181] After liberalising bank activities past 1910, banks started to significantly increase their financing of business firms and consumers. Banks allowed their customers to run up considerable debt, which they used to make risky investments.[182] During the 1920s, banks broadly entered the securities-underwriting business, evolving into universal banks.[183] In the summer of 1929, a recession began that was intensified by the stock market crash in October and that turned these investments unviable by a large scale.[184] The recession later became known as the Great Depression.[185]

The GSA was adopted because (i) the direct involvement of commercial banks with corporate securities was considered harmful to the financial system and because (ii) proponents argued that universal banking led to a considerable conflict of interest.[186] Large banks were criticised for motivating reckless speculation in two respects: firstly, they were accused of making excessive loans on securities as well as investments in securities with their own funds. Secondly, they were accused of convincing retail investors and small correspondent banks of converting deposits and safe investments into risky investments underwritten by their securities affiliates.[187]

The Pecora Hearings in 1933 shed a light on *"terrible abuses of trust and conflicts of interest"* by the *National City Bank*, the most important bank engaged in securities activities, and its securities affiliate. They caused public outrage and set the political environment for the adoption of such a strict law as the GSA.[188]

---

181 *Carpenter/Murphy* (2010) Permissible Securities Activities, 2.

182 *Wilmarth* (2005) Universal Banks, 560–561.

183 *Wilmarth* (2016) Glass-Steagall, 1291.

184 *Wilmarth* (2005) Universal Banks, 560–561.

185 *Carnell/Macey/Miller* (2017) Financial Institutions, 19.

186 *Kroszner/Rajan* (1994) Glass-Steagall Act, 810.

187 See *Wilmarth* (2005) Universal Banks, 565, citing remarks of certain proponents of the GSA.

188 *Benston* (1994) Universal Banking, 122. For a detailed discussion of abusive practices of the National City Bank, see also *Wilmarth* (2016) Glass-Steagall, 1301–1327 (*Wilmarth* sets out in detail how*"National City and Chase encouraged unsophisticated investors to purchase risky securities through highpressure sales techniques and misleading prospectuses. Both banks used stock pools and other manipulative techniques to promote the sale and boost the price of their own stocks as well as*

2. Full separation

The GSA's four provisions[189] established the separation of commercial and investment banking that left its mark on the United States banking landscape up until today.[190]

The separation is accomplished through provisions that on the one hand prohibit an affiliation of banks with securities firms,[191] and on the other hand the sharing of personnel with securities firms.[192] The GSA further restricts banks from underwriting and dealing with securities and purchasing them for their own account. There is, however, an exception for certain government securities, such as United States obligations.[193] Vis-à-vis,

---

stocks of favored clients. Both banks incurred large losses after making hazardous loans and investments to support the activities of their securities affiliates. Senior executives at both banks reaped extraordinary personal gains by exploiting their managerial positions").

189 Most authors consider the Glass-Steagall Act to refer to Sects. 16, 20, 21, 32 of the Banking Act of 1933, (e.g. *Masciandaro/Suardi* (2014) Public Interest and Lobbies, 308; *Pace* (2012) Business of Banking, 12; *Manasfi* (2013) Systemic Risk, 185 Fn 9); *Wilmarth* also includes Sec. 5(c) (*Wilmarth* (2005) Universal Banks, 564 Fn 8). This provision extends the securities limitations for national banks on state-chartered banks (see *Carpenter/Murphy* (2010) Permissible Securities Activities, 5 Fn 27). For a detailed discussion of the provisions, see e.g. *Felsenfeld/Glass* (2011) Banking Regulation, 307 et seqq.

190 See *Carpenter/Murphy* (2010) Permissible Securities Activities, 2. The full separation of the GSA was finally abolished by the Gramm-Leach-Bliley Act (Gramm-Leach-Bliley Act, Publ. L. No. 106–102, 113 Stat. 1338 (1999) (GLBA)). It repeals two provisions of the GSA, namely the prohibition for banks to affiliate with securities firms and the prohibition on the sharing of personnel (Sec. 101, Gramm-Leach-Bliley Act). However, it leaves the other provisions of the GSA intact, thereby maintaining the prohibition for banks from offering the entire spectrum of securities, and the prohibition for securities firms from accepting deposits (*Carpenter/Murphy* (2010) Permissible Securities Activities, 15, The GLBA does not repeal Sec. 16 and Sec. 21 of the GSA). The GLBA therefore permits a new category of holding company, the "financial holding company". It is allowed to own subsidiaries that engage in (i) banking, (ii) securities activities, (iii) insurance activities. *Barth/Brumbaugh/Wilcox* (2000) Glass-Steagall, 193; see also *Carpenter/Murphy* (2010) Permissible Securities Activities, 16.

191 Sec. 20, Glass-Steagall Act.

192 Sec. 32, Glass-Steagall Act.

193 Sec. 16, Glass-Steagall Act. Similar provisions can be found in modern-day structural reforms, e.g. the European Commission's draft regulation (Chapter II.II.C.a: Prohibitions) or the Volcker Rule (Chapter I.IV.D.a: Digression: The Volcker Rule).

the GSA prohibits securities firms from engaging in the deposit-taking business.[194]

The GSA is enforced and interpreted by regulating authorities via regulations, guidelines and orders.[195] This leeway for enforcement led to its demise when regulators *"adopted creative statutory interpretations"*.[196]

The GSA's full separation prohibits banking groups from affiliating with securities firms and investment banking activities. It thereby limits universal banking. Full separation can thus, for the purpose of this dissertation, be defined as *a bank structural reform that prohibits a broad set of investment banking activities, which are considered high-risk, for the whole banking group, thereby limiting universal banking.*

3. Criticism and impact of the Glass-Steagall Act

Among the modern-day criticism, *Wilmarth* highlights three arguments commonly brought forward: firstly, it is often said that the GSA was "interest group legislation", in that it shielded traditional investment banks from competition with commercial banks.[197] Secondly, it is argued that universal banks were indeed less risky and that they did not jeopardize the financial system.[198] Thirdly, the basis for the belief of lawmakers that universal banking led to severe conflicts of interest is contested.[199]

The GSA nevertheless had a massive impact on the United States' banking landscape, as the mandated separation of commercial and investment banking was in principle maintained for most of the 20th century.[200] The resulting differentiation of regulation for securities firms on the one hand

---

194 Sec. 21, Glass-Steagall Act.

195 *Carpenter/Murphy* (2010) Permissible Securities Activities, 8.

196 See e.g. *Wilmarth* (2016) Glass-Steagall, 445, 456 et seqq.

197 This is, for example, argued by *Shughart* (1988) Public Choice Perspective, 103–104.

198 One of the main advocates of this argument is e.g. *White* (1986) Glass-Steagall Act, 51–52; *Wilmarth*, however, criticises *White's* data and conclusions, see *Wilmarth* (2005) Universal Banks, 591–592.

199 *Wilmarth* (2005) Universal Banks, 585 et seqq.; see also *Barth/Brumbaugh/Wilcox* (2000) Glass-Steagall, 192 (discussing reasons for the repeal of the Glass-Steagall Act).

200 *European Commission* (2014) Impact Assessment Part 2, 5; *Akhigbe/Whyte* (2004) Gramm Leach-Bliley Act, 435.

and banks on the other hand emanated from the U.S. and influenced regulation around the world.[201]

Since the global economic crisis in 2008, the GSA has again attracted attention in politics and academics. In search of a solution for the structural problems of the financial system, many voices called for a reinstallation of full separation.[202] This became particularly visible during the 2016 presidential election, in which the GSA was a central part of various candidates' campaigns.[203] What contributed to the almost legendary status of the Act and what is indeed remarkable, is that during the long reign of the GSA, there was no major crisis in the United States; and that, although it had before been watered down considerably, the global economic crisis hit only shortly after its full repeal.[204]

---

201 See *Carpenter/Murphy* (2010) Permissible Securities Activities, 2. On the significant influence of the regulatory divide between securities law and banking regulation, that also left its traces on the European Union, see *Armour et al.* (2016) Financial Regulation, 3–5.

202 See e.g. *Johnson*, Resurrecting Glass-Steagall, Project Syndicate: The World's Opinion Page (October 25, 2015); It is interesting to see that the GSA to this day has considerable significance to the American people, as observable in the political discussion. It is also visible in the recognisable orientation of the VR along the GSA, (see Chapter I.IV.D.a: Digression: The Volcker Rule). There may be a number of possible reasons for that: (i) a regulation, which governs an important sector like the banking business for such a long time has the potential of leaving marks on society; (ii) The GSA is based on a concept that is simple, radical and easy to grasp; (iii) the full repeal of the GSA was only 8 years before the economic crisis, a possible linkage (regardless of whether true or false) is therefore easy to establish for the general public.

203 Especially *Bernie Sanders* was promoting a new form of GSA and made it a central part of his campaign during the 2016 US presidential elections (see *Escow*, 5 Reasons Glass-Steagall Matters, (November 16, 2015) https://berniesanders.com/yes-glass-steagall-matters-here-are-5-reasons-why/; *The Economist*, Bernie Sanders's obsession with Glass-Steagall is misplaced (February 18, 2016)). *Donald Trump* also spoke out for a new form of the GSA during the elections. See *Reuters*, Trump calls for '21st century' Glass-Steagall banking law (October 26, 2016).

204 This is, for instance, indicated by the *Financial Crisis Inquiry Commission* (2011) Financial Crisis, 52–56; *Lehmann* (2014) Ring-Fencing, 6; see also *Merkley/Levin* (2011) 518–520; *Armour et al.* (2016) Financial Regulation, 505; *Wilmarth* (2016) Glass-Steagall, 444 Fn 7 (pointing out multiple sources discussing the connection between the Glass-Steagall Act repeal and the economic crisis). See also e.g. *Reich*, Hillary Clinton's Glass-Steagall, (July 14, 2015) http://robertreich.org/post/124114229225 (*"To this day some Wall Street apologists argue Glass-Steagall wouldn't have prevented the 2008 crisis because the real culprits were nonbanks like Lehman Brothers and Bear Stearns. Baloney. These nonbanks got their funding from*

b. Differences between ring-fencing and full separation

Ring-fencing is influenced by the full separation of commercial banking and investment banking and its most prominent emanation, the Glass-Steagall Act. They both share the idea that certain commercial banking activities need to be separated from certain investment banking activities (one of ring-fencing's core characteristics).[205] This is likely the reason why it is sometimes associated with ring-fencing.

The following paragraphs first outline important differences between ring-fencing and full separation in general, taking the form of the other two core characteristics established above. Subsequently, differences between ring-fencing as a 21st century structural reform and the Glass-Steagall Act shall be discussed.

The first difference is ring-fencing's core characteristic of striking a balance between the separation on the one hand, and universal banking on the other hand. While full separation taking the form of the Glass-Steagall Act, to quote *Vickers*, virtually *"end[ed] universal banking"*,[206] all methods of ring-fencing maintain the freedom of banks to offer unlimited financial services.[207]

---

the big banks [...] If the big banks hadn't provided them the money, the nonbanks wouldn't have got into trouble"); see also e.g. *Reid*, We were wrong about universal banking, Financial Times (November 11, 2015) (in which former chairman and CEO of Citigroup, *John Reid*, considers universal banking, as introduced with the repeal of the GSA *"inherently unstable and unworkable"*). The Glass-Steagall period is thus referred to by some as the "Quiet Period". See *Crawford* (2017) Glass-Steagall, 8.

205 See Chapter I.IV.B: Ring-fencing as a structural reform.

206 See *Vickers* (2016) Banking Reform Presentation, 20.

207 As an example for the attitude towards universal banking, see *ICB* (2011) Vickers Report, 138 (*"Leaving aside the diversification benefits, the proposed ring-fence would also preserve the other synergies which full separation would remove. Customers would be able to receive their banking services together in one place. The ring-fence would not require separation of the operational provision of all services to customers – rather it would require separation of the financial transactions to which these give rise. Further, the ring-fence itself would place no restriction on the sharing of information and expertise between ring-fenced banks and the rest of the banking group"*); see Chapter I.IV.B: Ring-fencing as a structural reform. As will be discussed, a literal interpretation of the word ring-fencing already produces that (i) a ring-fenced part and (ii) a part that may unwantedly influence the ring-fenced part need to be combined under the same roof (see Chapter I.VII.A: Origins of the term "ring-fencing"; Chapter I.VII.B: Ring-fencing outside banking regulation). This is also a pervasive element of all uses of ring-fencing outside banking regulation (see Chapter I.VII.B: Ring-fencing outside banking regulation).

The second difference is ring-fencing's core characteristic of establishing a fence: a prohibition cannot be equated with a system of provisions that aims to ensure legal, financial and operational independence of two entities within the same group.[208]

Regarding differences between ring-fencing as a 21st century structural reform and the Glass-Steagall Act, the following can be found: the goals of ring-fencing are not the same as the ones of Glass-Steagall. One could describe it as an evolution of the regulations' ambitions: Glass-Steagall aimed primarily to protect the individual depositor (i) from conflicts of interest within the bank which could occur due to the *"easy access to large numbers of unsophisticated depositors"* who could easily be defrauded by misrepresenting the quality of underwritten securities; and (ii) from the failure of a bank due to the risky nature of investment banking.[209] While unsound universal banks were thought of as *"undermining the safety of the banking system"* for their risk of causing bank runs,[210] it can be concluded that the protection of the individual has been the focus of attention.

As will be set out, modern-day ring-fencing rules aim much more at the protection of the system, namely the financial system and the real economy as a whole.[211] This is largely due to the developments in the banking sector, with banks growing in size, complexity and interconnectedness.[212] Ring-fencing rules aim at enhancing the resolvability and by that reducing implicit subsidies of large universal banks. Conflicts of interest are also addressed but play a much lesser role compared to Glass-Steagall's full separation. Ultimately, ring-fencing attempts to tackle the too-big-to-fail problem.[213]

In addition, it can be found that there is an altered threat situation. While the Glass-Steagall Act is characterised by a distrust towards "simple"

---

208 See *ICB* (2011) Vickers Report, 63–66 (noting that *"the right approach is not to require full separation, but instead to impose through ring-fencing the degree of separation required to secure the benefits"*).

209 See *Kroszner/Rajan* (1994) Glass-Steagall Act, 811, 814–815; see also *White* (1986) Glass-Steagall Act, 38; *Armour et al.* (2016) Financial Regulation, 512.

210 See *White* (1986) Glass-Steagall Act, 39; see also *Kroszner/Rajan* (1994) Glass-Steagall Act, 811. The stability of the banking system was furthermore backed up by the introduction of a federal deposit insurance to discourage "runs" on banks. See *Wilmarth* (2017) Glass-Steagall Repeal, 450.

211 *Armour et al.* (2016) Financial Regulation, 512; see Chapter I.V: The Basic Rationale and Goals of Ring-fencing.

212 See Chapter I.II: Changes in the Realm of International Banking; Chapter I.III: Bailouts and Too-Big-to-Fail.

213 See Chapter I.V: The Basic Rationale and Goals of Ring-fencing.

investment banking activities, in particular underwriting,[214] the focus of modern-day ring-fencing rules is on complex, international trading activities, with some even considering underwriting not risky enough to justify a separation from the retail entity.[215] This is, of course, also due to developments in the banking industry, which has become faster, more complex, more technologically advanced and more international.

D. Ring-fencing and the activities ban

Ring-fencing needs to be contrasted against another form of structural reform: the *activities ban* which is most prominently featured in the Volcker Rule (VR). A short digression is considered important because, as will be discussed, (i) the *activities ban* is sometimes attributed to ring-fencing. While it in some instances is (ii) applied together with ring-fencing, it is a different structural reform and should be identified as such. The VR is also a (iii) warning example for the difficulties in defining proprietary trading.

a. Digression: The Volcker Rule

1. Section 619 Dodd-Frank Act

The Dodd-Frank Act is a central part of the Obama administration's response to the economic crisis. Its aim is to make the financial system stronger and to limit risk-taking at banking entities.[216] Its 848 pages bring about important changes for the financial sector.[217]

---

214 See Chapter I.IV.C.a: Digression: The Glass-Steagall Act.

215 This is typically the case in jurisdictions that the containment method (see Chapter I.VI: Different Methods of Ring-Fencing), for example Germany (see Chapter III.IV.B: Germany); according to the Liikanen Report, underwriting would also remain in the ring-fenced entity (see Chapter II.I.C: Avenue 2).

216 *Financial Stability Oversight Council* (2011) Proprietary Trading, 1. See also e.g. *Cooper,* Obama Signs Overhaul of Financial System, NY Times, (2010, July 21). It also aims at avoiding future tax money bailouts. This is emphasized by a *"prohibition of taxpayer funding"*. See Sec. 214 Dodd-Frank Act; see also *Sester* (2010) Bank Restructuring Law, 515 Fn 11.

217 *Krawiec* (2013) Joe the Plummer, 54–55; *Doyle et al.* (2010) Volcker Rule, 692 (underscoring the Volcker Rule's *"significant effects"* on banking entities and FED-supervised firms).

"Volcker Rule" refers to Section 619 of the Dodd-Frank Act that added a new section to the Bank Holding Company Act of 1956.[218] Although the Dodd-Frank Act was adopted already in 2010, the final regulations, i.e. rules specifying the implementation of the VR, jointly released by the regulating authorities, were officially adopted as late as 2014.[219]

The VR's core elements are (i) a prohibition of certain relationships with hedge funds and private equity funds and (ii) a prohibition of proprietary trading.[220] These are realized by the stipulation that a *"banking entity"* is forbidden to (i)*"acquire or retain any equity, partnership, or other ownership interest in or sponsor a hedge fund or a private equity fund"* or to (ii) *"engage in proprietary trading"*.[221]

The term "banking entity" is designed to cover not just a particular depository institution but the whole banking group.[222] The VR thereby takes a group perspective,[223] i.e. prohibited activities cannot be performed by any member of a group that includes a bank.

The VR defines proprietary trading as *"engaging as a principal for the trading account [...] in any transaction to purchase or sell, or otherwise acquire or dispose of any [financial instrument]"*.[224] Trading account means *"any account used for acquiring or taking positions in [financial instruments] principal-*

218 Sec. 619 of the Dodd-Frank Act adds a new Sec. 13 to the Bank Holding Company Act of 1956, 12 U.S.C. 1851.

219 *U.S. Agencies* (2014) Final Rule. The Final Rule was already released in December 2013. See homepage of the U.S. Securities and Exchange Commission, https://www.sec.gov/rules/final/finalarchive/finalarchive2013.shtml.

220 See title of Sec. 619 Dodd-Frank Act.

221 Sec. 619(a)(1) Dodd-Frank Act.

222 It is defined as *"any insured depository institution [...], any company that controls an insured depository institution, or that is treated as a bank holding company [...], and any affiliate or subsidiary of any such entity"*. Sec. 619(h)(1) Dodd-Frank Act.

223 See e.g. *Binder* (2015) Ring-Fencing, 109.

224 *"[E]ngaging as a principal for the trading account [...] in any transaction to purchase or sell, or otherwise acquire or dispose of any security, any derivative, any contract of sale of a commodity for future delivery, any option on [any of the just mentioned] or any other security or financial instrument"* that a federal regulator determines. Sec. 619(h)(4) Dodd-Frank Act; Trading account is defined as *"any account used for acquiring or taking positions in securities and [financial] instruments [...] principally for the purpose purpose of selling in the near term (or otherwise with the intent to resell in order to profit from short-term price movements)"* and any other accounts regulators may determine. Sec. 619(h)(6) Dodd-Frank Act.

ly for the purpose of selling in the near term (or otherwise with the intent to resell in order to profit from short-term price movements)".[225]

The VR's general prohibition therefore forbids banks from owning or running hedge funds and private equity funds[226] and from engaging in trading activities for own account with the purpose of (i) selling in the near term or to (ii) profiting from short-term price movements.[227]

In a second step, the VR stipulates a number of exemptions for activities related to proprietary trading[228] that are considered beneficial to society. Among these "permitted activities" are proprietary trading in government securities, market making, and risk-mitigating hedging activities.[229] Further exemptions are set down for proprietary trading outside the U.S.[230] and certain investments through insurance company affiliates.[231]

In a third step, the VR limits the permitted activities insofar as no activity is to profit from the exemptions, (i) that would result in a material conflict of interest between the bank and counterparties, (ii) that would result in a material exposure by the bank to high-risk assets or high-risk trading strategies, (iii) that would pose a threat to the safety and soundness of the

225 *"[A]ny account used for acquiring or taking positions in [financial instruments] principally for the purpose of selling in the near term (or otherwise with the intent to resell in order to profit from short-term price movements)"* and any other accounts regulators may determine. Sec. 619(h)(6) Dodd-Frank Act.

226 *Elliott/Rauch* (2014) Volcker Rule, 4.

227 The terms "near term" and "short-term" have, for good reason, been criticised for their vagueness. See for a discussion *Whitehead* (2011) Volcker Rule, 48–49, 48 Fn 43; The Final Rules stipulate a rebuttable presumption that financial positions are presumed to be for the trading account, if a bank holds the financial instrument for less than 60 days, or if it substantially transfers the risk of the financial instrument within 60 days. This means that banks need to hold financial instruments for longer than 60 days to avoid qualification as proprietary trading (they can, however, demonstrate that they held a financial instrument for other purposes). See Final Rules, §_.3(b)(2).

228 For a discussion of the relation of market making to proprietary trading, see Chapter I.II.B: Proprietary trading and market making.

229 See Sec. 619(d)(1)(A)-(C).

230 See Sec. 619(d)(1)(H).

231 See Sec. 619(d)(1)(F); some of the exemptions were included during the final negotiations of the bill due to a campaign of the financial industry, which was *"lobbying vigorously to weaken the Volcker Rule"*. *Cassidy*, The Volcker Rule: Obama's economic adviser and his battles over the financial-reform bill, The New Yorker (July 26, 2010); See further on the lobbying efforts and successes of the banking industry, *Wilmarth* (2011) Dodd-Frank Act, 1028.

bank, or (iv) that would pose a threat to the financial stability of the United States.[232]

2. Activities ban

The Volcker Rule introduces an outright ban on activities which are considered not compatible with the business of banking. By that, it *"reflects the Glass-Steagall philosophy that certain activities should not, for political or practical reasons, coexist in the same corporate structure"*.[233] This ban prohibits the bank and, in case of a banking group, all entities from providing activities identified by it, thereby effecting a full separation from banking entities comparable to the one of the GSA.[234] This is rightly pointed out by the Vickers Report, noting that the Volcker Rule is *"a form of full separation"*.[235]

Similarly to the Glass-Steagall Act, the *activities ban* therefore limits the universal banking model by fully separating certain activities from the whole banking group. In contrast to the full separation of the Glass-Steagall Act however, its restrictions aim only to separate certain specified activities and not securities activities as a whole: not all investment banking is prohibited for affected banks – only certain activities that are considered so high-risk that they should not be performed by banking groups at all.[236]

232 Sec. 619(d)(2)(A).

233 *Dombalagian* (2012) Proprietary Trading, 399.

234 See Chapter I.IV.C.a: Digression: The Glass-Steagall Act; *European Commission* (2014) Impact Assessment Part 2, 8 (noting that the *"Volcker Rule entails full ownership separation, thus the cease and divestment of the prohibited activities"*); The ostensible orientation towards Glass-Steagall is intentional and is portrayed by the policy essay of *Merkley/Levin*, who introduced the VR in Congress (see *Manasfi* (2013) Systemic Risk, 197), and characterized its goal as *"restor[ing] the spirit of regulations that followed the Great Depression"* (*Merkley/Levin* (2011) Dodd-Frank Act, 516). See also *Gary* (2012) Economic Crisis, 1341–1342, 1386 (underscoring the Glass-Steagall spirit of the Volcker Rule). The orientation towards the GSA has been criticised by *Whitehead* as *"a fixture of the past"* and has been called *"a financial Maginot Line"* (*Whitehead* (2011) Volcker Rule, 43) – outdated, inflexible and expensive.

235 *ICB* (2011) Vickers Report, 45.

236 The VR aims at preserving the *"synergistic benefits of bundling such services"*, thereby *"striking a compromise"* between the GSA and the Gramm-Leach-Bliley Act. See *Dombalagian* (2012) Proprietary Trading, 388.

It can therefore be regarded as a subcategory of full separation.[237] The key difference to the Glass Steagall Act's full separation is the scope of the prohibition.

Being a subcategory of full separation justifies a generalized term. Volcker Rule-style activities restrictions are, for the purpose of this dissertation, referred to as *activities ban*. The *activities ban* is defined as *a bank structural reform that prohibits a limited set of investment banking activities, which are considered high-risk, for the whole banking group, thereby limiting universal banking.*[238]

3. Criticism

The VR can be regarded as a relatively unsuccessful banking regulation. It was ill-fated from the beginning and has attracted criticism from both proponents and opponents of strict banking regulation. The following paragraphs outline some of the key points of criticism that the author regards as most valuable for the discussion of European bank structural reforms.[239]

Especially with regard to the distinction of prohibited proprietary trading and the various exemptions, the provisions of the VR are, to speak with *Dombalagian*, *"frustratingly vague"*[240] and leave open a number of questions. This is mainly due to the difficulties in the separation of proprietary trading and related activities, market making and hedging in particular. The VR is not applicable by itself, but requires specification by regulators. Regarding that, regulators are given so much discretion that one could describe their duty rather as shaping the law.[241]

---

237 *ICB* (2011) Vickers Report, 45 (referring to the Volcker Rule as a *"form of full separation in that it prevents common ownership of banks and entities which conduct such activities"*).

238 Key difference to full separation is the limited scope of the *activities ban*, which is emphasized by the note that it only comprises the prohibition of *"a limited set"* of investment banking activities. To underscore that the *activities ban* is besides that a *"form of full separation"* (*ICB* (2011) Vickers Report, 45), the definition is aligned with the definition of full separation (see Chapter I.IV.C.a.2: Full separation). For a discussion of other differences, see *Möslein* (2013) Trennung, 360–362.

239 For a good overview of perceived costs and benefits of the VR, see *Elliott/Rauch* (2014) Volcker Rule, 5–8.

240 See *Dombalagian* (2012) Proprietary Trading, 403.

241 The reason why the Volcker Rule's 11 page idea turned into 489 page agency proposal is because it *"asks regulators to do something that is difficult in practice"*: to

Furthermore, *Whitehead* criticises that the VR does not take into account today's connectedness of banks and the shadow banking sector. By causing proprietary trading to move from the former to the latter, it shifts it to a much less regulated industry. Due to the interconnectedness, banks remain exposed to the dangers of proprietary trading.[242]

Duffie predicts that the attempt to unravel activities with market making intent and proprietary trading would result in an overall reduction of market making activities by banks, leading to a loss of liquidity, higher costs of capital for corporations and eventually also for the government.[243] Indeed, *Dombalagian* claims that *"[e]ven as its full implementation remains incomplete, [the VR] has unquestionably had a dramatic impact on the market for financial services"* and that it appears to have adversely affected liquidity.[244] *Bao/O'Hara/Zhou* find that it has a detriment effect on liquidity in corporate bond markets, and that dealers subject to it *"become less willing to provide liquidity during stress times"* with illiquidity in stress periods *"now approaching levels seen during the financial crisis"*.[245]

However, there are also proponents of the VR: *Coates*, for instance, defends it to be more than just a *"'watered down' version of the [GSA]"*. He notes that it is tackling the *"casino-like speculative culture of banks"* and that the importance of such a change, for example by a change of remuneration policies, should not be underestimated.[246]

The future of the VR has considerably darkened with the election of President Trump, who attacked the Dodd-Frank Act during his campaign and promised to dismantle it. Besides a change of regulators' enforce-

---

separate market making from proprietary trading. (*Schultz* (2013) Conclusions, 226). Moreover, even the extensive final rules, which set out the relation between proprietary trading and the exemptions, pose new issues. *Krawiec/Liu* (2015) Volcker Rule, 510–511.

242 *Whitehead* (2011) Volcker Rule, 44–46, 73; see also *Duffie* (2012) Market Making, 5–6. For a general discussion of the exposure of the banking sector to risks emanating from shadow banking, see *Hoeck* (2018) Schattenbanken, 334–341.

243 *Duffie* (2012) Market Making, 4–5.

244 *D ombalagian* (2015) Volcker Rule, 470.

245 *Bao/O'Hara/Zhou* (2016) Volcker Rule, 29–30.

246 *Coates* (2015) Volcker Rule, 15–17; See also *Reid*, We were wrong about universal banking, Financial Times (November 11, 2015) (in which former chairman and CEO of Citigroup *John Reid* emphasizes the importance of culture and the dangers of mixing incompatible cultures); *Richardson* (2012) Volcker Rule, 15–18; *Richardson/Smith/Walter* (2011) Large Banks, 207–208.

ment,[247] there are currently legislative efforts to amend the VR that start to gather bipartisan support.[248]

b. Differences between ring-fencing and the activities ban

Ring-fencing needs to be differentiated from the *activities ban*, which most prominently takes the form of the Volcker Rule.[249] The *activities ban* has since been discussed in many jurisdictions, often in connection with ring-fencing.[250] Despite the considerations above, some authors have characterised the *activities ban* as ring-fencing.[251]

This is likely due to three reasons: both ring-fencing and the *activities ban* (i) aim to distance risky activities from activities that are to be protected (thereby sharing the first core characteristic of ring-fencing);[252] (ii) the *activities ban* is often applied in combination with ring-fencing. This, for example, is the case for the European Commission's draft regulation; (iii) as discussed above, the *activities ban* only mandates full separation of selected activities and in this aspect differs from a Glass-Stagall Act full separation, which potentially blurs the awareness of it being a subcategory of full separation.

247 See *Hamilton,* Trump Watchdog Tells Banks He Really, Really Likes Them, Bloomberg (April 9, 2018); *Tracy/Carney,* How to Kill the Volcker Rule? Don't Enforce It, Wall Street Journal (November 28, 2016).

248 *Mont,* Push for Volcker Rule reforms gains momentum, Compliance Week (April 16, 2018); *Dexheimer,* Volcker Rule Change Backed in House Panel's Dodd-Frank Remedy, Bloomberg (March 21, 2018).

249 See Chapter I.IV.D: Ring-fencing and the activities ban; The European Commission's draft regulation also includes elements of this approach. See Chapter II.II.C: Separation of proprietary trading (The European Commission's draft regulation sets forth elements of the *containment method* of ring-fencing and the *activities ban* of full separation).

250 See e.g. *ICB* (2011) Vickers Report, 45–46; *HLEG* (2012) Liikanen Report, 84–85; *European Commission* (2014) Impact Assessment Part 2, 7–9; *Expertenkommission* (2010) Schlussbericht, 125–126.

251 See e.g. *Masciandaro/Suardi* (2014) Public Interest and Lobbies, 307, 318 (*Masciandaro/Suardi,* however, then consider the Volcker Rule a form of full separation); *Brown* (2014) With this Ring, I Thee Fence, 1043; *Schwarcz* (2013) Ring-Fencing, 80–81 (*Schwarcz* discusses both Glass-Steagall, the Volcker Rule and UK ring-fencing under the term "ring-fencing"); *Schwarcz* (2016) Systemic Risk, 57.

252 See Chapter I.IV.B: Ring-fencing as a structural reform.

However, as pointed out explicitly by both the Vickers and the Liikanen Report, the *activities ban* cannot be regarded as ring-fencing.[253] This is in particular because, similarly to full separation,[254] the *activities ban* lacks two core characteristics of ring-fencing:

Firstly, ring-fencing aims at maintaining universal banking.[255] While ring-fencing allows for all activities to be provided within the same banking group, the *activities ban* removes certain activities completely from the group, thus limiting a bank's ability to engage in all respects of the banking, securities and insurance business.[256]

As will be discussed below, a literal interpretation of the word ring-fencing indicates that (i) a ring-fenced part and (ii) a part that may unwantedly influence the ring-fenced part need to be combined under the same roof.[257] This is also a pervasive element of all uses of ring-fencing outside banking regulation.[258] As the *activities ban* effectively bans certain activities from the banking group, it cannot be properly subsumed under the term "ring-fencing".

Secondly, there is no fence: a prohibition cannot be equated with a system of provisions that aims to ensure legal, financial and operational independence of two entities within the same group. Arguing that there was a fence, only a much higher one taking the form of a prohibition, is in the author's opinion far-fetched. It would furthermore logically entail that also full separation, such as the Glass-Steagall Act (which also takes the form of a prohibition, however a broader one) would be ring-fencing.[259] This is ex-

253 Both the Vickers Report and the Liikanen Report differ between their own structural recommendations and the *activities ban.* See *ICB* (2011) Vickers Report, 45 (*"The Volcker Rule is a form of full separation in that it prevents common ownership of banks and entities which conduct such activities. […] However, prohibiting only those activities caught by the Volcker Rule would not achieve all of the objectives of ring-fencing"*); *HLEG* (2012) Liikanen Report, 83 (The Liikanen Report attributes the Volcker Rule to a category of structural reforms it refers to as *"activities restrictions"*).

254 See Chapter I.IV.C.b: Differences between ring-fencing and full separation.

255 See Chapter I.IV.B: Ring-fencing as a structural reform.

256 See Chapter I.IV.D.a.2: Activities ban; Chapter I.I.A.a: Definition.

257 See Chapter I.VII.A: Origins of the term "ring-fencing"; Chapter I.VII.B: Ring-fencing outside banking regulation.

258 See Chapter I.VII.B: Ring-fencing outside banking regulation.

259 *Schwarcz* seems to argue in this direction, including both Glass-Steagall and the Volcker Rule into his concept of ring-fencing. See *Schwarcz* (2013) Ring-Fencing, 79–80; *Schwarcz* (2016) Systemic Risk, 57.

plicitly disagreed with by e.g. the Vickers Report, which dedicates a whole chapter on the question *"why not full separation"*.[260]

V. The Basic Rationale and Goals of Ring-Fencing

This chapter addresses the basic rationale of ring-fencing and subsequently explains what objectives may also be reached by its implementation. This structure is considered useful as it highlights that the protection of systemically important activities, described in the first step, is an essential precondition for the achievement of the other objectives, expanded on as a second step.

A. The basic rationale of ring-fencing

As discussed in previous chapters, the global economic crisis brought with it a series of unprecedented bailouts and shed light on the fact that the banking sector had evolved in a direction that was far from socially optimal: banks had become so big, complex, interconnected and fragile that governments had little choice but to bail them out in times of stress to avert major damages to the real economy as well as bank runs.

The central problem that ring-fencing rules are trying to address is the danger that bank deposits and the provision of services considered vital to the real economy are jeopardized by risky activities.[261] The basic rationale of ring-fencing is therefore that banks shall be prevented from risking their deposits and their ability to provide these services to avert negative consequences for the financial system as a whole, and for the continuity of financial services.[262]

---

260 See *ICB* (2011) Vickers Report, 63–66 (noting that *"the right approach is not to require full separation, but instead to impose through ring-fencing the degree of separation required to secure the benefits"*).

261 Cf. *Gambacorta/Van Rixtel* (2013) Structural Bank Regulation Initiatives, 1 (*Gambacorta/Van Rixtel* do not use the term "ring-fencing" but simply use the term "structural reform"; see Chapter I.IV.B: Ring-fencing as a structural reform.).

262 *Proctor* (2014) International Banking, 16; *Armour et al.* (2016) Financial Regulation, 507. In contrast to older structural reforms, the focus of ring-fencing is hence the protection of the system, namely of financial stability. See *Armour et*

The Liikanen Report explains this pointedly, noting that *"the key objective is [...] to ensure a banking sector that is capable of financing the real economy and to persue its other functions that contribute to the prosperity of [...] citizens and the economy"*.[263]

Ring-fencing aims to insulate these functions from others deemed riskier and less important. The various initiatives all put up a fence somewhere between commercial and investment banking. This segregation nevertheless maintains the universal banking model.[264]

The Vickers Report points this out clearly, noting that *"[t]he purpose of the [...] ring-fence is to isolate those banking activities where continuous provision of service is vital to the economy and to a bank's customers in order to ensure, first, that this provision is not threatened as a result of activities which are incidental to it and, second, that such provision can be maintained in the event of the bank's failure without government solvency support"*.[265]

Some jurisdictions highlight more than others the protection of deposit-taking and services essential to the real economy as the basic rationale.

---

al. (2016) Financial Regulation, 512; see also the considerations in Chapter I.IV.C.b: Differences between ring-fencing and full separation.

263 See *HLEG* (2012) Liikanen Report, 88; See also e.g. *ICB* (2011) Vickers Report, 35 (emphasizing *"those activities where continuous provision of services is vital to the economy and to a bank's customers"*); *Expertenkommission* (2010) Schlussbericht, 38 (stressing the importance of the continuation of systemically important functions, namely the domestic deposit-taking, loans business and payment services, to avoid government bailouts); *Deutscher Bundestag* (2013) Gesetzesentwurf Trennbankengesetz, 2 (noting that customer business needs to be separated while putting particular focus on deposits); *European Commission* (2014) Impact Assessment Part 1 (noting that it is the *"key objective of structural reform [...] to make banks that provide essential services to the real economy more resilient in the event of endogenous or exogenous shocks but also more resolvable in the event of a failure, thus reducing the severity of future financial crises"*).

264 Cf. *Gambacorta/Van Rixtel* (2013) Structural Bank Regulation Initiatives, 1 (discussing structural reforms, thus including the *activities ban* of full separation (see Chapter I.IV.D: Ring-fencing and the activities ban). See Chapter I.I.A.a.2: Universal banking after ring-fencing.

265 *ICB* (2011) Vickers Report, 35 (While the Vickers Report describes the "retail ring-fence", its description applies to all methods of ring-fencing (see Chapter I.VI: Different Methods of Ring-Fencing)).

Some point it out explicitly,[266] others tend to commingle it with the other goals that they argue can be reached by its implementation.[267]

B. Other benefits of ring-fencing

Proponents of ring-fencing claim that its implementation can tackle a number of problems in today's financial world. Some of these problems are inherent in the universal banking model and are laid out in Chapter I.I.B.[268] They have been discussed for decades, usually mentioning full separation as the alternative form of structure. Other problems ring-fencing aims to tackle are new and reflect recent developments of the financial sector.[269]

The benefits below are intertwined and influence each other. How much they materialize depends on the ring-fencing method and the strength of separation.[270] Altogether, they should reduce the probability of future tax payer bailouts and tackle systemic risk and the too-big-to-fail problem.[271]

266 The Vickers Report points out the basic rationale very clearly. *ICB* (2011) Vickers Report, 35 (see above); On an EU level, the HLEG similarly notes: "*The central objectives of the separation are to make banking groups, especially their socially most vital parts mainly deposit-taking and providing financial services to the non-financial sectors in the economy), safer and less connected to high-risk trading activities and to limit the implicit or explicit stake of taxpayer in the trading parts of banking groups*". *HLEG* (2012) Liikanen Report, 100.

267 See, for instance, *European Commission* (2014) Proposal for a Regulation, 15 (noting that among other goals such as the reduction of competition distortions, "*[i]t also intends to shield institutions carrying out activities that deserve a public safety net from losses incurred as a result of other activities.*", omitting that this is a prerequisite for tackling competition distortions). However, in the impact assessment to the draft regulation, the European Commission underscores the importance of making banks that provide "essential services to the real economy" more resilient. See *European Commission* (2014) Impact Assessment Part 1, 26.

268 See Chapter I.I.B: Benefits and costs of universal banking.

269 See Chapter I.II: Changes in the Realm of International Banking; Chapter I.III: Bailouts and Too-Big-to-Fail.

270 See e.g. the European Commission's assessment of the impact of the various reforms on moral hazard, *European Commission* (2014) Impact Assessment Part 1, 47–48.

271 See *European Commission* (2014) Impact Assessment Part 1, 26; see also *FSB* (2014) Structural Banking Reforms, 3; *ICB* (2011) Vickers Report, 163; *Expertenkommission* (2010) Schlussbericht, 54.

a. Resolvability

Ring-fencing aims to enhance the resolvability of a banking group.[272] In resolution, it has to be decided what activities of a failing bank are continued and how. Resolution involves ex post structural action, such as transferring activities onto a bridge bank. To maintain an orderly procedure, contagion onto other banks and tax payer assistance have to be avoided. The continuation of vital banking services must be ensured.[273]

Ring-fencing is thought to facilitate a resolution, because vital banking services are separated ex ante.[274] A simpler group structure with a fence somewhere between commercial banking and investment banking should make the assessment and allocation of losses easier. Furthermore, the entities are smaller and more simply structured, so that regulators are provided with more options regarding resolving only parts of the banking group or the group as a whole. Trading activities are found to regularly impede a resolution due to their complexity and interconnectedness. Separating them, proprietary trading and complex forms of securisation and derivatives in particular, should facilitate a swift resolution.[275]

b. Subsidies and moral hazard

Ring-fencing aims to end the subsidisation of risky activities, in particular by implicit subsidies.[276] Separate funding requirements and restricted interconnections between the ring-fenced part and the non-ring-fenced part of the banking group are considered to *"impose a significant increase in market discipline"* on the non-ring-fenced trading entity. Due to legal, economic and governance requirements, intra group exposure limits and credible resolvability, trading activities are thought not to benefit from the im-

272 See *FSB* (2014) Structural Banking Reforms, 3.

273 *ICB* (2011) Vickers Report, 9.

274 *ICB* (2011) Vickers Report, 24.

275 See *European Commission* (2014) Impact Assessment Part 1, 44–45. Likewise, see *Deutscher Bundestag* (2013) Gesetzesentwurf Trennbankengesetz, 2, 42 (noting that the separation of trading activities and their provision by a financial trading institution facilitates their resolution); *Expertenkommission* (2010) Schlussbericht, 38–39 (The Swiss approach contains resolvability as an own category. It notes that the unbundling of financial, personnel, operational and structural interdependencies facilitates the resolution of the banking group).

276 For a discussion of implicit subsidies, see Chapter I.III.C: Implicit subsidies.

plicit public subsidies (to the same extent). Increasing funding costs for the trading entity would reflect riskiness of the activity. Readjusting the costs of risk-taking should decrease moral hazard in the respective areas of operation.[277]

The application of prudential requirements onto each entity, which are otherwise applied on consolidated group level, such as capital and liquidity buffers, is also believed to contribute to ending the cross-subsidy from deposits to trading. This is because the cost of regulation would be better aligned with the actual risk.[278] Depending on the strength of the separation, trading activities would furthermore be distanced from explicit subsidies deriving from public safety net coverage.[279]

c. Complexity and size

Ring-fencing aims to mitigate the complexity and potentially the size of banks, which should improve their manageability, transparency, and resolvability.[280] The separation of activities into different entities combined with further requirements is thought to considerably improve market discipline and to enhance the transparency of the stand-alone performance of the different entities of the banking group. Banks would no longer be allowed to unrestrictedly shift profits and losses within the group.[281] It should make banking groups simpler and more transparent, which again would facilitate supervision, recovery and resolution.[282]

---

277 See *European Commission* (2014) Impact Assessment Part 1, 47–48; See also *Gambacorta/Van Rixtel* (2013) Structural Bank Regulation Initiatives, 2; *ICB* (2011) Vickers Report, 20; *Deutscher Bundestag* (2013) Gesetzesentwurf Trennbankengesetz, 2; *Expertenkommission* (2010) Schlussbericht, 50.

278 See *European Commission* (2014) Impact Assessment Part 1, 48.

279 See *European Commission* (2014) Impact Assessment Part 1, 50; see also *Gambacorta/Van Rixtel* (2013) Structural Bank Regulation Initiatives, 2 (emphasizing explicit subsidies such as deposit guarantees and central bank lending); *HLEG* (2012) Liikanen Report, 94, 95 (emphasizing that the separation would curb the cross subsidy arising from explicit guarantees for deposits).

280 *Gambacorta/Van Rixtel* (2013) Structural Bank Regulation Initiatives, 2; see also *ICB* (2011) Vickers Report, 76–77.).

281 See *European Commission* (2014) Impact Assessment Part 1, 47.

282 *HLEG* (2012) Liikanen Report, 100.

d. Culture and competition

Ring-fencing furthermore aims to distance the ring-fenced bank from the aggressive risk culture often associated with investment banking.[283] While the Vickers Report acknowledges that corporate culture cannot be directly mandated, ring-fencing *"should assist in building a separate, consumer-focused culture".*[284]

As set out above, the improved resolvability should entail a decrease of implicit subsidies, which again is thought to entail a normalisation of competition. Bigger and more unsound institutions should not benefit from a competitive advantage anymore.[285] A level playing field between large and small institutions would be established.[286]

C. Differences to recovery and resolution

In their objectives, ring-fencing rules are similar and to a certain extent overlapping with certain tools of recovery and resolution initiatives such as the *Key Attributes of Effective Recovery and Resolution Regimes* and their national and transnational realisations, such as the BRRD and the SRMR: this is particularly the case where such rules authorise regulators to ex ante mandate certain changes to the structure of banks, notably Art. 17(5) BRRD and Art. 10(11) SRMR.[287] The Swiss emergency plan and the corresponding resolvability assessment are also based on the recovery and resolution framework.[288] *Binder* rightly notes that *"both developments are clearly*

---

283 See *FSB* (2014) Structural Banking Reforms, 3; see also *HLEG* (2012) Liikanen Report, 99; *ICB* (2011) Vickers Report, 76; *European Commission* (2014) Impact Assessment Part 1, 49.

284 *ICB* (2011) Vickers Report, 76.

285 See *ICB* (2011) Vickers Report, 160; see also *Deutscher Bundestag* (2013) Gesetzesentwurf Trennbankengesetz (noting that the risk premium will be restored to market conditions); *Expertenkommission* (2010) Schlussbericht, 54.

286 *European Commission* (2014) Impact Assessment Part 1, 51.

287 For a discussion of the ability of the provisions to constitute a basis for the introduction of ring-fencing, see Chapter II.IV.C.c: Existing regimes.

288 Expert Interview, Affected Bank, September 28, 2017; *Schiltknecht* (2013) Schweizerisches Bankeninsolvenzrecht, 67 (noting that the emergency plan is an important element of the global recovery and resolution planning); *Hofer* (2014) Structural Reforms, 347. See also *Schiltknecht* (2015) Internationale Standards, 606 (noting that both the emergency plan and the resolvability assessment are based on the FSB's key attributes). In contrast to "living wills", the

related from a functional perspective", arguing that *"one of the motives for structural reforms, in addition to the preservation of certain systemically relevant business functions has been to remove impediments to effective crisis resolution"*.[289]

Due to the similarities, it is necessary to clarify the relationship between ring-fencing and recovery and resolution and to differentiate the former from the latter.

The central difference between the two regulatory initiatives is their nature: ring-fencing describes a certain structure banking groups have to implement. The requirements of ring-fencing are therefore static. Recovery and resolution in contrast, can be regarded as a process: This process involves *inter alia* recovery planning, resolution planning and, in case of an emergency, regulators' use of tools for orderly resolution. It aims at ensuring that a bank *"can be stabilised, restructured or removed from the marketplace in orderly fashion"*.[290] The process is dependent on the actions of regulators for individual banks,[291] hence "enforcement-based". Once regulators make use of tools to ex ante influence the structure of banks, the two regulatory initiatives converge. Regulators' use of these tools may lead to a ring-fencing structure, however, it might not.[292]

Swiss emergency plan does not aim to enhance the resolvability of a bank, but to ensure the continuation of systemically important functions. *Von der Crone/Beeler* (2012) Systemrelevante Finanzinstitute, 15.

289 *Binder* (2014) Resolution Planning, 4 (with a view to tools to tackle resolvability impediments).

290 *Finma*, Recovery and resolution planning for systemically important banks, https://www.finma.ch/en/supervision/banks-and-securities-dealers/supervisory-instruments/recovery-and-resolution-planning/.

291 See *European Commission* (2014) Impact Assessment Part 1, 21.

292 In this dissertation, the use of the term "enforcement-based" in connection with ring-fencing thus refers to an approach, in which powers are delegated to regulatory authorities that allow them to influence a banking group's structure and to ultimately establish a ring-fencing structure, for example Finma's assessment of the Swiss emergency plan (see Chapter III.IV.D.b.1: Basis of the exclusion) or the powers proposed by Liikanen's Avenue 1 (see Chapter II.I.B: Avenue 1). Such powers can differ in strength and authorities can have leeway of various extent in administering them: they may make use of these powers, pushing for the establishment of far reaching bank structural reform, they may, however, also accept more lenient forms of bank structural reform or even decide not to exert their powers at all (see e.g. the discussion of whether full ring-fencing can be established through the provisions of the BRRD and SRMR in Chapter II.IV.C.c: Existing regimes). While there may be certain overlaps, the term "enforcement-based" is to be distinguished from regulatory authorities' enforcement actions concerning breaches of financial market law, such as unauthorized

As far as recovery and resolution tools substantially affect a banking group's legal entity structure, its size, its management organization or its ability to provide activities, they can be regarded as a structural reform (that aims to improve resolvability).[293] Once its implementation fulfils the core characteristics of ring-fencing, namely (i) the separation of certain commercial banking activities from certain investment banking activities, (ii) the maintenance of universal banking and (iii) the stipulation of requirements that aim to ensure that the separated activities can be provided independently from each other, it can be regarded as ring-fencing.

Besides this theoretical discourse, it should be stressed that ring-fencing initiatives regularly set out their relation with recovery and resolution initiatives themselves, welcoming them as *"an essential part of the future regulatory structure"*.[294] The Vickers Report, for instance, notes that ring-fencing and recovery and resolution *"are complements, not substitutes"*[295] and that considering them as alternatives would be *"misleading"*.[296] Ring-fencing is generally emphasized to facilitate recovery and resolution.[297]

VI. Different Methods of Ring-Fencing

This chapter attempts to categorise the ring-fencing initiatives pursued in different jurisdictions according to the strategies they use. It aims at establishing key methods of ring-fencing and a uniform terminology. This will allow a better illustration of ring-fencing strategies in use and will set a framework to which potential future ring-fencing initiatives can be set in relation.

---

business activities and market manipulation. See e.g. Finma, Enforcement division, https://www.finma.ch/en/finma/organisation/finma-s-divisions/enforcement-division/; PRA, Enforcement, (March 21, 2018) https://www.fca.org.uk/about/enforcement; For a description of Finma's enforcement, see also Wyss (2014) Finanzmarktenforcement, 83 et seqq.

293 See the definition of structural reform in Chapter I.IV.A: Structural reform as an umbrella term.

294 See *HLEG* (2012) Liikanen Report, iv (with regard to the BRRD).

295 *ICB* (2011) Vickers Report, 26.

296 *ICB* (2011) Vickers Report, 66.

297 See e.g. the considerations regarding their relation in *European Commission* (2014) Impact Assessment Part 1, 21–22; *HLEG* (2012) Liikanen Report, vii; *ICB* (2011) Vickers Report, 66; cf. *Armour et al.* (2016) Financial Regulation, 528.

As they are all based on the same underlying assumption, this will be outlined in a first step. Subsequently, the two different methods of ring-fencing will be explored one after the other.

A. Underlying assumption

All ring-fencing methods are based on the premise that, firstly, there are activities that are important for the real economy and are simultaneously less risky compared to other activities. Secondly, that some activities are severely risky and simultaneously less important for the real economy. Third, that there is a remaining quantity of other activities that may or may not carry any risks but are not especially important for the real economy.[298]

Universal banks of today provide a large variety of different services. They may be divided into three groups according to the standards mentioned above:[299] The first group, which can be referred to as "desired activities", usually comprises of commercial banking activities for ordinary customers and small and medium-sized enterprises, namely deposit-taking and lending, and the provision of payment services.[300] These services are considered the *"socially most vital"* parts of a banking group.[301]

The second group, which can be referred to as "risky activities", typically consists of certain activities that are attributed to investment banking, particularly trading.[302] What activities it comprises depends on where the fence is located: typical activities distrusted by legislators and authorities

298 See e.g. *ICB* (2011) Vickers Report, 36–38, 51–52, 54 (this is reflected in the Vickers Report's differentiation between mandated, prohibited and permitted services); *HLEG* (2012) Liikanen Report (emphasizing that *"it is necessary to require legal separation of certain particularly risky financial activities from deposit-taking banks within a banking group"*). *Armour et al.* criticise this understanding as *"naïve"*. *Armour et al.* (2016) Financial Regulation, 507; cf. *Gordon/Ringe* (2015) Bank Resolution, 20 (noting that investment banking is not the major threat to the stability of banks).

299 *Britton et al.* choose a similar approach identifying three groups in their illustration of where activities have to be provided, according to the Banking Reform Act 2013 and secondary legislation. See *Britton et al.* (2016) Ring-fencing, 167.

300 See *ICB* (2011) Vickers Report, 11, 35 et seqq.; *HLEG* (2012) Liikanen Report, 100; *Expertenkommission* (2010) Schlussbericht, 12–13, 38; *Deutscher Bundestag* (2013) Gesetzesentwurf Trennbankengesetz, 2.

301 *HLEG* (2012) Liikanen Report, i.

302 See Chapter I.II.A.c: Market-based banking.

are proprietary trading and certain investments in hedge funds and private equity funds.[303] Market making and underwriting are exceptional cases, as the ring-fencing models of the various jurisdictions do not consistently attribute them to the group.[304]

The third group contains all other activities whose provision is neither considered *"vital to the economy and to a bank's customers"*[305] nor a *"high risk trading activity"*.[306] It regularly includes activities such as wealth management[307] or corporate financing such as trade finance.[308]

The universal banking model allows these three groups of activities to be performed by a single banking group. Ring-fencing rules maintain this freedom, but mandate a certain structure for it.[309]

B. Two methods

In principle, the various ring-fencing models can be divided into two methods aiming to achieve the insulation of universal banks' desired activities from activities deemed risky: (i) separation of desired activities from the rest of the banking group, or (ii) separation of risky activities from the rest of the banking group.[310] Both methods require that the separation is executed and maintained ex ante and that sufficient independence of the two groups of activities is ensured.

A logical result of the different methods of ring-fencing is that banking groups – with a view to the banking activities they perform – end up somewhere between a large ring-fenced entity and a small trading entity, or, on the other end of the spectrum, a small ring-fenced entity and a large trad-

303 See e.g. *ICB* (2011) Vickers Report, 54; *HLEG* (2012) Liikanen Report, v; Chapter III.IV.A.b.1: Excluded activities.
304 See e.g. *Deutscher Bundestag* (2013) Gesetzesentwurf Trennbankengesetz, 41.
305 *ICB* (2011) Vickers Report, 4.
306 *European Commission* (2014) Proposal for a Regulation, 2.
307 See e.g. Chapter III.IV.C.c.3: Conclusio.
308 See e.g. Chapter III.IV.A.c: Summary.
309 See the considerations in Chapter I.I.A.a.2: Universal banking after ring-fencing.
310 This conceptual division is also pointed out by the European Commission in its assessment of national structural reforms in with the context of the adoption of its draft regulation. *European Commission* (2014) Impact Assessment Part 1, 28–30; It has also been identified by the academia, see e.g. *Binder*, who distinguishes between ring-fencing *"of core banking functions"* and ring-fencing *"of certain investment banking activities"*. *Binder* (2015) Ring-Fencing, 106, 108.

ing entity.[311] However, all ring-fencing rules give affected parties considerable leeway in their implementation of the fence.[312]

a. The defensive method

The first method focuses on the desired activities described above: it insulates them by separating them from the rest of the bank. After the separation, they can be conducted within a separate legal entity that can, however, remain part of the banking group. The separate legal entity must be legally, economically and operationally independent, i.e. able to sustain the failure of the rest of the group. A prohibition on risky activities completes the model and keeps these out of the now "ring-fenced" entity.

The United Kingdom pioneered this method with the Vickers Report and followed up on it with the Banking Reform Act in 2013. Although the Swiss Expert Commission explicitly decided against far-reaching structural requirements,[313] the organizational measures of the Swiss Too-Big-to-Fail Regime implement a similar form of ring-fencing.[314]

As this approach focuses on defending core banking activities by isolating them from the rest of the banking group, it will hereafter be referred to as the *defensive method* of ring-fencing. The *defensive method* fully maintains the universal banking model, but interferes with it by mandating a certain structure for the provision of activities.

b. The containment method

The second method focuses on risky activities. While it pursues the same basic rationale of ring-fencing identified in the chapter above,[315] it works the other way around by separating the risky activities from the rest of the

---

311 See *European Commission* (2014) Impact Assessment Part 1, 28.

312 See e.g. Chapter III.IV.A.d: Affected banks (in which it is set out, how differently affected banks in the UK chose to implement the ring-fence); Chapter III.IV.A.c: Summary (setting out activities that can be provided by both the ring-fenced entity and non-ring-fenced rest of the banking group).

313 See *Hofer* (2014) Structural Reforms, 351; see also *Expertenkommission* (2010) Schlussbericht, 48–49, 121.

314 This is discussed in detail in the third part of the dissertation. See Part III: Legal Comparative Analysis.

315 See Chapter I.V.A: The basic rationale of ring-fencing.

bank. This shall ensure that the rest of the banking group cannot be negatively affected by the activities.

Banks can be obliged to assign risky activities to a trading entity within a banking group. This entity must be legally, economically and operationally separate. All other activities can be performed by the now ring-fenced entity. Parallel to the defensive method, a prohibition on desired activities for the trading entity completes the model.

This method of ring-fencing has been proposed by the EU's Liikanen Commission[316] and has since been adopted in a diluted form by a number of EU member states.[317]

By stipulating this kind of separation, it is attempted to contain the risky activities in a trading entity. Therefore, it will hereafter be referred to as the *containment method* of ring-fencing. The *containment method* fully maintains the universal banking model. It only interferes with it by mandating a certain structure for the provision of activities.

VII. Attempt at a Definition

The term ring-fencing has been in use for a long time, its meaning, however, has not been static but has been used for a variety of contexts. Since the global economic crisis, ring-fencing has become a buzzword for structural reform measures across the globe.[318] Reviewing academic literature on ring-fencing, one finds that there is a scattered number of definitions shaped by the respective author's understanding of the term. Furthermore, there is ambiguity in the notation.[319]

This chapter will briefly introduce the origins of the term "ring-fencing" and some of the ideas that the term has referred to outside of banking regulation. Subsequently, the chapter will narrow down to definitions in

316 See *HLEG* (2012) Liikanen Report, 100–103.

317 For Germany, see Chapter III.IV.B.a: Non-ring-fenced body.

318 See *Binder* (2015) Ring-Fencing, 98; *Binder* (2014) To ring-fence or not, and how?, 2.

319 While some authors spell it "ring-fencing" (see e.g. *Schwarcz* (2013) Ring-Fencing; *Hardie/Macartney* (2016) EU Ring-Fencing; *Zaring* (2014) Ring-Fencing; see also *European Commission* (2014) Impact Assessment Part 3, 89 Fn 81), others spell it "ring fencing" (see e.g. *Masciandaro/Suardi* (2014) Public Interest and Lobbies), or even "ringfencing" (see e.g. *Brown* (2014) With this Ring, I Thee Fence). This dissertation falls in line with the original spelling of the word described below, namely "ring-fencing".

the field of banking regulation. Ultimately, the chapter will try to establish its own definition reflecting the three core characteristics identified above.

A. Origins of the term "ring-fencing"

To better understand the term and learn about its character, the following paragraphs, as a starting point, explore the definition of ring-fencing outside financial and legal discussion.

The *Oxford Dictionary* defines ring-fencing as "*a fence completely enclosing a farm or piece of land*". It further refers to it as "*an effective or comprehensive barrier*".[320] A literal interpretation of the word therefore already suggests two important characteristics: first, there is a defensive element, in that a fence represents a barrier or an obstacle, second, there is a valuing element, in that something precious needs protection.

The *Cambridge Dictionary* already relates to its use in the financial discussion, defining it as "*something that protects a sum of money or area of spending so that it cannot be reduced or is kept separate from other amounts or areas*".[321] The two characteristics identified above have thus remained unchanged. What is more, as will be shown, they pervade all regulatory concepts that are referred to as ring-fencing.

The finding that there is both a defensive and a valuing element inherent in the word has important implications for the definition of ring-fencing: the literal sense of the word does not permit its use concerning, for instance, risky activities. The frequent use of the phrase "ring fencing of investment banking activities" in academic literature referring to the *containment method* of ring-fencing can therefore be regarded as inaccurate, as it ignores (if not contrasts) the valuing element: risky activities cannot be considered precious and in need of protection. Ring-fencing indeed aims at protecting deposit-taking and services essential to the real economy from risky activities.

---

320 https://en.oxforddictionaries.com/definition/ring_fence; *Stevenson* (2010) Oxford Dictionary of English, 1532. This definition relates to the noun. As a verb, the *Oxford Dictionary* describes "to ring-fence" used with an object as (i) "*enclose (a piece of land) with a ring fence.*" (ii) "*British: guarantee that (funds allocated for a particular purpose) will not be spent on anything else*" with the example sentence "*the government failed to ring-fence the money provided to schools*". *Stevenson* (2010) Oxford Dictionary of English, 1532.

321 http://dictionary.cambridge.org/dictionary/english/ring-fence.

Furthermore, the defensive and the valuing element suggest that a potential external influence needs to be fought off or hindered from entering something valuable:[322] This puts both the ring-fenced valuable and the imminent external influence on the map, only separated by a fence. It is inherent to the word "fence" that it can theoretically be breached or gotten over.[323]

Applied to the legal discussion, this indicates that it is inherent to the term "ring-fencing" to combine under the same roof (i) a ring-fenced part and (ii) a part that could unwantedly influence the ring-fenced part (the imminent external influence) if it was not for the fence. This can be used to contrast ring-fencing from full separation: there is no need for a fence, as the external influence is completely eliminated.[324] A literal interpretation of the term ring-fencing therefore suggests that the attribution of full separation or its sub-form, the *activities ban*, to "ring-fencing" is already in the literal sense inaccurate.

B. Ring-fencing outside banking regulation

Besides its use in banking regulation, ring-fencing has been used in a variety of contexts. Two particularly prominent applications of ring-fencing are public utility companies and securitisation arrangements. The following paragraphs briefly describe these, aiming to deepen the understanding of the term.

---

322 A fence completely enclosing a farm or piece of land may for instance hinder unwanted travellers from entering the piece of land. An effective or comprehensive barrier may protect against a flood. A sum of money is kept separately from other sums of money or from being reduced by an external influence.

323 Compared e.g. with a neutral word such as "separation", which does not imply the possibility of a breach.

324 Taking up the dictionaries' descriptions, there is no need for a fence completely enclosing a farm or piece of land if there are no unwanted travellers. There is no need for an effective or comprehensive barrier if there is no looming flood. There is no need for a sum of money to be kept separate if there are no other sums of money, or no need for it to be protected from being reduced by an external influence if there is none. This is also reflected by the neutral term "separation", which, in contrast to "ring-fencing", does not imply a possible breach.

a. From public utility companies to securitisations

As a regulatory concept, ring-fencing is often used in relation to public utility companies. Regulators regularly oblige public utility companies, i.e. private-sector companies that provide the public with essential utilities such as power, clean water and communication, to separate their risky assets and activities from the ones deemed necessary for society.[325]

It is further used in securitization and covered bonds transactions. If a firm is interested in raising financing, usually a special purpose entity is established which issues securities independently from the firm. This way, the special purpose entity and therefore the creditors are unimpaired by a bankruptcy of the associated firm, thus lowering funding costs and allocating risk better. In other words, the special purpose entity is ring-fenced from dangers emanating from the associated firm. Securities transactions usually realize ring-fencing contractually.[326] In covered bonds transactions, the same goal is pursued but is in most countries realized by laws stipulating ring-fencing.[327]

b. Results

The paragraphs above briefly mention two important contexts in which the term "ring-fencing" has been used outside of banking regulation. Drawing from this use, it can be found that (i) the use of the term is not limited to a certain field of activity. Public utility companies and securitisations are quite different areas of application.

There are, however, similarities: one finds that (ii) the valuing element (be it electricity, water or securities) and the defensive element (a separation of some sort to ward off a threat) are omnipresent. Additionally, in all cases, (iii) both the ring-fenced part and the non-ring-fenced part are in some way connected, but separated by a fence.

---

325 See *Schwarcz* (2013) Ring-Fencing, 71, 74; see also *Möslein* (2013) Trennung, 363.

326 *Schwarcz* (2013) Ring-Fencing, 74–75; See further about covered bonds *Schwarcz* (2011) Covered Bonds, 566–567.

327 *European Covered Bond Council* (2009) European Covered Bond Factbook, 97–98; See also *Schwarcz* (2011) Covered Bonds, 566–567; See also *Schwarcz* (2013) Ring-Fencing, 74–75.

C. Ring-fencing in banking regulation

The following paragraphs discuss the use of ring-fencing in banking regulation. They set out the concept of jurisdiction-oriented ring-fencing and *Binder's* activities-oriented ring-fencing.[328] Subsequently, they establish an own definition of ring-fencing taking into account the findings from the chapters above.

a. Jurisdiction-oriented ring-fencing

In the context of banking regulation, ring-fencing has been used to describe strategic actions of authorities during cross-border insolvency resolution. In case of insolvency of a transnational bank, local authorities may feel competent to shield local depositors and other local creditors of the bank from insolvency administration and liquidation of foreign authorities. For a foreign owned branch, ring-fencing is achieved by seizing all assets; for a foreign owned subsidiary, it is realized by separate insolvency proceedings and by obstructing foreign interference. The strategic actions consist of ex ante and ex post measures and can collectively be referred to as "jurisdiction-oriented ring-fencing".[329]

While the focus of this dissertation is on the functional separation of activities and not on jurisdiction-oriented ring-fencing, it must be mentioned that the former always entails elements of the latter: all of the ring-fencing rules examined in this dissertation bring with them certain territorial effects that shield local assets from foreign influence.[330]

---

328 *Binder* (2015) Ring-Fencing, 98. See also *Binder* (2014) To ring-fence or not, and how?, 2–3.

329 See *Binder* (2015) Ring-Fencing, 98; Other terms in use are: "geographical ring-fencing", "territorial approaches", and "home bias", (see *D'Hulster* (2014) Ring-Fencing, 2; see also *D'Hulster/Oetker-Robe* (2014) Ring-Fencing, 1–2); "geographical perspective of ring-fencing" (see *Cerrutti/Schmieder* (2014) Ring Fencing, 1).

330 This is reflected in e.g. the prohibition for UK ring-fenced banks from having branches and subsidiaries outside the EEA (see Chapter III.IV.A.b.2: Prohibitions; *Armour et al.* (2016) Financial Regulation 518 (noting that such a geographic restriction does not reduce risk)) or the Swiss emphasis on domestic systemically important functions (see Chapter III.IV.C.a.2: Systemically important functions). The FSB discusses potential negative cross-border implications of structural reforms in *FSB* (2014) Structural Banking Reforms, 1–2.

b. Activities-oriented ring-fencing

The most accurate definition of ring-fencing within the focus of this dissertation is established by *Binder*. He summarizes bank structural reforms that aim at separating deposit-taking and other functions important to the economy from certain investment banking services under the term "activities-oriented ring-fencing".[331]

Binder describes it as *"the legal and commercial isolation of systemically important activities within a banking group, with a view to protecting such activities against the risks emanating from less economically important functions"*.[332] The creation of a summarizing term for ring-fencing that allows to delimit it from the older "jurisdiction-oriented" form is to be welcomed.[333]

For the purpose of this dissertation however, *Binder*'s description requires modification: this is mainly because his definition does not differentiate ring-fencing from the *activities ban* of full separation, taking the form of the Volcker Rule.[334] It thus does not reflect all of the three core characteristics of ring-fencing established above.

Other definitions are more detached from the functional separation of commercial and investment banking activities and aim to define ring-fencing as a general financial regulatory concept, comprising either uses outside banking regulation,[335] or a combination of jurisdiction-oriented and

331 *Binder* (2015) Ring-Fencing, 98. See also *Binder* (2014) To ring-fence or not, and how?, 2–3.

332 *Binder* (2015) Ring-Fencing, 98.

333 Another expression, parallel to activity-based ring-fencing, is "functional" ring-fencing. In an article about jurisdiction-based ring-fencing, *D'Hulster* differentiates it from functional ring-fencing and explains the latter noting that *"trading book assets need to be separated from retail assets"*. See *D'Hulster* (2014) Ring-Fencing, 2 Fn 2. This dissertation's focus on functional separation of activities, however, falls in line with the consistent practice of using the general term "ring-fencing". (See e.g. *Gordon/Ringe* (2015) Bank Resolution, 20; *Schwarcz* (2013) Ring-Fencing; *Hardie/Macartney* (2016) EU Ring-Fencing; *Zaring* (2014) Ring-Fencing; *Masciandaro/Suardi* (2014) Public Interest and Lobbies *Brown* (2014) With this Ring, I Thee Fence). For a short discussion of its relation to "jurisdictional-oriented ring-fencing", see Chapter I.VII.C.a: Jurisdiction-oriented ring-fencing.

334 See *Binder* (2015) Ring-Fencing, 108. For a discussion of the character of the *activities ban* and its differences to ring-fencing, see Chapter I.IV.D: Ring-fencing and the activities ban.

335 *Schwarcz* defines ring-fencing in financial regulation by examining its core functions: he states that in financial regulation it frequently (i) has the purpose of making firms bankruptcy-remote, i.e. protecting a firm from liabilities and oth-

activities-oriented ring-fencing.[336] Both definitions are too comprehensive for the focus of this dissertation.[337]

c. Establishing a definition

To establish a definition of ring-fencing that delimits it against other structural reforms and reflects the three core characteristics established above, it is necessary to take stock of the findings regarding its character:

Regarding the literal use of the term "ring-fencing" outside of financial and legal discussion, it was found that it entails (i) a valuing and a defensive element. Ring-fencing therefore needs to specify activities that are to be protected (the valuing element) and that there is a fence of some sort (the defensive element). Furthermore, it has to indicate that risky activities

---

er risks connected to a bankruptcy. It also (ii) aims at enabling firms to operate on a standalone basis – even if affiliated firms fail -, and (iii) at enabling them to protect their business and assets from being taken advantage of by associated firms. Ring-fencing also (iv) allows to limit a firm's risky activities and investments (see *Schwarcz* (2013) Ring-Fencing, 73–81). While the application of ring-fencing is voluntary in some contexts such as securitization and covered bond transactions, the regulatory application is required by government regulation (*Schwarcz* (2013) Ring-Fencing, 82–83). In conclusion, *Schwarcz* defines the financial regulatory concept of RF as *"legally deconstructing a firm in order to more optimally reallocate and reduce risk"*. *Schwarcz* (2013) Ring-Fencing, 108.

336 *Binder* uses *Schwarcz*'s definition as a starting point and develops a comprehensive definition of ring-fencing in banking regulation. It includes both jurisdiction-oriented ring-fencing, and ring-fencing which aims at protecting banks deposits and the provision of services deemed necessary to the real economy. He finds that, although they on the first sight have little in common, there are, in fact, common features and defines ring-fencing as *"a generic concept that involves the segregation of assets, liabilities and/or business activities from specific risks with a view to protecting markets and counterparties either directly or indirectly."* See *Binder* (2015) Ring-Fencing, 115; *Binder* (2014) To ring-fence or not, and how?, 32–34.

337 While ring-fencing of activities often features elements of jurisdiction-oriented ring-fencing, this dissertation clearly focuses on the separation of activities. This dissertation's definition should reflect this emphasis. In addition, *Binder*, as discussed, also includes the Volcker Rule in his definition (*Binder* (2015) Ring-Fencing, 108). In the author's opinion it should be attributed to full separation and should therefore not be considered activities-oriented ring-fencing. *Schwarcz's* definition is very broad, in that it includes both the Glass-Steagall Act and the Volcker Rule. (see *Schwarcz* (2013) Ring-Fencing, 79–80). It is furthermore detached from banking regulation in that it strives to include all uses as a financial regulatory concept. See *Schwarcz* (2013) Ring-Fencing, 72.

(the potential external influence) are allowed to be provided under the same roof.[338]

From the use of ring-fencing as a regulatory concept outside banking regulation it can be derived that (ii) a definition should clearly reflect ring-fencing as a concept of banking regulation. It should furthermore reflect that (iii) both desired and risky activities are permitted to be provided under the same roof.[339] "Structural reform" was found to be an (iv) umbrella term.[340] The definition of ring-fencing thus must delimit it from other structural reforms.

It derives from the underlying assumption of ring-fencing that its definition must reflect (v) the classification of activities as "desired", "risky" and not belonging to any of the two.[341] It was furthermore established that (vi) the basic rationale of all ring-fencing initiatives is protecting deposits and services essential for the functioning of the real economy.[342]

In summary, the three core characteristics comprising the concept of ring-fencing can be reiterated: (i) separation of commercial banking activities and certain investment banking activities, (ii) the establishment of a fence, (iii) allowing for universal banking to be fully maintained.[343]

Taking into account the findings and core characteristics above, as well as *Binder's* definition,[344] ring fencing can be defined as *a bank structural reform that aims to shield deposits and services essential for the functioning of the real economy from services deemed riskier and less socially important by ensuring they are provided legally, financially and operationally separately from each other within a banking group, thereby preserving universal banking.*

VIII. Results

The first part of the dissertation laid the foundation for the other parts. It addressed the first research question, namely what comprehensive concept of ring-fencing as a category of bank structural reform can be established

338 This was found in Chapter I.VII.A: Origins of the term "ring-fencing".
339 This was found in Chapter I.VII.B: Ring-fencing outside banking regulation.
340 This was found in Chapter I.IV.A: Structural reform as an umbrella term.
341 This was found in Chapter I.VI.A: Underlying assumption.
342 This was found in Chapter I.V.A: The basic rationale of ring-fencing.
343 These three core characteristics of ring-fencing as a structural reform are already set out in Chapter I.IV.B: Ring-fencing as a structural reform.
344 *Binder* (2015) Ring-Fencing, 98; Chapter I.VII.C.b: Activities-oriented ring-fencing.

and how its definition can be contributed to. The following paragraphs reiterate selected findings.

Examining a number of well-established definitions of universal banking, it was found that they all highlight the ability of a banking group to provide unlimited financial services. Ring-fencing interferes with the universal banking model as it mandates a certain structure. However, it maintains universal banking, as it does not restrict the ability of a banking group to provide unlimited financial services. The interference is reflected in the definition of universal banking: after introducing ring-fencing, universal banks can be defined as *financial institutions that can engage, through ring-fenced and non-ring-fenced entities, in all respects of the banking, securities and insurance business.*[345]

Bank structural reform is an umbrella term that refers to a variety of regulations that intervene with the organisation of banks. The broadness of the concept is reflected in the definition of bank structural reform for this dissertation as *any regulatory reform that substantially affects the legal entity structure, the size, the management organization or the ability to provide activities.*[346]

Ring-fencing is a structural reform. While its relation to "structural reform" is somewhat blurred due to the synonymous use, it should be regarded as its own concept, because it can be clearly delimited from other structural reforms. For the purpose of this dissertation, three core characteristics that identify ring-fencing as a structural reform on its own were established: (i) the separation of commercial banking activities from investment banking activities; (ii) the preservation of universal banking; and (iii) the establishment of a fence, i.e. provisions that aim to ensure that the separated activities can be provided independently from each other.

---

345 This definition is based on the ones of *Benston* (*Benston* (1994) Universal Banking, 121) and *Wilmarth* (*Wilmarth* (2002) U.S. Financial Services Industry, 223 Fn 23), taking into account the specifics of ring-fencing; see Chapter I.I.A.a: Definition.

346 This definition is based on *Hofer*'s, but includes activity restrictions, such as the Volcker Rule and full separation (see *Hofer* (2014) Structural Reforms, 218 (defining structural reform as *"any regulatory reform substantially affecting either the legal entity structure, the size or management organization of [large and complex financial institutions]"*). *Hofer* excludes activity restrictions, such as the Volcker Rule from his concept of structural reform but includes full separation (*Hofer* (2014) Structural Reforms, 251–257). This is inconsistent, as activity bans are to be seen as a subcategory of full separation. See Chapter I.IV.D: Ring-fencing and the activities ban.

Ring-fencing needs to be delimited against two related structural reforms that are sometimes associated with it: The first is full separation, featured in the Glass-Steagall Act, and its subcategory the *activities ban,* featured in the Volcker Rule. The latter differs from the former mainly by its limited scope: while the Glass-Steagall Act prohibited all securities activities for banking groups, the Volcker Rule only prohibits selected investment banking activities.[347] Both thus share the core characteristic of a separation of commercial banking activities from investment banking activities with ring fencing. They, however, lack the criteria of the preservation of universal banking and the establishment of the fence.

The basic rationale of ring-fencing is the protection of deposit-taking and services essential to the real economy. It precedes all other benefits and is inherent in all ring-fencing initiatives. Benefits of ring-fencing, such as enhanced resolvability and the tackling of complexity and size, are intertwined and influence each other. Together they aim to tackle systemic risk, TBTF and tax payer bailouts.

While in some respects *"clearly related from a functional perspective"*,[348] there is a key difference between ring-fencing and recovery and resolution initiatives. Ring-fencing is static: it mandates a certain structure, dictated by the core characteristics above. Recovery and resolution, in contrast, can be understood as an enforcement-based process. Where the process includes provisions that authorise regulators to extensively influence a banking group's structure, it has the potential to lead to a ring-fencing structure of a banking group. Once the implementation results in a structure that fulfils the core characteristics of ring-fencing established above, it can be considered as such.

Ring-fencing initiatives can be categorised according to strategies they use. Two methods of ring-fencing were established: the *defensive method* and the *containment method.* They both are based on the underlying assumption that there are activities that are important for the real economy and are simultaneously less risky (desired activities) than other activities, which are severely risky and simultaneously less important for the real economy (risky activities). The *defensive method* insulates desired activities by separating them from the rest of the bank. The *containment method* insu-

347 This is reflected in their definitions. See Chapter I.IV.C.a.2: Full separation; Chapter I.IV.D.a.2: Activities ban.

348 *Binder* (2014) Resolution Planning, 4 (with a view to tools to tackle resolvability impediments).

lates desired activities by separating the risky activities from the rest of the bank.

Taking into account the findings of the first part of the dissertation, ring-fencing can be defined as *a bank structural reform that aims to shield deposits and services essential for the functioning of the real economy from services deemed riskier and less socially important by ensuring they are provided legally, financially and operationally separately from each other within a banking group, thereby preserving universal banking.*[349]

---

349 This definition is based on *Binder's* description of activities-based ring-fencing as *"the legal and commercial isolation of systemically important activities within a banking group, with a view to protecting such activities against the risks emanating from less economically important functions"* (see *Binder* (2015) Ring-Fencing, 98). However, as he also includes the *activities ban* of full separation in his definition, it is modified. See *Binder* (2015) Ring-Fencing, 108. It furthermore reflects the findings obtained in the first part of the dissertation.

Part II – Legal Developments on EU Level

This part of the dissertation explores legal developments on a European Union level. In February 2012, the European Commission put in place a High-Level Expert Group (HLEG)[350] with the assignment of considering possible bank structural reforms for the European Union.[351] Eight months later, the Final Report of the HLEG (Liikanen Report)[352] set off the EU's undertaking of implementing a common approach on structural reform. In January 2014, the European Commission adopted its draft regulation[353] after reviewing the proposal, consulting stakeholders and conducting a comprehensive impact assessment.[354] According to the EU's legislative process, the next step following the submission of draft legislation by the European Commission would have been the adoption of a position by the European Parliament.[355] The events in the European Parliament, however, led to the situation that no position was adopted. The Council of the EU

350 The official title of the expert group is "High Level Expert Group on reforming the structure of the EU banking sector".

351 *HLEG* (2012) Liikanen Report, i.

352 The HLEG was chaired by Erkki Liikanen, Governor of the Bank of Finland.

353 *European Commission* (2014) Proposal for a Regulation.

354 *European Commission* (2014) Impact Assessment Part 1, 6–8.

355 The EU's bank structural reform was supposed to take the form of a regulation, as set down in Art. 288 Treaty on the Functioning of the European Union, C 326/47 (TFEU), and thus was exemplary for the general trend of the EU financial market law towards full harmonisation (see *Sester* (2015) Neue Generation, 420 et seqq. (describing the impact of the financial crisis on the EU's legislation, leading to a trend towards full harmonization); *Sester* (2018) EU-Finanzmarktrecht, 54–56). Art. 114 TFEU stipulates that the European Parliament and the Council of the EU shall adopt legislation concerning the internal market (see Art. 26 TFEU) according to the ordinary legislative procedure which is set down in Art. 289 TFEU: the European Parliament and the Council jointly adopt a regulation based on the proposal of the European Commission. The legislative procedure demands that after a European Commission's proposal, the European Parliament is to adopt a position in a first reading, which it then communicates to the Council of the EU. Depending on the Council of the EU's decision to approve or not approve this position, the legislative procedure continues (in case of a rejection the Council is to adopt its own position and to communicate it to the Parliament). As the European Parliament was not able to adopt its position, the legislative procedure was halted until finally being withdrawn.

made use of the possibility of adopting a general approach.[356] In late 2017, the European Commission made public its decision to withdraw the controversial file as part of its Work Programme 2018 and by that end, the legislative process.[357]

In spite of the withdrawal, research on the developments above continues to be of special importance, as they (i) have strongly influenced the academic and political discourse on structural reforms of banking both internationally and nationally and (ii) have considerably shaped already adopted national legislation. Due to the advanced stage of the legislative process, they will (iii) remain a benchmark for structural reform proposals in the EU and abroad. There is, furthermore, (iv) still the chance that parts of the structural reform file are adopted with other regulatory initiatives.[358] These likely orientate towards the discussed approaches.[359] Alternative options for introducing a union-wide ring-fencing requirement may set the foundation for a possible approximation of the EU's to the Swiss solution.

This part of the dissertation therefore discusses the contentious steps of the legislative process, the events in the European Parliament and the withdrawal by the European Commission, and subsequently explores alternative ways of introducing a union-wide ring-fencing requirement.

---

356 The Council of the EU may issue a general approach, which is a political agreement reached by the Council before the European Parliament has adopted its position in the first reading. A general approach serves the goal of accelerating the legislative procedure and facilitating an agreement by informing the European Parliament of the Council's views, which would otherwise take the form of a Council's position. See http://www.consilium.europa.eu/en/council-eu/decision-making/; The general approach of the Council is therefore referred to as "negotiating stance", *Council of the EU* (2015) Negotiating Stance.

357 *European Commission* (2017) Commission Work Programme 2018: Annex 4, 2. The European Commission has yet limited its explanation for the withdrawal to the comment that there was *"no foreseeable agreement"* on the matter and that *"the main financial stability rationale"* had in the meantime been addressed by other regulatory measures. *European Commission* (2017) Commission Work Programme 2018: Annex 4, 2.

358 This applies for example to the negotiations on the EU intermediate parent undertaking (IPU), which is part of the CRRII/CRD IV package. For a discussion of the EU IPU, see *Nemeczek/Pitz* (2016) Intermediate EU Parent Undertaking. See also the proposed amendments to CRDV, reflecting a (more stringent) European Commission's proposal, Chapter II.IV.C.b: Legislative options.

359 See e.g. the proposed amendments to CRDV, reflecting the Liikanen recommendations. See Chapter II.IV.C.b: Legislative options.

I. Liikanen Report

This chapter enlarges on the findings of the HLEG considering structural reform of the EU banking sector. In a first step, these findings shall be presented. Subsequently, their reception by the various stakeholders shall be examined. Then they shall be discussed and put in perspective to the methods of ring-fencing established above.

A. Mandate and structure

The HLEG's mandate commissioned it to *"consider in depth whether there is a need for structural reform [...] or not and to make any relevant proposals as appropriate, with the objective of establishing a safe, stable and efficient banking system serving the needs of citizens, the EU economy and the internal market"*. The HLEG was thereby instructed to take into account structural reform measures already proposed in the United States and the United Kingdom.[360]

The Liikanen Report outlines developments of the EU bank sector before and after the crisis,[361] and analyses the EU bank sector's composition.[362] It subsequently evaluates other regulatory reforms, such as Basel III, EMIR,[363] MiFID II[364] and BRRD. Many of them, however, were still at an early stage at the time of the report. Furthermore, it sums up other structural reform efforts of the time, namely the United States' Volcker Rule and the United Kindom's Vickers Report.[365] Finally, it assesses the necessity of further reform and then presents its own structural reform proposal.[366]

---

360 *European Commission* (2011) Mandate of the HLEG; *HLEG* (2012) Liikanen Report, i; See also *European Commission* (2014) Structural Reform Press Release.

361 See further *HLEG* (2012) Liikanen Report, 3 et seqq.

362 See further *HLEG* (2012) Liikanen Report, 32 et seqq.

363 EMIR's counterpart in Switzerland is the Financial Market Infrastructure Act. See Chapter I.II.C.c: Post-crisis response. On central counterparties and their emergence, see *Brändli* (2011) Zentrale Gegenpartei, 3 et seqq.

364 Directive 2014/65/EU of the European Parliament and of the Council of 15 May 2014 on markets in financial instruments, L 173/349 (MiFID II). MiFID II's counterpart in Switzerland is the Bundesgesetz über die Finanzdienstleistungen (Swiss Financial Services Act) which is yet to be adopted. See *Bundesrat* (2015) Gesetzesentwurf Fidleg.

365 See further *HLEG* (2012) Liikanen Report, 67 et seqq.

366 See further *HLEG* (2012) Liikanen Report, 88 et seqq.

The HLEG comes to the conclusion that further reform measures are needed to complement the reforms mentioned above, to further reduce the chance of bank failures, to further raise the chance of bank resolvability and to further avert tax payer bailouts.[367]

B. Avenue 1

To achieve these goals, the HLEG developed two models of functional separation. Under the term "Avenue 1" the Liikanen Report presents, apart from increased capital requirements on trading activities, the *"separation of banking activities subject to a supervisory evaluation of the credibility of the recovery and resolution plans"*.[368]

a. Outline

By making the separation conditional on the decision of a supervisory authority, structural separation is linked to the recovery and resolution plans (RRP) mandated by the BRRD. Banks with significant trading activity exceeding a certain threshold would need to prove to supervisors as part of their RRP that they are capable of separating retail banking activities from trading activities in case of distress. They would need to show that trading activities could be wound down without danger to the retail activities. The supervisor would then have to decide whether the RRP is credible. If an RRP is considered not credible, functional separation would come into force: banks would have to reallocate their trading activities into a separate legal entity. This entity would have to be legally, economically and operationally separate, and thus be allowed to fail. The remaining retail entity would be prohibited to engage in trading activities except liquidity management and own hedging.[369]

---

367 *HLEG* (2012) Liikanen Report, 94.
368 *HLEG* (2012) Liikanen Report, 95–97.
369 *HLEG* (2012) Liikanen Report, 94–97.

b. Costs and benefits

The Liikanen Report addresses some benefits and potential costs of Avenue 1. In its favour, it argues that an evolutionary approach may be better suited to the continuing weakness of the financial system as discontinuities to the provision of financial services could be avoided. It would further give banks the chance of taking the initiative for structural reform themselves, while allowing supervisors to make the ultimate decision on banks' proposals. As some banks have endured the financial crisis without major problems, Avenue 1 would allow flexible decisions concerning individual banks and would avoid a separation in cases where it is not necessary. Furthermore, it is in line with other regulatory initiatives and is considered by the HLEG to complement them smoothly. The main criticism identified by the Liikanen Report is, apart from questions of the calibration of the capital requirements, that there may be difficulties establishing an even and harmonised implementation.[370]

C. Avenue 2

Under the term "Avenue 2" the Liikanen Report puts forth the model of structural reform that is favoured by the HLEG and which constitutes its final proposal. Similar to the structural reform model mentioned above, Avenue 2 establishes increased capital requirements on trading activities and their functional separation from the rest of the bank. However, unlike Avenue 1, the separation is mandatory and does not involve the decision of a supervisor.[371]

a. Outline

Banks that exceed a certain threshold would have to separate trading activities from the rest of the bank and place them in a legally, economically

---

370 *HLEG* (2012) Liikanen Report, 97. This argument lost weight due to the common supervision and resolution, in particular for G-SIBs. (On the SSM and SRM, see Chapter II.II.A.a: Importance of a harmonized approach). The competence of ECB and SRB likely enhance the harmonised and consistent application of recovery and resolution, free from national biases. See e.g. *Binder* (2014) Resolution Planning, 20.

371 *HLEG* (2012) Liikanen Report, 97–98.

and operationally separate trading entity. This would be achieved by requirements such as separate capital bases, separate funding, individual responsibility for the compliance with prudential regulatory requirements, separate reporting, independent results and balance sheets, independent management and governance, and the necessity of transacting at arm's length. A holding company structure would be required to combine trading activities and commercial banking activities under the same roof.[372]

b. Costs and benefits

Also with respect to Avenue 2, the Liikanen Report addresses costs and benefits. The HLEG argues that the most effective way of tackling complexity, interconnectedness and implicit subsidies for trading activities remains their separation from commercial banking. A separation of balance sheets would also support recovery and resolution procedures by making it easier to get rid of the risky part in case of distress. Overall, bank structures would be more aligned with their activities, which would increase transparency for both the banks themselves and the regulators and would keep different management cultures apart. Once a bank is split up in a trading and a retail entity, further regulation such as activities restrictions would, moreover, be easier to impose. The main points of criticism, as presented by the Liikanen Report, are the apprehension that rules may be eroded over time and that they may not work as intended. Furthermore, the Report notes that the requirement of arm's length transactions between the different entities may be hard to enforce. Important additional arguments against mandatory separation are the difficulty of the task of identifying which activities must be separated and, in particular, the high costs arising by its implementation.[373]

c. Final proposal

In the proposal, the HLEG recommends the separation of *"proprietary trading and all assets or derivative positions incurred in the process of market-making"*.[374] These activities must be performed by the separate trading entity

372 *HLEG* (2012) Liikanen Report, 98.
373 *HLEG* (2012) Liikanen Report, 98–99.
374 *HLEG* (2012) Liikanen Report, 101.

that can be constituted as an investment firm or bank. This entity alone would be allowed to engage in relationships with hedge funds, private equity funds and structured investment vehicles.[375] The Liikanen Report recommends that all other activities be allowed to remain with the rest of the bank, now the retail entity[376], except if, for instance, RRPs demanded something else. Securities underwriting and certain hedging services would not have to be segregated, but closely monitored by supervisors. The trading entity would further be prohibited from accepting deposits and providing retail payment services, but could engage in all other banking services.[377]

Regarding the scope, the HLEG recommends introducing thresholds to ensure that mandatory separation would only be necessary *"if the activities to be separated amount to a significant share of a bank's business, or if the volume of these activities can be considered significant from the viewpoint of financial stability"*. It endorses a two-stage process: in the first stage, the focus is on banks' assets held for trading and available for sale. If they exceed a relative threshold of 15–25% or an absolute threshold of 100 billion €, those banks would proceed to the second stage. In the second stage, the trading activities that were to be separated are assessed. The HLEG handed it over to the Commission to calibrate an appropriate threshold, which would be a share of the banks' total assets. If activities to be separated exceed the share, all of these activities would need to be separated.[378]

D. Results and discussion

The following paragraphs first consider the reception of the HLEG's proposals by the various stakeholders. Subsequently, criticism by both supporters and opponents shall be discussed. Then, the underlying character

---

375 *"Any loans, loan commitments or unsecured credit exposures to hedge funds (including prime brokerage for hedge funds), SIVs and other such entities of comparable nature, as well as private equity investments, should be assigned to the trading entity"*. *HLEG* (2012) Liikanen Report, 101. This definition implies that secured credit exposures, i.e. fully collateralised transactions are not prohibited for the retail entity. A similar exception exists in Germany, see Chapter III.IV.B.a.1: Excluded activities.

376 The Liikanen Report refers to the retail entity as "deposit bank". *HLEG* (2012) Liikanen Report, 101.

377 *HLEG* (2012) Liikanen Report, 101–102.

378 *HLEG* (2012) Liikanen Report, v.

shall be explored and the method of RF proposed by the Liikanen Report identified.

a. Reception by stakeholders

The Liikanen Report has overall received rather positive responses from the press and the world of politics.[379] On March 6th 2013, the College of Commissioners discussed the need for structural reform and in particular the findings of the Liikanen Report. President *Barroso* noted *"broad consensus in favour of an approach at European level"*.[380] The European Parliament also welcomed the findings of the Liikanen Report, considering it a *"sound and welcome basis for structural reform"*[381] and almost unanimously[382] adopted a resolution welcoming the European Commission's *"intention to bring forward a directive for structural reform of the EU banking sector"* in its Committee on Economic and Monetary Affairs.[383]

Although the Liikanen Report has been greeted by some as a *"step forward for EU banks"*[384] and *"a good second best"*[385] to a Glass-Steagall-oriented separation, it has also been criticised by both supporters and opponents of bank separation.

---

379 See *ZEW* (2013) Trennbanken, 23–24. See also *Wolf*, Liikanen is at least a step forward for EU banks, Financial Times (October 4, 2012); *The Economist*, The Liikanen Review: Into the ring (October 6, 2012); *Krahnen* (2013) Rettung durch Regulierung?, 179 (pointing out that the banking industry predominently rejected the recommendations of the Liikanen Report).

380 See *European Commission* (2013) Meeting of the Commission, 17–20. See also *European Commission* (2014) Impact Assessment Part 1, 6. Other commentators considered the European Commission's response not as positive, e.g. *The Economist*, The Liikanen Review: Into the Ring, (October 6, 2012) (noting *"a cool reception from the European Commission, which says it wants to reflect on how they fit with its other regulatory proposals"*).

381 *European Parliament* (2013) Report on Structural Reform, 14.

382 The final vote of the committee resulted in 36 votes of consent, 3 dissenting votes and 4 abstained from voting. *European Parliament* (2013) Report on Structural Reform, 15.

383 *European Parliament* (2013) Report on Structural Reform, 8.

384 *Wolf*, Liikanen is at least a step forward for EU banks, Financial Times (October 4, 2012).

385 *Financial Times*, EU sets out vision for safer banking: Liikanen report on structural reforms is a promising start (October 3, 2012).

b. Criticism of the Liikanen Report

One of the main points of critique by supporters is the height of the threshold. For some commentators it has been set too high, missing in its scope a number of systemically important banks. Furthermore, as the European Commission is to specify the threshold, they argue that there is too much room left for banks to exercise pressure and thus to water it down.[386]

In addition, there is doubt about the permission for the retail entity to engage in hedging services for non-banking clients and securities underwriting, as they *"naturally belong to the 'casino' rather than the 'deposit' arm of a bank"*.[387] In this context, *Vickers* points out certain inconsistencies of the Liikanen Report, namely that securities underwriting in particular *"by its nature creates large exposures"*. These exposures are far higher than the ones of market making and regular derivatives trading, which are prohibited for the retail entity. He also notes that although relationships with hedge funds, private equity funds and structured investment vehicles are limited to the trading entity, the retail entity could still engage in a number of worrisome relationships with other kinds of financial institutions or non-European entities.[388]

Opponents, on the other hand, claim that costs for bank clients such as corporate bond issuers would increase. Furthermore, they argue that European banks would face a competitive disadvantage against banks from the United States, where structural reform is considered to be less stringent.[389] In relation to the threshold, they identify a different problem, namely that banks may be confronted with the incentive to retain trading activities beneath the thresholds, while engaging in riskier trades to keep up the ex-

---

386 See *Wolf*, Liikanen is at least a step forward for EU banks, Financial Times (October 4, 2012); See *Financial Times*, EU sets out vision for safer banking: Liikanen report on structural reforms is a promising start (October 3, 2012).

387 *Financial Times*, EU sets out vision for safer banking: Liikanen report on structural reforms is a promising start (October 3, 2012). See also *Wolf*, Liikanen is at least a step forward for EU banks, Financial Times (October 4, 2012). In the UK, such transactions face limitations, see Chapter III.IV.A.b: Non-ring-fenced bodies.

388 *Vickers* (2012) Banking Reform, 19. See in this regard the prohibitions for certain transactions set down by the UK regime, Chapter III.IV.A.b: Non-ring-fenced bodies.

389 *Jenkins/Barker*, Big banks face hardest hit from ringfencing, Financial Times (October 2, 2012). See also *European Commission* (2012) Replies to the Consultation, 3.

pected return. They further identify uncertainties regarding the evaluation of the recovery and resolution plans of Avenue 1.[390] Other points of criticism are that the consistency of the different structural reforms in other countries (U.S. and UK) may not be ensured and that there is a lack of clarity regarding the implementation (for example with regard to the measurement of the thresholds).[391]

In the author's opinion, it could further be criticised that the Liikanen Report lacks explanation in some of its key points. Recollecting the HLEG's mandate, which included *"paying particular attention"* to other structural reforms, notably the Volcker Rule and the Vickers Report, [392] the HLEG's observations concerning them are of a rather basic form: first, the Liikanen Report provides merely an outline of both regulatory approaches. Only with regard to the Volcker Rule does it describe some concerns expressed by respondents during the consultation process.[393] Furthermore, there is no reflection on why the HLEG decided against those approaches, and where it detects the benefits that make its own proposal superior.[394]

Similarly, it can be criticised that the HLEG provides two avenues and rationale for each of them, but does not offer a substantial reasoning on why it considered Avenue 2 to be superior. A further explanation balancing the two avenues would have been desirable, making the HLEG's choice more transparent.

---

390 See *ZEW* (2013) Trennbanken, 22–23 (pointing out uncertainties regarding the supervisory competence and noting that the HLEG stresses the need of a single supervisory authority). With the adoption of the Single Supervisory Mechanism, this fundament has been set. See Chapter II.II.A.a: Importance of a harmonized approach.

391 *European Commission* (2012) Replies to the Consultation, 3. This has been addressed by the European Commission (see Chapter II.II.E.e: Exemption for the United Kingdom) and the Council of the EU (see Chapter II.III.E.c: Exemption for the United Kingdom) in their proposals.

392 *European Commission* (2011) Mandate of the HLEG.

393 See *HLEG* (2012) Liikanen Report, 84.

394 More detailed considerations would likely have contributed better to a well-founded discussion of structural reforms. They would likely have prevented the European Commission from recommending measures the Liikanen commission did not consider worth pursuing, in particular the prohibition of proprietary trading. Enlightening in this regard is *Krahnen/Kemmerer* (2013) Gesprächsreihe Strukturreformen, 7, 18 (clarifying intentions of the Liikanen commission's recommendations).

c. Characterisation and method of ring-fencing

The Liikanen Report is clearly inspired by the Vickers Report's ring-fencing model and subsequent legal developments in the United Kingdom.[395] However, the Liikanen Report proposes a separation that works the other way around, namely a separation of risky activities from the rest of the bank. Since the separation is only relative – risky activities can still be performed from an independent trading entity, the Liikanen Report recommends the *containment method* of ring-fencing.[396]

In the author's opinion, the HLEG deserves acknowledgement for pioneering this form of ring-fencing, which presents a different approach than the one chosen by the ICB while maintaining many of its benefits. Particularly, it shows consideration for the universal banking model, as it does not propose a total ban on certain activities. Given the experiences with the Volcker Rule, it further seems sensible not to differentiate between proprietary trading and market making. Delimiting both activities has proven to be a considerable challenge.[397]

Although the European Commission did not fully pick up its recommendations, the Liikanen Report has had a course-setting impact on structural reform efforts on a national level, shaping ring-fencing laws across Europe.[398]

II. Commission Draft Regulation

This chapter explores the European Commission's draft regulation,[399] which was adopted following the Liikanen proposal at the end of January

395 On similarities and differences see e.g. *Vickers* (2012) Banking Reform, 19 et seqq.

396 The Liikanen Report forces affected banks to separate activities which are considered risky. The separated trading entity is prohibited from providing desired activities such as deposit takting. This typically characterises the *containment method* of ring-fencing. See Chapter I.VI: Different Methods of Ring-Fencing.

397 See Chapter I.IV.D.a: Digression: The Volcker Rule. *Krahnen* describes the separation of market making as the *"potentially most important detail"* of the Liikanen Report. Own translation from German original, see *Krahnen* (2013) Rettung durch Regulierung?, 174.

398 Germany and France in particular adopted legislation on the basis of the Liikanen Report. See *Lehmann* (2014) Ring-Fencing, 8–9; *Hardie/Macartney* (2016) EU Ring-Fencing, 512–513; Chapter III.II.C: Germany.

399 *European Commission* (2014) Proposal for a Regulation.

2014. As it provided the basis for the negotiations of the European Parliament and the Council of the European Union, it shall be presented in greater detail. To avoid redundancies, a critical evaluation shall be performed synchronously to its presentation. This chapter will, after an introduction, examine the draft regulation with a view to its key elements, namely its scope, the separation of proprietary trading and of other trading activities, and the bundle of provisions governing the strength of the separation. Concludingly, its underlying character and possible implications shall be analysed, its reception and criticism by the various stakeholders shall be discussed, and the method of ring-fencing decided on by the European Commission shall be identified.

A. Introduction

a. Importance of a harmonized approach

As several Member States had already implemented or were in the process of implementing their own structural reform,[400] the European Commission found a need for a harmonized European Union approach.[401] This was in particular to avoid regulatory arbitrage[402] and to make sure that banks could be supervised through the Single Supervisory Mechanism

400 This includes Germany, France, the United Kingdom and Belgium. See e.g. *De Vogelaere* (2016) Bank Structure Reforms; *Binder* (2014) To ring-fence or not, and how?, 29 et seqq.

401 *European Commission* (2014) Proposal for a Regulation, 5.

402 The EU fundamental freedoms can facilitate regulatory arbitrage concerning national regulation: the freedom to provide services allows banks to offer financial services across the European Union. The freedom of establishment allows them to establish both subsidiaries – legally independent entities subject to the regulation of the Member State they are established in, and branches – legally dependent units of a bank subject to the regulation of the Member State their parent bank is established in, in every Member State. National legislation only applies to banks and subsidiaries that are established in the specific country. Branches of banks from other Member States are not covered. Therefore, there may be inconsistencies in a certain market when banks established in the Member State and subsidiaries, which are both covered by national regulation, compete against branches of banks established in other Member States, which are not covered by national regulation. Banks may be tempted to relocate and offer their services through a local branch to avoid regulation or move certain activities to Member States with more lenient legislation. *European Commission* (2014) Impact Assessment Part 1, 22–23.

(SSM)[403] on a consistent basis. Furthermore, the European Commission argued that the effectiveness of the Single Resolution Mechanism (SRM)[404] would make a harmonized approach necessary.[405]

Although a number of other EU financial sector reforms had already been launched and were at an advanced stage at the time of the adoption, the European Commission considered its draft regulation "*a critical part of the Union response to tackling the TBTF dilemma*",[406] "*complement(ing) the overarching reforms already undertaken*".[407]

This highlights how important the European Commission considered an EU-wide structural reform and is particularly interesting when compared to later messages reflecting the development towards a watered-down version,[408] ultimately even the withdrawal of the draft regulation.[409] At the time, the European Commission set a tone that has since been exerting pressure on law-making institutions, including, in particular, the European Commission itself. With the withdrawal and the brief explanation, the high hopes for structural reform have turned into a considerable loss of image and credibility for the European Union.

403 The SSM constitutes the first pillar of the European Banking Union. It consists of national authorities of the euro area, national authorities of non-euro Member States that have chosen to participate in the SSM, and of the European Central Bank. It is in charge of the prudential supervision of all credit institutions in the participating Member States. If credit institutions fulfil certain criteria and thresholds, they are considered 'significant' and are thus supervised directly by the ECB (*European Central Bank* (2014) Banking Supervision, 4–5, 10–11). This direct supervision by the ECB applies to Europe's biggest banks and as of April 1, 2017 includes 124 significant entities (*European Central Bank* (2017) List of supervised entities). The ECB's direct supervision can be seen as part of a general trend of the EU towards full harmonisation, which can also be observed with regard to its legislation. See *Sester* (2015) Neue Generation, 420 et seqq.; *Sester* (2018) EU-Finanzmarktrecht, 54–56.

404 The SRM constitutes the second pillar of the European Banking Union. It aims at improving the management of a bank resolution through a Single Resolution Board (SRB) and a Single Resolution Fund (SRF). *European Commission* (2015) Banking Union, 2; On the functioning of the SRM, see e.g. *European Commission* (2015) Single Resolution Mechanism.

405 *European Commission* (2014) Impact Assessment Part 1, 22–25.

406 *European Commission* (2014) Proposal for a Regulation, 2.

407 *European Commission* (2014) Structural Reform Press Release.

b. Structure

The European Commission adopted its draft regulation after conducting two public stakeholder consultations and entering into discussion with Member States. Furthermore, an extensive impact assessment[410] was conducted and repeatedly revised.[411]

The draft regulation consists of three major elements that are to establish a common structural reform in Europe: firstly, as the European Commission targets only large banks, it establishes criteria and thresholds to identify the banks subject to the regulation. Secondly, the draft regulation stipulates a prohibition on proprietary trading. Thirdly, it mandates a potential separation of certain trading activities. This last element entails a great many other provisions governing the implementation and the upholding of the separation.[412]

---

408 E.g. *European Commission* (2015) Speaking Notes of Commissioner Hill (in which Commissioner *Hill* speaks about the draft regulation on the occasion of the adoption of the Council of the EU's negotiating stance, saying *"I know this has not been a straightforward proposal, in some Member States in particular. The proposal was never aimed – although some thought it was – at calling into question the important role that universal banks play in supporting the financing of the wider economy. The text has changed substantially since the Commission's original proposal. [...] However, overall, we believe today's text is a reasonable and pragmatic compromise which forms a solid basis for future trilogues."*); *European Commission* (2017) Commission Work Programme 2018: Annex 4 (in which the European Commission claims that *"the main financial stability rationale of the proposal has in the meantime been addressed by other regulatory measures in the banking sector and most notably the entry into force of the Banking Union's supervisory and resolution arms"*).

409 *European Commission* (2017) Commission Work Programme 2018: Annex 4, 2. The limited explanation for the withdrawal provides a sharp contrast to the comprehensive work done on the file.

410 The impact assessment explains why the European Commission chose to adopt the draft regulation in its present form. Among other things, it considers existing structural reform, including legislation in Germany, France, the United States and the United Kingdom in detail and weighs them against each other. By doing that, it compensates for the lack of evaluation of the Liikanen Report, criticised in Chapter II.I.D.B: Criticism of the Liikanen Report. *European Commission* (2014) Impact Assessment Part 1, 34 et seqq.; *European Commission* (2014) Impact Assessment Part 2, Annex A1.

411 *European Commission* (2014) Proposal for a Regulation, 3–4.

412 *European Commission* (2014) Proposal for a Regulation, 7–8.

B. Scope of the draft regulation

The first elements of the draft regulation are the criteria and thresholds that identify the banks that are subject to its provisions. Art. 3 stipulates that the draft regulation applies to European banks that are identified as global systemically important institutions (GSIIs). It further applies to banks exceeding two thresholds for three consecutive years: the first threshold is fulfilled if a bank's total assets exceed 30 billion €.[413] The second threshold is fulfilled if a bank's total trading assets and liabilities[414] exceed 70 billion € or 10 percent of its total assets.[415]

In contrast to the Liikanen Report,[416] the draft regulation exempts all banks with total assets of less than 30 billion €. This general exemption allows for such banks to have a more trading-oriented business model. Even if trading assets and liabilities constitute a high percentage of such a bank's total assets, neither the prohibition of proprietary trading nor the conditional separation of trading activities apply.

The draft regulation casts a wide net[417] as it applies to Union credit institutions and their EU parents, their subsidiaries and branches, including in third countries. It further applies to EU branches and EU subsidiaries of banks established in third countries.[418]

C. Separation of proprietary trading

a. Prohibitions

The prohibition on proprietary trading is set down in Art. 6 in the second chapter of the draft regulation.[419] For the definition of proprietary trading,

413 The threshold of 30 billion € also constitutes the threshold for the ECB supervision. See Chapter II.II.A.a: Importance of a harmonized approach.

414 Art. 22 and 23 of the draft regulation comprise rules on the calculation. Assets and liabilities of insurance and reinsurance undertakings and other non-financial undertakings are not included in the calculation. The EBA is called upon to draft implementing technical standards. See *European Commission* (2014) Proposal for a Regulation, Art. 22, 23.

415 *European Commission* (2014) Proposal for a Regulation, 7, Art. 3.

416 See Chapter II.I.C.c: Final proposal.

417 There are, however, possible exemptions set down in Art. 4; See *European Commission* (2014) Proposal for a Regulation, Art. 4.

418 *European Commission* (2014) Proposal for a Regulation, 7, Art. 3.

419 *European Commission* (2014) Proposal for a Regulation, Art. 6(1)(a).

it refers to Art. 5(4), which specifies proprietary trading as "*using own capital or borrowed money to take positions in any type of transaction to purchase [or] sell [...] any financial instrument or commodities for the sole purpose of making profit for own account, and without any connection to actual or anticipated client activity or for the purpose of hedging the entity's risk as a result of [...] client activity, through the use of desks, units, divisions or individual traders specifically dedicated to such position taking and profit making [...]*".[420]

To avert banks from bypassing the proprietary trading prohibition, they are also forbidden from engaging in certain relations with alternative investment funds,[421] in particular hedge funds and other entities engaging in proprietary trading.[422] In contrast to the Liikanen report however, there is no prohibition for loans or guarantee business with alternative investment funds.[423]

There are exemptions for trading in government bonds and cash management processes.[424]

b. Discussion

It is remarkable that the European Commission chose to include a prohibition on proprietary trading – something that was not recommended by the Liikanen Report – and that it chose a very narrow definition,[425] especially compared to the U.S. Volcker Rule, which stipulates a much broader pro-

420 *European Commission* (2014) Proposal for a Regulation, Art. 5(4).

421 For a definition of „alternative investment funds", the draft regulation refers to Art. 4(1)(a) Directive 2011/61/EU of the European Parliament and of the Council of 8 June 2011 on Alternative Investment Fund Managers and amending Directives 2003/41/EC and 2009/65/EC and Regulations (EC) No 1060/2009 and (EU) No 1095/2010. Alternative investment funds include hedge funds, private equity funds, commodity funds, real estate funds and infrastructure funds. *European Commission* (2009) Alternative Investment Fund Managers, 2. However, Art. 6(3) of the draft regulation stipulates far reaching exemptions to unleveraged and closed-ended funds, mainly private equity, venture capital and social entrepreneurship funds, because of their relevance for financing the real economy. *European Commission* (2014) Proposal for a Regulation, 8.

422 *European Commission* (2014) Proposal for a Regulation, Art. 6(1)(b). This provision is clearly orientated towards the Volcker Rule's prohibition on the relations with certain funds, see Chapter I.IV.D.a: Digression: The Volcker Rule.

423 See Chapter II.I.C.c: Final proposal; for the German Ring-fencing Act, see Chapter III.IV.B.a.1: Excluded activities.

424 *European Commission* (2014) Proposal for a Regulation, Art. 6(1)(a) and (b).

425 See *European Commission* (2014) Proposal for a Regulation, 8.

hibition.[426] As shown above, the draft regulation only prohibits trading on own account through sections of a bank that are *"specifically dedicated"* to such an activity. E contrario, all proprietary trading happening in other, not-specifically dedicated elements of a bank is not covered by the general prohibition.

This leads to the situation that the proposed prohibition per se would only have a limited force over bank's business models of today, not only because of the very narrow scope,[427] but also because banks cut back on dedicated proprietary trading operations after the crisis.[428]

The European Commission itself finds this prohibition in its impact assessment to be of *"limited effectiveness"*. Nevertheless, it claims that the separation of additional trading activities would improve the effectiveness, as the supervisor would have the possibility to require the separation of further activities.[429]

The Commission chose this approach for practical reasons, namely because it acknowledges the difficulty of distinguishing between proprietary trading from other permitted activities such as treasury management or market making. It points out that a broad definition of proprietary trading would most likely have the undesired effects of identifying activities that should not have been identified and not identifying activities that should have been identified. A choice for a narrow definition therefore had its reason in the feasibility.[430]

For the advantage of the European Commission, it is to note that the proprietary trading prohibition may, in contrast to the reception of the Volcker Rule, be indeed less criticised for being *"frustratingly vague"*[431] and remains rather clear in its scope. By avoiding a too broad definition, regu-

---

426 Chapter I.IV.D.a: Digression: The Volcker Rule; see also *Armour et al.* (2016) Financial Regulation, 524.

427 *Barker*, Banking groups push Brussels to ditch overhaul of big lenders, Financial Times (November 23, 2014).

428 This has also been acknowledged by the European Commission. However, it argues that the current cut back is far from a guarantee that proprietary trading will not increase again in the future. *European Commission* (2014) Impact Assessment Part 1, 45; *European Commission* (2014) Impact Assessment Part 3, 56, 248. See also *PwC* (2014) AFME: Bank Structural Reform Study, 7 (noting that *"[a]lmost 90% of banks studied announced reductions in proprietary trading activities since the financial crisis, with over half exiting these businesses"*).

429 See *European Commission* (2014) Impact Assessment Part 1, 62–63.

430 See *European Commission* (2014) Impact Assessment Part 1, 60–61; see also *Armour et al.* (2016) Financial Regulation, 524.

431 *Dombalagian* (2013) Proprietary Trading, 403.

lators are spared the difficult and possibly unreasonable unravelling of prohibited proprietary trading and permitted activities, in particular market making.[432] Whether this provision may achieve the desired effect or may be considered a farce, only application in practice would show.

D. The conditional separation of trading activities

The second major element of the European Commission's proposal for structural reform is the potential separation of certain trading activities. It is stipulated in the third chapter of the draft regulation.[433]

a. Trading activities

Art. 8 specifies activities that are not part of the trading activities and can therefore under no circumstances be separated. These include retail activities such as deposit-taking, retail lending and retail payment services. All other activities[434] are considered trading activities.[435]

This negative definition of trading activities comprises a large variety of activities. It grants the competent authority the competence to review a significant part of a bank's operations and thus contributes to the strong position of the authority.

---

432 See Chapter I.II.B: Proprietary trading and market making.

433 *European Commission* (2014) Proposal for a Regulation, Chapter III.

434 There is an exemption for the buying and selling of European Union government bonds from the potential separation in Art. 8(2), that goes hand in hand with the exemption from the prohibition on proprietary trading stipulated in Art. 6(2). These exemptions are set down to *"prevent possible negative consequences in these crucial markets"* (*European Commission* (2014) Proposal for a Regulation, 8). It is beyond the scope of this dissertation to criticise these provisions. It should, however, be pointed out that comparable provisions existed already in the Glass-Steagall Act (See Chapter I.IV.C.a: Digression: The Glass-Steagall Act) and that they can also be found in the Volcker Rule. See Chapter I.IV.D.a: Digression: The Volcker Rule.

435 *European Commission* (2014) Proposal for a Regulation, Art. 8(1).

b. Review of trading activities

The draft regulation then tasks the competent authority with the review of these activities and highlights among them market making, investing in and acting as a sponsor for securitisation and trading in derivatives,[436] as these are activities particularly prone to risks. The competent authority – for systemically important banks included in the SSM, this would be the European Central Bank –[437] shall therefore use a number of metrics, including relative size of trading assets, leverage of trading assets, relative complexity of trading derivatives, relative profitability of trading income and the interconnectedness to assess the activities with regard to a separation. The measurement of these metrics shall be specified by the EBA,[438] and adopted by the European Commission as a delegated act.[439] There are, however, exemptions for risk management and the provision of risk management services to customers.[440]

The competence to separate market making is especially very controversial. It is a significant increase in scope and thus in strictness compared to approaches adopted in European Member States, namely Germany and France, after the Liikanen Report.[441]

c. Separation procedure

Art. 10 empowers the competent authority to separate trading activities by requiring the core credit institution, i.e. the deposit-taking entity,[442] to stop providing them. This decision can be made after a procedure stipulat-

436 Investing in and acting as a sponsor for securitisation and trading in derivatives are activities that have especially contributed to the financial crisis (*European Commission* (2014) Proposal for a Regulation, 9). Market making is one of the activities that are especially close to proprietary trading and therefore difficult to distinguish. See *European Commission* (2014) Impact Assessment Part 1, 60.

437 See Chapter II.II.A.a: Importance of a harmonized approach.

438 *European Commission* (2014) Proposal for a Regulation, Art. 9(1), 9(2), 9(4).

439 *European Commission* (2014) Proposal for a Regulation, Art. 10(6).

440 *European Commission* (2014) Proposal for a Regulation, Art. 11–12.

441 *Barker*, EU bank reforms set out to reduce complexity and curb speculation, Financial Times (January 29, 2014). See also *Hardie/Macartney* (2016) EU Ring-Fencing, 504 et seqq. (discussing the question why France and Germany chose to pursue much softer ring-fencing laws); Chapter III.IV.B.a: Non-ring-fenced body.

442 See *European Commission* (2014) Proposal for a Regulation, Art. 5(16).

ed by the draft regulation: first, the review by the authority, described above, must reveal that the metrics are fulfilled, and the authority must "*deem [...] that there is a threat to the financial stability of the core credit institution or the Union financial system as a whole*".[443] In a second step, the authority notifies the affected bank. Thirdly, the bank then has the chance to demonstrate that the reasons leading to the authority's conclusion are not justified. Fourthly, the authority decides whether or not it accepts the demonstration of the bank. Fifthly, the authority states the reasons for its decision and publicly discloses it.[444]

If the review by the authority reveals that the metrics are not fulfilled, it can still initiate the procedure leading to the separation of a particular activity if it considers the activity to "*pose[] a threat to the financial stability of the core credit institution or the Union financial system as a whole*".[445]

This provision is particularly notable as it allows the competent authority to engage a separation even if the metrics are not fulfilled. That means that an authority may also order a separation if it concludes that the financial stability is at risk and takes into account the rather imprecise objectives[446] of the draft regulation. This provision, therefore, provides the authority with wide discretion.

The authority's decision to separate a bank is, therefore, an ultima ratio, applied only if the authority doubts the bank's ability to manage its risk properly. *Krahnen/Noth/Schüwer* point out that the authority thereby has significant discretion in its decision-making, as the conditions for its intervention refer to financial stability in very general terms.[447]

---

443 *European Commission* (2014) Proposal for a Regulation, Art. 10(1).

444 *European Commission* (2014) Proposal for a Regulation, Art. 10(3).

445 *European Commission* (2014) Proposal for a Regulation, Art. 10(2); see also the detailed explanation of the draft regulation, *European Commission* (2014) Proposal for a Regulation, 9. However, the wording of the draft regulation itself is somewhat obscure, as Art. 10(2) allows the competent authority to "*start the procedure leading to a decision as referred to in the third subparagraph of paragraph 3 [of Art. 10]*", whereas the procedure leading to such a decision is stipulated in the second subparagraph. *European Commission* (2014) Proposal for a Regulation, Art. 10(2).

446 These objectives include, for example, the reduction of excessive risk-taking, the removal of conflict of interest, the reduction of interconnectedness, the facilitation of an orderly resolution and recovery. *European Commission* (2014) Proposal for a Regulation, Art. 1.

447 *Krahnen/Noth/Schüwer* (2016) Structural Reforms, 15.

E. Rules following a separation

Art. 13 of the draft regulation stipulates that the trading entity has to be *"legally, economically and operationally separate [...] from the core credit institution"*,[448] but may remain in the same banking group. This provision gives rise to a number of questions and is in need of further determination. The following articles set down rules governing the strength of separation between the deposit-taking entity and the trading entity.

a. Activities restrictions

The deposit-taking entity is naturally no longer allowed to perform the trading activities separated by the decision of the competent authority.[449] The draft regulation further stipulates a prohibition for the trading entity to engage in the activities of deposit-taking and payment services.[450]

b. Subgroups

In case of separation, two subgroups have to be established which contain either only deposit-taking entities or only trading entities.[451] Both subgroups have to comply with prudential requirements of the CRR concerning own funds, capital requirements, large exposures, liquidity, leverage and disclosure on an individual basis.[452] They are further subject to large

---

448 *European Commission* (2014) Proposal for a Regulation, Art. 13(1).

449 There are, however, exceptions, as the deposit-taking entity may continue to carry out certain trading activities: permitted are trading activities *"to the extent that the purpose is limited to only prudently managing its capital, liquidity and funding"*, i.e. for managing its own risk. Several safeguards, such as a limitation to certain derivatives, a specified remuneration policy and a duty to demonstrate that it is indeed hedging, shall prevent proprietary trading (*European Commission* (2014) Proposal for a Regulation, 9, Art. 11); Furthermore, the deposit-taking entity is allowed to provide certain risk management services to non-financial, non-banking clients. It is thereby limited regarding the potential customers, with regard to the potential financial instruments it may use, and with regard to the risks it may address. *European Commission* (2014) Proposal for a Regulation, 9–10, Art. 12.

450 *European Commission* (2014) Proposal for a Regulation, Art. 20.

451 *European Commission* (2014) Proposal for a Regulation, Art. 13(3).

452 *European Commission* (2014) Proposal for a Regulation, 10, Art. 13(11)-(13).

exposure limits[453] on both intra- and extra-group exposures, contributing significantly to the economic separation.[454] In addition, both subgroups are each to issue their own debt.[455]

These provisions increase the distance between deposit-taking entities and trading entities, and serve the goal of making the former more resistant to dangers of the latter (for example by limiting their exposure to each other). They also enforce that trading entities can be excluded from implicit subsidies of the deposit-taking entities. Furthermore, the provision that both subgroups would need to comply with the CRR's capital standards traps capital and would significantly shrink[456] the activities of the trading entity.

c. Exercise of power

A deposit-taking entity is not allowed to hold voting rights or capital instruments in a trading entity.[457] They may enter into contractual relations, but only on arm's length basis, i.e. they *"shall be as favourable to the core credit institution as are comparable contracts and transactions with [...]entities not belonging to the same sub-group"*.[458]

---

453 Large exposure limits aim at preventing institutions from suffering disproportionately large losses following the failure of an individual client or a group of connected clients. See *European Banking Authority,* Large exposures and structural measures, https://www.eba.europa.eu/regulation-and-policy/large-exposures.

454 *European Commission* (2014) Proposal for a Regulation, 10, Art. 14, 15.

455 *European Commission* (2014) Proposal for a Regulation, Art. 13(6).

456 See for an example of how far-reaching the effects of the need to comply with capital standards on an individual basis on the scale of trading activities can be (*Blundell-Wignall/Atkinson/Roulet* (2013) Bank Business Models, 78–80). *PwC* conducted a study for the bank interest group *AFME* in which it came to the same conclusion. However, in contrast to *Blundell-Wignall/Atkinson/Roulet,* it considers its findings detrimental to the public good: if trading entities face higher funding and capital costs, banks would not be able to offer market making services at today's conditions. This, in turn would reduce the number of market makers and liquidity in the market, which would then lead to higher costs for corporate borrowers in the corporate bond markets. See *PwC* (2014) Bank Structural Reforms, 51 et seqq.

457 *European Commission* (2014) Proposal for a Regulation, Art. 13(5).

458 *European Commission* (2014) Proposal for a Regulation, Art. 13(7).

Furthermore, the management body[459] of the deposit-taking entity and the trading entity shall not be composed of the same persons, but shall each consist of a majority of persons not engaged in the managing body of the other entity. No member of the management body, apart from the parent undertaking's risk management officer, shall occupy an executive function in both entities.[460] In addition, the management bodies of all entities of the group just mentioned, including the parent, are under the obligation to "*uphold the objectives of the separation*".[461]

d. Designation

The separation of the two entities is further emphasized by a provision stipulating that the character of each entity has to be reflected in its designation, so that "*the public can easily identify which entity is a trading entity and which entity is a core credit institution*".[462]

This provision is especially interesting. It shows that the independency of the two entities shall also be emphasized in their appearance before the public. The effect of such a designation should not be underestimated.

e. Exemption for the United Kingdom

Art. 21 allows for a derogation of the third chapter of the draft regulation, i.e. the separation of trading activities. A credit institution that takes deposits can be excluded from the provisions concerning separation if it is "*subject to national primary legislation adopted before 29 January 2014*" and if

459 The term "management body" is defined in Art. 3(1)(7) of the CRDIV Directive (Directive 2013/36/EU). It refers to "*an institution's body or bodies, [...] which are empowered to set the institution's strategy, objectives and overall direction, and which oversee and monitor management decision-making, and include the persons who effectively direct the business of the institution*". *European Commission* (2014) Impact Assessment Part 3, 99 Fn 98.

460 *European Commission* (2014) Proposal for a Regulation, Art. 13(8).

461 *European Commission* (2014) Proposal for a Regulation, Art. 13(9). This provision resembles the prohibitions on the sharing of personnel of the Glass Steagall Act (see Chapter I.IV.C.a: Digression: The Glass-Steagall Act). The management body, particularly executive functions, has significant influence on the conduct of an entity. Conflicts of interest can be avoided only through a truly independent management body.

462 *European Commission* (2014) Proposal for a Regulation, Art. 13(10).

several criteria are met. The European Commission decides on the request of the Member State.[463] For third countries, Art. 27 stipulates that the European Commission may regard their legal situation as equivalent to the requirements of the draft regulation.[464]

F. Results and discussion

The following paragraphs characterise the draft regulation with regard to other structural reforms, in particular the proposal of the Liikanen Report. Subsequently the implications of its adoption as proposed by the European Commission, shall be assessed. In a third step it shall be explored how the draft regulation has been perceived by stakeholders. Concludingly, the method of ring-fencing chosen by the Commission shall be identified.

a. Characterisation

In summary, it can be found that the European Commission decided against the main proposal (Avenue 2) of the Liikanen Report: in contrast to the HLEG's recommendations, the draft regulation does not stipulate a mandatory separation of trading activities: the Commission chose to empower the competent authority to decide about it. This may be understood as a watered-down approach that is more lenient than the Liikanen proposal;[465] it may, however, also be understood as a more flexible approach that allows for a tailor-made assessment of each bank subject to the regulation.

With regard to proprietary trading and relations with certain funds, the draft regulation stipulates an *activities ban* for the whole banking group. It thereby strikes out in a new direction orientating towards the United States' Volcker Rule. As pointed out above, the draft regulation, however,

463 *European Commission* (2014) Proposal for a Regulation, Art. 21. This provision is tailored to the UK ring-fencing regime (other Member States that had at the time implemented structural reforms, e.g. Germany, are not within its scope). It addresses the risk that banks in the UK could be affected by both national and transnational bank structural reform and thus required to split into three parts. See e.g. *Haynes* (2015) Banking Reform, 122–133.

464 *European Commission* (2014) Proposal for a Regulation, Art. 27.

465 See e.g. *Barker*, EU bank reforms set out to reduce complexity and curb speculation, Financial Times (January 29, 2014); *Jenkins*, Ringfencing will make it harder to wind up failing banks, The Financial Times (January 29, 2014).

differs from it by prohibiting proprietary trading only in specifically dedicated units of the bank, i.e. it does not attempt to define proprietary trading functionally.

Considering that the potential separation of trading activities is subject to the competent authority's decision, the European Commission decided to follow the Liikanen Report's Avenue 1. As *Krahnen/Noth/Schüwer* put it, the draft regulation therefore *"combines the logic of Liikanen's Avenue 1 [...] with the Volcker Rule"*.[466]

b. Implications

The European Commission's decision to create a more enforcement-based approach, conforming to Liikanen Avenue 1, may lead to a similar result as the mandatory separation proposed by the HLEG in Avenue 2: *Krahnen* emphasizes that one should not be fooled by the limited reach of the draft regulation, separating only proprietary trading. *"At second sight [...] [the draft regulation] may prove to be more effective than many believe today"*, as the competent authority may end up exercising a lot of influence on the structure of banks through its risk assessment. Although the risk assessment is not specified in the draft regulation, he expects the competent authority to have a lot of discretion in its decision-making. As part of the risk assessment, the competent authority would require banks to prepare effective recovery and resolution plans.[467]

Because transparency and planning security is of utmost importance to both the competent authority and banks themselves, banks may therefore implement structures that almost achieve factual separation of trading activities themselves, even if it has not been demanded from them by the competent authority. Therefore, in case of an implementation of the draft regulation it may be possible that *"there will be a factual separation in the self-interest of financial institutions, rather than a forced one"*.[468]

466 *Krahnen/Noth/Schüwer* (2016) Structural Reforms, 15.

467 See *Krahnen* (2014) Structural Reform, 2 (*"The fencing of trading business from other banking activities may play a crucial role in signalling stability and resolvability vis-à-vis the supervisor"*).

468 *Krahnen* (2014) Structural Reform, 2. This form of separation has a lot in common with the Swiss approach. See Chapter III.IV.C: Switzerland.

c. Reception and criticism

The draft regulation was welcomed with mixed emotions by stakeholders. Germany and France expressed their concern that its measures are too stringent and therefore might hurt the economy and lead to a relocation of activities to the shadow banking sector.[469] The United Kingdom also took an opposing stance against the draft.[470]

The fact that the European Commission adopted the draft regulation shortly before the European Parliament breaks for election, thus at a very inconvenient time in the EU legislative calendar, was criticised heavily by Members of Parliament.[471] Furthermore, the draft regulation is not supported by all Members of Parliament and was criticised by some to be a *"purely symbolic political act"*.[472]

Representatives of the industry warned that the draft regulation could prove disruptive and damaging to both banks and the economy.[473] Furthermore, they criticised that the draft regulation was inconsistent with the European Commission's aim to ensure the flow of credit to the real economy, supporting the Capital Market Union (in particular because of the looming separation of market making), and to abstain from excess EU interventions. Banks were said to have become much safer, making further reform unnecessary. Moreover, data from the European Commission's impact assessment was considered outdated and it was pointed out that in some Member States, national structural reform legislation had already been implemented.[474] The *Association for Financial Markets in Europe*

469 *Barker*, EU bank reforms set out to reduce complexity and curb speculation, Financial Times (January 29, 2014).

470 *Barker*, EU's Hill considers shelving bank structural reforms, Financial Times (December 4, 2014).

471 *Barker*, EU bank reforms set out to reduce complexity and curb speculation, Financial Times (January 29, 2014).

472 *Barker*, Europe set to ease reform on bank splits, Financial Times (January 5, 2014).

473 *Barker*, EU bank reforms set out to reduce complexity and curb speculation, Financial Times (January 29, 2014).

474 *Barker*, Banking groups push Brussels to ditch overhaul of big lenders, Financial Times (November 23, 2014). See *British Bankers' Association/Federation Bancaire Francaise*, Letter to Frans Timmermans, First Vice President Better Regulation, Interinstitutional Relations, the Rule of Law and Charter of Fundamental Rights, (November 13, 2014), http://www.fbf.fr/fr/files/9R6M5Q/Letter-EU-Structural-Reform-Better-Regulation.pdf.

(AFME),[475] one of the most active lobbying groups concerning the EU's structural reform, commissioned *PwC* to conduct an extensive study on the consequences of an implementation of the draft regulation. The study's findings[476] supported the interest group's claims mentioned above.[477] Furthermore, it was argued that the draft regulation would lead to significant disadvantage for European banks' competition, in particular with regard to U.S. banks, and would harm Europe's *"economic sovereignty"*.[478]

Opponent interest groups such as *Finance Watch*,[479] on the other hand, contested most of these arguments and argued that separation would, on the contrary to bank interest group claims, lead to numerous benefits, such as cheaper funding and a better functioning Capital Markets Union.[480]

The draft regulation was further hit by a change of personnel in the European Commission, with *Jonathan Hill*[481] succeeding *Michael Barnier* as Commissioner responsible for Financial Stability, Financial Services and Capital Markets Union. *Jonathan Hill* was called upon by banks to recon-

475 http://www.afme.eu.

476 Among other things, the study found that the draft regulation would entail significant costs for companies interested in borrowing, and would have a detrimental effect on economic growth and jobs in the EU. It would further reduce the number of viable capital market banks, decrease market liquidity and would increase end-user costs. Furthermore, it found that implicit subsidies that were *"once considerable"* are now *"statistically insignificant"* and concluded, that *"while costs […] are clearly substantial"*, *"it is much harder to quantify incremental benefits"*. *PwC* (2014) Bank Structural Reforms, 1–3.

477 *PwC* (2014) Bank Structural Reforms, 1–3.

478 See opinion by Frédéric Oudéa, CEO of Société Générale and president of the European Banking Federation, *Oudéa,* Europe needs homegrown bulge bracket banks, Financial Times (October 11, 2015). As a response, *Finance Watch* noted they *"[understood] concerns among big banks about competitiveness, but Europe's need for sustainable prosperity must come first"*. Big banks should *"recognise financial stability as a prerequisite for sustainable growth and job creation in the rest of the economy"*. See opinion by *Christophe Nijdam*, Secretary General of *Finance Watch*, *Nijdam,* Need for sustainable prosperity comes first, Financial Times (October 15, 2015).

479 http://www.finance-watch.org/home.

480 See *Lallemand*, Bank Reforms will help lift Europe's struggling economy, Financial Times (November 26, 2014).

481 *Jonathan Hill* was European Commissioner from 2014 to 2016 (*European Commission*, Jonathan Hill, http://ec.europa.eu/commission/2014-2019/hill_en). He resigned in the aftermath of Brexit. *Rankin,* UK's European Commissioner quits in wake of Brexit vote, The Guardian (June 25, 2016).

sider the draft regulation, which took form under his predecessor.[482] Indeed, *Hill* already considered a withdrawal in November 2014 but decided to await future developments.[483]

d. Method of ring-fencing

Considering the question which method of ring-fencing the draft regulation represents, one comes to the conclusion that the European Commission decided for the *containment method*, because it chose to separate risky activities from the rest of the bank. It is, however, enforcement-based: similarly to the Liikanen Report – although dependent on an authority's decision –, the draft regulation stipulates in its third chapter that trading activities can be separated and assigned to a trading entity. In particular Art. 13 to Art. 17, presented above, enable the trading entity to be legally, economically and operationally separate. All other activities can be performed by the now ring-fenced entity. Art. 20 of the draft regulation stipulates a prohibition on desired activities for the trading entity, thereby completing the model.

However, the European Commission further proposed a prohibition on proprietary trading in the second chapter of the draft regulation, which took the form of an outright ban. The mandatory segregation of designated proprietary trading from the banking group as a whole qualifies as an *activities ban* of full separation.

In conclusion, it can be noted that the European Commission's proposal is characterised by an enforcement-based *containment method* of ring-fencing in combination with an *activities ban* concerning proprietary trading.

482 *Barker,* Banking groups push Brussels to ditch overhaul of big lenders, Financial Times (November 23, 2014).

483 *Barker,* EU's Hill considers shelving bank structural reforms, Financial Times (December 4, 2014); See, in particular, *Hill,* Letter to Frans Timmermans, (November 18, 2014) http://www.eunews.it/wp-content/uploads/2014/12/Letter-to-VP-Timmermans_Hill.pdf.

III. Council of the European Union Negotiating Stance

This chapter addresses the negotiating stance of the Council of the European Union.[484] It presents and assesses its main modifications of the European Commission's draft regulation. In conclusion, the results shall be summed up and the concept of RF chosen by the representatives of the European Member States shall be identified.

A. Introduction

On June 19th 2015, the Council of the European Union adopted its negotiating stance on the EU bank structural reform. It is based on draft regulation of the European Commission and provides the foundation for the negotiations with the European Parliament. If the European Parliament had adopted its position, negotiations would have commenced.[485] As the European Parliament did not reach agreement on its own position, the negotiating stance of the Council remains the most recent step in the almost tragic story of the European Union bank structural reform.

The Council claims to *"aim[] at strengthening financial stability by protecting the deposit-taking business of the largest and most complex EU banks from potentially risky trading activities"*.[486] Identically to the draft regulation, the negotiating stance acknowledges the still pending too-big-to-fail problem of *"a limited subset of the largest and most complex Union banking groups"*, which requires structural reform as a complement to the ongoing banking regulatory reform agenda.[487] However, the negotiating stance comprises a number of important modifications to the draft regulation, leading to a much softer proposal.

---

484 For better readability and in line with the Council's own terminology, this dissertation refers to the general approach as "negotiating stance" (see *Council of the EU* (2015) Restructuring Risky Banks Press Release). As explained above, a general approach is a position of the Council, already adopted during the first reading. It will serve as the Council Presidency's negotiating mandate in the negotiations with the European Parliament on the final version of the regulation *Council of the EU*, Structural reform of EU banking sector: improving the resilience of credit institutions, http://www.consilium.europa.eu/en/policies/banking-structural-reform/.

485 *Council of the EU* (2015) Restructuring Risky Banks Press Release.

486 *Council of the EU* (2015) ECOFIN Council Meeting, 4.

487 *Council of the EU* (2015) Negotiating Stance, 4; *European Commission* (2014) Proposal for a Regulation, 14.

B. Scope

The negotiating stance identifies entities that are to be covered by its provisions and subsequently allocates them into two tiers. While the scope remains unchanged regarding the Commission's draft regulation,[488] the introduction of tiers is a new feature.

a. Tiers

The negotiating stance's tiers are based on the size of an entity's trading activities and on the presence of excessive risks: if an entity's trading activities[489] have exceeded 100 billion € over the last three years, it is automatically included into Tier 2.[490] This provision is aimed at banks with especially large trading activities. Entities with smaller trading activities can be included into Tier 2 if an assessment reveals the presence of excessive risks.[491] All other entities are included into Tier 1.[492]

The allocation of banks into different tiers correlates with different efforts of supervision: an entity included into Tier 2 has to comply with a broader assessment of its trading activities and stricter reporting requirements.[493]

b. Negative scope

Furthermore, the negative scope, which stipulates exemptions from the proposed regulation, was changed by the Council by adding exemptions to the draft regulation.

---

488 Although the wording of the scope has changed compared to the draft regulation, there are no significant changes concerning the scope. In particular, the thresholds and the link to the qualification of being a G-SII has stayed exactly the same. See *Council of the EU* (2015) Negotiating Stance, Art. 3; *European Commission* (2014) Proposal for a Regulation, Art. 3.

489 The calculation of the trading activities follows the provisions of the European Commission's draft regulation. See *European Commission* (2014) Proposal for a Regulation, Art. 23; *Council of the EU* (2015) Negotiating Stance, Art. 3b.

490 *Council of the EU* (2015) Negotiating Stance, Art. 4a(2).

491 See *Council of the EU* (2015) Negotiating Stance, Art. 8(4).

492 *Council of the EU* (2015) Negotiating Stance, Art. 4a(3).

493 See *Council of the EU* (2015) Negotiating Stance, Art. 6b, 8a.

Art. 4(1)(d) and (e) set forth exemptions both for groups with at least one credit institution established or authorised in the European Union as well as for credit institutions that are neither a parent undertaking nor a subsidiary, if they fulfil at least one of two conditions: if they either hold total eligible deposits of less than three per cent of their total assets or if their total eligible retail deposits amount to less than 35 billion euros.[494]

This provision is aimed at banks that only engage in deposit-taking to a limited extent, either in relation to their balance sheets or in total numbers. This arguably refers to big investment banks that do not engage in retail banking,[495] presumably in particular to non-EU investment banks operating from the UK.[496]

C. Separation of proprietary trading

a. Mandatory separation

One of the most important changes is the handling of proprietary trading.[497] In contrast to the draft regulation, proprietary trading is not prohibited by the negotiating stance. Instead of a total ban from the banking group as a whole, proprietary trading can be performed in a trading entity that is legally, economically and operationally separate from core credit institutions.[498] This is effected by the Council opting in Art. 6 for a mandatory separation from the core credit institution,[499] i.e. the deposit-taking entity.

Regarding the prohibition of relations with certain funds, the negotiating stance emphasizes that it only covers funds employing leverage on a substantial basis.[500] Similarly to proprietary trading, they can, however, be

494 *Council of the EU* (2015) Negotiating Stance, Art. 4(1)(d), 4(1)(e).
495 *BBVA Research* (2015) Financial Regulation Outlook, 5.
496 *Barker*, EU finance ministers back drive to tackle 'too big to fail' banks, Financial Times (June 19, 2015).
497 However, the perception of its quality remains unchanged, as the negotiating stance states that it has *"limited or no added value for the public good and [...] [is] inherently risky". Council of the EU* (2015) Negotiating Stance, 9.
498 *Council of the EU* (2015) Negotiating Stance, 9.
499 *Council of the EU* (2015) Negotiating Stance, Art. 6(1)(a).
500 *Council of the EU* (2015) Negotiating Stance, Art. 6(1)(b) (referring for a definition of "substantial basis" to Art. 111 of the Commission Delegated Regulation (EU) No. 231/2013, which uses the term, if exposure of a fund exceeds three times its net asset value).

conducted in a trading entity. Furthermore, the fully collaterized loans and guarantee business is not prohibited.[501]

b. Three-step procedure

This separation is enforced in a three-step procedure: first, core credit institutions are prohibited from performing proprietary trading and from certain relations with funds. Second, several activities close to proprietary trading are exempted. It is clarified in the process that they do not constitute proprietary trading. Third, to make sure the core credit institution does not engage in proprietary trading, a procedure to identify the activity and require the core credit institution to cease it, is created.

1. First step: prohibition of proprietary trading

As described above, the first step is the mandatory separation of proprietary trading, which is achieved by a prohibition for core credit institutions to perform it. [502] Regarding its definition, the negotiating stance only slightly changes the wording of the draft regulation; however, it omits an important part: the European Commission limited its prohibition of proprietary trading to sections of a bank which are specifically dedicated to perform such activities.[503] This limitation was dropped by the Council, leading to a much broader definition of proprietary trading,[504] which

---

501 See *Council of the EU* (2015) Negotiating Stance, Art. 6(1)(b)(iv). A similar exemption was introduced in Germany by BaFin. See Chapter III.IV.B.a.1: Excluded activities.

502 *"A core credit institution shall not: (a) engage in proprietary trading"*. *Council of the EU* (2015) Negotiating Stance, Art. 6(1)(a).

503 *"[...] through the use of desks, units, divisions or individual traders specifically dedicated to such position taking and profit making, [...]"* *European Commission* (2014) Proposal for a Regulation, Art. 5(4). See also Chapter II.II.C: Separation of proprietary trading.

504 Proprietary trading is, therefore, defined as *"using own capital or borrowed money to enter into any type of transaction to purchase, sell or otherwise acquire or dispose of any financial instrument or commodities for the sole purpose of making a profit for own account, and without any connection to actual or anticipated client activity or for the purpose of hedging the entity's risk as result of actual or anticipated client activity"*. *Council of the EU* (2015) Negotiating Stance, Art. 5(4). Apart from the omission described above, only a minor change in the wording can be found.

again leads to a much broader prohibition. Relations with certain funds are also prohibited for the core credit institution.[505]

2. Second step: exemptions

The negotiating stance then explicitly stipulates several activities that are not to be considered proprietary trading, including the provision of funding, hedging, investment services to clients, market making and the buying and selling of financial instruments acquired for long term investment purposes.[506]

These activities, in particular market making, are difficult to distinguish from proprietary trading.[507] By broadening the scope of the definition, the problem arises that proprietary trading is very hard to distinguish from the other trading activities.[508]

3. Third step: identification procedure

As a result, core credit institutions have to provide *"detailed reporting"* on these activities *"to demonstrate that they do not constitute proprietary trading"*. Competent authorities have to perform an assessment and order the credit institution to *"cease carrying out these activities"* if they turn out to indeed constitute proprietary trading.[509]

The reporting requirements and the assessment concerning the possible performance of proprietary trading are stipulated in Art. 6b and Art. 8 of the negotiating stance. Core credit institutions have the duty to at least annually make information on the activities mentioned above available to

505 *Council of the EU* (2015) Negotiating Stance, Art. 6(1)(b)(iv).

506 *Council of the EU* (2015) Negotiating Stance, Art. 6(2). These exemptions are very similar to the ones of the German Ring-fencing Act. See Chapter III.IV.B.a.2: Exceptions.

507 See Chapter I.II.B: Proprietary trading and market making.

508 The negotiating stance acknowledges this problem and aims to tackle it with enhanced reporting. See *Council of the EU* (2015) Negotiating Stance, 10 (*"It is difficult to distinguish proprietary trading from other trading activities, especially market making. To overcome this difficulty and to dissuade core credit institutions from engaging in proprietary trading, core credit institutions should provide detailed reporting […]"*). Similar problems arise concerning the Volcker Rule's proprietary trading prohibition. See Chapter I.IV.D.a: Digression: The Volcker Rule.

509 *Council of the EU* (2015) Negotiating Stance, 10.

the competent authority. This information includes qualitative information and quantitative information. As mentioned above, Tier 2 core credit institutions have stricter reporting requirements. If the competent authority finds the core credit institution to engage in proprietary trading, it can require it to cease that activity.[510]

c. Results

The negotiating stance, on the one hand, mitigates the separation of proprietary trading proposed by the European Commission by allowing it to be performed in a separate entity. On the other hand, it decides against the European Commission's limited scope of proprietary trading, thereby broadening the scope of proprietary trading that has to be separated.

The broadened scope combined with the exemptions for trading activities, including market making, imports the problems of delimitation discussed in the context of the Volcker Rule: comprehensive and complex reporting.[511] If authorities want to ensure this separation takes place, they have to identify it first. The burden of identifying it is therefore placed on the regulators: the draft regulation spared authorities the task of identifying it by addressing units specifically dedicated to proprietary trading. The negotiating stance tasks them with the elaborate obligation of finding it and differentiating it from other activities.

The negotiating stance recommends a separation very similar to the one adopted in Germany and France.[512] As it combines the scope of the Volcker Rule with a more lenient form of separation, it can be considered *"Volcker-lite"*.[513]

---

510 *Council of the EU* (2015) Negotiating Stance, Art. 6b, 8.

511 See Chapter I.IV.D.a: Digression: The Volcker Rule. See also *Krahnen/Kemmerer* (2013) Gesprächsreihe Strukturreformen 15–16 (explicitly warning that such a system was deliberately not recommended by the Liikanen Commission).

512 For example, as pointed out above, with regard to the prohibition and exemptions. For the German and French national ring-fencing legislation, see *Lehmann* (2014) Ring-Fencing, 8–9; *De Vogelaere* (2016) Bank Structure Reforms, 72–76; see also Chapter III.IV.B.a: Non-ring-fenced body.

513 *Vickers* uses this term to describe German and French national ring-fencing legislation. See *Vickers* (2016) Banking Reform Presentation, 22.

D. The conditional separation of trading activities

The conditional separation of trading activities is linked to the allocation of entities into the different tiers. Core credit institutions that are included into Tier 2 (trading assets of over 100 billion € or excessive risks according to an assessment) are subject to an assessment to identify excessive risk in their trading activities.[514]

a. Assessment of other trading activities

In this assessment, the competent authority has to evaluate the information provided by the Tier 2 core credit institution in accordance with Art. 6b, which includes both qualitative information[515] and quantitative information[516]. The EBA is ordered to issue guidelines to specify a methodology for assessing the level of risk.[517]

If the assessment reveals highly risky trading activities or conditions facilitating them, the competent authority has to *"carry out due diligence to verify whether those trading activities are excessively risky"*. If it turns out that the risks are indeed excessive, the competent authority has to make a decision as set down in Art. 10.[518]

Art. 10 stipulates the power of a competent authority to impose certain measures on a Tier 2 core credit institution. These measures include, apart from other prudential measures,[519] an increase of the core credit institu-

---

514 *Council of the EU* (2015) Negotiating Stance, Art. 8a.

515 Qualitative information that needs to be provided to the competent authority at least annually includes, *inter alia*, a description of the governance structure of the trading activities, a description of mandates, activities, strategies and procedures of each trading unit, and a description of internal control measures. See *Council of the EU* (2015) Negotiating Stance, Art. 6b(2).

516 Quantitative information that needs to be provided to the competent authority quarterly includes, *inter alia*, daily profit and loss and quarterly transaction volumes. See *Council of the EU* (2015) Negotiating Stance, Art. 6b(3).

517 *Council of the EU* (2015) Negotiating Stance, Art. 8a.

518 *Council of the EU* (2015) Negotiating Stance, Art. 8a(4).

519 These prudential measures are set down in Art. 104 of the CRDIV Directive (Directive 2013/36/EU) and include, for example, requiring an institution to present a plan to restore compliance and set a deadline for it, requiring the reduction of the risk inherent in the activities, products and systems of an institution, or requiring an institution to use net profits to strengthen own funds.

tion's own fund requirements, and the separation of the trading activities.[520]

b. Results

Conclusively, it can be said that the competent authority reviews trading activities of Tier 2 banks. If it finds them to be of high risk, it has to make absolutely sure they are excessively risky. If they indeed turn out to be excessively risky, the authority may choose separation of the many remedies provided by the negotiating stance.

However, there is number of newly introduced backstops that keep the competent authority from making decisions that might be too far-reaching. If, for example, the competent authority finds during its assessment that market making activities carry high risks, it shall *"consider the importance of those activities for the well-functioning of the financial system or real economy [...] and weigh the additional benefits of a separation against other measures that may be taken to reduce the risks of the core institution"*.[521]

During the assessment, the competent authority shall furthermore take into account a number of principles,[522] which include that *"decision[s] shall be proportionate to the aim pursued and appropriate as regards the need for, and the choice of any measures [...]"*, *"the need to balance the interests of the various Member States involved [...]"*.[523] Art. 10, which empowers the competent authority to impose separation, also calls the competent authority to take *"appropriate action"*, which shall be *"proportionate to the risk identified"*.[524]

This emphasis on proportionality pervades the entire negotiating stance.[525] It is complemented by a strong call for the compliance with fun-

520 *Council of the EU* (2015) Negotiating Stance, Art. 10.
521 *Council of the EU* (2015) Negotiating Stance, Art. 8a(4).
522 *Council of the EU* (2015) Negotiating Stance, Art. 8a(4). Art. 8a(4) refers for the principles, obviously by mistake, to Art. 26(6), which does not constitute any principles. Only a reference to Art. 26(7) makes sense, as this provision sets forth principles for decision-making.
523 *Council of the EU* (2015) Negotiating Stance, Art. 26(7).
524 *Council of the EU* (2015) Negotiating Stance, Art. 10.
525 *"Following the assessment, where the competent authority concludes that excessive risk exists [...], it should impose an effective and proportionate measures to address that risk. The proportionality principle should apply [...]"*. *Council of the EU* (2015) Negotiating Stance, 15.

damental rights and fundamental freedoms[526] as well as the regular confirmation that trading activities are *"generally beneficial to the real economy and the public good"*.[527] It can be assumed that the unlikely case of an implementation of the negotiating stance in this form would lead to a very reluctant enforcement of separation.

E. Rules following a separation

Considering the rules following a separation, the Council decided for comparatively minor changes. Trading entities still must be legally, economically and operationally separate from core credit institutions.[528]

The requirements for separated entities to issue their own debt, engage with each other at arm's length, maintain separated management bodies, individually comply with capital requirements of the CRR and to carry distinct designations also remain unchanged.[529]

a. Corporate structure

The council, however, added the provision that groups may choose the appropriate legal corporate structure for their operations. The requirement to create subgroups, as set down by the draft regulation, should *"not necessarily result in a requirement to adopt a holding structure or other specific corporate legal structures"*. After a separation, core credit institutions and trading entities should still be able to be parent undertakings of both trading entities and core credit institutions.[530] This explains why the Council also decided

526 See *Council of the EU* (2015) Negotiating Stance, 26, stressing that the application of the negotiating stance has to be in accordance with, *inter alia*, the freedom to conduct business, the rights of shareholders, the right to property, the right to a fair trial.

527 See, for instance, *Council of the EU* (2015) Negotiating Stance, 10. See also *Council of the EU* (2015) Negotiating Stance, 13 (describing trading activities as *"often related to client activity"* and emphasizing the *"potentially useful nature of such activities"*).

528 *Council of the EU* (2015) Negotiating Stance, Art. 13(1); *European Commission* (2014) Proposal for a Regulation, Art. 13(1).

529 See *Council of the EU* (2015) Negotiating Stance, Art. 13.

530 *Council of the EU* (2015) Negotiating Stance, 16, Art. 13(4).

to skip the prohibition of holding capital instruments or voting rights in a trading entity for core credit institutions.[531]

b. Activity-restrictions

A further change was made to the activity-restrictions for trading entities. Whereas the draft regulation prohibits them from taking deposits in general,[532] the negotiating stance only prohibits them from taking "retail deposits", i.e. deposits held by natural persons and micro, small and medium sized enterprises. It thereby allows trading entities to accept non-retail deposits eligible for deposit insurance.[533] Trading entities can therefore fund themselves with deposits from e.g. institutional investors.[534]

c. Exemption for the United Kingdom

Concerning the legal situation in the United Kingdom, the controversial exemption of Art. 21 of the draft regulation was amended: the negotiating stance stipulates in Art. 5a that a separation of trading activities can be either achieved by the measures set down in its provisions, or by *"the requirement [...] that core retail banking activities [...] are located in a legally, economically and operationally separate entity"*. It thereby essentially describes the United Kingdom's structural reform model.[535]

The provision is formulated in a way that opens up the alternative for every Member State. Essentially, however, it constitutes a *"rare UK derogation from [an] EU regulation"*.[536] Interestingly, the negotiating stance, as requested by French negotiators, emphasizes that *"the way chosen is due to the*

531 Cf. *European Commission* (2014) Proposal for a Regulation, Art. 13(5).
532 See *European Commission* (2014) Proposal for a Regulation, Art. 20.
533 *Council of the EU* (2015) Negotiating Stance, 17, Art. 5(18), Art. 5(19), Art. 20.
534 A similar exception can be found in the German Ring-fencing Act. See Chapter III.IV.B.b.2: Other activity restrictions for the financial trading institution.
535 See *Council of the EU* (2015) Negotiating Stance, Art. 5a.
536 *Barker*, EU finance ministers back drive to tackle 'too big to fail' banks, Financial Times (June 19, 2015) (This article also cites *George Osborne*, former UK chancellor saying: *"What we have had to come up with is a regulation which is rather unusual in design and basically allows the European Central Bank to have a single resolution, while allowing the UK to take a different and tougher course"*).

special circumstances of the regulation. It is in no way a precedent for future financial services regulation".[537]

F. Results and discussion

a. Negotiating manifest

Because of the events in the European Parliament depicted in the next chapter, the Council's negotiating stance remains the latest step in the European Union's failed Bank Structural Reform file. Evaluating its provisions, one has to note that they constitute a negotiating manifest for negotiations with the European Parliament rather than a final legal text. However, in the author's opinion, its provisions are already indicative of the following developments of the EU's bank structural reform, namely the withdrawal by the European Commission.

b. Watered down

The negotiating stance is characterised by a systematic watering down of previous legislative proposals.[538] While the draft regulation has already been criticised by proponents of tougher structural reform for not taking up the path of mandatory separation of trading activities recommended by

537 *Council of the EU* (2015) Negotiating Stance, 7. See *Barker*, EU finance ministers back drive to tackle 'too big to fail' banks, Financial Times (June 19, 2015). See for an insight into French banks' interest group work *Federation Bancaire Francaise* (2015) Bank Structural Reform.

538 This is noted by the media, (see e.g. *Barker*, EU finance ministers back drive to tackle 'too big to fail' banks, Financial Times (June 19, 2015)), but is also indicated by leading actors: Commissioner *Hill* described the content as *"a reasonable and pragmatic compromise"*, which changes a proposal that *"has not been [] straightforward"*. *European Commission* (2015) Speaking Notes of Commissioner Hill. See also *Hogan*, Bank Ring-Fencing Edges Closer in Europe: Finance Ministers have agreed on their version of ring-fencing heaping pressure on MEPs to complete their discussions, (June 28, 2015) https://home.kpmg.com/xx/en/home/insights/2015/06/bank-ring-fencing-edges-closer.html (noting that, although the negotiating stance is seen as watered down, it would still place considerable requirements on banks).

the Liikanen Report,[539] the negotiating stance reduces the importance of the separation measure considerably.

This is in particular because, with regard to trading activities that are found to be excessively risky, separation is only one of several possible remedies. As discussed above, several backstops ensure that a separation becomes highly unlikely. The grandly announced bank structural reform is therefore reduced to only one alternative, notably a very unlikely one.[540]

Furthermore, the number of affected banks was decreased dramatically. Only banks allocated to Tier 2, i.e. banking groups with trading assets of over 100 billion € or excessive risks according to an assessment, are subject to the potential separation of trading activities.[541]

Regarding proprietary trading the Council decided, on the one hand, to follow the problematic direction towards the Volcker Rule set by the draft regulation and assimilate it even more by adopting a similarly broad definition. On the other hand, it decided against a full separation in the form of the *activities ban* for the whole banking group.

c. Method of ring-fencing

The Council's negotiating stance proposes a mandatory *containment method* of ring-fencing for proprietary trading and relations with certain funds. It thus decided against the *activities ban* of full separation proposed by the European Commission.

Regarding other trading activities, a subset of banks are subject to an authority's decision, drawing from a number of measures, of which the *containment method* of ring-fencing constitutes one. Regarding the other trading activities, it is thus enforcement-based.

d. Influence of Germany and France

Hardie/Macartney emphasize that the powerful Member States Germany and France were already advocating for lighter ring-fencing requirements

539 See Chapter I.II.F: Results and discussion.
540 See Chapter I.III.D: The conditional separation of trading activities.
541 See Chapter II.III.D: The conditional separation of trading activities.

during the Liikanen process and later on during negotiations with the European Commission.[542]

Looking at the ring-fencing model set out by the Council in the negotiating stance, one finds that it orientates clearly towards the national ring-fencing legislation adopted in the two countries. In particular with regard to the handling of proprietary trading, the negotiating stance is inspired by national legislation of Member States.[543] The far-reaching exemptions for hedging, investment services to clients, market making and the buying and selling of financial instruments acquired for long term investment purposes[544] also reflect adopted ring-fencing legislation of the Member States.[545] As it combines, similarly to Germany and France, the scope of the Volcker Rule with a more lenient form of separation, it can be considered "*Volcker-lite*".[546]

It is indeed comprehensible that the two countries did not manage to achieve their domestic interests with regard to the Liikanen Commission or the European Commission, as these two bodies are to act independently from interests of the Member States. However, it is not surprising that the position of the Council, which constitutes the institution on a European Union level that represents interests of the Member States, much more reflects their interests and national legislation.

IV. Withdrawal of the File and Alternatives

A. European Parliament

At the end of January 2014, the draft regulation of the European Commission was passed on to the European Parliament,[547] where the Committee

---

542 *Hardie/Macartney* (2016) EU Ring-Fencing, 513. See also *Götz/Krahnen/Tröger* (2017) Liikanen-Bericht, 208 (noting disputes in the Council of the EU due to the different impacts of concrete rules on Member States according to the respective design of the rules).

543 For the German and French national ring-fencing legislation, see *Lehmann* (2014) Ring-Fencing, 8–9; *De Vogelaere* (2016) Bank Structure Reforms, 72–76; see also Chapter III.IV.B.a.1: Excluded activities.

544 *Council of the EU* (2015) Negotiating Stance, Art. 6(2).

545 For the German exceptions, see Chapter III.IV.B.a.2: Exceptions.

546 *Vickers* uses this term to describe German and French national ring-fencing legislation. See *Vickers* (2016) Banking Reform Presentation, 22.

547 *EUR-Lex*, Procedure 2014/0020/COD, http://eur-lex.europa.eu/procedure/DE/2014_20.

for Economic and Monetary Affairs (ECON) became responsible for the file. *Gunnar Hökmark*, a member of parliament of the centre right European People's Party, was appointed rapporteur.[548] *Hökmark* himself left no doubt that the European Commission's draft regulation was in his opinion the wrong way to go and prominently argued against a separation of trading activities.[549]

While in 2013 the Liikanen Report was welcomed by ECON as *"sound and welcome basis for structural reform"*,[550] the European Commission's draft regulation became a highly controversial matter: particularly between centre left and centre right parties, the views diverged considerably and no agreement could be reached.[551]

One of the most controversial issues was whether or not a separation should to be mandatory or in the discretion of the regulator. Centre right parties rejected the idea of automatically splitting up a bank once a threshold is exceeded. Centre left parties, in contrast, demanded such a requirement to avoid, the risk of an in their opinion lenient approach of regulators.[552]

Another highly discussed issue was whether separation could be avoided in the case of increased capital requirements for banks. Opponents of the draft regulation pushed for a risk-based approach instead of structural measures.[553]

---

548 *European Parliament*, 2014/0020(COD), http://www.europarl.europa.eu/oeil/popups/ficheprocedure.do?lang=en&reference=2014/0020(OLP).

549 This is reflected, e.g. in the rapporteur's explanatory statement, in which he argues that *"there is nothing telling us that trading is more risky than lending, rather the opposite. [...] Trading in covered bonds or options in transparent markets is often more secure than lending to shopping galleries or office centres"*. See *European Parliament Committee on Economic and Monetary Affairs* (2013) Draft Report, 54.

550 *European Parliament* (2013) Report on Structural Reform, 14.

551 See *Jones,* Stand-off traps EU's 'too big to fail' bank reform in limbo, Reuters (October 26, 2016); *European Parliament,* Banking Structural Reform, (February 20, 2018), http://www.europarl.europa.eu/legislative-train/theme-deeper-and-fairer-internal-market-with-a-strengthened-industrial-base-financial-services/file-banking-structural-reform. See also *Götz/Krahnen/Tröger* (2017) Liikanen-Bericht, 208 (noting disputes in the European Parliament due to the different impacts of concrete rules on Member States according to the respective design of the rules).

552 See *Jones,* Stand-off traps EU's 'too big to fail' bank reform in limbo, Reuters (October 26, 2016).

553 *European Parliament,* Banking Structural Reform, (February 20, 2018), http://www.europarl.europa.eu/legislative-train/theme-deeper-and-fairer-internal-market-with-a-strengthened-industrial-base-financial-services/file-banking-structural-reform.

In May 2015, the draft report was rejected by ECON, with only one vote difference,[554] for being too lenient.[555] Since then, the positions hardened on both sides.[556] In September 2016, Commission Vice-President *Dombrovski* tried to kick-start the bill without success.[557]

The fact that the European Parliament was not able to reach a position is remarkable: as the draft report was rejected by ECON, the European Parliament had to restart its negotiations, something that has not occurred on any other major financial reform package.[558]

What is also interesting is that the draft report was rejected by the center left parties for being too lenient.[559] Proponents of a strict functional separation were in the awkward position of either accepting the changes proposed by opponents, which mitigated the draft regulation considerably or rejecting the draft report as a whole.

B. Withdrawal

In late 2017, the European Commission made public its decision to withdraw the controversial file as part of its Work Programme 2018 and by that end the legislative process. It has limited its explanation for the withdrawal to the comment that there was *"no foreseeable agreement"* on the matter and that *"the main financial stability rationale"* had in the meantime been addressed by other regulatory measures, *"most notably the entry into force of the Banking Union's supervisory and resolution arms"*.[560]

554 *European Parliament Committee on Economic and Monetary Affairs* (2015) Minutes: Meeting of 26 May 2015, 3 (The result of the vote was 29 in favour and 30 against the draft report).

555 See further *Moshinski*, EU Bank-Structure Rules Falter with Parliament Divided, Bloomberg (May 26, 2015).

556 *Gunnar Hökmark* for instance noted: *"I think there will be a stalemate for quite some time"* and *"[e]ither the socialists accept our offer or we will still be where we are"*. *Jones*, Stand-off traps EU's 'too big to fail' bank reform in limbo, Reuters (October 26, 2016).

557 *Weber*, EU Bank-Breakup Push Still 'Locked' After Dombrovskis Effort, Bloomberg (October 25, 2016).

558 *Hogan*, Bank Ring Fencing Edges Closer in Europe, KPMG Insights, (June 28, 2015), https://home.kpmg.com/xx/en/home/insights/2015/06/bank-ring-fencing-edges-closer.html.

559 See *Moshinski*, EU Bank-Structure Rules Falter with Parliament Divided, Bloomberg (May 26, 2015).

560 *European Commission* (2017) Commission Work Programme 2018: Annex 4, 2.

The reception of the decision has been as divided as the positions in the ECON: while rapporteur *Hökmark* applauded the Commission,[561] shadow rapporteur *von Weizsäcker* of the S&D emphasized that the withdrawal *"marks an unfortunate turning point in the European agenda on regulating large banks"*.[562]

The withdrawal of the file by the European Commission is remarkable. In the author's opinion, it can be criticised for two reasons: firstly, the medium chosen by the European Commission to inform the public, does not seem to be fitting. To announce the withdrawal of *"a critical part of the Union response to tackling the TBTF dilemma"*[563] over the Work Programme 2018 seems inappropriate. One would think that the intention to withdraw a major EU reform project would merit a press release.

Secondly, there seems to be insufficient reasoning of the intention to withdraw. While it is likely true that there is *"no foreseeable agreement"* – the file has indeed *"not progressed since 2015"* – the argumentation that the main financial stability rationale has *"in the meantime been addressed by other regulatory measures in the banking sector"* requires substantiation. That it is addressed *"most notably [by] the entry into force of the Banking Union's supervisory and resolution arms"*[564] is also questionable. The EU's bank structural reform has since the Liikanen Report been designed to complement these initiatives.[565] A more detailed explanation would have been desirable.

The withdrawal of the file can rightly be considered a *"long-sought victory for the banking industry"*, as affected banks and interest groups have lobbied

---

561 *"As a rapporteur, I welcome the decision. I achieved a majority with me against the core of the original proposal [...] It was my firm belief that splitting up universal banks by separating retail from trade, investment and market making, would create instability and hinder investments and a more dynamic banking sector. [...] The original proposal wouldn't have strengthened the European banking sector, but rather made it less resilient in times of crisis." Hökmark,* Commission withdraws proposal on Banking Structural Reform (BSR), (October 24, 2017), http://hokmark.eu/commission-withdraws-proposal-on-banking-structural-reform-bsr/.

562 *Helin-Villes,* The withdrawal of the Bank Structural Reform file marks an unfortunate turning point in the European agenda on regulating large banks, say S&Ds, (October 25, 2017), http://www.socialistsanddemocrats.eu/newsroom/withdrawal-bank-structural-reform-file-marks-unfortunate-turning-point-european-agenda.

563 *European Commission* (2014) Proposal for a Regulation, 2.

564 *European Commission* (2017) Commission Work Programme 2018: Annex 4, 2.

565 The Liikanen Report, for instance, discusses extensively the at the time proposed recovery and resolution plans (*HLEG* (2012) Liikanen Report, 81–83) and the Banking Union and Single Supervisory Mechanism (*HLEG* (2012) Liikanen Report, 80–81).

hard against its adoption.[566] As discussed with regard to the negotiating stance,[567] it also reflects the interests of Member States that advocated for lighter structural reform rules.

In summary, it can be stated that the winds seem to have turned in Brussels. Both in the Council of the EU and the European Parliament, the necessary support for stringent structural reform measures could not be gathered. While in the UK and Switzerland, the largest banks are already in the process of implementing far-reaching structural changes,[568] a common European Union approach has not been realizable.

C. Alternatives

Due to the withdrawal of the file by the European Commission, alternative ways of imposing a ring-fence are expected to become more important. The following paragraphs will set out the expected starting position in the EU institutions and subsequently discuss legislative options for reintroducing a structural reform bill. Finally, they will explore the possibility of introducing bank structural reform through existing provisions.

a. Starting position

Considering the close vote in the European Parliament to reject the draft position,[569] the reaction of the political groups[570] and the number of seats

566 *Brush/Glover*, Banks Win as EU Scraps Proposal to Split Off Trading Units, Bloomberg (October 25, 2017). *Christian Stiefmueller*, Senior Policy Analyst at Finance Watch, commentated this rather dramatically: *"The demise of the bill is as regrettable as it was – by now – predictable. The fact that not even Vice-President Dombrovskis' intervention one year ago succeeded in reviving the effort is testimony to the iron grip the financial industry's lobby still exerts on governments and legislators."* See *Finance Watch*, Too-big-to-regulate: The EU's bank structural reform proposal failed, (October 25, 2017), http://www.finance-watch.org/press/press-releases/1468.

567 See Chapter II.III.F: Results and discussion.

568 See Part III: Legal Comparative Analysis.

569 *European Parliament Committee on Economic and Monetary Affairs* (2015) Minutes: Meeting of 26 May 2015, 3 (The result of the vote was 29 in favour and 30 against the draft report).

570 See *Helin-Villes*, The withdrawal of the Bank Structural Reform file marks an unfortunate turning point in the European agenda on regulating large banks,

by political group,[571] it can be assumed that there is still considerable support for a structural reform of banking in the European Parliament.[572]

As discussed in the context of the European Council's negotiating stance, the Member States, notably France and Germany, do not seem to be interested in a stringent union-wide bank structural reform at the moment.[573] It is hard to tell the position of the European Commission in its current form. The withdrawal and especially its reasoning suggest, however, that it does not see the need for another attempt to revive the project.[574]

b. Legislative options

The first option would be a legislative proposal by the European Commission based on the regular legislative process of the European Union.[575] Due to the position of the European Commission discussed above, this option can currently be regarded as improbable.

The second option would be a request by the European Parliament to the European Commission to submit an appropriate legislative proposal. The treaties set down the possibility for the European Parliament to adopt such a request with a majority of Members of Parliament. The adoption of such a request would be conceivable, however it is questionable whether it could gather enough momentum to achieve a majority vote. In addition, the European Commission is not bound to submit a proposal following the request.[576]

---

say S&Ds, (October 25, 2017), http://www.socialistsanddemocrats.eu/newsroom/withdrawal-bank-structural-reform-file-marks-unfortunate-turning-point-european-agenda.

571 *European Parliament*, Seats by Political Group, http://www.europarl.europa.eu/meps/en/hemicycle.html.

572 This is also indicated by contributions of Members of Parliament in other matters, in which they stress the importance of reviving the bank structural reform project. See e.g. *Marco Valli* of the EFDD, in a debate on March 1st 2018 on the annual report on the banking union. *European Parliament*, 2017/2072(INI), http://www.europarl.europa.eu/sides/getDoc.do?pubRef=-//EP//TEXT+CRE+20180301+ITEM-002+DOC+XML+V0//EN&language=EN.

573 See Chapter II.III.F: Results and discussion.

574 See *European Commission* (2017) Commission Work Programme 2018: Annex 4, 2; see also Chapter II.IV.B: Withdrawal.

575 Art. 294 TFEU.

576 See Art. 224 TFEU.

The third option would be that the proponents of structural reform in the European Parliament attempt to slip parts of their agenda into the negotiations of other legislative initiatives. Suitable for such actions at the moment is in particular the CRRII/CRDV package.[577] This option can currently be considered as the most probable.

Indeed, in February 2018, Members of Parliament proposed as an amendment to CRDV an additional chapter on bank structural reform: it features a prohibition of proprietary trading and relations with certain funds. Deposit-taking entities are allowed only to engage in deposit-taking, lending, payment services and certain activities necessary for hedging. Other trading activities are to be separated into a trading entity, which may remain part of the banking group based on the decision of regulators.[578] This proposal reflects the European Commission's draft regulation's recommendations but is more stringent: it picks up elements of the *activities ban* of full separation (however, with a wider scope than the draft regulation and a reverse burden of proof). Regarding other trading activities, it constitutes an enforcement-based *containment method* of ring-fencing.

While the chances of the proposal to make it through the legislative process are rather small,[579] it demonstrates that proponents of ring-fencing have not yet given up on the project. Elements of the EU's bank structural reform will likely appear in connection with banking regulation packages for a long time.

---

577 *European Commission*, Proposal for a Regulation of the European Parliament and of the Council amending Regulation (EU) No 575/2013 as regards the leverage ratio, the net stable funding ratio, requirements for own funds and eligible liabilities, counterparty credit risk, market risk, exposures to central counterparties, exposures to collective investment undertakings, large exposures, reporting and disclosure requirements and amending Regulation (EU) No 648/2012, COM(2016) 850 final; *European Commission*, Proposal for a Directive of the European Parliament and of the Council amending Directive 2013/36/EU as regards exempted entities, financial holding companies, mixed financial holding companies, remuneration, supervisory measures and powers and capital conservation measures, COM(2016) 854 final.

578 *European Parliament Committee on Economic and Monetary Affairs* (2018) Amendments CRDV, 81–89.

579 The distribution of votes likely has not materially changed in the European Parliament. The coming election in 2019 will, however, create a new situation that can not yet be predicted.

c. Existing regimes

With the withdrawal of the bank structural reform, other, already existing, ways of imposing a ring-fence are likely to become more important in the discourse. Certain provisions of the BRRD and the SRMR are considered by some as potential gateways for union-wide ring-fencing,[580] and may approximate the EU's solution to the Swiss'.

1. BRRD

Binder underscores that the BRRD's concept of recovery and resolution planning exceeds mere planning. It could be used *"in a way that drastically interferes with the institution[s'] business portfolio, financial and organisational structure, including group structures"*.[581]

Central provision regarding the organisation of banks are the *"powers to address or remove impediments to resolvability"* stipulated in Art. 17(5) BRRD. The provision sets down considerable powers for regulators to influence the organisational structure of a banking group, in case the resolvability assessment has found substantive impediments: the resolution authority is empowered, *inter alia,* to require the institution to cease certain activities, to divest assets and to conduct changes to legal or operational structures.[582] As *Kern* notes, *"this could [indeed] involve changes to the legal, operational, and financial structure of institutions or the group itself and their business activities"*.[583] The resolution authority is not limited to measures listed in Art. 17(5) BRRD, as the list is to be understood as non-exhaustive.[584]

Far-reaching structural changes can certainly not be ordered out of the blue. The BRRD sets down processes that leads to such a decision. The res-

580 In particular Art. 17 BRRD and Art 10 SRMR are considered such gateways. See e.g. *Alexander* (2015) Universal Model Banking, 496; *Binder* (2014) Resolution Planning, 16 (noting with regard to the BRRD that *"[o]n the basis of their powers given under this part of the Directive, authorities could go a long way towards implementing fully-fledged structural reforms of banking in the relevant jurisdictions, even without a more specific formal mandate to do so"*). See also *Binder* (2015) Gleichung, 165 (noting that a segregation of commercial and investment banking may be introduced via these provisions).

581 *Binder* (2014) Resolution Planning, 16.

582 Art. 17(5) BRRD.

583 *Alexander* (2015) Universal Model Banking, 496.

584 *EBA* (2014) Guidelines Impediments Resolvability, 6.

olution authority's measures in particular have to meet a proportionality test.[585] While this test is only *"vaguely defined"*,[586] a decision to require a bank to remove impediments for resolvability is subject to the right of appeal.[587] The EBA clarified that *"depending on the individual case, certain measures may be less intrusive than others"*. Resolution authorities should therefore *"assess which measure is the least intrusive for removing the firm-specific impediment"*.[588]

2. SRMR

Another provision that provides regulators with similarly broad powers to influence the organisation of banking groups is Art. 10(11) SRMR. It can be regarded as *"equivalent"* to Art. 17(5) BRRD.[589] If the SRB determines that there are *"substantive impediments"* to the resolvability, it may instruct national resolution authorities to take measures that include far-reaching structural interventions.[590]

Similar to the BRRD, the instruction to take certain measures requires a process.[591] In addition to balancing the effect of the measures on with cer-

---

585 Once a resolvability assessment finds *"substantive"* impediments to resolvability, a resolution authority informs the institute (Art. 17(1) BRRD). Within four months, the institute may propose possible measures to *"address or remove"* these impediments. The resolution authority then assesses whether this is the case (Art. 17(3) BRRD). If not, the resolution authority may require the institute to conduct the measures discussed above (including structural measures). It has to demonstrate how the measures proposed by the institution *"would not be able to remove the impediments to resolvability"* and how its own measures *"are proportionate in removing them"*. It has to take into account *"effect of the measures on the business of the institution, its stability and its ability to contribute to the economy"* (Art. 17(4) BRRD).

586 *Binder* (2014) Resolution Planning, 21.

587 Art. 17(6) BRRD.

588 *EBA* (2014) Guidelines Impediments Resolvability, 6.

589 *Alexander* (2015) Universal Model Banking, 498. The framework of the recovery and resolution planning of the SSMR and SRMR *"do not deviate substantially from the relevant procedures and sustantive requirements of the BRRD"*. *Binder* (2014) Resolution Planning, 19.

590 See Art. 10(7)-(10) SRMR.

591 This process is set down in Art. 10(7)-(10) SRMR: If the SRB finds *"substantive impediments to the resolvability"*, it first prepares a report to inform the bank about its findings. It should recommend *"any proportionate and targeted measures"* that are *"necessary or appropriate"* to remove them (Art. 10(7) SRMR).

tain costs,[592] the SRB must take into account *"the need to avoid any impact on the institution or the group concerned which would go beyond what is necessary to remove the impediment to resolvability or would be disproportionate"*[593] – a provision that does not have a counterpart in the BRRD. Decisions by the SRB based on Art. 10(10) SRMR, can be appealed at the Appeal Panel.[594] Its decisions can be appealed at the ECJ.[595]

3. Results

The argument that the EU's bank structural reform legislation is unnecessary because *"tools for structural change already explicitly exist"* has been put forward by industry groups during the legislative process.[596] Indeed, there are important tools for structural change that can be used to influence banks' structure. However, whether they will be used to establish credible ring-fencing is in the author's opinion questionable.

The idea of implementing bank structural reform via authorities' decisions within the framework of recovery and resolution planning is not new: it is clearly set out in Avenue 1 of the Liikanen Report[597] and the European Commission's draft regulation.[598] The Swiss emergency plan and resolvability assessment are also enforcement-based and set within the framework of recovery and resolution.[599] The main argument against Avenue 1, the poten-

---

Within four months, the bank shall propose possible measures *"to address or remove"* the impediments. If they *"do not effectively reduce or remove the impediments"*, the SRB makes a decision. Similar to the BRRD, the SRB has to demonstrate that the measures proposed by the bank are not able to remove the impediments and that its own measures are *"proportionate in removing them"* (Art. 10(10) SRMR). In the assessment of impediments, the SRB is furthermore dependent on information provided by the bank itself and the national resolution authority. See *Schoenmaker* (2016) Euro-Area Banks, 10.

592 *Inter alia*, the effect of the measure on the *"business of the institution, [...], its ability to contribute to the economy, on the internal market for financial services"*. Art. 10(10) SRMR.

593 Art. 10(10) SRMR.

594 Art. 85 SRMR.

595 Art. 86 SRMR.

596 See e.g. *PwC* (2014) Bank Structural Reforms, 3.

597 See Chapter II.I.B: Avenue 1.

598 See Chapter II.II.D: The conditional separation of trading activities.

599 See Chapter III.IV.D.c.2: Method of ring-fencing; Chapter III.V.D.b.5: Switzerland as a role model for the EU?.

tial lack of a harmonised and consistent application,[600] lost weight due to the common supervision and resolution, in particular for G-SIBs.[601] However, in contrast to the Liikanen Report and the draft regulation, the existing provisions of the BRRD and the SRMR exhibit the effort of intervening with the structure of banking groups only as little as possible.

In the author's opinion, the obstacles for comprehensively implementing ring-fencing or other bank structural reforms via the existing provisions of the BRRD and the SRMR should not be underestimated: one thing that pervades preparatory documents of ring-fencing initiatives around the world is that it is hard to quantify the benefits and costs of ring-fencing. Similar problems are likely to arise with impediments of resolvability. It can therefore be assumed that (i) a clear assessment of the proportionality as it is stipulated by both the BRRD and the SRMR is hard to obtain with regard to establishing a fully realized ring-fence. The (ii) obligation only to apply the least intrusive measure, which is set out by the EBA for the BRRD and in Art. 10(10) SRMR is also a considerable constraint. As the (iii) list of measures in both legal sources is non-exhaustive, it can moreover be assumed that other measures, such as capital increases, will play an important role.

The considerations above should not be understood as criticism of the powers of regulators to impose structural requirements to enhance the resolvability. They merely question whether full ring-fencing such as the Liikanen recommendations can be established through the existent provisions.

While with the provisions of the BRRD and the SRMR potential gateways for ring-fencing were created, it remains to be seen how far authorities are willing or able to go with regard to structural requirements. Critics even call into question whether authorities will exercise their powers to ensure *"at the very least"* resolvability[602] – effectively separating commercial banking and investment banking activities seems to be a long shot from this.

600 See Chapter II.I.B: Avenue 1.

601 The competence of ECB and SRB likely enhance the harmonised and consistent application of recovery and resolution, free from national biases. See e.g. *Binder* (2014) Resolution Planning, 20.

602 *"In practice, however, it remains to be seen if any of these new powers are exercised, let alone enforced, in the face of relentless resistance by the industry and rapidly declining political support."* *Finance Watch*, Too-big-to-regulate: The EU's bank structural reform proposal failed, (October 25, 2017), http://www.finance-watch.org/press/press-releases/1468.

It can therefore be concluded that an enforcement-based implementation of ring-fencing, as defined for the purpose of this dissertation,[603] via the resolvability assessment would ideally require an additional legal basis that justifies far-reaching intervention with banking groups' organisation.[604]

V. Results and Outlook

The second part of the dissertation discussed the European Union's bank structural reform initiative addressing the question what the current developments concerning ring-fencing on a EU level are and in what direction it is expected to evolve. The following paragraphs reiterate selected findings and provide a short outlook.

The Liikanen Report is evidently inspired by the Vickers Report and subsequent legal developments in the UK. However, it proposes the separation of risky activities with the possibility of providing them in a trading entity, thereby recommending the *containment method* of ring-fencing. The Liikanen Report considered a separation based on an authority's decision (Avenue 1), but ultimately decided for a mandatory separation (Avenue 2).

The European Commission draft regulation deviates from the Liikanen Report in that it does not stipulate a mandatory separation, but one based on an authority's decision. In addition, it orientates towards the U.S. Volcker Rule, albeit applying a much narrower scope for the prohibition of proprietary trading. It therefore *"combines the logic of Liikanen's Avenue 1 [...] with the Volcker Rule"*.[605] In spite of the decision for an enforcement-based approach, the effect of a bank structural reform in the form of the European Commission's draft regulation would likely be material.[606] The European Commission thus decided for an enforcement-based *containment method* of ring-fencing. It complemented this with another structural reform, namely with a variant of the *activities ban* of full separation regarding proprietary trading.

603 See Chapter I.VII.C.c: Establishing a definition.

604 Such a basis could also include thresholds for larger banks, and a clearer specification of requirements that collectively aim at ensuring the independence of the separated entities (thereby constituting a fence). See Chapter II.I.B: Avenue 1.

605 *Krahnen/Noth/Schüwer* (2016) Structural Reforms, 15.

606 See *Krahnen* (2014) Structural Reform, 2.

After the publication of the draft regulation, the battle for and against a structural reform of banking in the European Union reached its peak so far, with interest groups and Member States making their case for and against it.

The Council's negotiating stance remains the latest step of the legislative process. As a negotiating manifest for dialogues with the European Parliament, it is characterised by a systematic watering down of the European Commission's draft regulation. This is most obvious regarding trading activities that are not proprietary trading: only a subset of banks (the riskiest ones and the ones with the largest trading operations) are subject to a potential separation. This separation, however, is only one of many possible measures and becomes highly unlikely due to a number of backstops inserted in the legal text.

The Council's negotiating stance proposes a mixture between a mandatory *containment method* of ring-fencing for proprietary trading and an enforcement-based *containment method* for other trading activities. In particular with regard to proprietary trading, the negotiating stance follows closely national ring-fencing legislation in Germany and France. As it combines the limited scope of the Volcker Rule with a more lenient form of separation, it can be considered *"Volcker-lite"*.[607]

Due to the events in the European Parliament and the withdrawal of the file by the European Commission, alternative ways of imposing a ring-fence in the European Union are expected to become more important. Assessing legislative options, taking into account the starting positions in the institutions of the European Union, it was found that the most probable way of adopting ring-fencing legislation in the European Parliament was via other regulatory reform packages. Indeed, Members of Parliament have already proposed amendments to CRDV, effectively slipping bank structural reform elements into the negotiations.

Among existing regimes, provisions on impediments of resolvability in particular can be considered potential gateways for imposing union-wide ring-fencing. Such an enforcement-based approach would approximate the EU solution to the Swiss. However, in the author's opinion, the provisions of the BRRD and SRMR lack the determination to be used to introduce fully realized ring-fencing: they both prominently reiterate the need for proportionality and comprise a number of obstacles for the introduction of comprehensive structural reform. In particular when taking into ac-

607 *Vickers* uses this term to describe German and French national ring-fencing legislation. See *Vickers* (2016) Banking Reform Presentation, 22.

count the particularities of the EU banking sector,[608] their suitability for introducing comprehensive and solid ring-fencing can be questioned. To ensure an effective and legally dependable enforcement-based implementation of ring-fencing, in the author's opinion, an additional legal basis such as the one proposed by Liikanen's Avenue 1 would be desirable.

The European Union's bank structural reform project has an almost tragic character: embarking in 2012 with the formation of the Liikanen commission, there were high hopes for a union-wide ring-fencing regime. Structural reform was generally seen as a *"a critical part of the Union response to tackling the TBTF dilemma"*.[609] Since then, however, the file has lost support in all European Union institutions. This is particularly visible in the European Parliament, where the Liikanen Report was at the time almost unanimously welcomed as a *"sound and welcome basis for structural reform"*,[610] and where two years later no agreement could be reached on the file; something that has not happened in any other major financial reform package.[611] With the announced withdrawal by the European Commission, the legislative process of the bank structural reform ends.

However, the idea of union-wide bank structural reform was planted deep, and it can be reasonably assumed that it will continue to emerge in negotiations on other banking regulations. Furthermore, existing regimes such as provisions of the BRRD and SRMR may be used to establish a union-wide ring-fencing regime based on authorities' demands. Other soft factors such as the potential ECB presidency of *Erkki Liikanen* might also breathe new life into this controversial project.[612]

---

608 See the considerations on Switzerland as a role model for the enforcement-based introduction of ring-fencing in Chapter III.V.D.b.5: Switzerland as a role model for the EU?.

609 *European Commission* (2014) Proposal for a Regulation, 2.

610 *European Parliament* (2013) Report on Structural Reform, 14.

611 See *Hogan*, Bank Ring Fencing Edges Closer in Europe, KPMG Insights, (June 28, 2015), https://home.kpmg.com/xx/en/home/insights/2015/06/bank-ring-fencing-edges-closer.html.

612 See *Jones*, European Central Bank's marathon man moves to front of the pack, Financial Times (April 3, 2018).

Part III – Legal Comparative Analysis

While the fate of the European Union's regulation has long been uncertain, a number of countries in Europe already adopted structural reform legislation, with some of them even having applied it already. This part of the dissertation comparatively analyses and discusses national legislation of the jurisdictions of Europe's most important financial centres, namely the United Kingdom, Germany and Switzerland.

The conducted aspect-to-aspect comparative analysis will outline the major differences of the national approaches.[613] It thus provides an understanding of each nation's plan for structural reform while ensuring that the dissertation does not lose its perspective of the bigger picture. The legal comparative analysis is conducted as a micro comparison as described by *Zweigert/Kötz*.[614]

The unique approach of Switzerland makes it necessary for the comparative analysis to refer in some areas to the separation process of its largest banks, *UBS* and *Credit Suisse*. As G-SIBs, they fall in the particular research focus of this dissertation. While Switzerland's organisational measures apply to several banks, these two banks considerably shaped the legislation and were the first ones to implement it. They moreover are exemplary for the primary target group of structural reform measures, as they are large globally active universal banks that provide the whole range of banking services (including substantial investment banking services). As will be discussed, Swiss regulation has a different impact on them than on their domestically oriented competitors.

This part of the dissertation further examines whether the jurisdictions fulfil or defer from the definition and concept of ring-fencing established in the first part, and if so, what method of ring-fencing was chosen. This is especially important with regard to the unique Swiss approach, whose similarity is not consistently acknowledged.

---

613 The aspects used, (e.g. the height of the fence, what activities fall on which side of the fence), are in line with the general practice. See e.g. *ICB* (2011) Vickers Report, 35, 36, 62; *Brown* (2014) With this Ring, I Thee Fence, 1047, 1049, 1053; *Hofer* (2014) Structural Reforms, 477, 479, 488.

614 *Zweigert/Kötz* (1996) Rechtsvergleichung, 4, 42; See also *Zweigert/Kötz* (1998) Comparative Law, 5, 43–44.

I. Banking Landscape

This chapter explores the characteristics of the three financial centres of interest. It sets the factual foundation for the legal analysis in subsequent chapters. The chapter first explores the importance of the financial centre and financial services to the respective home country. Subsequently the banking sectors' composition and nature is illustrated. Finally, the countries' G-SIBs are put on the map with a short view to particularities in their coping with the global financial crisis.

A. United Kingdom

a. Importance of the financial centre

The United Kingdom as a financial centre has since the end of the 18th century been of worldwide importance.[615] It is a global financial hub with significant international relations, which is underscored by it having the largest global share of cross-border bank lending and foreign exchange trading.[616] The UK financial centre is also the European headquarters for a great many of the world's financial firms.[617]

---

615 *Carney* (2017) High Road, 2; For a short summary of the emergence of the UK's financial centre, see *Djankov* (2017) City of London, 3–4.

616 *Carney* (2017) High Road, 2 (in which *Carney* emphasizes the UK's international orientation also by pointing out that it is has the second largest asset management industry and fourth largest insurance industry in the world). It is interesting that the particularly large share of international activity can be traced back to banks from outside the UK, which have affiliates in the country. *Koch* illustrates that the cross-border business of banks with a location in the UK is "*notably bigger*" than the cross-border business of banks that have their headquaters in the UK. See *Koch* (2016) United Kingdom, 30–31.

617 See *HM Treasury*, EU referendum: 6 reasons why the EU is good for financial services jobs (Archived), (May 12, 2016), https://www.gov.uk/government/news/eu-referendum-6-reasons-why-the-eu-is-good-for-financial-services-jobs; *Hill*, Speech at Chatham House, the Royal Institute of International Affairs, Speech by Commissioner Hill, (June 9, 2016) https://ec.europa.eu/commission/commissioners/2014-2019/hill/announcements/commissioner-hills-speech-chatham-house-royal-institute-international-affairs_en (in which Commissioner *Hill* stressed the importance of the UK financial centre noting that „*[h]alf the world's financial firms have chosen to base their European headquarters in the UK. At the moment, one quarter of financial services income in the EU is generated in the UK*"); See also *Euro-*

The *Global Financial Centres Index* currently ranks London as the number one financial centre in the world, leading in all of its categories.[618] It is undoubtedly the leading financial centre of the European Union with a large percentage of the EU's financial market activities located in the UK.[619] The UK financial services sector contributes 7% to the country's GDP.[620] Another way of estimating the importance of financial services to the national economy is to take into account its share of gross value added (GVA):[621] the financial sector has contributed 6.6% GVA. Financial services alone accounted for 4.1% GVA.[622] Within the financial centre, banking services generate by far the highest revenues.[623]

---

pean Parliament (2016) Brexit, 1; *IMF* (2016) Financial Stability Assessment: United Kingdom, 9.

618 *Z/Yen Group/China Development Institute* (2017) GFCI Nr. 22, 4 (these categories include (i) business environment (ii) human capital (iii) infrastructure (iv) financial sector development and (v) reputation).

619 This was emphasized by Bank of England Governor *Mark Carney* during a press conference, when he stressed that "*[i]t is important to recognise that the United Kingdom is effectively the investment banker for Europe.*" *Reuters*, Highlights – Bank of England's Carney speaks on UK banking risks (November 30, 2016). For the UK share of the EU's various financial market activities, see *TheCityUK* (2016) International Financial Centre, 9.

620 *Norton Rose Fulbright/Association of Foreign Banks* (2017) Brexit survey, 4; *Bank of England* (2017) Authorisation and Supervision of International Banks, 1; Other sources note a contribution of 7.2% in 2016, see *SIF* (2017) Swiss financial Centre: Key figures; *EIU* (2017) Financial Services: United Kingdom, 2.

621 Gross value added refers to the value of all services and goods produced in an economy. Key difference to GDP is that it does not take into account taxes and subsidies on products.

622 Own calculation based on *Office for National Statistics* (2017) Gross Value Added. The Office for National Statistics estimated the total GVA of all sectors in 2016 1747.647 billion £, the GVA of financial and insurance activities (the financial centre) 115.280 billion £, and the GVA of financial services alone 72.204 billion £. See *Office for National Statistics* (2017) Gross Value Added; Cf. *Tyler* (2017) Financial Services, 5 (indicating a GVA of 7.2%). The author's result is matched by Eurostat, which mentions 6.7% financial centre contribution. See *Eurostat*, Gross value added and income by A*10 industry breakdowns, (January 31, 2018), http://appsso.eurostat.ec.europa.eu/nui/show.do?query=BOOKMARK_DS-406765_QID_-4FCE2BB0_UID_-3F171EB0&layout=NACE_R2,B,X,0;TIME,C,X,1;GEO,L,Y,0;UNIT,L,Z,0;NA_ITEM,L,Z,1;INDICATORS,C,Z,2;&zSelection=DS-406765NA_ITEM,B1G;DS-406765UNIT,PC_TOT;DS-406765INDICATORS,OBS_FLAG;&rankName1=UNIT_1_2_-1_2&rankName2=INDICATORS_1_2_-1_2&rankName3=NA-ITEM_1_2_-1_2&rankName4=NACE-R2_1_2_0_0&rankName5=TIME_1_0_1_0&rankName6=GEO_1_2_0_1&rStp=&cStp=&rDCh=&cDCh=&rDM=true&cDM=true&footnes=false&empty=false&wai=false&

At the end of 2016, the financial services and insurance industry employed 1.1 million people, equalling 3.1% of the total workforce.[623] Regarding the tax receipts of the financial sector, calculations range from 24.4 billion £[624] to 71.4 billion £, equalling 11.5% of total tax receipts.[625]

b. Number of banks their nature

The number of banks in the UK has declined considerably due to consolidation in the domestic retail bank market and foreign banking groups acquiring UK entities.[626] The ECB lists 390 monetary financial institutions at the end of 2016[627] (down from 393 in December 2015).[628]

---

time_mode=NONE&time_most_recent=false&lang=EN&cfo=%23%23%23%2C%23%23%23.%23%23%23.

623 *Tyler* (2017) Financial Services, 8. The percentage of UK workforce employed by the financial centre corresponds to Eurostat, which assumes 3.2%. See *Eurostat*, Employment by A*10 industry breakdowns, (January 31, 2018), http://appsso.eurostat.ec.europa.eu/nui/show.do?query=BOOKMARK_DS-406759_QID_-48796ABF_UID_-3F171EB0&layout=NACE_R2,B,X,0;TIME,C,X,1;GEO,L,Y,0;UNIT,L,Z,0;NA_ITEM,L,Z,1;INDICATORS,C,Z,2;&zSelection=DS-406759NA_ITEM,EMP_DC;DS-406759UNIT,PC_TOT_PER;DS-406759INDICATORS,OBS_FLAG;&rankName1=UNIT_1_2_-1_2&rankName2=INDICATORS_1_2_-1_2&rankName3=NA-ITEM_1_2_-1_2&rankName4=NACE-R2_1_2_0_0&rankName5=TIME_1_0_1_0&rankName6=GEO_1_2_0_1&rStp=&cStp=&rDCh=&cDCh=&rDM=true&cDM=true&footnes=false&empty=false&wai=false&time_mode=NONE&time_most_recent=false&lang=EN&cfo=%23%23%23%2C%23%23%23.%23%23%23.

624 *HM Revenue & Customs* (2016) Tax Receipts Banking Sector, 2; See also *Tyler* (2017) Financial Services, 10.

625 *PwC* (2016) Tax Contribution of UK Financial Services, 5; See also *Tyler* (2017) Financial Services, 10.

626 *Casu/Gall* (2016) Building Societies, 8.

627 The term monetary financial institutions (MFI) is defined in Art. 1 of ECB Regulation 1071/2013 of 24 September, 2013 concerning the balance sheet of the monetary financial institutions sector (ECB/2013/33). MFIs comprise (i) central banks, (ii) deposit-taking corporations and (iii) money market funds. The number above excludes the Bank of England as the UK central bank and is drawn from ECB statistics. See *ECB*, Number of monetary financial institutions (MFIs) in the non-participating Member States: December 2016, https://www.ecb.europa.eu/stats/ecb_statistics/escb/html/table.en.html?id=JDF_MFI_MFI_LIST_NEA&period=2016-12.

628 *ECB*, Number of monetary financial institutions (MFIs) in the non-participating Member States: December 2015, https://www.ecb.europa.eu/stats/ecb_statistics/e

The UK banking sector is highly concentrated, with the seven largest banks being responsible for over 75% of total assets.[629] The big, long-established institutes are often referred to as "high street banks"[630] Four particularly large banks, namely *Barclays, Lloyds, HSBC* and *RBS*, lead the UK's commercial banking segment and are followed by a second tier of smaller institutes, that comprises the UK subsidiary of *Santander, Standard Chartered* and *Nationwide Building Society*.[631]

In 2015, the country's three largest commercial banks' assets amounted to 48.4% of total assets. Since the financial crisis, this number has considerably decreased (from 60.3% in 2007).[632] The 5-bank asset concentration rate, which measures assets of the five biggest banks as a share of total commercial banking assets, was 71.4% in 2015 (down from 76.7% in 2007).[633]

High street banks can be differentiated from so called "challenger banks",[634] smaller institutes which mostly focus on specific segments and in particular on retail banking, and which increasingly demand their share of the market.[635] As of now, this share continues to be small[636] with only 5% of the lending market share,[637] however, challenger banks are constantly growing their lending book.[638]

Another group of banks includes large retailers such as *Tesco* or *Sainsbury's* which provide relatively simple services, such as unsecured products

---

scb/html/table.en.html?id=JDF_MFI_MFI_LIST_NEA&period=2015-12 (excluding the Bank of England as the UK central bank, in line with the above).

629 *IMF* (2016) Financial Stability Assessment: United Kingdom, 10.

630 *Casu/Gall* (2016) Building Societies, 8 (also noting that another term frequently used is "Major British Banking Groups" or "MBBG").

631 *EIU* (2017) Financial Services: United Kingdom, 4; *KPMG* lists the UK subsidiary of *Santander* as part of the big banks and thusly refers to them as "the big five". *KPMG* (2016) New Landscape, 1.

632 See *Worldbank* (2017) Global Financial Development Database.

633 See *Worldbank* (2017) Global Financial Development Database.

634 These challenger banks are often contrasted with the long-established big banks, see e.g. *Molyneux* (2016) Banking in the UK, 517. They can be subdivided into large and smaller challengers, see *KPMG* (2016) New Landscape, 1. The term "challenger bank" derives from the fact that they compete in a market that is dominated by few very long-established banks. *Casu/Gall* (2016) Building Societies, 2.

635 See *EIU* (2017) Financial Services: United Kingdom, 4; *IMF* (2016) Financial Stability Assessment: United Kingdom, 10.

636 *EIU* (2017) Financial Services: United Kingdom, 4.

637 *IMF* (2016) Financial Stability Assessment: United Kingdom, 10.

638 *KPMG* (2016) New Landscape, 4 (pointing out that challenger banks increased lending in 2014–2015 by 31.5% while the "big five" reduced theirs by 4.9%).

and savings accounts. Some of them have extended their offer to mortgages and current accounts, thus competing with big banks.[639]

One can also distinguish banks according to the location of their head offices. As mentioned above, the UK is home to a large number of foreign banks. This is illustrated by the fact that of 313 authorized banking institutions in 2015, only 155 were incorporated in the UK (which is less than half). Of the 158 institutions incorporated abroad, 77 were incorporated within the European Economic Area.[640] These banks are also in charge of a significant share of the banking sector's total assets.[641]

Another UK specialty are building societies,[642] i.e. mutual financial institutions which can be described as *"specialist financial institutions that are owned by their customers"*.[643] They may only be established if their purpose is making loans which are secured on residential property and are funded substantially by its members.[644] By November 2017, the Bank of England listed 45 building societies authorized in the UK.[645]

c. HSBC, Barclays, RBS, Standard Chartered

The UK is currently home to four G-SIBs, namely *HSBC*, *Barclays*, *Royal Bank of Scotland* and *Standard Chartered*. While the last two are allocated in the first bucket of the GSIB framework, *Barclays* is in the second and *HSBC* even in the third.[646]

---

639 See *KPMG* (2016) New Landscape, 1. See also *Casu/Gall* (2016) Building Societies, 15; *Molyneux* (2016) Banking in the UK, 518.

640 *Casu/Gall* (2016) Building Societies, 8. These numbers are supported by *Claessens/Van Horen* who suggest a rate of 58% of foreign banks among all banks for 2013. See *Claessens/Van Horen* (2015) Global Financial Crisis, 909; See also *Worldbank* (2017) Global Financial Development Database.

641 For 2013, *Claessens/Van Horen* suggest a rate of 14% of total assets held by foreign owned banks. See *Claessens/Van Horen* (2015) Global Financial Crisis, 913; *Worldbank* (2017) Global Financial Development Database.

642 Building societies are governed by the Building Societies Act 1986, c. 53.

643 *Casu/Gall* (2016) Building Societies, 23, 59.

644 Sec. 5(1) Building Societies Act 1986.

645 *Bank of England* (2017) List of Building Societies: November, 1.

646 *FSB* (2017) Global Systemically Important Banks, 3. Banks of the first bucket are subject to the comparatively "light" capital buffer of 1.0%. Banks of the second bucket are subject to 1.5% and banks of the third bucket of 2.0% capital buffer. *FSB* (2017) Global Systemically Important Banks, 3; Apart from *Standard Chartered*, UK G-SIBs have continuously been included in the G-SIB assessment. See *FSB* (2011) Systemically Important Financial Institutions, 4.

The global financial crisis caused severe stress for UK banks and forced authorities to intervene unprecedentedly to maintain stability in the banking system.[647] These actions related not just to small banks but to many of the country's biggest institutions.[648]

Among the most prominent measures was the recapitalization of the *Royal Bank of Scotland*, one of UK's G-SIBs, and of *Lloyd's Banking Group*, a major commercial bank, through a series of transactions which led to HM Treasury acquiring large percentages of both banks. Other well-known measures were the nationalising of *Bradford & Bingley* and of *Northern Rock* to ensure the protection of depositors and an orderly unwinding of obligations and HM Treasury's guarantees.[649]

Other G-SIBs managed better to overcome the crisis and joined the global efforts of balance sheet repair. However, in its 2016 *Financial Sector Assessment Program* on Germany, the IMF found that *HSBC* was the second biggest contributor to systemic risks in the global banking system.[650] In late 2017, the Bank of England proclaimed that for the first time since the beginning of its stress testing, no participating bank (all G-SIBs and *Lloyds Banking Group*, *Nationwide* and *Santander UK*) needed to improve its capital position.[651]

In 2016, the G-SIBs' balance sheets still equalled high percentages of UK's GDP: Total assets of *HSBC* equalled 90%,[652] *Barclays* 62%[653], *Royal*

647 The estimate of public funds committed to the financial sector in 2008 and 2009 accounted for about 60% of UK GDP. See *Schildbach* (2010) Financial Crisis, 2; *Krahnen/Noth/Schüwer* (2016) Structural Reforms, 12.

648 *EIU* (2017) Financial Services: United Kingdom, 4.

649 *HM Treasury* (2010) Maintaining the Financial Stability of UK Banks, 4.

650 See *IMF* (2016) Stress Testing, 42.

651 *Bank of England* (2017) Stress Testing, 5.

652 Own calculation based on *HSBC* (2017) Annual Report 2016 (At the end of 2016, *HSBC* had assets of 2375 billion $ on its balance sheet); *Worldbank*, GDP (current US$), https://data.worldbank.org/indicator/NY.GDP.MKTP.CD (UK's 2016 GDP was 2648 billion $).

653 Own calculation based on *Barclays* (2017) Annual Report 2016, 242 (In 2016 *Barclays*' balance sheet size was 1213 billion £); *Office for National Statistics* (2017) Gross Domestic Product (In 2016, UK's GDP was 1963 billion £).

Bank of Scotland 41%[654] and *Standard Chartered* 33% of UK GDP.[655] The balance sheets of all UK G-SIBs together equalled almost 2.3 times UK GDP.[656]

B. Germany

a. Importance of the financial centre

Frankfurt, Germany's banking hub, is consistently ranked in the top 20 financial centres.[657] It has *"broad and deep financial services activities"* and is connected to most other financial centres.[658] It is widely seen as one of the main profiteers of Brexit and will likely become the leading financial centre within the EU after the UK's exit from the Union.[659]

According to DESTATIS, Germany's financial centre (consisting of financial services and insurance services) contributed around 3.9% of GDP in 2016.[660] With regard to GVA, the financial centre contributed 3.9%.[661]

---

654 Own calculation based on *Royal Bank of Scotland* (2017) Annual Report 2016, 242 (In 2016 *RBS's* balance sheet size was 799 billion £); *Office for National Statistics* (2017) Gross Domestic Product (In 2016, UK's GDP was 1963 billion £).

655 Own calculation based on *Standard Chartered* (2017) Annual Report 2016, 242 (In 2016 *Standard Chartered's* balance sheet size was 647 billion £); *Office for National Statistics* (2017) Gross Domestic Product (In 2016, UK's GDP was 1963 billion £).

656 Own calculation based on the above.

657 *Z/Yen Group/China Development Institute* (2017) GFCI Nr. 22, 4 (in which Frankfurt ranked 11th); see also former GFCI Reports, e.g. and *Z/Yen Group/China Development Institute* (2008) GFCI Nr. 8, 9, (rank 11).

658 *Z/Yen Group/China Development Institute* (2017) GFCI Nr. 22, 13; *Z/Yen Group/China Development Institute* (2008) GFCI Nr. 8, 6–7.

659 While at this point no final conclusion is to be drawn, there is a recognisable trend of internationally active banks to strengthen their presence in EU financial centres, in particular in Frankfurt. *Sester* (2018) EU-Finanzmarktrecht, 52.

660 See *DESTATIS* (2017) Bruttoinlandsprodukt, 11 (To be precise, *Destatis* does not take into account subsidies and taxes in its "GDP ratio". It therefore incorrectly refers to the GVA ratio as GDP. This is also the reason why the result equals the GVA ratio below); *SIF* (2017) Swiss financial Centre: Key figures.

661 Own calculation, based on *DESTATIS* (2017) Bruttowertschöpfung. In 2016, the gross value added by the financial centre equalled 111.469 billion € in current prices, the total GVA of all economic sectors equalled 2831.942 billion €, see *DESTATIS* (2017) Bruttowertschöpfung. The results are matched by the ones of Eurostat. See *Eurostat*, Gross value added and income by A*10 industry break-

The contribution of financial services alone can be estimated around 2.5% of the total GVA.[662] This makes the financial centre a relatively small but important pillar of the German economy.[663]

The German banking sector, however, should not be underestimated: in absolute terms it is – alongside the French one – the largest in the Eurozone,[664] with 7.8 trillion € total assets at the end of 2016.[665] German banks employed 609.100 people in 2016.[666] According to Eurostat, the financial centre employs 2.7% of the total German workforce.[667]

---

downs, (January 31, 2018), http://appsso.eurostat.ec.europa.eu/nui/show.do?query=BOOKMARK_DS-406765_QID_-4FCE2BB0_UID_-3F171EB0&layout=NACE_R2,B,X,0;TIME,C,X,1;GEO,L,Y,0;UNIT,L,Z,0;NA_ITEM,L,Z,1;INDICATORS,C,Z,2;&zSelection=DS-406765NA_ITEM,B1G;DS-406765UNIT,PC_TOT;DS-406765INDICATORS,OBS_FLAG;&rankName1=UNIT_1_2_-1_2&rankName2=INDICATORS_1_2_-1_2&rankName3=NA-ITEM_1_2_-1_2&rankName4=NACE-R2_1_2_0_0&rankName5=TIME_1_0_1_0&rankName6=GEO_1_2_0_1&rStp=&cStp=&rDCh=&cDCh=&rDM=true&cDM=true&footnes=false&empty=false&wai=false&time_mode=NONE&time_most_recent=false&lang=EN&cfo=%23%23%23%2C%23%23%23.%23%23%23.

662 Own calculation, based on *DESTATIS* (2017) Bruttowertschöpfung. Numbers for the 2016 gross value added of financial services sector have not been published yet. In the previous years, however, the contribution remained relatively stable. Gross value added is therefore estimated based on 2015 numbers: the gross value added by the financial services sector alone equalled 69.567 billion € in current prices, the total of all economic sectors equalled 2740.226 billion €.

663 See *EIU* (2017) Financial Services: Germany, 6.

664 *European Central Bank* (2017) Financial Structures, 24. See also *Mersch* (2016) German Banking Market, 2–3.

665 *Deutsche Bundesbank* (2017) Monthly Report February, Statistical Section 24.

666 *AGV Banken* (2017) Bericht 2016, 91; *Bankenverband* (2017) Kreditwirtschaft, 7.

667 See *Eurostat*, Employment by A*10 industry breakdowns, (January 31, 2018), http://appsso.eurostat.ec.europa.eu/nui/show.do?query=BOOKMARK_DS-406759_QID_-48796ABF_UID_-3F171EB0&layout=NACE_R2,B,X,0;TIME,C,X,1;GEO,L,Y,0;UNIT,L,Z,0;NA_ITEM,L,Z,1;INDICATORS,C,Z,2;&zSelection=DS-406759NA_ITEM,EMP_DC;DS-406759UNIT,PC_TOT_PER;DS-406759INDICATORS,OBS_FLAG;&rankName1=UNIT_1_2_-1_2&rankName2=INDICATORS_1_2_-1_2&rankName3=NA-ITEM_1_2_-1_2&rankName4=NACE-R2_1_2_0_0&rankName5=TIME_1_0_1_0&rankName6=GEO_1_2_0_1&rStp=&cStp=&rDCh=&cDCh=&rDM=true&cDM=true&footnes=false&empty=false&wai=false&time_mode=NONE&time_most_recent=false&lang=EN&cfo=%23%23%23%2C%23%23%23.%23%23%23.

b. Number of banks and their nature

Consolidation in the German banking sector continued in 2016. At the end of the year, the Bundesbank kept a count of 1711 banks[668] (down from 1775 in December 2015).[669] There is high concentration in the German banking sector. In 2015, the country's three largest commercial banks' assets have amounted to 74.8% of total assets. Since the financial crisis, this number has increased (from 72.4% in 2007).[670] The 5-bank asset concentration rate is 83.8% in 2015 (down from 85.4% in 2007).[671]

Banks in Germany are usually categorised into three groups: (i) private banks, (ii) publicly owned savings banks and (iii) cooperative banks. In addition, there are a few special purpose banks[672] that specialise in certain banking services[673] and are not universal banks.[674] This system, which in its basic structure dates back to the 19th century, is often referred to as "Three-Pillar-System".[675]

---

668 See *Deutsche Bundesbank* (2017) Monthly Report February, Statistical Section 24.

669 *Deutsche Bundesbank* (2016) Monthly Report February, Statistical Section 24.

670 See *Worldbank* (2017) Global Financial Development Database.

671 See *Worldbank* (2017) Global Financial Development Database.

672 Special purpose banks comprise (i) mortgage banks, (ii) buildings and loan associations and (iii) banks that offer funding to encourage investments in specific sectors of the economy. The latter include *Deutsche Industrie Bank (IKB)* (*Detzer et al.* (2017) German Financial System, 65), which became one of the first victims of the global financial crisis in Germany and which was bailed out and privatized later on (see *Goldstein/Veron* (2011) Too Big To Fail, 7; For a description of *IKB*'s involvement in mortgage-related securities and the financial crisis, see *Financial Crisis Inquiry Commission* (2011) Financial Crisis, 246–248; *Bobek et al.* (2011) Ökonomische Analyse, 6–8); The organisational decision to provide only limited services as a special purpose bank is made internally, either as a business strategy or to profit from special laws, e.g. Bau-SparkG, that entitle to the use of a specific designation, e.g. "Bausparkasse". Special purpose banks are often subsidiaries of universal banks and parts of larger banking groups. *Grundmann* (2016) Bankvertragsrecht, 14–15.

673 *Detzer et al.* (2017) German Financial System, 56; See also *Grundmann* (2016) Bankvertragsrecht, 14–15; *Deutsche Bundesbank* (2015) Monatsbericht April, 34.

674 *Detzer et al.* (2017) German Financial System, 56; *Hackethal* (2004) German Banks, 73; See also *Grundmann* (2016) Bankvertragsrecht, 14–15; *Deutsche Bundesbank* (2015) Monatsbericht April, 34.

675 *Behr/Schmidt* (2015) German Banking System, 2–3, *Deutsche Bundesbank* (2015) Monatsbericht April, 34.

Regarding the first group, the Bundesbank currently totals up 266 private banks,[676] which it subdivides into "big banks", "regional and other commercial banks" and "branches of foreign banks".[677]

There are four banks that qualify as "big banks", namely *Deutsche Bank AG, Commerzbank AG, UniCredit Bank AG* and *Deutsche Postbank AG.*[678] Big banks' business operations and funding models have a strong international focus and emphasize capital markets.[679] They provide the full range of banking activities, including retail corporate and investment banking.[680] At the end of 2016, the balance sheets of these banks in sum amounted to 1.8 trillion €,[681] equalling 23% of all assets held by banks.[682]

While the category "regional and other commercial banks" consists of *"an extremely heterogenous set"* of banks,[683] most of them are considerably smaller and have a regional focus.[684] They provide specific business services, in particular mortgage loans, financing of specific industries and wealth management,[685] and generally focus on loans to non-financial corporations and households.[686] At the end of 2016, the Bundesbank totalled up 156 banks of this category. Their total assets amounted to 962.8 billion €,[687] equalling 12.3% of all assets in the German banking sector.[688]

---

676 *Deutsche Bundesbank* (2017) Monthly Report: October, Statistical Section 24; The Bundesbank refers to private banks in its public statistics as "commercial banks". *Detzer et al.* (2017) German Financial System, 56.

677 *Deutsche Bundesbank* (2017) Monthly Report: October, Statistical Section 25 Fn 7.

678 *Deutsche Bundesbank* (2017) Monthly Report February, Statistical Section 24.

679 *Deutsche Bundesbank* (2015) Monthly Report April, 36; see also *IMF* (2016) Germany, 11.

680 *IMF* (2016) Germany, 11.

681 *Deutsche Bundesbank* (2017) Monthly Report February, Statistical Section 24.

682 Own calculation based on *Deutsche Bundesbank* (2017) Monthly Report February, Statistical Section 24 (Ratio between the banks' assets amounting to 1819.7 billion € and total assets of all banks amounting to 7836.2 billion €).

683 *Deutsche Bundesbank* (2015) Monthly Report April, 36 Fn 5 (underscoring that the group comprises also central counterparties and Germany-based subsidiaries of international banks); Banks in this group are either smaller joint stock banks or privately-owned banks, often with a long history. *Detzer et al.* (2017) German Financial System, 61.

684 *Deutsche Bundesbank* (2015) Monthly Report April, 36.

685 *IMF* (2016) Germany, 12.

686 *Deutsche Bundesbank* (2015) Monthly Report April, 36–37.

687 *Deutsche Bundesbank* (2017) Monthly Report February, Statistical Section 24.

688 Own calculation based on *Deutsche Bundesbank* (2017) Monthly Report February, Statistical Section 24 (Ratio between the banks' assets amounting to 962.8 billion € and total assets of all banks amounting to 7836.2 billion €).

The second pillar of the German banking sector comprises of the publicly owned savings banks[689] consisting of (i) savings banks, also called "Sparkassen", (ii) "Landesbanken" and the (iii) *DekaBank*.[690]

Sparkassen, which are incorporated as institutions under public law, have regional operations and are not primarily focused on profits. Tasked with supporting regional economic development, they mainly serve the needs of retail customers and small- and medium-sized businesses.[691] The total assets of 408 Sparkassen amounted to 1172.9 billion € at the end of 2016,[692] equalling 15.0% of all assets held by banks.[693]

Landesbanken, which are either incorporated as corporations or public law institutions,[694] can be regarded as central institutions of Sparkassen.[695] They benefited for a long time from state-guarantees[696] and have become *"major players in the wholesale banking and capital market business, where they go head to head with [...] the big banks"*.[697] Due to various crises over the past decades, many Landesbanken were merged,[698] so that at the end of

689 *IMF* (2016) Germany, 12; see also *Detzer et al.* (2017) German Financial System, 56; *Behr/Schmidt* (2015) German Banking System, 9.

690 *Detzer et al.* (2017) German Financial System, 62.

691 *IMF* (2016) Germany, 12.

692 *Deutsche Bundesbank* (2017) Monthly Report February, Statistical Section 24.

693 Own calculation based on *Deutsche Bundesbank* (2017) Monthly Report February, Statistical Section 24 (Ratio between the banks' assets amounting to 1172.9 billion € and total assets of all banks amounting to 7836.2 billion €).

694 *Behr/Schmidt* (2015) German Banking System, 11.

695 See *Deutsche Bundesbank* (2015) Monthly Report April, 37; Ownership of Landesbanken is divided to a various extent between state governments Sparkassen. *IMF* (2016) Germany, 12; Traditionally, Landesbanken acted as (i) clearing banks for local Sparkassen of the region, (ii) principal relationship banks for the state(s) and made available services the local Sparkassen were to small to provide. *Behr/Schmidt* (2015) German Banking System, 11.

696 See *Detzer et al.* (2017) German Financial System, 63; see also *IMF* (2011) Germany, 22.

697 *Deutsche Bundesbank* (2015) Monthly Report April, 37 (also noting that Landesbanken provide services that Sparkassen cannot provide, due to their small size and regional focus, in particular investment and wholesale banking activities); see also *IMF* (2011) Germany, 22 (underscoring that the termination of government guarantees did not lead to downsizing but to continued wholesale funding and investment in risky overseas securities, which led to severe problems during the crisis.). Indeed, after the termination of government guarantees in 2005, Landesbanken increased their investments in foreign securities dramatically. See *IMF* (2011) Banking Sector Structure: Germany, 6–8 (in particular the chart on page 8).

698 *Behr/Schmidt* (2015) German Banking System, 12.

2016 only 9 remain, with total assets of 879.1 billion €,[699] equalling 11.2% of all assets.[700]

Cooperative banks constitute the third pillar of the German banking sector.[701] They outnumber all other pillars with a number of 976 at the end of 2016,[702] but are (together with Sparkassen) under the most severe consolidation pressure.[703] Cooperative banks mainly have local or regional operations[704] and are mostly small to medium-sized. Their business model is raising local deposits and lending to households and SMEs. They do not maximize profits but support business activities of their members.[705] With 850.3 billion €[706] cooperative banks held 10.9% of all assets in the German banking sector.[707]

At the end of 2016, there were 138 foreign owned banks in Germany. With 1088.8 billion €[708] they were in charge of 13.9% of total assets.[709]

---

699 *Deutsche Bundesbank* (2017) Monthly Report February, Statistical Section 24.

700 Own calculation based on *Deutsche Bundesbank* (2017) Monthly Report February, Statistical Section 24 (Ratio between the banks' assets amounting to 879.1 billion € and total assets of all banks amounting to 7836.2 billion €).

701 *IMF* (2016) Germany, 12.

702 *Deutsche Bundesbank* (2017) Monthly Report February, Statistical Section 24.

703 *Deutsche Bundesbank* (2015) Monthly Report April, 37.

704 *IMF* (2016) Germany, 12.

705 *Behr/Schmidt* (2015) German Banking System, 12. Among the cooperative banks, *DZ Bank*, a large institute, provides asset management, clearing services and liquidity funding for the others. *IMF* (2016) Germany, 13; It merged with the second provider in 2016, thus, became the *"joint central institution of the local cooperative banks"*. *DZ Bank* (2017) Annual Report 2016, 14.

706 *Deutsche Bundesbank* (2017) Monthly Report February, Statistical Section 24.

707 Own calculation based on *Deutsche Bundesbank* (2017) Monthly Report February, Statistical Section 24 (Ratio between the banks' assets amounting to 850.3 billion € and total assets of all banks amounting to 7836.2 billion €).

708 *Deutsche Bundesbank* (2017) Monthly Report February, Statistical Section 24.

709 Own calculation based on *Deutsche Bundesbank* (2017) Monthly Report February, Statistical Section 24 (Ratio between the banks' assets amounting to 1088.8 billion € and total assets of all banks amounting to 7836.2 billion €). See also *Claessens/Van Horen* (2015) Global Financial Crisis, 909, 912.

c. Deutsche Bank

*Deutsche Ba*nk is by far Germany's largest financial institute[710] and its only G-SIB. It is currently allocated to the third bucket of the G-SIB-framework.[711] Since the global financial crisis, *Deutsche Bank* has faced rough headwinds – on the one hand caused by external factors such as subdued economic growth, negative interest rates and rigorous regulation, on the other hand caused by internal factors, including mismanagement and legacies from the crisis. These factors in particular put pressure on *Deutsche Bank*'s investment bank unit, making necessary severe cuts of workforce and the balance-sheet, but also led to a generally depressed profitability of the bank.[712]

Uneased market sentiment peaked after U.S. authorities announced looming fines amounting to 14 billion $ with regard to *Deutsche Bank*'s pre-crisis mortgage backed securities business.[713] As this amount threatened the existence of the institute,[714] *Deutsche Bank*'s share prices hit a historic low.[715] In its 2016 *Financial Sector Assessment Program*, the IMF found that *Deutsche Bank* was not just one of the largest contributors of interconnectedness and systemic risks in the German banking and insurance sector, but that it also appeared to be "*the most important net contributor to systemic risks in the global banking system*".[716]

710 In 2016 *Deutsche Bank* was, with assets of 1590 billion €, more than three times bigger than Germany's second largest bank, *DZ Bank*. See *Kuck* (2017) Deutsche Kreditwirtschaft, 14; see also *Deutsche Bank* (2017) Annual Report 2016, 38.

711 See *FSB* (2017) Global Systemically Important Banks, 3. Banks of the third bucket are subject to a capital buffer of 2% (*FSB* (2017) Global Systemically Important Banks, 3); *Deutsche Bank* has continuously been considered G-SIBs since the first G-SIB assessment. See *FSB* (2011) Systemically Important Financial Institutions, 4.

712 *EIU* (2017) Financial Services: Germany, 6.

713 See *EIU* (2017) Financial Services: Germany, 6–7; *Financial Times*, Deutsche Bank and Credit Suisse pay billions to settle US probe (December 23, 2016); *Schultz*, US Regierung gegen Deutsche Bank: Der 14 Milliarden-Schock, Der Spiegel (September 16, 2016); The highly tense situation was resolved after a settlement between *Deutsche Bank* and U.S. authorities that was assessed by the majority as favourable to *Deutsche Bank* compared to the intial claims. *EIU* (2017) Financial Services: Germany, 7.

714 On the post-crisis situation, in particular the credible threat of a failure of *Deutsche Bank*, see exemplarily *Burghof* (2016) Deutsche Bank, 784–785.

715 *Financial Times*, Deutsche Bank and Credit Suisse pay billions to settle US probe (December 23, 2016).

716 *IMF* (2016) Stress Testing, 41–42.

In 2016, *Deutsche Bank* had assets of 1591 billion € on its balance sheet.[717] Set in relation to Germany's 2016 GDP of 3144 billion €,[718] its assets thus amount to approximately half of the German GDP.

C. Switzerland

a. Importance of the financial centre

Over the course of history, banking has been one of the key Swiss industries and has played an important role for Switzerland's economy and reputation in the world. Switzerland's financial system is highly developed and its institutions conduct business globally as well as domestically.[719]

The *Global Financial Centres Index* continuously lists both Zurich and Geneva in the top 20 of global financial centres.[720] The Swiss financial centre (consisting of financial services and insurance services) contributed a considerable 9.1% to the country's GDP in 2016, of which financial services made up 4.6%.[721] However, the contribution of the sector has declined since before the global financial crisis, when in 2007 financial ser-

717 See *Deutsche Bank* (2017) Annual Report 2016, 73.

718 See DESTATIS (2018) Deutsche Wirtschaft 2017, 3.

719 *EIU* (2017) Financial Services: Switzerland, 2.

720 *Z/Yen Group/China Development Institute* (2017) GFCI Nr. 22, 4 (in which Zurich was ranked 9th and Geneva 15th); See also former GFCI Reports, e.g. *Z/Yen Group/China Development Institute* (2014) GFCI Nr. 16, 5 (ranking Zurich 7th and Geneva 13th); and *Z/Yen Group/China Development Institute* (2008) GFCI Nr. 8, 9, (ranking Zurich 8th and Geneva 9th).

721 See *SIF* (2017) Swiss financial Centre: Key figures; Other calculations produce even higher results: in contrast to the FSO, *UBS* finds the contribution of the financial sector in 2015 at around 12% of GDP, taking not just into account direct added value, but also indirect added value *"in other sectors through orders to industry and the purchasing of services"*. (*UBS* (2017) Switzerland and UBS, 9; See also *BAKBASEL* (2016) Schweizer Finanzsektor, 22–23). The author's own calculation based on (*FSO* (2017) Industries production account) comes to a similar result: in 2016, the gross value added by the financial services sector equalled 30.261 billion CHF in current prices, the gross value added by the insurance sector was at 29.541 billion CHF, the total of all economic sectors after adjustments (subsidies and taxes, which allow for it to correspond to the GDP) equalled 658.978 billion CHF. There nevertheless needs to be a caveat: this can only be regarded as a rough illustration, as neither the author's calculation nor, as it seems, the *SIF's* calculation take into account the actual share of subsidies and taxes belonging to the financial services sector).

vices alone accounted for 8.2% of Swiss GDP.[722] The Swiss financial centre contributed 9.4% to the total GVA. Financial services alone accounted for 4.7%.[723]

Swiss banks employed 120.843 people[724] in 2016, of which 101.382 were employed in the country and 19.461 abroad.[725] According to Eurostat, the financial centre employs 4.7% of the total Swiss workforce.[726] Despite the elimination of tax secrecy for international clients,[727] Switzerland remains

---

722 Own calculation based on *FSO* (2017) Industries production account (for a description of the calculation, see Fn above).

723 Own calculation based on *FSO* (2017) Industries production account. The calculation resembles the one of Fn above. However, it uses the gross value added of all economic sectors *before* adjustments, which amounts to 638.981 billion CHF. The result of the calculation is matched by the one of Eurostat. See *Eurostat*, Gross value added and income by A*10 industry breakdowns, (January 31, 2018), http://appsso.eurostat.ec.europa.eu/nui/show.do?query=BOOKMARK_DS-406765_QID_-4FCE2BB0_UID_-3F171EB0&layout=NACE_R2,B,X,0;TIME,C,X,1;GEO,L,Y,0;UNIT,L,Z,0;NA_ITEM,L,Z,1;INDICATORS,C,Z,2;&zSelection=DS-406765NA_ITEM,B1G;DS-406765UNIT,PC_TOT;DS-406765INDICATORS,OBS_FLAG;&rankName1=UNIT_1_2_-1_2&rankName2=INDICATORS_1_2_-1_2&rankName3=NA-ITEM_1_2_-1_2&rankName4=NACE-R2_1_2_0_0&rankName5=TIME_1_0_1_0&rankName6=GEO_1_2_0_1&rStp=&cStp=&rDCh=&cDCh=&rDM=true&cDM=true&footnes=false&empty=false&wai=false&time_mode=NONE&time_most_recent=false&lang=EN&cfo=%23%23%23%2C%23%23%23.%23%23%23.

724 Measured in full time equivalents.

725 *SNB* (2017) Banks in Switzerland, 28. Also with regard to employment, there are much bolder calculations, e.g. *BAKBASEL* (2016) Schweizer Finanzsektor, 23–24 (expecting an employment multiplicator of 2.0, due to significant indirect employment effects of the banking sector); *UBS* (2017) Switzerland and UBS, 10–11.

726 See *Eurostat*, Employment by A*10 industry breakdowns, (January 31, 2018), http://appsso.eurostat.ec.europa.eu/nui/show.do?query=BOOKMARK_DS-406759_QID_-48796ABF_UID_-3F171EB0&layout=NACE_R2,B,X,0;TIME,C,X,1;GEO,L,Y,0;UNIT,L,Z,0;NA_ITEM,L,Z,1;INDICATORS,C,Z,2;&zSelection=DS-406759NA_ITEM,EMP_DC;DS-406759UNIT,PC_TOT_PER;DS-406759INDICATORS,OBS_FLAG;&rankName1=UNIT_1_2_-1_2&rankName2=INDICATORS_1_2_-1_2&rankName3=NA-ITEM_1_2_-1_2&rankName4=NACE-R2_1_2_0_0&rankName5=TIME_1_0_1_0&rankName6=GEO_1_2_0_1&rStp=&cStp=&rDCh=&cDCh=&rDM=true&cDM=true&footnes=false&empty=false&wai=false&time_mode=NONE&time_most_recent=false&lang=EN&cfo=%23%23%23%2C%23%23%23.%23%23%23.

727 *Nobel/Brändli* (2017) Can Banks Still Keep a Secret?, 308. For a compact description of the process of the removal of tax secrecy in an international context, the reasons for it the and the specialities in Swiss law that gave rise to controversies,

world leader in global cross-border private banking with a market share of 24.0%.[728]

b. Number of banks and their nature

In 2016, the trend of bank consolidation continued. At the end of the year, the SNB counted 261 banks (down from 266 in 2015) which it divides in groups such as "cantonal banks", "regional banks and savings banks", "Raiffeisen banks" and "big banks".[729]

The Swiss banking sector is highly concentrated: Assets of the country's three largest commercial banks amounted to 79.7% of total assets in 2015. Before the financial crisis, numbers were even higher with them in charge of 91.8% of total assets.[730] In 2015, the five biggest banks had an asset share of 89.2% (down from 93.7% in 2007).[731]

Currently the SNB qualifies four banks as "big banks",[732] namely (i) *UBS AG*, (ii) *UBS Switzerland AG*, (iii) *Credit Suisse AG* and (iv) *Credit Suisse (Switzerland) AG*. These are *"economically important"* banks that are active in all business areas and engage *"in particular [in] investment banking"*. They are part of financial groups, namely *UBS* and *Credit Suisse*, that have a global network of branches and subsidiaries.[733]

Cantonalbanks are part of a *"large, respected second tier of domestic banks"*.[734] Most of them are institutions under public law with their own legal personality[735] and are owned wholly or in part by the cantons.[736] Although a cantonal guarantee is not a constitutive feature anymore,[737] the

in particular with the United States, in the first place, see *Nobel/Brändli* (2017) Can Banks Still Keep a Secret?, 308–336.

728 *SwissBanking* (2017) Banking Barometer, 8.

729 *SNB* (2017) Banks in Switzerland, 5–6.

730 See *Worldbank* (2017) Global Financial Development Database.

731 See *Worldbank* (2017) Global Financial Development Database.

732 *SNB* (2017) Banks in Switzerland, 5–6.

733 *SNB*, Notes on the Banking Statistics, (September 28, 2017), https://data.snb.ch/en/topics/banken#!/doc/explanations_banken.

734 *EIU* (2017) Financial Services: Switzerland, 6.

735 *SNB*, Notes on the Banking Statistics, (September 28, 2017), https://data.snb.ch/en/topics/banken#!/doc/explanations_banken.

736 *EIU* (2017) Financial Services: Switzerland, 6.

737 The constitutive features of a cantonalbank are set down in Art. 3a Swiss Banking Act and include that the bank is (i) an establishment or limited-liability company on the basis of a Cantonal legal ordinance and that the (ii) Canton

majority of cantonalbanks retain one.[738] Even though most of them focus particularly on savings and mortgage business, they provide a range of banking services, including in some cases asset management for domestic clients. Most cantonalbanks focus on their own canton.[739] In 2016 the balance sheets of the 24 cantonalbanks accounted for 17.8% of Swiss banks' total assets.[740]

Raiffeisen banks, which together form the *Raiffeisen Switzerland Cooperative*,[741] account of 6.9% of total assets.[742] In addition, there are 62 regional and savings banks, which account for 3.7% of total assets.[743] For the most part, both groups concentrate on traditional banking services, such as mortgages and corporate loans,[744] and can, together with the cantonalbanks be characterised as *"domestic retail banks"*. All three have in common that they only have limited diversification and are largely dependent on the domestic mortgage market.[745]

81 foreign controlled banks,[746] some of which specialise in asset management and investment banking, are internationally active[747] and made up 8.0% of total assets in 2016.[748]

---

must hold more than one third of the capital and more than one third of the voting rights.

738 22 of 24 cantonalbanks retain a full Cantonal guarantee. In case of an insolvency the respective Canton is fully liable and bails out the bank. *Verband Schweizer Kantonalbanken*, Die Kantonalbanken, https://www.kantonalbank.ch/getmedia/ca3e1371-6405-432e-b9fa-37ccd9935325/Portrait_KB_Gruppe_2016_d.pdf.

739 *SNB*, Notes on the Banking Statistics, (September 28, 2017), https://data.snb.ch/en/topics/banken#!/doc/explanations_banken.

740 *SNB* (2017) Banks in Switzerland, 6, 9.

741 *SNB*, Notes on the Banking Statistics, (September 28, 2017), https://data.snb.ch/en/topics/banken#!/doc/explanations_banken.

742 *SNB* (2017) Banks in Switzerland, 9.

743 *SNB* (2017) Banks in Switzerland, 6, 9.

744 *SNB*, Notes on the Banking Statistics, (September 28, 2017), https://data.snb.ch/en/topics/banken#!/doc/explanations_banken; *Schiltknecht* (2013) Stabilität und Instabilität, 463.

745 *Schiltknecht* (2013) Stabilität und Instabilität, 463.

746 *SNB* (2017) Banks in Switzerland, 6.

747 *SNB*, Notes on the Banking Statistics, (September 28, 2017), https://data.snb.ch/en/topics/banken#!/doc/explanations_banken.

748 *SNB* (2017) Banks in Switzerland, 9.

c. UBS and Credit Suisse

UBS and *Credit Suisse* (*CS*) are the main players in the Swiss banking sector. In 2016, the balance sheets of *UBS* and *CS* accounted for 46.9% of Switzerland's balance sheet total, with 1.45 trillion CHF total assets.[749] Mainly due to regulatory pressure however, they have reduced their sizes considerably since the global financial crisis, when their balance sheets of 2.2 trillion CHF[750] accounted for a staggering 68.8% of Swiss banks' total assets.[751] *CS* and *UBS* are Switzerland's two G-SIBs and are currently part of the first bucket of the G-SIB framework.[752]

Both banks were heavily hit by the global financial crisis and incurred massive losses, which, in case of *UBS*, resulted in government intervention.[753] After two capital increases involving private investors,[754] which were followed by significant losses for these new shareholders,[755] Swiss authorities stepped in and bailed out the bank.[756] This was achieved by (i) the SNB financing the transfer of illiquid assets to a special purpose vehicle for

749 *SNB* (2017) Banks in Switzerland, 6, 9.

750 *SNB*, Data portal, https://data.snb.ch/en/topics/banken#!/doc/.

751 Own calculation based on *SNB*, Data portal, https://data.snb.ch/en/topics/banken#!/doc/ (In 2006, assets of the two banks amounted to 2.2 trillion CHF, all banks' assets amounted to 3.19 trillion CHF). See also *EIU* (2017) Financial Services: Switzerland, 5–6.

752 *FSB* (2017) Global Systemically Important Banks, 3; Banks of the first bucket subject to the comparatively "light" capital buffer of 1% (*FSB* (2017) Global Systemically Important Banks, 3); *UBS* and *CS* have continuously been considered G-SIBs since the first G-SIB assessment. See *FSB* (2011) Systemically Important Financial Institutions, 4.

753 *EIU* (2017) Financial Services: Switzerland, 6.

754 *Schiltknecht* (2010) "Too Big to Fail", 436.

755 *Bundesrat* (2008) Botschaft Massnahmenpaket schweizerisches Finanzsystem, 8955.

756 *Schiltknecht* (2010) "Too Big to Fail", 436; *EIU* (2017) Financial Services: Switzerland, 6. Interestingly, in its dispatch on the package of measures to strengthen Switzerland's financial system to Parliament, the Federal Council notes that the "*existence*" of *UBS* was, at the time of the adoption of the measures, "*not immediately threatened*". However, because of its vulnerability and the difficult environment, Swiss authorities could not rule out an exacerbation of the confidence crisis, which would have had a massive impact on the Swiss financial system and economy (*Bundesrat* (2008) Botschaft Massnahmenpaket schweizerisches Finanzsystem, 8955). This assessment is largely shared in academic literature (see e.g. *Sethe* (2011) Finanzmarktkrise und Steuerstreit, 108; *Jordan* (2010) SNB-Stabfund, 823). Drawing from the remarks on the vast size of *UBS* (especially at that time) and its importance for the Swiss economy above, it is evident that

a maximum amount of 60 billion \$.[757] Furthermore, (ii) direct financial aid was provided in the form of mandatory convertible notes amounting to 6 billion CHF, which were purchased by the Swiss Confederation.[758] *CS*, on the other hand, made it through the global financial crisis much less affected and avoided direct government support.[759] However, in its 2016 *Financial Sector Assessment Program* on Germany, the IMF found that *CS* was the third biggest contributor to systemic risks in the global banking system.[760]

In 2016, *UBS* had total assets of 935 billion CHF on its balance sheet,[761] *CS* had 820 billion CHF.[762] Compared with Switzerland's 2016 GDP of 659 billion CHF,[763] the balance sheet of *UBS* is thus 1.4 times the Swiss GDP, *CS*'s balance sheet 1.2 times, together accounting for 2.6 of Switzerland's GDP.[764]

D. Results

a. Importance of the financial centre

As a first step, it makes sense to compare the financial centres of interest according to their global importance. Undoubtedly, the United Kingdom, Switzerland and Germany are Europe's biggest and most important financial capitals. To reflect this, the author referred in the respective chapters to the *Global Financial Centres Index*,[765] which lists all the countries' finan-

---

Swiss authorities took the right decision and there was little room for alternatives.

757 *Bundesrat* (2008) Botschaft Massnahmenpaket schweizerisches Finanzsystem, 8945; *SNB*, Chronicle of monetary events 1848–2017, https://www.snb.ch/en/iabout/snb/hist/id/hist_wpc#t14.

758 *Bundesrat* (2008) Botschaft Massnahmenpaket schweizerisches Finanzsystem, 8945; *Bundesrat,* Federal Council takes decision on measures to strengthen Switzerland's financial system (October 16, 2008), https://www.admin.ch/gov/en/start/documentation/media-releases.msg-id-22019.html.

759 *EIU* (2017) Financial Services: Switzerland, 6.

760 See *IMF* (2016) Stress Testing, 42.

761 See *UBS* (2017) Annual Report 2016, 169.

762 See *Creditsuisse* (2017) Annual Report 2016, 173.

763 See *FSO* (2017) Gross domestic product.

764 Own calculations based on *UBS* (2017) Annual Report 2016, 169; *UBS* (2017) Annual Report 2016, 169; *FSO* (2017) Gross domestic product.

765 *Z/Yen Group/China Development Institute* (2017) GFCI Nr. 22.

cial centres within the global top 20. Apart from Luxembourg,[766] the next European country whose financial centre is listed is France, with Paris at rank 26. It can thus be concluded that London, Zurich and Frankfurt are by far the leading financial centres in Europe.

Assessing their positions however, it quickly becomes clear that there are considerable differences in their global rank: the United Kingdom currently leads the entire ranking and is thus far ahead of all other European financial centres. The next financial centre is Zurich (9th place), followed closely by Frankfurt (11th place).[767]

External factors influence the importance of financial centres. Interestingly, London remained on the first place with minimal losses in spite of the ongoing Brexit negotiations. While Zurich and Geneva fell in the ratings, Frankfurt rose, which is attributed to it being considered one of the main profiteers of Brexit.[768] It is also remarkable that Switzerland is represented by both Zurich and Geneva among the world's leading 20 financial centres. Summarizing, it can be stated that while London leads the ranking in the distance, Frankfurt is in the process of catching up to Zurich in the run for Europe's second place.

In a second step, it is considered useful to compare the financial centres importance from a national perspective. Which of the financial centres of interest is most important for the respective nation? As an indicator, the author used the GDP and GVA ratio of the financial services sector as well as the number of employees and tax contribution. Because of discrepancies in the contribution of the financial centres to GDP, the GVA ratio is considered best suited for a comparison.

Looking at the GVA contribution of the various financial centres, Switzerland's has by far the highest rate with 9.4%.[769] Luxembourg aside, this is the highest rate in Europe.[770] Switzerland's economy thus relies

766 Luxembourg is at rank 14, followed by Geneva at rank 15. *Z/Yen Group/China Development Institute* (2017) GFCI Nr. 22, 4.

767 See *Z/Yen Group/China Development Institute* (2017) GFCI Nr. 22, 4.

768 See *Z/Yen Group/China Development Institute* (2017) GFCI Nr. 22, 2, 4; see also *Sester* (2018) EU-Finanzmarktrecht, 52 (pointing out the recognisable trend of internationally active banks strengthening their presence in EU-financial centres, in particular Frankfurt, and not expanding operations in Switzerland).

769 See Chapter III.I.C.a: Importance of the financial centre.

770 *Eurostat*, Employment by A*10 industry breakdowns, (January 31, 2018), http://appsso.eurostat.ec.europa.eu/nui/show.do?query=BOOKMARK_DS-406759_QID_-48796ABF_UID_-3F171EB0&layout=NACE_R2,B,X,0;TIME,C,X,1;GEO,L,Y

heavily on financial and insurance services. The UK follows with 6.6% and Germany with 3.9%.[771]

Focussing on financial services alone, Switzerland is still ahead with financial services adding 4.7% of gross value. The UK, however, follows closer with considerable 4.1%. The reduced gap is due to Switzerland's strong insurance sector, which contributes strongly to the financial centre. In Germany, financial services contribute only 2.5% to the total GVA.[772] Both in Switzerland and the UK, financial services thus contribute a great deal and to a comparable degree to the economy. The gross added value of financial services in Germany is significantly smaller.

Comparing employment rates, Switzerland is again in the lead with 4.7% of the total workforce employed by the financial centre. It is followed by the UK with 3.1% and Germany with 2.7% of the total workforce.[773] With regard to employment, the financial centres of the UK and Germany thus employ similar percentages of the workforce, whereas in Switzerland financial services employ by far the most people of the respective countries.

b. Number of banks and their nature

There is considerable consolidation in the banking markets of all three countries of interest, which is reflected by the constant decline in the number of banks since the global financial crisis. In absolute numbers, Germany has by far the most banks, followed by the UK, which has noticeably

,0;UNIT,L,Z,0;NA_ITEM,L,Z,1;INDICATORS,C,Z,2;&zSelection=DS-406759NA_ITEM,EMP_DC;DS-406759UNIT,PC_TOT_PER;DS-406759INDICATORS,OBS_FLAG;&rankName1=UNIT_1_2_-1_2&rankName2=INDICATORS_1_2_-1_2&rankName3=NA-ITEM_1_2_-1_2&rankName4=NACE-R2_1_2_0_0&rankName5=TIME_1_0_1_0&rankName6=GEO_1_2_0_1&rStp=&cStp=&rDCh=&cDCh=&rDM=true&cDM=true&footnes=false&empty=false&wai=false&time_mode=NONE&time_most_recent=false&lang=EN&cfo=%23%23%23%2C%23%23%23.%23%23%23.

771 See Chapter III.I.A.a: Importance of the financial centre (and the corresponding chapters of Germany and Switzerland).

772 See Chapter III.I.A.a: Importance of the financial centre (and the corresponding chapters of Germany and Switzerland).

773 See Chapter III.I.A.a: Importance of the financial centre (and the corresponding chapters of Germany and Switzerland).

fewer banks relative to its size (roughly less than double the number of banks in Switzerland).[774]

Comparing bank concentration, the three largest commercial banks' share of total assets were in 2015 the highest in Switzerland (79.7%), followed by Germany (74.8%). In the UK the share was only 48.4%.[775] With regard to the 5-bank-asset concentration rate, Switzerland is still ahead with 89.3%, followed by Germany with 83.8% and the UK with 71.4%.[776] The order thus remains the same. In the UK the concentration share increases the most compared to the previous concentration rate (more than 20%), but is still comparatively low, which can be attributed to a higher number of large banks, namely the "high street banks".

In a 2013 dataset comparing the number of foreign banks among total banks, the UK leads with striking 58%. In Switzerland the share is 20% and in Germany only 14%.[777]

c. G-SIBs

Comparing the countries' G-SIBs, one finds that Switzerland is the most exposed to its biggest banks' balance sheets: total assets of its two G-SIBs alone amount to 2.6 times the nation's GDP. The UK is closely following with total assets amounting to 2.3 times the GDP, but with the important difference that it takes four banks to put this vast number together. While *Deutsche Bank* is considerably bigger than the Swiss banks, it equals only half of the German GDP.[778] Germany can therefore be regarded as the least exposed.

---

774 See Chapter III.I.A.b: Number of banks and their nature (and the corresponding chapters of Germany and Switzerland).

775 See *Worldbank* (2017) Global Financial Development Database; see also Chapter III.I.A.b: Number of banks and their nature (and the corresponding chapters of Germany and Switzerland).

776 See *Worldbank* (2017) Global Financial Development Database; see also See Chapter III.I.A.b: Number of banks and their nature (and the corresponding chapters of Germany and Switzerland).

777 See *Claessens/Van Horen* (2015) Global Financial Crisis, 909; *Worldbank* (2017) Global Financial Development Database; see also Chapter III.I.A.b: Number of banks and their nature (and the corresponding chapters of Germany and Switzerland).

778 See Chapter III.I.A.c: HSBC, Barclays, RBS, Standard Chartered (and the corresponding chapters on G-SIBs of Germany and Switzerland).

Looking at the G-SIBs individually, one finds that *HSBC* is undisputedly the biggest bank, followed by *Deutsche Bank* and *Barclays*. The differences between the banks' balance sheets are noteworthy. Take *Credit Suisse* as an example: although *Credit Suisse* is a huge bank in itself with an enormous importance for Switzerland, its total assets amount to only around a third of *HSBC's*.[779] Together, the countries are home to Europe's largest banks.[780]

During the global financial crisis, none of the countries was spared the distress of witnessing at least one of its G-SIBs face an existential threat. Considering the vast sizes of these banks and their systemic importance both nationally and globally, a failure would have caused massive disruption and could have posed an existential threat to both the countries[781] and the international community.

II. Preparatory Work and Legal Sources

This chapter traces the evolution of the structural reform models of the respective countries: it presents the preparatory work and the final product deriving from it. This is important, because (i) it shows that structural reform is a process and not just the final legislation. Structural reform evolves over time. The final legislative outcome is often very different from the initial idea. This is particularly visible regarding the Swiss organisational measures.[782] It also (ii) highlights issues of the final product. Most of them already exist in the preparatory works. It is thus interesting to see how, and if, they are addressed in the course of the legislative process. The chapter furthermore (iii) sets the scene for the subsequent examination by

779 Own calculation based on *HSBC* (2017) Annual Report 2016 (At the end of 2016, *HSBC* had assets of 2375 billion $ on its balance sheet); *Creditsuisse* (2017) Annual Report 2016, 173 (At the end of 2016, *Credit Suisse* had a balance sheet of 820 billion CHF, equalling around 805 billion $ in December 2016). However, one has to mind fluctuations due to changes in the exchange rate.

780 *Deutsche Bank* and *HSBC* are Europe's only third bucket G-SIBs. *FSB* (2017) Global Systemically Important Banks, 3.

781 *Waibel*, for example, discusses bank insolvency as an important channel linking the balance sheets of banks and countries and notes that *"[t]he largest ticking bomb for public balance sheets is the debt of the banking sector"*. *Waibel* (2011) Bank Insolvency, para 13.03.

782 See Chapter III.IV.D.e: Relation to expert commission recommendations. The intensity of transformation can also be observed in the various stages of the EU's structural reform. See Part II: Legal Developments on EU Level.

introducing the various sources of law. This facilitates the understanding of the legal design of the respective structural reform.

Switzerland's path to structural reform requires particular attention, as it reveals the discomfort of the Swiss legislator and authorities with clear ring-fencing rules on the one hand, and the awareness that stringent organisational requirements are necessary on the other hand. In the author's opinion highlighting this tension is vital to grasp the uniqueness of the Swiss approach.

A. United Kingdom

Following the UK Government's unprecedented intervention to stabilise the financial system described in the chapter above, an expert commission was formed to *"consider structural and related non-structural reforms to the UK banking sector to promote financial stability and competition"*.[783] The commission, which was headed by *Sir John Vickers*, was soon referred to as the "Vickers Commission", its final report as the "Vickers Report".[784] This report gained global prominence and considerably contributed to the discussion in many other countries.[785]

The Vickers Commission found that *"a package of measures"* was needed to (i) improve the loss-absorbing ability of banks, to (ii) facilitate the resolution of banks that still got into difficulties and to (iii) keep in check incentives for excessive risk taking. It recommended that this package should consist on the one hand of capital measures and measures to prop up the loss-absorbing ability and on the other hand of structural reform.[786]

783 *ICB* (2011) Vickers Report, 19. The commission was formed on June 16, 2010. See *ICB* (2011) Interim Report, 11. This was remarkable, as historically banking regulation in the UK was largely non-structural. See *Korotana* (2016) Banking Reform Act, 197–198.

784 See e.g. *Binder* (2015) Ring-Fencing, 98; *Chambers-Jones* (2011) Vickers Report, 280; *Dombalagian* (2012) Proprietary Trading, 394 Fn 41; *Elliott/Rauch* (2014) Volcker Rule, 1; *Gambacorta/Van Rixtel* (2013) Structural Bank Regulation Initiatives, 23; *Krahnen/Noth/Schüwer* (2016) Structural Reforms, 1.

785 See e.g. *Blundell-Wignall* (2011) Necessity, 298; Boot (2011) Banking, 29–30; *Chow/Surti* (2011) Making Banks Safer, 22–23; *Brandi/Gieseler* (2013) Entwurf des Trennbankengesetzes, 741; *European Commission* (2014) Impact Assessment Part 2, 2; *ZEW* (2013) Trennbanken, 10 et seqq.

786 *ICB* (2011) Vickers Report, 8.

The UK Government welcomed the Vickers Report, vowing to *"remain[] strongly committed to implementing these proposals"*[787] and accepted the majority of the proposed measures,[788] which became part of UK law with the adoption of the Financial Services (Banking Reform) Act 2013.[789] The Banking Reform Act 2013 amends a number of provisions of the Financial Services and Markets Act 2000[790] and more importantly adds a new Part 9B with the title "ring-fencing".[791] It is complemented by four pieces of secondary legislation, adopted by HM Treasury,[792] which make use of the generously delegated powers. In addition, supervisory material by the regulator sets out details and expectations.[793]

B. Germany

In Germany, legislative efforts to adopt ring-fencing rules are part of the post-crisis regulatory regime[794] and can be understood as a reaction to the EU's Liikanen Proposal.[795] According to *Hardie/Macartney*, the German Government pushed for such measures both for international and domestic political reasons, namely (i) to avoid the application of a more stringent

787 *HM Treasury* (2012) Banking Reform, 7.

788 See *Britton et al.* (2016) Ring-fencing, 166; see also *HM Treasury* (2012) Banking Reform, 15–33.

789 Financial Services (Banking Reform) Act 2013, c. 33.

790 Financial Services and Markets Act 2000, c. 8 (FSMA 2000).

791 See Banking Reform Act 2013, Sec. 4.

792 See *Britton et al.* (2016) Ring-fencing, 166; This includes FSMA 2014 Order No. 1960, FSMA 2014 Order No. 2080, FSMA 2015 Regulations No. 547; FSMA 2016 Order No. 1032.

793 Supervisory material includes in particular the PRA's Supervisory Statement on ring-fenced bodies and the PRA Rulebook. See *PRA* (2017) Ring-fenced Bodies; *PRA* (2016) PRA Rulebook: Ring Fenced Bodies; see also *Thomson Reuters Practical Law,* PRA Rulebook, supervisory statements and other supervisory material, https://uk.practicallaw.thomsonreuters.com/5-573-3805?__lrTS=20171230004551129&transitionType=Default&contextData=(sc.Default)&firstPage=true&bhcp=1.

794 See *Braun* (2016) Geschäftsorganisation, para 1; *Deutscher Bundestag* (2013) Gesetzesentwurf Trennbankengesetz, 2.

795 *Schwennicke* (2016) Verbotene Geschäfte, 196. For a discussion of the Liikanen Report, see Chapter II.I: Liikanen Report.

EU approach and (ii) to forestall demands of the main challenger party in the run-up of the federal elections.[796]

The provisions of the draft bill[797] were adopted by the German parliament as part of a law[798] that was soon referred to as "Trennbankengesetz".[799] Its name, however, is rather misleading, as it falsely suggests it would stipulate a full separation for banks.[800] In the author's opinion, the term "Abschirmungsgesetz" that is also used by BaFin[801] is more suitable, because in contrast to "Trennbankengesetz", (i) it derives from the official title of the law and (ii) does not overstate the content of the German provisions. It furthermore (iii) relates to the English term "ring-fencing", which is to some extent used by BaFin in English translations.[802] It would be desirable if German authorities and the academic discourse would use the term "Abschirmungsgesetz" and, if necessary, the term "Ring-fencing Act" in English translations.

The law entered into force on August 13, 2013.[803] The German Ring-fencing Act amends and adds provisions to the German Banking Act, in particular § 3 and § 25f.[804] It is complemented by an Interpretative Guid-

---

796 See *Hardie/Macartney* (2016) EU Ring-Fencing, 505–506, 512–513. This was also to some exent argued by the opposition parties SPD and Bündnis 90/Die Grünen, see *Deutscher Bundestag* (2013) Bericht Finanzausschuss, 3 (noting that the German Ring-fencing Act is of limited scope compared to the Liikanen Report); *Deutscher Bundestag* (2013) Stenografischer Bericht, 28615–28616 (in which *Joachim Poß* of the SPD accuses the Government of adopting the Act only to forestall demands of the SPD).

797 See *Deutscher Bundestag* (2013) Gesetzesentwurf Trennbankengesetz.

798 Gesetz zur Abschirmung von Risiken und zur Planung der Sanierung und Abwicklung von Kreditinstituten und Finanzgruppen, August 7, 2013, Bundesgesetzblatt Part I, 3090 (German Ring-fencing Act).

799 The term "Trennbankengesetz" was used by the German Government itself (see *Deutsches Bundesministerium für Finanzen* (2013) Trennbankengesetz) and has since been used by most authors. See e.g. *Brandi/Gieseler* (2013) Entwurf des Trennbankengesetzes. *Schelo/Steck* (2013) Trennbankengesetz;; *Schaffelhuber/Kunschke* (2015) Trennbankengesetz.

800 BaFin uses the term "Bank Separation Act" in the English version of its Interpretative Guidance. See e.g. *BaFin* (2016) Interpretative Guidance, 1.

801 See e.g. *BaFin* (2016) Auslegungshilfe, 1.

802 See e.g. *BaFin* (2016) Interpretative Guidance, 1.

803 *Deutscher Bundestag*, Gesetz zur Abschirmung von Risiken und zur Planung der Sanierung und Abwicklung von Kreditinstituten und Finanzgruppen, http://dipbt.bundestag.de/extrakt/ba/WP17/508/50871.html. See also the considerations regarding the application of the law, Chapter III.VI.B: Germany.

804 Gesetz über das Kreditwesen, July 10, 1961, Bundesgesetzblatt Part I, 2776 (German Banking Act).

ance of BaFin and Deutsche Bundesbank that was published in late 2016.[805]

C. Switzerland

In Switzerland structural reform became a topic of interest after the bailout of *UBS*[806] and the subsequent discussion of too-big-to-fail.[807] In 2009, the Federal Council set up an expert commission on the topic, which was chaired by *Peter Siegenthaler*[808] and which published its final report in late 2010.[809]

a. Decision against structural reforms

In its report, the expert commission explicitly decided against certain measures that were discussed globally, among them size caps, the full dismantling of large banks, i.e. cutting up large banks into several smaller institutes, and the prohibition of proprietary trading.[810] Regarding the latter, the expert commission pointed out the difficulties of defining such activities and the risk of their shifting into the shadow banking sector.[811]

Interestingly, it also rejected other structural requirements for banks: first it mentioned as an example the requirement to form a holding struc-

---

805 See *BaFin* (2016) Auslegungshilfe.

806 For the government intervention for the benefit of *UBS*, see Chapter III.I.C.c: UBS and Credit Suisse.

807 See e.g. *Hofer* (2014) Structural Reforms, 294; *Bahar/Peyer* (2013) Systemrelevante Banken, 378; see also *Achermann* (2018) Organisation, 272–273.

808 *EFD* (2009) Expertenkommission Medienmitteilung, 1.

809 See *Expertenkommission* (2010) Schlussbericht. References in this dissertation relate to the German version of the expert commission's report, because (i) the English translation stipulates that the German original prevails in case of discrepancies (*Expertenkommission* (2010) Final Report, 1), (ii) there are indeed discrepancies leading to slight deviations of the meaning. However, in some cases it may be appropriate to refer to the English version (when there is no deviation) or simultaneously point out the referenced parts of the English version.

810 For an explanation of proprietary trading, see Chapter I.II.B.a: Proprietary trading.

811 See *Expertenkommission* (2010) Schlussbericht, 49. The expert commission rightly identified the issue of drawing the line between proprietary trading and other desired trading activities. For the problem of an effective delimitation, see e.g. Chapter I.IV.D.a: Digression: The Volcker Rule.

ture and emphasized that such a structure would neither limit corporate group liability,[812] nor improve crisis management, nor facilitate the recovery[813] of an institute.[814]

The report then argued that a holding structure would only limit corporate group liability if there was a complete operative, legal separation of the various group entities that also included the workforce.[815] This is remarkable as it relatively well describes the end result of the Swiss regulation, as will be demonstrated in the following chapters.

According to the expert commission, (i) such requirements, however, would mostly eliminate economies of scope of a globally active banking group. In addition, it emphasized that in case of a crisis, (ii) it would be probable that Switzerland would be pressured into rescuing foreign based subsidiaries of Swiss banks by countries negatively affected by their bankruptcy.[816]

In the annex to the final report, the expert commission furthermore noted, with a view to a holding structure with subsidiaries for each country of business operations, that such an organization would be beneficial to the separation of systemically important functions. However, they argued that such requirements would come close to the full dismantling of banks described above and then pointed out that the main issue of such requirements would be *"a very extreme form of intervention to meet the criterion C2 [i.e. simplified resolution and restructuring of systemically important banks], which in turn makes it hardly justifiable with respect to criteria C3 [i.e. func-*

---

812 Corporate group liability is a special feature of Swiss law: Entities of a banking group are liable for each others' debt under certain conditions. The liability can be based on a contract, say a guarantee, which could be referred to in English as "legal corporate group liability". Moreover, there is a concept which could be referred to as "factual corporate group liability", that mandates that entities are liable for each other's debt if there is interdependence with regard to personnel or finances or if the entities use the same name or appear together on the market. Corporate group liability is set out in Art. 3c Swiss Banking Act and Art. 21(2) Swiss Banking Ordinance. For a more detailed explanation, see *Maurenbrecher/Kramer* (2013) Geschäftsbetrieb, 144–145.

813 In the English version "Sanierbarkeit" is mistakenly translated as "resolvability". *Expertenkommission* (2010) Schlussbericht, 48; *Expertenkommission* (2010) Final Report, 46.

814 *Expertenkommission* (2010) Schlussbericht, 48, 121.

815 See *Expertenkommission* (2010) Schlussbericht, 48–49. For further explanation of these arguments, see *Hofer* (2014) Structural Reforms, 411–412.

816 See *Expertenkommission* (2010) Schlussbericht, 48–49. For further explanation of these arguments, see *Hofer* (2014) Structural Reforms, 411–412.

tioning and efficiency of the financial system] and C4 [i.e. competitive neutrality]."[817]

b. Policy mix and core measure organization

Instead of the direct structural requirements described in the chapter above, the expert commission decided to propose a policy mix consisting of four *"core measures"*, namely (i) capital, (ii) liquidity, (iii) risk diversification, and (iv) organisation.[818] Collectively, these measures constituted the expert commission's proposals to effectively tackle too-big-to-fail.[819]

1. Organisational measures

i. Emergency plan

The expert commission found that organisational measures were necessary to protect the continuation of systemically important functions (*inter alia* domestic lending and deposit-taking, as well as payment transactions) in case of an insolvency of a bank. It recommended for banks not to be required to implement a specific organisation but that they be tasked solely with demonstrating that a continuation of these activities was ensured.[820]

Banks could in principle do this by coming up with a credible emergency plan, i.e. a plan that would show how – in case of its activation – it was ensured that, within a short period of time – this typically means a weekend – the functions could be continued. However, the expert commission already hinted that certain changes to the organisation of the affected institutes would possibly be necessary to ensure the credibility of the emergency plan.[821]

---

817 *Expertenkommission* (2010) Final report, 109, 118; see also *Expertenkommission* (2010) Schlussbericht, 112, 121.

818 *Expertenkommission* (2010) Schlussbericht, 2; *Expertenkommission* (2010) Final report, 2.

819 *Expertenkommission* (2010) Schlussbericht, 5; *Expertenkommission* (2010) Final report, 5 (noting that the implementation of all the core measures is necessary *"if the TBTF problem is to be tackled effectively"*).

820 *Expertenkommission* (2010) Schlussbericht, 37–38, 40.

821 See *Expertenkommission* (2010) Schlussbericht, 40–41. The expert commission, for instance, noted that the *"emergency plan must be designed in such a way that it*

ii. Organisational measures to improve general resolvability

In addition to the emergency plan, organisational measures to improve the general resolvability were to *"boost the resolvability of systemically important banks and thereby reduce the repercussions of insolvency"*. These organisational precautions that exceed the minimum requirements of the emergency plan were also considered to have a positive effect on ensuring the continuation of the systemically important functions.[822] To reward banks for such measures, capital rebates were to be awarded.[823]

2. Subsidiarity principle

Organisational measures are highly invasive regarding fundamental rights, international competitiveness and competition in general. The expert group recommended the solution outlined above, because it considered it the least invasive. It intended to ensure this by introducing a *"rigorous subsidiarity principle"*: it is based on the thought that functional requirements are less invasive than specific requirements:[824]

Banks are required to organise themselves in a way that makes certain that the functional goal of the continuation of systemically important functions can be ensured in the case of insolvency. Finma can only impose specific organisational measures if the bank fails to prove this with its emergency plan. Banks should thus have a considerable range of choices regarding the organisational measures.[825]

The expert commission furthermore decided to recommend only to require the minimum goal and not to mandate additional measures that would be in the interest of the country and third countries. The implemen-

---

can be implemented within a very short space of time in the face of a crisis. The timing at which implementation would need to begin, as well as the question of what further organisational measures would need to be taken in addition to the emergency plan itself and even before its implementation, depend on the existing organisation of the bank, the specific emergency plan in question, and the remaining capital cover." *Expertenkommission* (2010) Final report, 39; see also *Expertenkommission* (2010) Schlussbericht, 40.

822 *Expertenkommission* (2010) Final report, 36–37.

823 See *Expertenkommission* (2010) Schlussbericht, 43–44.

824 See *Expertenkommission* (2010) Schlussbericht, 39; *Expertenkommission* (2010) Final report, 38; For a discussion of this claim, see Chapter III.II.D.e: Invasiveness.

825 See *Expertenkommission* (2010) Schlussbericht, 38, 40.

tation of organisational measures that enhance the general resolvability is to be incentivised by capital rebates.[826]

3. TBTF evaluation

In 2015, the Federal Council met the obligation set down in Art. 52 Swiss Banking Act, by publishing its first evaluation of the TBTF package[827] based on the work of an expert commission under the lead of *Aymo Brunetti.*[828] It generally approved the Swiss TBTF package, in particular its organisational measures, and recommended a number of smaller changes,[829] including introducing the requirement for ex ante separated banks that provide systemically important functions to comply with capital requirements on a standalone basis.[830] In 2017, the Federal Council published its second evaluation, which did not find the need for any changes regarding the organisation requirements.[831]

c. Legal sources

1. Banking Act and Banking Ordinance

The Federal Council submitted the final draft of the Swiss too-big-to-fail package, which took the form of a partial revision of the Banking Act, to

826 See *Expertenkommission* (2010) Schlussbericht, 38.
827 See *Bundesrat* (2015) Bericht Too Big to Fail.
828 See *Expertenkommission* (2014) Schlussbericht; 39–40.
829 See *Bundesrat* (2015) Bericht Too Big to Fail, 1932. The recommendation of the expert group to include a deadline for the implementation of emergency planning (*Expertenkommission* (2014) Schlussbericht, 47–48) was followed and implemented by the Federal Council. See *Bundesrat* (2016) Änderung Bankenverordnung, 1738–1739.
830 See *Expertenkommission* (2014) Schlussbericht, 47; *Bundesrat* (2015) Bericht Too Big to Fail, 1939; Chapter III.V.C.b: Capital and Liquidity].
831 *Bundesrat* (2017) Bericht systemrelevante Banken.

parliament in April 2011.[832] It was approved in September[833] and entered into force in March 2012.[834]

As the adopted TBTF package is based on the expert commission's final report, it is strongly shaped by its recommendations.[835] The legal foundation for organisational measures was set in the fifth section of the Banking Act, which concerns systemically important banks.[836] As the provisions of the Swiss Banking Act can be considered *"relatively vague and open"*,[837] they are complemented by amendments[838] to the Swiss Banking Ordinance.[839] The seventh chapter of the Swiss Banking Ordinance in its current form[840] comprises the relevant provisions for systemically important banks.[841]

2. Finma emergency plan assessment

There is, however, another source not in the form of legislation, whose importance should nevertheless not be underestimated. The Swiss Banking Act and Swiss Banking Ordinance stipulate that affected banks have to prove that their emergency plans are workable[842] and that they took all necessary measures to protect systemically important functions.[843] Finma

832 *Bundesrat* (2011) Botschaft TBTF; *Bundesrat* (2011) Entwurf Bankengesetz.
833 *Bundesversammlung* (2011) Änderung BankG, 1. *Bundesrat* (2012) TBTF Press Release.
834 *Bundesrat* (2012) TBTF Press Release. For a detailed description of the legislative process, see *Hofer* (2014) Structural Reforms, 297.
835 See *EFD* (2012) Kommentar Bankenverordnung, 5; *Bahar/Peyer* (2013) Systemrelevante Banken, 378–379, 390, 418, 429–430; *Hofer* (2014) Structural Reforms, 297.
836 Art. 7–10a Swiss Banking Act. See also *Bundesversammlung* (2011) Änderung BankG.
837 *Hofer* (2014) Structural Reforms, 297.
838 See *Bundesrat* (2012) Botschaft Bankenverordnung; *EFD* (2012) Kommentar Bankenverordnung; *Bundesversammlung* (2012) Genehmigung Bankenverordnung.
839 Verordnung über die Banken und Sparkassen, May 17, 1972 SR 952.02.
840 Verordnung über die Banken und Sparkassen, April 30, 2014, SR 952.02 (Swiss Banking Ordinance).
841 Art. 60–66 Swiss Banking Ordinance.
842 Art. 9(2)(d) Swiss Banking Act; Art. 60(1) Swiss Banking Ordinance.
843 Art. 60(1) Swiss Banking Ordinance.

is tasked to verify this[844] and to mandate all necessary measures, in case they are not.[845]

Even before the first approval of an emergency plan, there is thus a close cooperation between Finma and the affected bank during the assessment of the current status of the emergency plan.[846] While this informal exchange does not necessarily qualify as a legal act on its own, it has to be identified as a source of information of utmost importance for banks regarding the question of how to design their new structure.[847]

Broken down, the process is the following: a bank subject to the TBTF requirement delivers its draft emergency plan to Finma. Finma then assesses the plan and highlights what has to be improved. This happened for the first time in 2015, when *UBS* delivered its emergency plan to Finma. *Credit Suisse* delivered its plan in early 2016. In both cases, Finma found the need for amendments due to *"strong operational and financial dependence of the Swiss subsidiaries on their parent companies"*.[848] When assessing, it pays a lot of attention to FSB Guidances.[849] The bank then applies the changes, and reflects them in the new the emergency plan. This process involves a close dialogue.[850]

The process may also result in changes to the structure of the bank: In the case of one affected institute, for instance, the first emergency plan was originally based on a bridge bank concept. Due to multiple reasons, in particular the capital rebate, and after a number of discussions within the

---

844 Art. 61(1) Swiss Banking Ordinance.

845 Art. 10(2) Swiss Banking Act.

846 Expert Interview, Affected Bank, September 28, 2017. The closeness of cooperation with *UBS* and *Credit Suisse* with regard to the ex ante separation of systemically important functions is also emphasized by Finma in its annual report. See *Finma* (2017) Jahresbericht 2016, 32.

847 The *"critical importance"* of the discussions between Finma and banks is identified by *Schöchli, as "due to the complexity of the matter in the details, neither a law nor an ordinance are able to provide more than a basic framework"*. Own translation from German original, *Schöchli,* Der lange Weg der Notfallplanung, NZZ (June 6, 2012); see also *Hofer* (2014) Structural Reforms, 332.

848 *Finma* (2017) Annual Report 2016, 33; *Finma* (2017) Jahresbericht 2016, 33.

849 Potential FSB Guidances Finma might possibly take into account are, e.g. *FSB* (2014) Key Attributes; *FSB* (2015) Obstacles to Resolvability; *FSB* (2016) Operational Continuity. For a summary of relevant *FSB* Guidances, see *Achermann* (2018) Organisation, 276–278; For a discussion of their legal character, see *Brändli* (2018) Internationale Standards, 47–50.

850 Expert Interview, Affected Bank, September 28, 2017.

bank and with Finma, the bank, however, decided to conduct an ex-ante separation.[851]

In the author's opinion, the powers of Finma in combination with the design of the process described above expectably lead to extensive steering capabilities for Finma. Even if it did not explicitly express its wishes, it would be able to significantly regulate banks' emergency plans and structures only by identifying selective needs for improvement. The assessment process should thus be considered a major source of information and regulation.

D. Results

a. Expert commissions

1. National focus

All three countries' legislation is based on the recommendations of expert commissions. Both the UK and Switzerland formed domestic expert commissions that drew up recommendations for the national banking sector. Germany, in contrast, based its legislation on the Liikanen Report,[852] which was formed on an EU level and whose recommendations were prepared with a view of a union-wide bank structural reform.

The German approach is somewhat peculiar: on the one hand (similarly to France)[853] it is based on a common EU expert commission and not on a tailor-made national commission focussing on the specialties of the German banking market. This could theoretically be argued for as having the advantage of a certain harmonisation of EU banking markets. On the other hand however, Germany did not await a common EU approach but decided for a solo run, considerably deviating from the EU recommendations.[854] Germany therefore neither profits from taking into account the

851 Expert Interview, Affected Bank, September 28, 2017.

852 For a detailled discussion of the Liikanen Report, see Chapter II.I: Liikanen Report.

853 For a short description of France's ring-fencing regime, see *Lehmann* (2014) Ring-Fencing, 8–10.

854 See also *Altvater/Von Schweinitz* (2013) Trennbankensystem, 633 (noting that national solo runs entail massive adverse competitive distortions within the internal market).

specialties of the German banking market, nor from a harmonisation due to common union-wide requirements.

2. Composition

The expert commissions themselves differ in their composition, in particular regarding the question whether or not banks are represented in the commissions. The UK expert group comprised five individuals from various fields of profession. While some of the members held senior positions in banking before joining the expert group, banks were not directly represented through group members.[855] The High Level Expert Group of the Liikanen Report consisted of 11 individuals from various fields. Banks were not directly included in the expert group.[856] The Swiss expert group, in contrast, comprised 14 members, of which two were direct representatives of banks.[857]

Including representatives of the affected banks has advantages and disadvantages: a key advantage is that such representatives provide up-to-date practical knowledge that is likely to benefit the resulting recommendations. They furthermore may be better suited to assess the feasibility of certain measures and to address questions that arise during implementation. In addition, it makes a good impression if measures agreed on are supported by the affected parties and not just imposed from above. At the same time, these members are subject to a considerable conflict of interest. As large banks have almost unlimited resources to support their members of the expert commission, including such members into the formal expert commission could shift a suboptimal amount of influence towards them. The question arises whether it is more expedient to place more weight on consultations than to include direct representatives in the expert commission.

855 For a short description of the members of the UK Vickers Commission, see *Gribben*, 'Wonderkid' and old girl form part of Sir John Vickers' Banking Commission team, The Telegraph (April 11, 2011); *ICB* (2011) Vickers Report, 19.

856 For a short descripition of the members of the High Level Expert Group, see *Bank of Finland* (2012) Expert Group; *HLEG* (2012) Liikanen Report.

857 See *Expertenkommission* (2010) Schlussbericht, 65–66 (they represented *UBS* and *Credit Suisse*).

b. Legal sources

1. Primary, secondary legislation, guidance

Comparing the legal sources, one can conclude that it seems to be hardly possible to address all relevant questions of ring-fencing in one legal act. The most extensive law was adopted in the UK. Part 9B of the FSMA 2000 on ring-fencing, which is included in the Banking Reform Act 2013, has almost 30 provisions.[858] The German Banking Act's main provisions on ring-fencing, in contrast, amount to two provisions.[859] In Switzerland primary legislation is rather short, comprising five provisions, of which only two relate to the emergency plan.[860]

While in both Switzerland and the UK secondary legislation is used to complement the respective acts, in Germany no secondary legislation has been adopted. The BaFin's Interpretative Guidance,[861] however, attempts to fill that gap, clarifying issues and ambiguities and in some instances forcefully reinterpreting provisions of the German Ring-fencing Act.[862]

Switzerland stands out, as it merely stipulates the functional goal of the continuation of systemically important activities and does not provide specific requirements on how to do so. This legislative technique, which is argued for with the strict subsidiarity principle, naturally requires much less detailed legislation. It, however, results in wide discretion of the regulator. For this reason, Switzerland's emergency plan assessment process[863] has to be underscored as an important legal source for banks.

2. Principle of legality

One major concern, with regard to the executive authority outlining key parts of the legal requirements, is the possible violation of the principle of

858 See Part 9B FSMA 2000.

859 See § 2, § 25f German Banking Act. The limited number of provisions, however, is offset by their length.

860 See Section 5 Swiss Banking Act; FSMA 2014 Order No. 1960, FSMA 2014 Order No. 2080, FSMA 2015 Regulations No. 547; FSMA 2016 Order No. 1032.

861 *BaFin* (2016) Auslegungshilfe; *BaFin* (2016) Interpretative Guidance.

862 A good example is the exemption of fully collateralised lending and guarantee business with hedge funds or AIFs from the excluded activities. See Chapter III.IV.B.a.1: Excluded activities.

863 See Chapter III.II.C.c.2: Finma emergency plan assessment.

legality.[864] It is beyond the scope of this dissertation to discuss the legal foundation of the principle in the respective countries and the question whether there are such violations. However, it is a fundamental understanding of a state under the rule of law, that administrative action should be based on and determined by the law. Once this basis or determination becomes questionable, a violation of the principle of legality is conceivable. The Swiss legislator tried to prevent such a violation with the need for parliamentary approval for the first sets of Ordinances specifying the Swiss Banking Act.[865] In the UK as well, secondary legislation was approved by Parliament.[866] Most problematic in this regard, however, remains Switzerland,[867] in particular due to the far-reaching powers of Finma,[868] and Germany, due to the vagueness of the German Ring-fencing Act[869] and missing secondary legislation.

3. Transparency

Another concern is the lack of transparency. Examining all three jurisdictions' legislation on ring-fencing as an outside party, one quickly learns that the easiest to grasp is the UK. This is because it uses the hierarchy of primary legislation, secondary legislation, interpretation guidance[870] most consequently. All these legal sources are publicly accessible and the goals articulated by the Vickers Report are pursued rather persistently. This has allowed for a public discussion of issues related to ring-fencing.

As discussed above, secondary legislation is missing in Germany. Only the Interpretative Guidance partially concretises the considerably vague provisions of the German Ring-fencing Act. What is important to understand regarding the Interpretative Guidance is that it was created in close

864 See *Hofer*'s critique of the Swiss solution regarding the principle of legality, *Hofer* (2014) Structural Reforms, 430–432.
865 Transitional provision of the amendment of September 30, 2011 Swiss Banking Act; see *Hofer* (2014) Structural Reforms, 298, 431.
866 See Sec. 142Z FSMA 2000.
867 See the critique of *Hofer*, *Hofer* (2014) Structural Reforms, 298, 430–432.
868 See Chapter Chapter III.II.C.c.2: Finma emergency plan assessment;.
869 A good example for the vagueness of the German Ring-fencing Act are the provisions on the independence of the financial trading entity. See Chapter III.V.B.a: Financial trading institution.
870 See Chapter III.II.A: United Kingdom.

cooperation with affected banks and interest groups.[871] Apart from a subsequent public consultation, these discussions are not publicly available. As the Interpretative Guidance by far does not address all questions arising from the German Ring-fencing Act,[872] transparency is not fully ensured.

The Swiss solution brings with it as well the burden of a considerable lack of transparency.[873] For an outside party, many obligations for affected banks are hard to grasp. This will be demonstrated in particular with regard to the question whether investment banking activities have to be separated from systemically important functions[874] and regarding the height of the fence:[875] In some areas, factual requirements for banks only derive from hints in the legislative materials or other sources of information.[876] To comprehend the Swiss solution, it does not suffice to take a look at the legislative provisions. An outside party has to dig into legislative materials and official statements, look at measures that affected banks implemented in response to TBTF, and to acquire information on the Finma's review process. The discussion of the structural reform measures thus takes place to a large extent between Finma and the affected banks and is therefore not easily available for outside parties.

c. Chronology

Comparing the preparatory work in the countries of interest one finds that, from a chronological point of view, the first country in which an ex-

---

871 This is explicitly stated by BaFin, see *BaFin* (2015) Begleitschreiben Konsultation Auslegungshilfe.

872 Among others, the Interpretative Guidance also does not comprehensively set out how the independence of the financial trading institution is to be ensured. See Chapter III.V.B.a: Financial trading institution.

873 See also *Hofer* (2014) Structural Reforms, 430–432, 450–452 (in particular his critique of (i) the risk of the introduction of more stringent requirements than recommended by the expert commission; and of (ii) the statements in legislative materials hinting the need for a separation of commercial banking and investment banking).

874 See Chapter III.IV.C.b: non-ring-fenced bodies.

875 See Chapter III.V.C: Switzerland.

876 See Chapter III.IV.C.a: Ring-fenced body; see also *Hofer* (2014) Structural Reforms, 431 (criticising the *"tendencies within official statements to aim at implementing some sort of a ring-fencing requirement"*).

pert commission was set up was Switzerland, in November 2009.[877] The Swiss expert commission already published its final report in September 2010.[878] This was just shortly after the UK Government had formed the Vickers Commission, in June 2010.[879] The Swiss expert commission's report thus only mentions the formation of the Vickers Commission as a marginal note.[880] The fact that Switzerland was that far ahead in tackling too-big-to-fail is an important detail in the comparison of the respective jurisdictions and considerably shaped the character of the Swiss solution.

The Vickers Commission published its interim report in April 2011[881] and the final report in September 2011.[882] This coincides with the adoption of the provisions on the emergency plan of the Swiss Banking Ordinance in Switzerland in June 2012.[883]

The EU's expert commission, on whose recommendations the German Ring-fencing Act is based, was set up February 2012[884] and published its final recommendations in October 2012.[885] The German Government introduced the draft bill in March 2013.[886]

In conclusion, it can be found that in the UK and Switzerland, motivation for structural reform of banking arose relatively shortly after the beginning of the global economic crisis. In Germany, it arose a great deal later. This is remarkable, as all three countries had to intervene massively through packages of aid for banks and had to witness the existence of national champions endangered.[887]

---

877 See *EFD* (2009) Expertenkommission Medienmitteilung, 1; Chapter III.II.C: Switzerland.
878 *Expertenkommission* (2010) Schlussbericht, 1.
879 *ICB* (2011) Interim Report, 11; Chapter III.II.C: Switzerland.
880 *Expertenkommission* (2010) Schlussbericht, 100.
881 *ICB* (2011) Interim Report.
882 *ICB* (2011) Vickers Report.
883 See *Bundesrat* (2012) Botschaft Bankenverordnung, 6669.
884 *HLEG* (2012) Liikanen Report, I; see Part II: Legal Developments on EU Level.
885 *HLEG* (2012) Liikanen Report.
886 *Deutscher Bundestag* (2013) Gesetzesentwurf Trennbankengesetz, 1.
887 See *Blundell-Wignall/Wehinger/Slovik* (2010) The Elephant in the Room, 14–15 (noting that the UK, Germany and Switzerland together with the U.S. had to put together *"massive packages of aid [...] on an unprecedented scale"* for too-big-to-fail banks in trouble).

d. Influence

The revision of the Swiss Banking Ordinance seems to be influenced by the emerging international discussions on bank separation, in particular by the recommendations of the Vickers Commission. This is hardly surprising, as the publication of the Vickers Commission's interim report in April 2011 was the focus of a lot of international attention.

The influence is especially visible in the legislative materials referring to the ex ante separation of systemically important functions as matching *"the example"*[888] of the UK Vickers Commission ring-fencing model.[889] The Swiss Banking Ordinance also seems to become significantly stricter, as it articulates explicitly the need to implement measures ex ante. This is insofar a first-time event, as the Swiss Banking Act referred only to planning.[890]

Another potential area in which Swiss legislation may have been influenced by international developments are the amendments following the Federal Council's first evaluation of the TBTF package in 2015.[891] The requirement for ex ante separated banks, which provide systemically important functions to comply with capital requirements on a standalone basis,[892] considerably assimilates Swiss organisational measures to other structural reform initiatives.

e. Invasiveness

Organisational requirements for banks are highly invasive and affect fundamental rights. In this regard it is interesting that there are considerable differences in the perception of the encroachment on fundamental rights and in the sympathy with the affected banks.

In the UK, a fundamental right encroachment is neither recognized by the Vickers Commission nor by the Government.[893] The German Government's proposal does not identify an encroachment on fundamental rights

---

888 Own translation from German original, see *EFD* (2012) Kommentar Bankenverordnung, 10 Fn 12.

889 *EFD* (2012) Kommentar Bankenverordnung, 10 Fn 12; see also *Hofer* (2014) Structural Reforms, 329.

890 This will be shown in Chapter III.IV.C.a.1: Ex ante separation.

891 See *Bundesrat* (2015) Bericht Too Big to Fail.

892 See *Expertenkommission* (2014) Schlussbericht, 47; *Bundesrat* (2015) Bericht Too Big to Fail, 1939; Chapter III.V.C.b: Capital and Liquidity.

893 See *HM Treasury* (2013) Impact Assessment, para 106.

either.[894] The Swiss expert commission and Government, in contrast, acknowledge the invasiveness of organisational measures. They stress the importance of the least invasive possible approach, emphasizing that structural measures therefore *"require particular justification"*.[895]

As set out in the chapter above, this is to be achieved through a subsidiarity principle and through requiring only a minimum goal.[896] The central idea is that *"functional requirements are significantly less of a burden than specific requirements"*. Finma may only impose structural requirements if a bank fails to prove it is *"appropriately organised"* and has reached the goal of maintaining systemically important functions.[897]

Exploring this central idea, one has to first ask why functional requirements are less burdensome than specific requirements. The idea is that the stipulation of a goal is less burdensome than to describe how an affected party has to reach it. This is because the party then can decide on its own how to do so.

This idea is certainly true, as long as (i) there is a variety of ways to reach a certain goal and as long as the goal (ii) can transparently be reached. Such a transparency can be assumed e.g. if a third party could without doubt consider a certain goal as reached. The idea, however, can be doubted once there are not many, or even just one certain way to reach a goal, or once it becomes non-transparent whether a goal is reached.

As will be demonstrated, the Swiss legal requirements do not allow for many ways of reaching the goal of the continuation of systemically important functions after all. There is, for example, hardly an alternative to an ex ante separation of systemically important functions.[898] It is furthermore hardly thinkable to include certain investment banking activities into such an entity.[899]

---

894 The legislative materials to the German Ring-fencing Act discuss the encroachment on fundamental rights with regard to other provisions (namely provisions on recovery and resolution) but not with regard to the ring-fencing provisions. From this follows that that the German Government acknowledges no human right violations with regard to § 3 and § 25f German Banking Act. See *Deutscher Bundestag* (2013) Gesetzesentwurf Trennbankengesetz, 36.

895 See *Expertenkommission* (2010) Final Report, 38. See also *Bundesrat* (2011) Botschaft TBTF, 4731.

896 See Chapter III.II.C.b.2: Subsidiarity principle.

897 *Expertenkommission* (2010) Final Report, 38.

898 See Chapter III.IV.C.a.1: Ex ante separatiion.

899 See Chapter III.IV.C.b: Non-ring-fenced body.

The transparency of the goal can also be called into question. The Swiss Banking Ordinance stipulates that an affected bank has to prove that the systemically important functions can be continued in case of imminent insolvency based on *"common experience"* and the *"current state of knowledge"*.[900] The legislative materials to the Swiss Banking Act note that the subject of evidence is (i) the prediction of the efficacy of the organisational measures of the emergency plan and (ii) the implementation of certain preventive organisational measures as required by the emergency plan.[901] Regarding the former, proof can be established if the affected bank can demonstrate that measures reach the goal *"with a high level of probability"* based on the *"current state of knowledge"*.[902] Regarding the latter, namely the ex ante implementation of necessary measures, a high standard of proof is required concerning whether the respective measures are implemented comprehensively.[903]

Even though the expert commission's final report and the legislative materials to both the Swiss Banking Act and the Swiss Banking Ordinance acknowledge the difficulties in establishing such a proof and attempt to solve this problem, there remains considerable uncertainty for affected banks regarding their ability to prove that the continuation of systemically important activities is ensured.

Drawing from the above, one finds that there are considerable differences in the acknowledgement of the invasiveness of structural requirements for banks. While in Germany and the UK there seems to be the tendency to ignore this problem, it is highlighted in the Swiss discussion which must be appreciated. At the same time, it has to be pointed out that the principle of subsidiarity and the functional requirements mitigate the invasiveness only if (i) there is more than one way to reach a goal and as (ii) this goal can transparently be reached. Both can be somewhat reasonably questioned. The advantage of functional requirements may therefore be smaller than originally planned, in particular when taking into account that other jurisdictions also allow for a degree of flexibility in the structure of an affected bank.[904]

---

900 Own translation from German orginal, see Art. 60(2) Swiss Banking Ordinance.

901 *Bundesrat* (2011) Botschaft TBTF, 4760.

902 Own translation from German original, see *Bundesrat* (2011) Botschaft TBTF, 4760; see also *Schiltknecht* (2010) "Too Big to Fail", 443; *EFD* (2012) Kommentar Bankenverordnung, 10; *Expertenkommission* (2010) Schlussbericht, 40, 82.

903 See *Bundesrat* (2011) Botschaft TBTF, 4760.

904 This is visible e.g. in activities that can be provided by both the ring-fenced entities and the non-ring-fenced entities (see Chapter III.IV.A.c: Summary; Chapter

III. Who Is Subject to the Fence?

This chapter addresses the question of who is subject to the fence, examining the scope of the jurisdictions' structural reforms. It first explores the personal scope, then turns to thresholds and exemptions and finally identifies affected banks.

A. United Kingdom

The scope of the UK's ring-fencing regime is centred around so called "core activities". All UK institutions that carry out these activities have to be ring-fenced and are thus called "ring-fenced bodies".[905]

a. Personal scope

The FSMA 2000 only identifies accepting deposits as a core activity but authorizes the Treasury (i) to add other activities or (ii) to exempt deposit taking under certain circumstances.[906]

The Treasury has not made use of the authorization to add other core activities. However, it specified deposit-taking, which is not a core activity and therefore does not require a ring-fence. It does so by introducing a negative delimitation: only the acceptance of "core deposits" is a core activity, all other forms of deposit-taking do not require a ring-fence. Core deposits are all deposits held by an UK deposit-taker,[907] i.e. a legal entity incorporated in the UK[908] in an EEA account,[909] i.e. an account opened at a branch in an EEA state.[910] That means that only banks based in the UK are affected. Branches of banks which are based outside the UK are not affect-

---

III.IV.IV.B.c: Summary); Banks in the UK, for instance, have also chosen very different models of ring-fencing, see Chapter III.IV.A.d: Affected banks.

905 See Sec. 142A(1) FSMA 2000.

906 Sec. 142B(2)-142B(5) FSMA 2000.

907 Art. 2 FSMA 2014 Order No. 1960.

908 See Art. 1 FSMA 2014 Order No. 1960; Art. 2(2)(d) FSMA 2016 Order No. 1032.

909 Art. 2(2) FSMA 2014 Order No. 1960.

910 Art. 2(3)(b) FSMA 2014 Order No. 1960.

ed.[911] This applies particularly to branches of EU-based banks.[912] Furthermore, it means that accounts opened with UK based banks in subsidiaries outside the EEA, say in Brazil, Switzerland[913] or South Africa, do not have to be included in a ring-fenced body.[914]

Exempted are accounts that are held by, among others, one or more relevant financial institutions, eligible individuals or qualifying organisations. They are not considered core deposits.[915] The Explanatory Notes to the Banking Reform Act 2013 mention high net-worth individuals and large corporate entities as examples for a possible exemption.[916] It is apparent that this provision aims at exempting parties that, on the one hand, can be regarded as sophisticated investors and that are not particularly in need of protection and that, on the other hand, possibly demand services that exceed the means of a ring-fenced body.[917]

It is important to underscore that these exemptions from the definition of "core deposits", do not lead to the obligation to bank only with non-ring-fenced entities. On the contrary, these parties are allowed to bank outside the ring-fence, but can nevertheless choose to bank with a ring-fenced body.[918]

---

911 See Explanatory Note to the FSMA 2016 Order No. 1032, 9 (mentioning this as the goal of a modification of the original Order from 2014); see also *FSB* (2014) Structural Banking Reforms, 7.

912 Due to EU passporting they do not have to fulfil other requirements. See *FSB* (2014) Structural Banking Reforms, 8 (setting out requirements for non-EEA-based banks).

913 For branches of foreign banks in Switzerland, see *Finma*, Branches of Foreign Banks, https://www.finma.ch/en/authorisation/banks-and-securities-dealers/getting-licensed/branches-of-foreign-banks/.

914 See *FSB* (2014) Structural Banking Reforms, 7.

915 Art. 2(2) in conjunction with Art. 3–5, 8–10 FSMA 2014 Order No. 1960 as amended by Art. 2(3)-(6) FSMA 2016 Order No. 1032.

916 Explanatory Notes to the Banking Reform Act 2013, para 28.

917 This is also suggested in statements regarding high net-worth individuals and small and medium sized companies in the white paper of the UK Government, see *HM Treasury* (2012) Banking Reform, 16–17.

918 This is explained well in Explanatory Memorandum to FSMA 2014 Order Nr. 1960, Sec. 7.8 – 7.9.

b. Threshold and exemptions

As it is not the intention of the legislator to require all UK deposit-takers to implement a ring-fence,[919] he has authorized the Treasury to stipulate exemptions,[920] which most importantly take the form of thresholds for core deposits:[921] all banks with core deposits of less than 25 billion £ do not have to ring-fence. For banking groups, this is calculated by adding up the core deposits of each group entity.[922]

Another important reduction of scope is set down in Sec. 142A(2)(a) FSMA 2000. It exempts building societies[923] from the obligation to ring-fence. This is especially interesting, because (i) *Nationwide*, a building society, is among the UK's biggest lenders[924] and because (ii) the Vickers Report recommended to include building societies, due to the many similarities to banks and the majority of them being protected by deposit insurance.[925] The Explanatory Notes justify the exemption with the already *"significant restrictions"* for building societies based on the Building Societies Act 1986.[926] The Banking Reform Act 2013, however, authorises the

---

919 See Explanatory Notes to the Banking Reform Act 2013, para 27.

920 Sec. 142A(2)-(3) FSMA 2000.

921 Art. 11, 12 FSMA 2014 Order No. 1960; The introduction of a threshold is one of the main divergences from the Vickers Report. The Vickers Commission criticised the introduction of thresholds for several reasons, among them that complex small banks could still pose considerable difficulties with resolution and that risks from capital markets could still be transmitted to retail banking in case of a large number of banks operating below the thresholds. In addition, there was only a "minimal" impact of ring-fencing rules on small banks, as most of them do not provide excluded activities anyway. See *ICB* (2011) Vickers Report, 39; see also *De Vogelaere* (2016) Bank Structure Reforms, 22.

922 See Art. 11, 12 FSMA 2014 Order No. 1960.

923 For a short description of building societies, see Chapter III.I.A.b: Number of banks and their nature.

924 See Chapter III.I.C.b: Number of banks and their nature.

925 See *ICB* (2011) Vickers Report, 85, 109, 233.

926 See Explanatory Notes to the Banking Reform Act 2013, para 89. While the Explanatory Notes only mention restrictions based on the Building Societies Act 1986, the Vicker's report mentions restrictions of the Building Societies Act 1997 (Building Societies Act 1997, c. 32), namely restrictions on transactions involving derivatives (*ICB* (2011) Vickers Report, 60). These restrictions also contribute to the decision to exempt building societies from the ring-fencing regime.

Treasury to make provisions about ring-fencing for building societies, to align the principles of their regime with the one for ring-fenced bodies.[927]

Furthermore, the Treasury clarifies that UK deposit-takers are not ring-fenced bodies if they carry out the regulated activity of effecting or carrying out contracts of insurance as principal.[928]

c. Affected banks

In summary, it can be established that UK ring-fencing rules apply to all banks incorporated in the UK that accept core retail deposits in any EEA state exceeding 25 billion £ in total. According to the *Proudman*, this applies to the five largest UK banking groups,[929] namely *Barclays*, *HSBC*, *Lloyds*, *RBS* and *Santander UK*,[930] as well as some of their smaller competitors.[931] Due to the limited size of its UK retail banking operations, *Standard Chartered* does not fall within the scope of the rules.[932] It is thus the only UK G-SIB that does not have to establish ring-fence.

B. Germany

a. Personal scope

The scope of the German ring-fencing rule is set down in § 3(2) German Banking Act. Its addressees are twofold: it applies to all (i) CRR credit institutions and to all (ii) companies that belong to a group of institutions, a financial holding group or mixed financial holding group or a financial conglomerate to which a CRR credit institution belongs.[933]

CRR credit institutions are defined in § 1(3d) German Banking Act, which refers to Art. 4(1)(1) of the EU's Capital Requirements Regulation

927 See Sec. 7 Banking Reform Act 2013; Explanatory Notes to the Banking Reform Act 2013, para 89.
928 See Art. 11(1)(a) FSMA 2014 Order No. 1960.
929 See *Proudman* (2017) Putting Up a Fence, 3.
930 See *Binham/Dunkley*, Regulators get ready to authorise 'ringfenced' UK banks, Financial Times (August 19, 2017).
931 See *Proudman* (2017) Putting Up a Fence, 3.
932 *Nahmias* (2016) UK Banks, 5.
933 § 3(2) German Banking Act; See also *BaFin* (2016) Interpretative Guidance, 1–2.

(CRR).[934] CRR credit institutions can simply be understood as credit institutions that are active in both deposit-taking and lending.[935] This means that credit institutions that are active only in one of these businesses – say they only accept deposits or other repayable funds but do not grant credits for their own account – are not CRR credit institutions and thusly do not fall within the scope of German ring-fencing provisions.[936]

Companies of a group to which a CRR credit institution belongs are also within the scope. Included are (i) a group of institutions, (ii) a financial holding group or (iii) mixed financial holding group or (iv) a financial conglomerate.[937] The first three are defined in § 10a German Banking Act. According to *Möslein*, the purpose of the provision is simply to ensure that the whole group (of which a CRR credit institution is a part) is within the scope of the ring-fencing provisions.[938]

The interpretation of the financial conglomerate, however, is not as clear. For a definition of financial conglomerates, the German Banking Act refers to § 1(2) of the German Act on the Supervision of Financial Conglomerates.[939] A financial conglomerate according to § 1(2) German Act on the Supervision of Financial Conglomerates can best be understood as a group (or subgroup) whose companies both provide banking or investment services and insurance services.[940] *Möslein* legitimately concludes from the comprehensive definition of groups with a CRR credit institu-

934 Regulation (EU) No 575/2013 of the European Parliament and of the Council of 26 June 2013 on prudential requirements for credit institutions and investment firms and amending Regulation (EU) No 648/2012, OJ L 176, 27.6.2013, p. 1–337; § 1(3d) German Banking Act in conjunction with Art. 4(1)(1) CRR.

935 See Art. 4(1)(1) CRR; see also *Schwennicke* (2016) Verbotene Geschäfte, 196; In greater detail *Schäfer* (2016) § 3 Verbotene Geschäfte, para 33. For a discussion of the differences between the definition of credit institutions in German and EU law, see *Schäfer* (2016) § 1 Begriffsbestimmungen, para 9–16.

936 See *Schäfer* (2016) § 1 Begriffsbestimmungen, para 14; See also *Möslein* (2013) Spartentrennung, 401; *Schwennicke* (2016) Verbotene Geschäfte, 196.

937 § 3(2) German Banking Act; See also *BaFin* (2016) Interpretative Guidance, 1–2.

938 *Möslein* (2013) Spartentrennung, 401. This is also indicated by the Explanatory Notes to the draft bill, which emphasize that the whole endeavour serves the intention of the legislator to ensure the solvency of CRR credit institutions. See *Deutscher Bundestag* (2013) Gesetzesentwurf Trennbankengesetz, 27–28.

939 § 1(20) German Banking Act in conjunction with § 1(2) Finanzkonglomerate-Aufsichtsgesetz, June 27, 2013, Bundesgesetzblatt Part I, 1862 (German Act on the Supervision of Financial Conglomerates).

940 See *BaFin*, Supervision of financial conglomerates and groups, (January 01, 2016), https://www.bafin.de/EN/Aufsicht/VersichererPensionsfonds/FinanzkonglomerateGruppen/gruppenaufsicht_artikel_en.html.

tion that ring-fencing provisions also apply to insurance companies whose groups include a CRR credit institution.[941]

The BaFin, in contrast, clarified in its Interpretative Guidance that, concerning insurance companies, it interprets § 3(2) German Banking Act restrictively. In line with the above, it argues that the provision is to be understood within the meaning of § 10a(1) German Banking Act. It, however, does not mention § 1(20) German Banking Act and the German Act on the Supervision of Financial Conglomerates, and particularly argues that *"it would mean a breach of the system"* to apply the ring-fencing provisions to *"a group of companies which are otherwise not subject to the requirements of banking supervision law"*. Ring-fencing provisions therefore do *"not apply to insurance undertakings which belong to a financial conglomerate"*.[942]

With regard to the geographic scope, the ring-fencing provisions include all CRR credit institutions that require a licence according to § 32(1) German Banking Act, due to their business activities in Germany. This includes CRR credit institutions domiciled outside the EEA, which operate in Germany via a branch, other physical presence or cross-border provision of services. In each case, however, this is limited to the German business.[943] For EEA- based CRR credit institutions that fall within the EU's passport regime, both the cross-border provision of services and operating a branch in Germany are excluded from the scope of the ring-fencing provisions.[944] Subsidiaries in Germany, in contrast, are subject to the rules.[945]

941 See *Möslein* (2013) Spartentrennung, 401; Approvingly also *Schwennicke* (2016) Verbotene Geschäfte, 196.

942 See *BaFin* (2016) Interpretative Guidance, 2–3. While the BaFin's interpretation of the scope of § 3(2) German Banking Act is understandable from a teleological and systematic point of view, it is a restrictive interpretation against the wording of the law.

943 See *BaFin* (2016) Interpretative Guidance, 3–4.

944 See *BaFin* (2016) Interpretative Guidance, 3–4. BaFin argues that § 3(2)-(4) are not mentioned in § 53b(3) sentence 1 no.1, a provision that ensures that branches of EEA institutions (that would otherwise be exempted due to the passporting regime) can be regulated with regard to certain provisions, to safeguard public interest. See *BaFin* (2016) Interpretative Guidance, 3–4. See also *Lehmann* (2014) Extraterritorial Effects, 307–308.

945 See *Lehmann* (2014) Extraterritorial Effects, 308.

b. Threshold

The addressees set out above are only subject to ring-fencing if they exceed certain thresholds. § 3(2) stipulates an (i) absolute threshold and a (ii) relative threshold.[946] The legislator set down the thresholds with a view to the Liikanen Report,[947] however, departed from it in a number of aspects.[948]

The absolute threshold takes into account the total trading portfolio and liquidity reserves of a firm on the balance sheet date of the previous business year. If they exceed 100 billion €, the addressee falls within the scope of the provisions.[949] This provision has been criticised by a number of authors, as the separation of certain risky activities then applies no matter what their proportion is in relation to the total trading activities, which do not have to be separated. It is indeed a major deviation from the Liikanen Report.[950]

This is particularly inadequate for reaching the objectives of the regulation, taking into account that the banks themselves do not determine the amount of liquidity reserves.[951] For example, a banking group that provides substantial market making services and holds large liquidity reserves due to regulatory requirements is potentially subject to ring-fencing, even though risky activities (that then have to be separated) only account for a small amount of trading activities.

The relative threshold is met (i) if the total trading portfolio and liquidity reserves exceed 20% of the institute's balance sheet (ii) and the respec-

---

946 *Deutscher Bundestag* (2013) Gesetzesentwurf Trennbankengesetz, 41.

947 See *Deutscher Bundestag* (2013) Gesetzesentwurf Trennbankengesetz, 41; *Van Kann/Rosak* (2013) Regierungsentwurf des Trennbankengesetzes, 1476; *Schwennicke* (2016) Verbotene Geschäfte, 196.

948 See *Schelo/Steck* (2013) Trennbankengesetz, 238 (emphasizing deviations in the relative threshold); *Schwennicke* (2016) Verbotene Geschäfte, 197; *Schaffelhuber/Kunschke* (2015) Trennbankengesetz, 394–395.

949 § 3(2) German Banking Act; *Stubbe* (2016) Trennbanken, 2.

950 See *Brandi/Gieseler* (2013) Entwurf des Trennbankengesetzes, 746 (criticising that, in contrast to the Liikanen Report, the draft bill does not stipulate assessment of the ratio of risky trading activities to total trading activities as a second step. Due to the focus on all trading activities, ring-fencing can thus become obligatory, even though an institute provides activities that have to be separated only on on limited scale.); *Schelo/Steck* (2013) Trennbankengesetz, 239; *Schaffelhuber/Kunschke* (2015) Trennbankengesetz, 394–395; *Schwennicke* (2016) Verbotene Geschäfte, 197.

951 See *BaFin* (2016) Interpretative Guidance, 6.

tive institute's balance sheet in total amounts to at least 90 billion € on the balance sheet date in the last three business years.[952]

c. Affected banks

In summary, banks and companies of a group which a bank is part of, fall within the scope of the ring-fencing provisions if they (i) have substantial trading operations of over 100 billion € or (ii) if their trading operations exceed 20% of a total balance sheet of at least 90 billion €.

In 2016, BaFin noted that approximately 11 banks fall within the scope of the German Ring-fencing Act.[953] This corresponds with the response of the German Government to the query of a member of the Bundestag.[954] Germany's only G-SIB, *Deutsche Bank*, is affected by the Act.[955]

C. Switzerland

The scope of Switzerland's organisational measures is shaped by the scope of the Swiss TBTF package: it addresses systemically important banks. The central provisions are therefore Art. 7 Swiss Banking Act, which clarifies the character of such institutes, and Art. 8 Swiss Banking Act, which sets down criteria for systemic importance and their determination.[956]

a. Personal scope

Art. 7(1) Swiss Banking Act defines systemically important banks as (i) banks, financial groups and bank-dominated financial conglomerates, (ii) whose failure would do considerable harm to the Swiss economy and the Swiss financial system.[957]

---

952 See § 3(2) German Banking Act; *Deutscher Bundestag* (2013) Gesetzesentwurf Trennbankengesetz, 41; rather misleading *Stubbe* (2016) Trennbanken, 2.

953 *Stubbe* (2016) Trennbanken, 10.

954 *Deutscher Bundestag* (2016) Antworten der Bundesregierung, 42–43.

955 *Deutsche Bank* (2017) 2016 SEC Form 20-F, 25.

956 Art. 7 Swiss Banking Act.

957 Art. 7(1) Swiss Banking Act. The translation follows the English version of draft of the *Expertenkommission* (*Expertenkommission* (2010) Final Report, 65). The

The first condition for an entity to be considered systemically important is therefore that it is a bank, a financial group or a bank-dominated financial conglomerate within the meaning of the Swiss Banking Act.[958]

The assessment of systemic importance thus includes not just a single institute but the whole group. That allows for more flexibility because systemic importance can be determined not just for a single institute but also for a group of non-systemically important institutes that display systemic importance only as a group.[959]

While *Bahar/Peyer* rightly point out that the reduced scope excludes other financial intermediaries such as (pure) insurance companies, the exclusion of securities dealer is strictly speaking not so clear.[960] Furthermore, it can be assumed that in case of bank-dominated financial conglomerates, which can be understood as banking groups with significant insurance operations,[961] insurance operations may also influence the determination of systemic importance.[962]

---

original German draft was transposed verbatim. See *Expertenkommission* (2014) Schlussbericht, 67; *Bahar/Peyer* (2013) Systemrelevante Banken, 397.

958 See Art. 1, Art. 3(c)(1)-(2) Swiss Banking Act.

959 See *Bundesrat* (2011) Botschaft TBTF, 4744; *Bahar/Peyer* (2013) Systemrelevante Banken, 372.

960 See *Bahar/Peyer* (2013) Systemrelevante Banken, 373. As mentioned above, Art. 7(1) includes financial groups, which are defined in Art. 3c(1). The provision, however, also applies to financial groups of which no bank but only a securities dealer is part of. A literal interpretation of Art. 7(1) thus also includes financial groups without a bank. Due to the focus on banking activities in the determination of systemic importance set down in Art. 8, a systematic interpretation and teleological interpretation may exclude financial groups without a bank. However, as securities dealer also hold protected deposits within the meaning of Art. 37h Swiss Banking Act, a financial group could in theory fulfil the criterion of Art. 8(2)(b). (See Art. 36a Bundesgesetz über die Börsen und den Effektenhandel, 954.1; *Bundesrat* (2002) Botschaft Bankengesetz, 8107; *Winzeler* (2013) Einlagensicherung, 758–759, 762–763). This will remain likely theoretical, with securities dealers only in charge of 0.04% of protected deposits in 2015. *Esisuisse* (2017) Jahresbericht 2016, 7.

961 See *Maurenbrecher/Kramer* (2013) Geschäftsbetrieb, 145–146.

962 This could happen via the criteria of Art. 8(2), namely the relationship of balance sheet and Swiss GDP (lit. c) and the risk profile (lit. d).

b. Threshold and exemptions

Art. 8(2) Swiss Banking Act stipulates the factors that determine whether a bank is of systemic importance, namely its (i) size, (ii) interconnectedness with the financial system and the economy, and the (iii) short-term substitutability of its services.[963] These three factors are not cumulative, but can each on their own determine a bank as systemically important.[964]

Art. 8(2) Swiss Banking Act has to be interpreted in conjunction with Art. 7(1) Swiss Banking Act, so that together with the satisfaction of one of the factors of Art. 8(2)(i)-(iii) Swiss Banking Act, it has to be assessed whether a failure of the bank would do considerable harm to the Swiss economy and the Swiss financial system.[965] To clarify the factors of Art. 8(2)(i)-(iii) Swiss Banking Act, Art. 8(2)(a)-(d) Swiss Banking Act set down list of criteria that indicate systemic importance. As the list is non-exhaustive, other non-specified criteria can as well be included in an assessment.

The first criterion is the market share of systemically important functions a specific bank is in charge of.[966] It refers to Art. 8(1) Swiss Banking Act that deems functions systemically important if they are indispensable for the Swiss economy and cannot be substituted in the short term. Art. 8(1) Swiss Banking Act underscores the domestic deposits and loans business and payment transactions,[967] but is non-exhaustive.[968]

According to *Bahar/Peyer*, a competent authority methodically has to assess every function of which the specific bank has a considerable market share, with regard to whether or not it has to be considered systemically important.[969]

---

963 Art. 8(2) Swiss Banking Act. The translation follows the English version of the draft of the *Expertenkommission* (*Expertenkommission* (2010) Final Report, 65). The German version was transposed almost verbatim. See *Expertenkommission* (2014) Schlussbericht, 67.

964 See *Expertenkommission* (2014) Schlussbericht, 76; *Bundesrat* (2011) Botschaft TBTF, 4746; *Bahar/Peyer* (2013) Systemrelevante Banken, 384.

965 See *Bahar/Peyer* (2013) Systemrelevante Banken, 385.

966 See Art. 8(2)(a) Swiss Banking Act.

967 Art. 8(1) Swiss Banking Act. See also *Expertenkommission* (2010) Final Report, 65.

968 See *Bahar/Peyer* (2013) Systemrelevante Banken, 381.

969 See *Bahar/Peyer* (2013) Systemrelevante Banken, 385. However, it is also plausible for a competent authority to first establish a list of functions it deems systemically important and then check each bank's market share: *Bahar/Peyer*'s opinion reflects the understanding that every activity can potentially be systemi-

The second criterion is the amount of protected deposits within the meaning of Art. 37h(1) Swiss Banking Act, which supersedes the maximum amount of deposit insurance set down in Art. 37h(3)(b) Swiss Banking Act, which is 6 billion CHF.

To put that into perspective, it is worthwhile to take a look at the total amount of protected deposits: at the end of 2015, protected deposits amounted to 437 billion CHF. The share *UBS* and *CS* alone was 23.9% equalling 104.4 billion CHF.[970] This simple equation already suggests that the two banks easily fulfil the criterion.

The third criterion is the relationship between the bank's balance sheet and Switzerland's GDP and has the purpose of highlighting a bank's size.[971] While the academic value of a comparison of value added and bank size can be questioned,[972] it nevertheless allows for a rough illustration of a bank's size. It also allows for an illustration of whether or not the failure of the bank in question would considerably harm the Swiss economy and indicates whether such an event would exceed the country's capacity to rescue the institute.[973] As discussed above, the balance sheet total of *UBS* and *Credit Suisse* amounts to 2.6 times the Swiss GDP.[974]

The fourth criterion is the bank's risk profile, which is comprised of its (i) business model, (ii) balance sheet structure, (iii) quality of its assets, (iv) liquidity, and (v) leverage ratio.[975] According to the Federal Council, this provision takes into account that a higher risk profile leads to a higher probability of a failure and higher potential for damage.[976]

---

cally relevant including investment banking activities. However, as will be discussed, this can, in the author's opinion, only be agreed to with a major caveat (see the discussion in Chapter III.IV.C.b: non-ring-fenced bodies). Drawing from the practical experience of affected banks, it seems that the focus is clearly set on the domestic deposits and loans business and on payment transactions. (See Chapter III.IV.C.c: Affected banks). Therefore, an authority can simply check each bank's market share of these functions.

970 *Esisuisse* (2017) Jahresbericht 2016, 7. See also *Winzeler* (2013) Einlagensicherung, 763 (noting that due to the maximum amount of 6 billion, only small and medium-sized insolvencies can be solved. *Winzeler* furthermore argues that it is uncontested that failures of systemic relevant institutes cannot be absorbed by a private sector deposit insurance).

971 See Art. 8(2)(c) Swiss Banking Act; *Bundesrat* (2011) Botschaft TBTF, 4745.

972 See the critique of *Bahar/Peyer* (2013) Systemrelevante Banken, 386.

973 See *Bundesrat* (2011) Botschaft TBTF, 4745; *Bahar/Peyer* (2013) Systemrelevante Banken, 386.

974 See Chapter III.I.C.c: UBS and Credit Suisse.

975 See Art. 8(2)(d) Swiss Banking Act.

976 See *Bundesrat* (2011) Botschaft TBTF, 4745.

Bahar/Peyer argue that this criterion does not influence the systemic importance of a bank. This is because the risk profile of a bank does not impact the effect of its failure. They reason that the failure of bank with a low risk profile could lead to exactly the same impact as one of a bank that is especially risky. In contrast to Art. 8(2)(a-c) Swiss Banking Act, a bank that is not deemed systemically important by other criteria, could not be attributed this feature solely based on this criterion.[977]

Bahar/Peyer therefore suggest that the assessment of a bank's risk profile would be better situated as part of the stipulation of special requirements for banks that are already deemed systemically important, set down in Art. 9 Swiss Banking Act and not as part of their identification.[978]

c. Affected banks

The assessment of systemic importance is conducted by the SNB and involves a consultation of Finma.[979] According to Art. 8(3) Swiss Banking Act, the SNB then determines by order which banks and which of their functions are systemically important.

In November 2012, the SNB determined *UBS AG* and *CS Group AG* to be systemically important.[980] One year later, it added *Zürcher Kantonalbank*.[981] In June 2014, it issued an order of the same kind to *Raiffeisen*[982] and in September 2015 to *Postfinance*.[983] Altogether, Switzerland is home to five banking groups that its authorities consider systemically important.[984]

977 See *Bahar/Peyer* (2013) Systemrelevante Banken, 386–387.
978 See *Bahar/Peyer* (2013) Systemrelevante Banken, 386–387.
979 See Art. 8(3) Swiss Banking Act.
980 *SNB* (2012) Verfügungen Systemrelevanz.
981 *SNB* (2013) Verfügung Systemrelevanz.
982 *SNB* (2014) Verfügung Systemrelevanz.
983 *SNB* (2015) Verfügung Systemrelevanz.
984 As will be discussed, the manifestation of Swiss organisational requirements differ according to whether affected banks are domestically oriented or globally oriented. See Chapter III.IV.C.a.1: Ex ante separation.

D. Results

a. Focus of the scope

In all three jurisdictions of interest, the legislator chose to limit the application of structural reform requirements to banks that have certain characteristics. He therefore decided against the idea that structural reform requirements should apply to all banks, regardless of specific features such as size or importance for the domestic economy.[985]

While structural requirements in the three countries all aim at ensuring similar goals, each legislator chose a different focus for the scope: in the UK, the focus is set on core deposits. Only banks that are in charge of a certain amount of these deposits are affected by the ring-fencing requirement.[986] The UK ring-fencing regime thus concentrates on one of the activities it strives to protect.[987]

The German legislator, on the contrary, set the focus on trading activities. All banks that exceed certain thresholds with their trading portfolios and liquidity reserves are subject to the prohibition or the separation.[988] This reflects that according to the ring-fencing method chosen by the German legislator, certain risky activities should be kept at bay.[989]

The Swiss legislator chose a different approach: authorities have to conduct a general assessment to identify systemically important banks whose failure would do considerable harm to the Swiss economy and the Swiss financial system. As part of the assessment, however, authorities inspect, among other things, similar elements as those in focus of the German and the UK approach. They also take into account the amount of deposits held by the bank;[990] and they likely also consider the share of the trading portfolio and the trading activities in general as part of the assessment of the bank's risk profile.[991] The Swiss approach reflects that (i) it defines the pro-

985 Such a drastic scope was recommended e.g. by the Vickers report. See *ICB* (2011) Vickers Report, 39; see also the considerations regarding thresholds of the Liikanen Report, *HLEG* (2012) Liikanen Report 94–95.

986 See Chapter III.III.A: United Kingdom.

987 See Chapter III.IV.A.a: Ring-fenced body.

988 See Chapter III.III.C: Germany.

989 See Chapter III.IV.D.c: Ring-fencing method.

990 See Art. 8(2)(b) Swiss Banking Act; Chapter III.III.C.b: Thresholds and exemptions.

991 See Art. 8(2)(d) Swiss Banking Act; Chapter III.III.C.b: Thresholds and exemptions.

cess for identifying systemically important banks in general; and (ii) systemically important banks do not only have to comply with organisational measures but with a whole policy mix (including, in particular increased capital requirements).

b. Personal scope

In the UK, the personal scope of the ring-fencing regime includes all domestic legal entities that accept core deposits in EEA accounts. Such entities have to be ring-fenced if a certain threshold is exceeded.

The German Ring-fencing Act, in contrast, refers to the concept of a credit institution introduced by the EU's CRR: it applies to all CRR credit institutions and to all companies that belong to a group of institutions, a financial holding group or mixed financial holding group or a financial conglomerate to which a CRR credit institution belongs.[992] As set out in the chapter above,[993] CRR credit institutions are characterised by being active in both deposit-taking and lending.[994] It thusly does not include institutes that are active only in one of these businesses.[995]

Switzerland defines systemically important banks as banks, financial groups and bank-dominated financial conglomerates whose failure would considerably harm the Swiss economy and the Swiss financial system.[996] Banks are not just undertakings that are active in deposit-taking and lending. Undertakings that provide financing services and do not accept deposits but instead finance themselves over banks also fall within the definition of banks.[997] A literal interpretation of the respective provision would

---

992 See Chapter III.III.B.a: Personal scope.

993 See Chapter III.III.B.a: Personal scope.

994 See Art. 4(1)(1) CRR; see also *Schwennicke* (2016) Verbotene Geschäfte, 196; In greater detail *Schäfer* (2016) § 3 Verbotene Geschäfte, para 33. For a discussion of the differences between the definition of credit institutions in German and EU law, see *Schäfer* (2016) § 1 Begriffsbestimmungen, para 9–16.

995 See *Schäfer* (2016) § 1 Begriffsbestimmungen, para 14; See also *Möslein* (2013) Spartentrennung, 401; *Schwennicke* (2016) Verbotene Geschäfte, 196.

996 Art. 7(1) Swiss Banking Act. The translation follows the English version of draft of the *Expertenkommission* (*Expertenkommission* (2010) Final Report, 65). The original German draft was transposed verbatim. See *Expertenkommission* (2014) Schlussbericht, 67; *Bahar/Peyer* (2013) Systemrelevante Banken, 397.

997 See Art. 2(1)(b) Swiss Banking Ordinance; *Bahar/Stupp* (2013) Geltungsbereich, 18, 25. Banks that do not refinance themselves over deposits are in practice,

theoretically even allow for the inclusion of financial groups, which no bank but only a securities dealer is part of.[998]

Comparing the definitions of banks, one therefore finds that the German approach has the narrowest scope: it revolves around the CRR credit institution that cumulatively takes deposits and is active in lending. Switzerland and the UK do not require the cumulative provision of these services.

c. Thresholds

1. Clear cut thresholds?

Comparing the different jurisdictions, one finds that Germany and the UK use clear cut thresholds: in the UK, banks with core deposits of less than 25 billion £ are not required to ring-fence. In Germany, there is an absolute threshold for banking groups with a trading portfolio and liquidity reserves of at least 100 billion €; and a relative threshold for banks whose total trading portfolio and liquidity reserves exceed 20% of the balance sheet, which in total amounts to at least 90 billion €. All banks below these thresholds are exempted from complying with the German ring-fencing regime.

In Switzerland, in contrast, organisational measures apply if an assessment of the SNB results in finding a bank systemically important. As set out in the previous chapter, the assessment also includes taking into account the amount of deposits and the risk profile of a bank.[999] It also takes into account the ratio between a bank's balance sheet and Switzerland's GDP, and the market share of systemically important functions.[1000]

These criteria are theoretically suited to be used as thresholds. Most of them can be easily calculated on the basis of existing information. Only the risk profile includes a more detailed qualitative assessment of, *inter alia,* the business model. The Swiss expert commission and Government, however, decided against identifying certain thresholds and thus delegated

---

however, rare. For a detailed discussion, see *Bahar/Stupp* (2013) Geltungsbereich, 27–28.

998 Art. 7(1) in conjunction with Art. 3c(1) Swiss Banking Act. For the theoretical discussion of the inclusion of financial groups of which no bank but only a securities dealer is part of, see Chapter III.III.C.a: Personal scope.

999 Chapter III.III.D.a: Focus of the scope.

1000 For a detailed discussion of the assessment Chapter III.III.C: Switzerland.

the decision to the authorities. While this approach avoids some of the problems discussed below, it can be questioned with regard to transparency and possibly the principle of legality.[1001]

2. Consolidated basis

In both the UK and Germany, the thresholds are calculated on a consolidated basis. This means that the calculation takes into account the thresholds, i.e. either core deposits or the trading portfolio, of the whole banking group.[1002] For Switzerland, the assessment is also conducted on a consolidated basis. The Swiss approach is nevertheless much more focused on the systemic importance of a bank for Switzerland, which is reflected in the assessment process.[1003]

3. Setting the threshold

As the focus of the scope differs between the different jurisdictions (core deposits in the UK, trading portfolio in Germany and general assessment in Switzerland), the thresholds cannot be meaningfully compared. However, a few general observations on thresholds can be made.

A key problem of thresholds is how to set them. If a threshold is set arbitrarily, it discriminates against the affected parties (in this case banks that are then required to ring-fence); by that it adversely affects their competitiveness. Other banks would be given an advantage and general competition in the market would be reduced. Setting a threshold is therefore a difficult decision which should be well justified.

In the UK, the Government transparently set out its reasoning for the threshold and acknowledged that it may adjust over time to fall in line with banking practice.[1004] The argumentation of the Liikanen Report, on

---

1001 For a discussion of transparency and the principle of legality, see Chapter III.II.D.b: Legal Sources.

1002 See *De Vogelaere* (2016) Bank Structure Reforms, 32; see also Chapter III.III.A.a: Personal scope; Chapter III.III.B.a: Personal scope.

1003 For example, the majority of the criteria set out in Art 8(2) Swiss Banking Act are focused on Switzerland. See Chapter III.III.C.b: Threshold and exemptions.

1004 The UK Government chose the size of deposits, because it *"is most likely to reflect the level of benefit derived from ring-fencing vital banking services in a particular firm relative to the costs"*. With the threshold of 25 billion £, 90% of deposits

which the German Ring-fencing Act is based, in contrast is less convincing.[1005] The German Ring-fencing Act does not provide any information on the threshold, except referring to the Liikanen Report.[1006] This is particularly remarkable, as the Act does not completely transpose the threshold recommended by the HLEG, only parts of it.[1007]

Another key problem of thresholds is the risk of regulatory arbitrage. Due to the regulatory burden connected to exceeding a threshold, banks are incentivized to artificially remain below it. This can lead to distortion of the functioning of the market,[1008] such as if banks e.g. were not to accept deposits anymore to remain below the threshold. Thresholds have to take this into account. It can, however, also be in the interest of the public to incentivize banks not to exceed certain thresholds. For example, not to exceed the level of trading activities considered optimal.

In summary, thresholds have to be set in a way that ensures their goal is reached, either by identifying banks for which the application of requirements makes sense or by incentivizing other banks not to exceed certain thresholds.

---

protected by deposit insurance were held by ring-fenced banks and building societies. *HM Treasury* (2012) Banking Reform, 31, 31 Fn 19.

1005 In the Liikanen report, the absolute threshold of 100 billion € is reasoned with financial stability. The relative threshold, which is the ratio of the trading portfolio to total assets, aims at exempting banks with conservative business models. (See *HLEG* (2012) Liikanen Report, v; For an explanation of the Liikanen Report's thresholds, see Chapter II.I.C.c: Final proposal). In the author's opinion, more detailed explanation of the HLEG, why it recommends an absolute threshold of a trading portfolio of 100 billion € and the relative threshold, would have been desirable.

1006 The legislative materials note that the relative threshold of a trading portfolio of 20% of total assets is in the middle of the range for a relative threshold recommended by the HLEG. See *Deutscher Bundestag* (2013) Gesetzesentwurf Trennbankengesetz, 28.

1007 See Chapter III.III.D.e: Relation to expert commission recommendations; This has been criticised by many authors, see Chapter III.III.B.b: Threshold and exemptions.

1008 See e.g. Explanatory Memorandum to FSMA 2014 Order Nr. 1960, Sec. 7.5.

d. Other exemptions

Comparing the exemptions, one finds that there are similarities. In all three jurisdictions there are certain exemptions for insurance undertakings.[1009] Ring-fencing requirements are applicable only to banks.

In addition, in the UK and Germany, there are exemptions due to EU passporting. In both countries, banking groups which are headquartered in other EU Member States and provide services through a branch or cross-border, are exempted from the ring-fencing requirements. In case of subsidiaries, the requirements apply. In Germany, this derives from the BaFin's Interpretative Guidance,[1010] in the UK from the scope, which applies to all UK deposit-takers,[1011] i.e. a legal entity incorporated in the UK.[1012] The Swiss Banking Act applies to both foreign-controlled banks as they are organised in accordance with Swiss law[1013] and branches of foreign banks.[1014]

e. Affected G-SIBs

Comparing the affected banks in the various jurisdictions, one finds that G-SIBs are comprehensively covered by the structural reform requirements. Only in the UK, *Standard Chartered* does not have to ring-fence its deposit-taking business as it remains below the thresholds.[1015] All other G-SIBs in the respective jurisdictions are covered by domestic requirements.

1009 See the respective Chapters of III.III: Who Is Subject to the Fence?.

1010 The interpretation of BaFin is explained in more detail in Chapter III.III.B.a: Personal scope.

1011 Art. 2 FSMA 2014 Order No. 1960.

1012 See Art. 1 FSMA 2014 Order No. 1960; Art. 2(2)(d) FSMA 2016 Order No. 1032.

1013 *SNB*, Notes on the Banking Statistics, (September 28, 2017), https://data.snb.ch/en/topics/banken#!/doc/explanations_banken; Foreign-controlled banks are defined in Art. 3bis(3) Swiss Banking Act; see also Chapter III.I.C.b: Number of banks and their nature.

1014 See Art. 2(1) Swiss Banking Act; see also *Chapuis* (2013) Geltungsbereich, 47–54.

1015 *Nahmias* (2016) UK Banks, 5; See Chapter III.III.A.c: Affected banks.

f. Relation to expert commission recommendations

There are some key differences between the expert commissions' recommendations and adopted legislation regarding the scope of the structural reform requirements. While Switzerland stuck very closely to the recommendations, often transposing them verbatim,[1016] Germany and the UK applied some important changes.

The German Ring-fencing Act deviates in an important aspect from the Liikanen Report. The latter recommends an absolute threshold of a trading portfolio of 100 billion €, and provides for a range of possible percentages as relative thresholds. Importantly, however, these two factors only constitute a first assessment. In a subsequent second assessment, the share of activities to be separated is assessed. If they exceed a certain share of total assets not specified by the Liikanen Report, they would have to be separated.[1017] The German Ring-fencing Act, in contrast, does not stipulate a second stage assessment of the share of the activities to be separated. Therefore, such activities would also be prohibited or needed to be separated if they only account for a very small part of the trading portfolio. This is criticised by the majority of commentators and is indeed not expedient and desirable.[1018]

In the UK, the main deviation from the recommendations of the Vickers Report regarding the scope concerns the number of affected banks.[1019] The Vickers Commission balanced arguments for an introduction of a *de minimis* exemption for smaller banks, but ultimately recommended to include all banks.[1020] The adopted legislation, however, set down that all banks with core deposits of less than 25 billion £ do not have to ring-fence.[1021] This reflects the idea that ring-fencing is a costly regulatory burden for affected banks and that unrestricted universal banking is riskier for larger banks, because *"the impact of a failure and thus the importance of resolution and of reducing contagion, is greater the more customers and creditors are affect-*

1016 See e.g. the footnote on Art. 7(1) Swiss Banking Act, Chapter III.III.C.a: Personal scope.
1017 See Chapter II.I.C.c: Final proposal.
1018 For the critique, see the footnote in Chapter III.III.B.b: Thresholds and exemptions.
1019 See Chapter III.III.A.b: Threshold and exemptions; see also *De Vogelaere* (2016) Bank Structure Reforms, 22.
1020 See Chapter III.III.A.b: Threshold and exemptions; *ICB* (2011) Vickers Report, 39.
1021 See Chapter III.III.A.b: Threshold and exemptions.

ed".[1022] The exemption applies to a great number of banks and brings with it the problems of setting an effective threshold discussed in the chapter above.[1023]

IV. What Activities Fall on Which Side of the Fence?

This chapter addresses the question of what activities fall on which side of the fence, setting out the location of the fence. To facilitate the comparative analysis, the chapters on Germany and Switzerland orientate towards the UK structure:[1024] they differ between activities that are to be provided by the ring-fenced body and the non-ring-fenced body.[1025] Subsequently, the findings are summarized and the practical implementation of affected banks is discussed.

The chapter is of great importance to the assessment of whether or not the countries of interest implement ring-fencing as defined in the first part of the dissertation, as it sets out two core characteristics: (i) that it separates commercial banking activities from investment banking activities and (ii) that it at the same time seeks to maintain universal banking.[1026] These two characteristics are also key for identifying the method of ring-fencing used.[1027]

A. United Kingdom

a. Ring-fenced body

1. Core activities

The FSMA 2000 stipulates core activities that have to be provided by a ring-fenced body. As set out in the chapter above, currently the only core

---

1022 See *ICB* (2011) Vickers Report, 39.
1023 For a discussion of the problems when setting a threshold, see Chapter III.III.D.c.3: Setting the threshold.
1024 To underscore similarities, they also employ a similar terminology.
1025 Due to the different method of ring-fencing chosen in Germany, a modified order (beginning with the non-ring-fenced body) is justified.
1026 See Chapter I.IV.B: Ring-fencing as a structural reform.
1027 See Chapter I.VI: Different Methods of Ring-Fencing.

activity is accepting core deposits,[1028] which can be summed up as accepting deposits of retail clients and small businesses from the UK and all other EEA countries.[1029]

Both the Vickers Commission and the legislator decided against mandating that loans to individuals and small and medium-sized companies – a function important to the domestic economy – were to be considered core activities and could thus only be provided by ring-fenced banks.[1030] This is mainly because such a requirement would possibly lead to a reduced supply of credit.[1031]

Both the Vickers Commission and the UK Government, however, expect that a large proportion of the credit supply would be *"naturally"* provided by the ring-fenced banks, as banks need to match their liabilities.[1032]

2. Core services

Core services are services that are connected to core activities. As only the acceptance of core deposits is a core activity, core services currently include (i) facilities for the accepting of deposits or other payments into an account which is provided in the course of the acceptance of core deposits; (ii) facilities for withdrawing money or making payments from such an account; (iii) overdraft facilities for such an account.[1033] The Explanatory Notes to the Banking Reform Act 2013 clarify that it is not necessary for ring-fenced bodies to provide all of the core services. Some banks may, for example, *"choose not to provide overdraft facilities"*.[1034]

1028 See Chapter III.III.A.a: Personal scope.

1029 See *Britton et al.* (2016) Ring-fencing, 166. See also Chapter III.III.A.c: Affected banks.

1030 See *HM Treasury* (2012) Banking Reform, 16; *ICB* (2011) Vickers Report, 37–38.

1031 See *ICB* (2011) Vickers Report, 37–38.

1032 *ICB* (2011) Vickers Report, 37–38 (*"Naturally, if a large volume of deposits were placed within ring-fenced banks then a significant proportion of the credit supply would be expected to follow"*); *HM Treasury* (2012) Banking Reform, 16 (*"the Government's expectation is that where banks carry out other functions important to the domestic economy, such as the provision of domestic credit to households and SMEs [...], these will as a matter of practice be undertaken by their ring-fenced entities"*).

1033 Art. 142C FSMA 2000.

1034 Explanatory Notes to the Banking Reform Act 2013, para 32.

The continued provision of these core services by the ring-fenced body is protected by the regulators.[1035] They have the duty, when dealing with matters related to ring-fencing and in particular when making rules, to take the services into account and protect their uninterrupted provision.[1036]

3. Excluded activities and prohibitions

The FSMA 2000 and secondary legislation by the Treasury also identify (i) activities that are excluded and (ii) transactions that are prohibited for the ring-fenced bank.[1037] These activities must not be provided by the ring-fenced body.[1038] A violation results in disciplinary measures and penalties that can be imposed by the regulators on the basis of Part 14 of FSMA 2000.[1039] They can nevertheless be provided by other members of the group that the ring-fenced body belongs to.[1040]

b. Non-ring-fenced bodies

1. Excluded activities

The FSMA 2000 only mentions one excluded activity, namely dealing in investments as a principal,[1041] i.e. proprietary trading.[1042] It authorizes the

---

1035 See e.g. Sec. 2B(3)(c) FSMA 2000; Sec. 1IA, 1EA FSMA 2000; *PRA* (2017) Ring-fenced Bodies, 7 ("*The PRA seeks to ensure the continuity of the provision of core services by an [ring-fenced body]*").

1036 *HM Treasury* (2012) Sound Banking, 7.

1037 See below.

1038 See Sec. 142G FSMA 2000.

1039 See Sec. 142G(1) FSMA 2000; Explanatory Notes to the Banking Reform Act 2013, para 39.

1040 This follows from (i) the fact that there is no prohibition for the ring-fenced body to be part of a group that includes non-ring-fenced members; and from (ii) Sec. 142H, which sets down rules that specify the relationship of a ring-fenced body to non-ring-fenced group members.

1041 Sec. 142D(2) FSMA 2000.

1042 See *Britton et al.* (2016) Ring-fencing, 166; see also Chapter I.II.B.a: Proprietary trading.

Treasury to both set down exemptions for it[1043] and add other excluded activities by order.[1044]

The Treasury made use of the delegated power by clarifying that proprietary trading is to be understood within the meaning of the Regulated Activities Order 2001.[1045] It is thusly broadly defined as *"buying, selling, subscribing for or underwriting securities or contractually based investments [...] as principal"*.[1046] It, however, alters the definition by disallowing certain exemptions of that order,[1047] thus increasing the scope, as well as by introducing own exemptions,[1048] thus reducing the scope. The resulting broad definition *"excludes most derivatives and trading activity currently undertaken by wholesale and investment banks"*.[1049] It not just includes the trading of financial instruments, in particular market making, but also their underwriting.

The second activity excluded by the Treasury is the buying and selling of commodities as a principal, which can be understood as proprietary trading with commodities,[1050] for example oil or agricultural products.[1051] It may, however, be performed under certain circumstances, e.g. when commodities are required for the ring-fenced body's own consumption or use.[1052] Excluding commodities trading intends to shield the ring-fenced entity against unexpected changes in global commodities prices.[1053]

While the Explanatory Notes rightly point out that dealing with the ring-fenced body's own share is always permitted,[1054] the Order stipulates exceptions in which an activity is not considered excluded: among them is the management of risk for ring-fenced bodies, such as interest rate

1043 See Sec. 142D(2)-(3) FSMA 2000.

1044 See Sec. 142D(4)-(7) FSMA 2000.

1045 FSMA 2001 Order No. 544; see Art. 4 FSMA 2014 Order No. 2080.

1046 Art. 14 FSMA 2001 Order No. 544.

1047 Namely Art. 15, 19, 20 FSMA 2001 Order No. 544.

1048 See Art. 4 FSMA 2014 Order No. 2080.

1049 *HM Treasury* (2012) Sound Banking, 10; See also *Armour et al.* (2016) Financial Regulation, 517 (noting that it *"prevents [ring-fenced bodies] from engaging in almost all investment banking activities"*).

1050 See Art. 5 FSMA 2014 Order No. 2080.

1051 Another example for commodities would be precious metals, such as gold or silver. See Explanatory Memorandum to FSMA 2014 Order No. 2080, Sec. 7.4.

1052 See Art. 5 FSMA 2014 Order No. 2080.

1053 See Explanatory Memorandum to FSMA 2014 Order No. 2080, Sec. 7.4.

1054 This is due to to the exception of Art. 18A of FSMA 2001 exempting it from the scope of the proprietary trading definition. See Explanatory Note to the FSMA 2014 Order No. 2080, 19.

changes or exchange rate changes and the management of liquidity risk.[1055] This allows the ring-fenced body to hedge risks stemming from its principal business, the intermediation between savers and borrowers.[1056]

There is also an exception for transactions with a central bank,[1057] which ensures that a ring-fenced body can access central bank liquidity.[1058] In addition, there are provisions that regulate under which circumstances ring-fenced bodies can sell derivatives to their customers:[1059] they include quantitative limitations, for example limitations with regard to the ring-fenced body's own funds;[1060] and qualitative limitations such as specifications of the permissible financial products.[1061] Their intention is to allow for the provision of simple risk-management services business customers, including small businesses, often require.[1062]

In all these cases, activities that would otherwise qualify as proprietary trading and commodities trading are not considered excluded, and are thus permitted.

2. Prohibitions

The FSMA 2000 also delegates power to the Treasury to impose prohibitions on ring-fenced bodies via secondary legislation.[1063] This, of course, reminds of the excluded activities discussed above. The difference is, however, that the intention of the prohibitions is not to identify a specific activity a ring-fenced body must not engage in, but on *"captur[ing] transactions with specified counterparties or transactions in particular jurisdictions"*.[1064]

To shield it against intra-financial contagion, the Order prohibits ring-fenced bodies from having exposures to other financial institutions, in-

1055 See Art. 6(1)-(2) FSMA 2014 Order No. 2080, see also Explanatory Note to the FSMA 2014 Order No. 2080, 19.
1056 Explanatory Memorandum to FSMA 2014 Order No. 2080, Sec. 7.5.
1057 See Art. 8 FSMA 2014 Order No. 2080.
1058 Explanatory Memorandum to FSMA 2014 Order No. 2080, Sec. 7.5.
1059 See Art. 9–12 FSMA 2014 Order No. 2080 in conjunction with Art. 3(6) FSMA 2016 Order No. 1032; Explanatory Note to the FSMA 2014 Order No. 2080, 20.
1060 See in particular Art. 12 FSMA 2014 Order No. 2080 in conjunction with Art. 3(6) FSMA 2016 Order No. 1032.
1061 See in particular Art. 10–11 FSMA 2014 Order No. 2080.
1062 Explanatory Memorandum to FSMA 2014 Order No. 2080, Sec. 7.5.
1063 Sec. 142E FSMA 2000.
1064 See *HM Treasury* (2012) Sound Banking, 11.

cluding banks, investment firms and global systemically important insurers. A ring-fenced body may, however, have exposures to building societies and other ring-fenced bodies.[1065] It may also have exposures to other (non-ring-fenced) members of its own group under certain conditions, e.g. if transactions are conducted at arm's length.[1066]

Certain exceptions from the prohibition provide for the necessary flexibility for doing business. These include the following: analogously to the excluded activities,[1067] there is a provision allowing a ring-fenced body to have exposures for managing its own risk.[1068] It is also allowed to have exposures in connection with trade finance services[1069] and from loans or guarantees given in connection with the financing of infrastructure projects.[1070]

Another prohibition restricts ring-fenced bodies from having branches and subsidiaries outside the EEA. It may only have a subsidiary that provides services that are not regulated activities under the FSMA 2000.[1071]

c. Summary

In summary, it can be found that in banking groups that contain a ring-fenced body, a distinction between ring-fenced bodies and non-ring-fenced entities has to be made. There are substantial legal requirements governing which activities have to be provided by which group of entities.

1065 See Art. 14(1) in conjuntion with Art. 2(1) in conjunction with Art. 1(4) FSMA 2014 Order No. 2080. Exposures to subsidiaries of global systemically important insurers are also prohibited. See Art. 3(2)(c) FMSA 2016 No. 1032.

1066 See Art. 14(4) in conjuntion with Art. 2(1) in conjunction with Art. 1(4) FSMA 2014 Order No. 2080.

1067 Explanatory Memorandum to FSMA 2014 Order No. 2080, Sec. 7.6.

1068 See Art. 14(2)-(3) FSMA 2014 Order No. 2080.

1069 See Art. 15 FSMA 2014 Order No. 2080. Bank intermediated trade finance comprises services provided by banks (and often insurers or non-bank institutions) that allow importers and exporters in international trade to shift the risk of non-performance or non-payment to banks. See e.g. *Asmundson et al.* (2011) Trade and Trade Finance, 5. The Explanatory Memorandum notes as an example that the exception allows ring-fenced bodies to confirm letters of credit issued by foreign banks for the benefit of UK exporters. Explanatory Memorandum to FSMA 2014 Order No. 2080, Sec. 7.6.

1070 Art. 19A FSMA 2014 Order No. 2080; Art. 3(10) FSMA 2016 Order No. 1032.

1071 Art. 20 FSMA 2014 Order No. 2080; Explanatory Note to the FSMA 2014 Order No. 2080, 20.

A good way of illustrating this is to form groups of key activities according to where they have to be provided.[1072] The first group consists of activities that have to be provided within the ring-fenced body. This group currently only comprises core activities, namely accepting deposits of retail and small business clients.[1073]

The second group is made up of activities that are either excluded or prohibited for ring fenced bodies and can thus only be provided by the non-ring-fenced entity.[1074] These include the buying and selling, i.e. proprietary trading, of (i) securities, (ii) commodities and (iii) derivatives. It also includes market making services. In addition, it includes the underwriting of securities and having exposures to financial institutions that are neither ring-fenced bodies nor building societies. Moreover, only the non-ring-fenced entity can have branches and subsidiaries outside the EEA.[1075]

The third group includes activities that can be provided by both the ring-fenced body and the non-ring-fenced entity. They consist of all activities within the scope of the exemptions discussed in the chapters above. This group in particular includes the taking of deposits from high net-worth individuals, larger companies and relevant financial institutions;[1076] furthermore, deposit-taking of ring-fenced bodies and building societies, lending to individuals and companies.[1077] The group also contains the activity of risk managing, namely the hedging of liquidity, interest rate, currency, commodity and credit risks. In addition, transactions with central banks and trade finance, payment services[1078] and dealing in simple derivatives to its account holders.[1079] All these activities can be provided by both a ring-fenced body and a non-ring-fenced entity.

1072 See the illustration of *Britton et al.* (2016) Ring-fencing, 167.

1073 See Chapter III.III.A.a: Personal scope; see also *Britton et al.* (2016) Ring-fencing, 167; *HM Treasury* (2012) Sound Banking, 8–9.

1074 See Chapter III.IV.A.b: non-ring-fenced bodies.

1075 See Chapter III.IV.A.b: non-ring-fenced bodies; see also *Britton et al.* (2016) Ring-fencing, 167; Explanatory Memorandum to FSMA 2014 Order No. 2080, Sec. 7.4.

1076 See Chapter III.III.A.a: Personal scope; see also *HM Treasury* (2012) Sound Banking, 9; Explanatory Memorandum to FSMA 2014 Order Nr. 1960, Sec. 7.8.

1077 See Chapter III.IV.A.a.1: Core activities; Chapter III.III.A.a: Personal scope; see also *Britton et al.* (2016) Ring-fencing, 167.

1078 See Chapter III.IV.A.b: non-ring-fenced bodies. See also *Britton et al.* (2016) Ring-fencing, 167.

1079 See Chapter III.IV.A.b: non-ring-fenced bodies. See also *Britton et al.* (2016) Ring-fencing, 167; Explanatory Note to FSMA 2014 Order No. 2080, 20.

d. Affected banks

Beyond the limitations of the requirements set out above, banking groups have a degree of flexibility in structuring their business. Mortgage lending, for instance, can be conducted either by a ring-fenced body or by a non-ring-fenced entity. A banking group may thus decide to provide such activities by a ring-fenced body, close by the retail deposit-taking; others may decide to provide them from outside the ring-fence.[1080] A banking group's business model, as well as the choice where to put the fence, is reflected in the division of assets.[1081]

Barclays decided to place in its domestic bank, *Barclays UK*, approximately 25% of its risk-weighted assets, namely UK retail banking, UK consumer credit cards, UK wealth and corporate banking for smaller businesses. Outside the ring-fence, *Barclays International* will in particular provide services related to corporate, investment, and private banking. Risk-weighted assets outside the UK ring-fence total to approximately 75%.[1082]

HSBC chose to place only approximately 9% of its risk-weighted assets inside its ring-fenced body,[1083] *HSBC UK Bank*. It includes in particular the UK retail banking and wealth management business and the UK commercial banking business. Furthermore, it includes the UK based global private banking business and *Mark & Spencer's Financial Services*.[1084] The remaining 91% of risk-weighted assets are outside the ring-fence and include the investment bank operations in continental Europe, Asia and the Americas.[1085]

1080 *Britton et al.* (2016) Ring-fencing, 166.

1081 Depending on where a banking group decides to put the fence, there can be a smaller ring-fenced body and larger parts of the bank outside the ring-fence, or a larger ring-fenced body and only small parts outside the ring-fence.

1082 *Binham/Dunkley*, Regulators get ready to authorise 'ringfenced' UK banks, Financial Times (August 19, 2017). For a short description of the various activities mentioned above and an impression of the vast number of customer accounts that have to be moved to another entity, see *Byers* (2017) Barclays Ring-fencing Transfer Scheme, 13, 16–18.

1083 *Binham/Dunkley*, Regulators get ready to authorise 'ringfenced' UK banks, Financial Times (August 19, 2017).

1084 *Huertas* (2018) Scheme Report: HSBC, 3.

1085 *Binham/Dunkley*, Regulators get ready to authorise 'ringfenced' UK banks, Financial Times (August 19, 2017). For a more detailed list of segments within and outside the ring-fence, see *Huertas* (2018) Scheme Report: HSBC, 21–22.

RBS went for a considerably bigger ring-fenced body, with approximately 80% of its risk-weighted assets within the ring-fence.[1086] The current *RBS* PLC transfers its retail and commercial banking business, consisting of *inter alia* deposits, personal mortgages, personal unsecured loans, credit cards, business and commercial loans and trade finance services into the ring-fenced body *NatWest Holdings Limited.* Through a number of name changes, customers will continue to deal with *RBS.*[1087] The remaining 20% of risk-weighted assets are outside the ring-fence and consist of *RBS's* corporate and investment banking.[1088]

As discussed before, *Standard Chartered* does not have to apply the ring-fencing law.

B. Germany

Due to differences in the method of ring-fencing pursued by Germany, it makes sense to apply a modified structure, starting with the activities that have to be provided by the non-ring-fenced body, the financial trading institution, and subsequently discussing the activities that have to be provided by the ring-fenced body.

a. Non-ring-fenced body

1. Excluded activities

The German Banking Act stipulates that banking groups falling into the personal scope and exceeding thresholds set out in the chapter above[1089] must not conduct certain activities.[1090] These activities are considered particularly dangerous by the legislator[1091] and are listed exhaustively in the

1086 *Binham/Dunkley*, Regulators get ready to authorise 'ringfenced' UK banks, Financial Times (August 19, 2017).
1087 *Grundy* (2017) Ring-Fencing Scheme Royal Bank of Scotland, 7–8.
1088 *Binham/Dunkley*, Regulators get ready to authorise 'ringfenced' UK banks, Financial Times (August 19, 2017).
1089 For the personal scope and thresholds, as well as exemptions, see Chapter III.III.B: Germany.
1090 § 3(2) sentence 1 German Banking Act.
1091 *Deutscher Bundestag* (2013) Gesetzesentwurf Trennbankengesetz, 41; *Schwennicke* (2016) Verbotene Geschäfte, 197.

Act.[1092] To simplify the comparison, they will be referred to as "excluded activities".[1093] They may be conducted by a financial trading institution,[1094] i.e. a trading entity, which is allowed to remain a part of the group, but to which certain requirements apply.[1095]

The German Banking Act mentions as excluded activities: (i) proprietary business, (ii) a certain form of proprietary trading and (iii) the lending and guarantee business with certain counterparts.[1096]

The German Banking Act differentiates between proprietary business and proprietary trading. Delimiting these two excluded activities requires special attention because of the use of the term "proprietary business" for an activity that would usually be referred to as proprietary trading.[1097]

Proprietary business is to be understood within the meaning of § 1(1a) sentence 3 German Banking Act,[1098] namely all purchasing and selling of financial instruments on own account that is not proprietary trading.[1099] According to the German Banking Act, most proprietary trading, as will be shown below, is characterised by its service character; proprietary business, in contrast, is a bank's own short-term investment activity. This is underscored by examples given by the BaFin which include the purchase and sale of securities, money market instruments or derivatives on own account without service character, usually to benefit from *"existing or expected short-term differences between purchase and sale prices or movements of market prices, market values or interest rates"*.[1100] Such activities are excluded and thus have to be terminated or conducted outside the ring-fence.

1092 § 3(2) sentence 2 German Banking Act.

1093 This responds well to their character and to the designation used in the UK.

1094 § 3(3)(2) German Banking Act.

1095 See § 25f German Banking Act; The requirements and the relation to the banking group are discussed in Chapter III.V.B: Germany.

1096 § 3(2) sentence 2 German Banking Act; see also *BaFin* (2016) Interpretative Guidance, 7, 11.

1097 See Chapter I.II.B.a: Proprietary trading. These designations are used by the Bundesbank and BaFin in the English Interpretative Guidance and the translation of the German Banking Act. See *BaFin* (2016) Interpretative Guidance, 7; *Deutsche Bundesbank* (2014) Banking Act, 2–3.

1098 See *Deutscher Bundestag* (2013) Gesetzesentwurf Trennbankengesetz, 41 *BaFin* (2016) Interpretative Guidance, 7.

1099 *BaFin* (2016) Interpretative Guidance, 7.

1100 *BaFin* (2016) Interpretative Guidance, 7. See also *BaFin* (2018) Merkblatt Eigenhandel und Eigengeschäft; *Schwennicke* (2016) Begriffsbestimmungen, 67.

The German Banking Act defines four different kinds of proprietary trading,[1101] among the market making business and the business of systematic internalisers.[1102] What they generally have in common is their service character, which is the key characteristic of proprietary trading within the meaning of the German Banking Act.[1103] The service character does not require a certain legal structure for a transaction or an acquired financial instrument to be identical to the sold financial instrument. It is assumed if a client order is received before a specific transaction is entered into;[1104] service character can nevertheless also be given, if transactions are entered in anticipation of client orders.[1105]

Of the different kinds of proprietary trading, the German legislator only deemed one dangerous enough to exclude it from the ring-fence: high-frequency trading.[1106] It is the only kind of proprietary trading within the meaning of the German Banking Act that does not require a service character.[1107] It is characterised by the buying and selling of financial instruments on own account via high-frequency algorithmic trading technique, which can be understood as trading that involves *inter alia* a certain infrastructure to minimise network latencies and the ability of the system to trade without human intervention.[1108] All other forms of proprietary trading can be conducted within the fence.

To ensure that market making activities that potentially fall into the scope of the definition of high-frequency trading are not affected by its prohibition, the German Banking Act stipulates that high-frequency trading constitutes an excluded activity as long as it is not market making.[1109]

1101 § 1(1a)(4)(a)-(d) German Banking Act.

1102 See *BaFin* (2018) Merkblatt Eigenhandel und Eigengeschäft, 2 (The main difference between market makers and systemic internalisers is that the former trades on organised markets, multilateral or organised trading systems; the latter trades outside such market places without itself being a multilateral trading system).

1103 *BaFin* (2016) Interpretative Guidance, 7–8.

1104 *BaFin* (2016) Interpretative Guidance, 8; *BaFin* (2016) Auslegungshilfe, 8; *BaFin* (2018) Merkblatt Eigenhandel und Eigengeschäft, 4.

1105 *Schwennicke* (2016) Begriffsbestimmungen, 56; *Schwennicke* (2016) Verbotene Geschäfte, 197–198; *BaFin* (2016) Interpretative Guidance, 9.

1106 § 3(2) sentence 2 (3), in conjunction with § 1(1a)(4)(d) German Banking Act.

1107 *Schwennicke* (2016) Begriffsbestimmungen, 54, 56.

1108 See § 1(1a)(4)(d) German Banking Act; See also *BaFin* (2018) Merkblatt Eigenhandel und Eigengeschäft, 4–5. For a more detailed explanation of high frequency trading, see e.g. *Aldridge* (2010) High-Frequency Trading, 1–6, 21 et seqq.

1109 See § 3(2) sentence 2(3) German Banking Act.

The third excluded activity is the lending and guarantee business with certain counterparts: banks must not engage in lending and guarantee activities with certain hedge funds and alternative investment funds.[1110] Most authors consider this prohibition to apply to transactions without taking into account their actual risk potential, risk-mitigating factors[1111] or collateral.[1112] The BaFin's Interpretative Guidance, however, set down a major exemption: fully collateralised lending and guarantee business with hedge funds and AIFs is not prohibited.[1113]

BaFin's argumentation for a teleological reduction is based on the purpose of the German Ring-fencing Act and includes a comparative law reference to France and the EU Commission's draft regulation.[1114] The exemption of fully collateralised transactions with hedge funds and AIFs is one of the most important reliefs for banks in practice and mitigates the prohibition of the German Ring-fencing Act considerably.

Besides the excluded activities just mentioned, the German legislator sets down powers for the regulator to prohibit additional activities (and allow them only to be conducted within a trading entity). These powers can be exerted even if a banking group does not exceed the threshold. The condition is that the solvency of either the CRR credit institution or its group is endangered,[1115] which has to be proved by BaFin on the basis of objective criteria.[1116] Activities that can be prohibited are (i) market making,[1117] and (ii) other transactions within the meaning of the excluded activities above[1118] and (iii) other transactions involving financial instruments which are comparable with market making and the excluded activities above and in terms of their risk.[1119] While (ii) enables the BaFin to mandate a separation of excluded activities in situations where thresholds are

---

1110 See § 3(2) sentence 2(2) German Banking Act.

1111 See *Schelo/Steck* (2013) Trennbankengesetz, 240; *Schwennicke* (2016) Verbotene Geschäfte, 198.

1112 See *Kumpan* (2014) Verbot von Eigengeschäften, 208; *Schwennicke* (2016) Verbotene Geschäfte, 198.

1113 *BaFin* (2016) Auslegungshilfe, 12.

1114 *BaFin* (2016) Auslegungshilfe, 12; For a discussion of the EU Commission's draft regulation, see Chapter II.II.E.a: Activities restrictions.

1115 See § 3(4) German Banking Act.

1116 *Schwennicke* (2016) Verbotene Geschäfte, 202.

1117 § 3(4) German Banking Act.

1118 § 3(4) in conjunction with § 3(2) sentence 2 German Banking Act.

1119 § 3(4) German Banking Act.

not exceeded,[1120] (iii) is rather unclear due to its vague wording.[1121] It constitutes a possibly far-reaching delegation of power to BaFin.

2. Exceptions

The legislator then stipulates a number of exceptions, in particular regarding the prohibition of proprietary business. This is because he acknowledges that some transactions are associated with client business or are necessary for treasury and risk management.[1122]

The first exception concerns hedging transactions for transactions with clients. The German Banking Act allows such transactions, as long as they are not conducted for transactions with hedge funds and alternative investment funds.[1123]

This provision is criticised because its wording not only excludes the hedging of prohibited transactions with hedge funds and AIFs, but also the hedging of all transaction with such counterparties, including permitted transactions; for example, the sale of a stock option to an AIF client following its order,[1124] which would not be within the scope of the prohibition due to its service character. As this would counteract the aim of the provision, *Kumpan* suggests to teleologically reduce it to the hedging of prohibited transactions.[1125] The BaFin seems to partly agree and clarifies that hedging is allowed with regard to all transactions with AIFs and hedge funds that are not prohibited.[1126]

According to *Schelo/Steck*, hedging of prohibited transactions would also be desired in the interest of stability.[1127] That would also include the hedging of credit and guarantee business with hedge funds and AIFs. BaFin did

1120 *Schwennicke* (2016) Verbotene Geschäfte, 202.

1121 See *Schelo/Steck* (2013) Trennbankengesetz, 241.

1122 *Schelo/Steck* (2013) Trennbankengesetz, 240; *Schwennicke* (2016) Verbotene Geschäfte, 198.

1123 See § 3(2) sentence 3(1) German Banking Act; *BaFin* (2016) Interpretative Guidance, 36.

1124 See *Schelo/Steck* (2013) Trennbankengesetz, 240; *Kumpan* (2014) Verbot von Eigengeschäften, 210.

1125 See *Kumpan* (2014) Verbot von Eigengeschäften, 210.

1126 See *BaFin* (2016) Interpretative Guidance, 36, 37.

1127 See *Schelo/Steck* (2013) Trennbankengesetz, 240; *Kumpan* (2014) Verbot von Eigengeschäften, 210 (approving of this thought).

not take this up and clarifies that the hedging of prohibited transactions is not excepted from the prohibition.[1128]

The second exception concerns the management of interest rate, foreign exchange, liquidity and credit risk of the banking group.[1129] While the legislator did not explicitly mention the management of price risk,[1130] it is included by BaFin through a conclusion by analogy.[1131]

The third exception concerns transactions connected with long-term investments: it includes transactions (i) with the purpose of purchasing and selling long-term participations[1132] and transactions (ii) that are not conducted with the aim of exploiting actual or expected short-term differences between buying and selling prices or other price or interest rate movements in order to generate profits.[1133] Most authors emphasize the importance and extent of this exception.[1134]

According to the wording of the third exception, its transactions are not limited to certain counterparts and – as long as they are long-term – to a specific activity. *Kumpan* argues that they could therefore also include credits to hedge funds.[1135] *Kumpan*, however, then goes on to argue that this would counteract the purpose of the prohibition and that the exception should be understood only with regard to the prohibition of proprietary business.[1136] This argumentation would, incidentally, also apply to credits to AIFs. In the author's opinion, *Kumpan's* conclusion already results from a systematic interpretation of the provision. The BaFin, however, clarifies in its Interpretative Guidance that the exception does not ap-

1128 *BaFin* (2016) Auslegungshilfe, 38.

1129 See § 3(2) sentence 3(2) German Banking Act.

1130 *Möslein* identifies this rightly as an unintended gap in the legislation. See *Möslein* (2013) Spartentrennung, 403; *Schwennicke* (2016) Verbotene Geschäfte, 200.

1131 This is argued by the BaFin to close the unintended gap of banks not being able to manage price risks. See further *BaFin* (2016) Interpretative Guidance, 38.

1132 See § 3(2) sentence 2(3) German Banking Act; *Deutsche Bundesbank* (2014) Banking Act, 30.

1133 See § 3(2) sentence 2(3) German Banking Act; *Deutsche Bundesbank* (2014) Banking Act, 30; *BaFin* (2016) Interpretative Guidance, 38.

1134 See *Schwennicke* (2016) Verbotene Geschäfte, 200 (considering it the main exception of the Act); *Möslein* (2013) Spartentrennung, 403 (noting that the exception is particularly wide-ranging).

1135 *Kumpan* (2014) Verbot von Eigengeschäften, 210; *Schwennicke* (2016) Verbotene Geschäfte, 200.

1136 *Kumpan* (2014) Verbot von Eigengeschäften, 210; *Schwennicke* (2016) Verbotene Geschäfte, 200.

ply to lending and guarantee business with AIFs.[1137] It, however, does not mention hedge funds in the Interpretative Guidance, leaving room for further speculation.

b. Ring-fenced bodies

The German Ring-fencing Act does not explicitly mandate activities that have to be provided by the entities within the ring-fence.[1138] This relates to the method of ring-fencing pursued by the German legislator.[1139] It, however, derives from its scope that a CRR credit institution, i.e. a bank that provides both deposit-taking and lending, must remain within the ring-fence.[1140]

There are also activities that must not be provided by the financial trading institution. If a banking group chooses to provide such activities, it can thusly only provide them from within the ring-fence. These activities are either (i) listed explicitly by the German Ring-fencing Act, or (ii) derive from an interpretation of the law. The question what activities have to be provided by the ring-fenced entities is thus closely connected to the question what activities can and cannot be provided by a financial trading institution.

1. Explicit activity restrictions for the financial trading institution

Activities mentioned explicitly in the German Ring-fencing Act are payment services and e-money business. The financial trading institution is explicitly prohibited from providing such services.[1141] From a group perspective, payment services and e-money business can therefore only be provided from within the ring-fence.

1137 *BaFin* (2016) Interpretative Guidance, 38–39.

1138 In contrast to the UK ring-fencing model with one ring-fenced body (and potentially subgroups), the ring-fence of the German approach is much broader, comprising all entities except the non-ring-fenced financial trading institution. It is therefore appropriate to use the plural ("ring-fenced bodies" or "ring-fenced entities") regarding the German approach.

1139 See Chapter III.IV.D.c: Ring-fencing method.

1140 See Chapter III.III.B.a: Personal scope.

1141 § 25f(6) German Banking Act.

2. Other activity restrictions for the financial trading institution

Besides that, the German Banking Act is very unclear regarding what activities can and cannot be provided by the financial trading institution. *Möslein* notes that, unlike the Liikanen Report, the Act does not even stipulate a prohibition of deposit and credit business for the financial trading institution.[1142]

This is a remarkable flaw in the legal drafting of the Act. According to the wording of the Act, it would theoretically be conceivable that the trading entity would accept deposits.[1143] Moreover, as long as it would not provide loans and accept deposits cumulatively and would thusly be regarded as a CRR credit institution,[1144] it could accept retail deposits and provide banking services, such as guarantees and principal broking services.

It is obvious that it is not compatible with the purpose of the law that the trading entity accepts deposits and provides almost unlimited banking services. However, as also the BaFin's Interpretative Guidance does not set down clear rules, this unintended gap is to be closed by interpretation.

There are two starting points: (i) activities whose provision would be in conflict with the character of the financial trading institution, as indicated in the legislative materials; and (ii) activities whose provision would be in conflict with the purpose of the law.

i. First starting point: Financial service institution

The legislative materials to the German Ring-fencing Act characterise the financial trading institution as a financial service institution. This is also indicated by the German Banking Act.[1145]

1142 *Möslein* (2013) Spartentrennung, 405.

1143 See *Möslein* (2013) Spartentrennung, 405.

1144 This is also underscored by *Schaffelhuber/Kunschke* (2015) Trennbankengesetz, 400.

1145 *Deutscher Bundestag* (2013) Gesetzesentwurf Trennbankengesetz, 42; See *Auerbach/Schriever* (2016) CRR-Kreditinstitute, 849. The idea that the trading entity could be classified as a financial service institution is strengthened by § 1(1a) sentence 3 German Banking Act, which sets down that a trading entity that provides proprietary business is a financial service institution.

The German Banking Act traditionally[1146] differs between two categories of financial institutions: (i) the typical bank, which provides classic "banking services" and is referred to as "credit institution"; and (ii) a company that provides "financial services", which is referred to as "financial service institution".[1147]

A financial service institution within the meaning of § 1(1a) German Banking Act is defined as an *"undertaking[] which provide[s] financial services to others commercially or on a scale which requires commercially organised business operations, and which [is] not [a] credit institution[]".*[1148] The financial services provided by a financial service institution comprise for example the operation of a multilateral trading facility, proprietary trading, proprietary business in the case of a financial trading institution.[1149]

A credit institution as defined in § 1(1) German Banking Act, in contrast, conducts *"banking business"* which comprises *inter alia* the deposit business, credit business, guarantee business and underwriting business.[1150] Credit institutions are not mandated to report financial services because of their full license,[1151] if an undertaking provides at least one service attributed to banking business, it is considered a credit institution.[1152] The relation of financial service institutions to credit institutions is implied in their definition: an undertaking may be a financial services institution if it *"[is] not [a] credit institution[]"*,[1153] i.e. if it does not conduct banking business. Otherwise it is a credit institution.[1154]

ii. Deliberate decision or editorial error

The question arises whether this characterisation is an editorial error or a deliberate decision. If one considers it a deliberate decision, it follows that

---

1146 In addition, the German Banking Act recognises the concept of CRR credit institutions, see below.

1147 See below.

1148 § 1(1a) German Banking Act; *Deutsche Bundesbank* (2014) Banking Act, 2.

1149 See § 1(1a) German Banking Act. Regarding the provision on proprietary business (§ 1(1a) sentence 3 German Banking Act), the BaFin explains that it was created solely to secure the prohibition of § 3(2) sentence 2 German Banking Act. See *BaFin* (2016) Interpretative Guidance, 49–50.

1150 See § 1(1) German Banking Act; *Deutsche Bundesbank* (2014) Banking Act, 1.

1151 *Schäfer* (2016) § 1 Begriffsbestimmungen, Sec. 34.

1152 *Schäfer* (2016) § 1 Begriffsbestimmungen, Sec. 13.

1153 § 1(1a) German Banking Act; *Deutsche Bundesbank* (2014) Banking Act, 2.

1154 See e.g. *Deutsche Bundesbank* (2016) Merkblatt Finanzdienstleistungen, 5–6.

the German legislator did not intend to allow the financial trading institution the provision of banking business within the meaning of § 1(1) German Banking Act.[1155] Such a conclusion is, on the one hand, conceivable, as the trading entity's activities would thus be limited to financial services within the meaning of § 1(1a) German Banking Act.[1156] Core banking services, such as deposit-taking or lending, could not be provided by the trading entity. The legislator would thus have addressed the open question of the competence of the trading entity.

This conclusion on the other hand, creates problems with regard to some of the excluded activities, namely (i) credit and guarantee business with hedge funds and AIFs;[1157] and with regard to (ii) activities that should be allowed to be provided by the trading entity, according to the purpose of the Act, but would not be allowed due to the classification of the trading entity as a "financial services institution".

While the excluded activity of proprietary business is a financial service within the meaning of § 1(1a) German Banking Act and can therefore be provided by a financial service institution, the provision of credit and guarantee business (even if it is with hedge funds and AIFs) are typical banking services within the meaning of § 1(1) German Banking Act.[1158] Conducting credit and guarantee business with such entities would thusly require the trading entity to be a credit institution.[1159]

It furthermore creates problems with regard to activities that should be allowed to be provided by the trading entity. If the trading entity was deliberately considered a financial services institution by the legislator, it could not even voluntarily provide banking services within the meaning of § 1(1) German Banking Act. This includes investment banking services that can be considered risky, such as underwriting.[1160] While underwriting may not be risky enough to be prohibited for the ring-fenced entities, banks should nevertheless be allowed to voluntarily shift such activities to the trading entity.

1155 § 1(1) German Banking Act.

1156 § 1(1a) German Banking Act.

1157 See Chapter III.IV.B.a.1: Excluded activities.

1158 See § 1(1) German Banking Act; see also e.g. *BaFin* (2009) Merkblatt Garantiegeschäft; *Möslein* (2013) Spartentrennung, 402–403.

1159 For a similar argumentation, see *Schaffelhuber/Kunschke* (2015) Trennbankengesetz, 399.

1160 See § 1(1)(10) German Banking Act. As will be discussed, a legal comparative analysis finds that other jurisdictions do not allow for underwriting to take place within the ring-fence.

It can therefore be assumed that the characterisation of the trading entity as financial services institution in the legislative materials to the German Ring-fencing Act is indeed an editorial error. Taking into account the history of the Act, being drafted hastily in the run-up of the federal elections,[1161] the occurrence of such an editorial error is plausible. An interpretation suggests that there is therefore no prohibition of providing banking services for the trading entity.[1162]

iii. Second starting point: Objectives of the Act

Once it is established that the characterisation of the trading entity as financial services institution is an editorial error, the question of what activities the trading entity can and cannot provide resurfaces: activities it cannot provide can only be conducted within the ring-fence.

Technically, the answer could be found in § 32(2) German Banking Act. It allows BaFin to award an authorisation to provide banking services within the meaning of § 1(1) German Banking Act and financial services within the meaning of § 1(1a) German Banking Act only with regard to a particular service or subject to conditions.[1163]

BaFin could thusly award the trading entity the necessary authorisation, depending on what activities are to be provided by the trading entity. If the trading entity, for instance, was supposed to provide only proprietary business, BaFin could award an authorisation only for the financial service of proprietary business. The trading entity would in such a case be a financial services institute.

If the trading entity was supposed to only provide loans and guarantee business with hedge funds and AIFs, BaFin could award the respective authorisation only for the two banking services. The trading entity would in this case be a credit institute that can provide a limited number of banking services. If the trading entity was supposed to provide all excluded activities, BaFin could award the respective authorisation only for the excluded

1161 See *Hardie/Macartney* (2016) EU Ring-Fencing, 505–506, 512–513; *Deutscher Bundestag* (2013) Bericht Finanzausschuss, 3; Chapter III.II.B: Germany.

1162 This also seems to be suggested in the Annual Report of *Deutsche Bank*. *Deutsche Bank* (2018) 2017 SEC Form 20-F, 59 (noting that *"[t]he financial trading institution may be established in the form of an investment firm or a bank"*).

1163 See § 32(2) German Banking Act.

activities. The trading entity would in such a case be a credit institute that can provide a limited number of banking and financial services.[1164]

iv. Limitations

The trading entity's activities should, however, not be limited to the excluded activities alone. A certain flexibility is necessary for economic reasons (also the trading entity needs to be self-sufficient), to mitigate the invasiveness of the law, and to ensure that activities that may be considered risky can voluntarily be transferred to the trading entity.

The latter is especially true for market making. While the German Ring-fencing Act does not stipulate a prohibition or separation of market making services, it does authorize BaFin to order a separation under certain conditions.[1165] By this, the legislator acknowledges that market making may be risky as well. However, there is no provision that sets out that market making can voluntarily be provided by the trading entity. Similar considerations apply to underwriting.

At the same time, there must be limitations. Allowing the trading entity to provide, for example, unlimited deposit-taking services, would counteract the objectives of the German Ring-fencing Act, namely the insulation of deposits from risky activities, a higher resolvability of the latter and the reduction of tax payer-funded bailouts.[1166] *Schaffelhuber/Kunschke* come to a similar conclusion. They furthermore rightly note that this should not apply to deposits of institutional investors.[1167]

1164 This also seems to be suggested in the Annual Report of *Deutsche Bank*. *Deutsche Bank* (2018) 2017 SEC Form 20-F, 59 (noting that *"[t]he financial trading institution may be established in the form of an investment firm or a bank"*).

1165 This option is discussed in detail in Chapter III.IV.B.a.1: Excluded activities.

1166 For the objectives of the Trennbankengesetz, see *Deutscher Bundestag* (2013) Gesetzesentwurf Trennbankengesetz, 2, 27.

1167 *Schaffelhuber/Kunschke* (2015) Trennbankengesetz, 400; Institutional investors are not included in the German Banking Act's understanding of deposits. See *Schäfer* (2016) § 1 Begriffsbestimmungen, para 46; *BaFin* (2014) Merkblatt Einlagengeschäft, 2–3.

3. Conclusio

Drawing from the above, clearer rules setting out the legislator's and regulator's idea of both the trading entity's character and the scope of activities it can and cannot provide are desirable. Based on the historical interpretation, which was complemented by a systematic and teleological interpretation, it can be established that the qualification of the trading entity as a financial trading institution in the legislative materials is an editorial error. The trading entity is therefore not limited to financial services.

However, from a teleological and systematic interpretation it can be drawn that certain limitations are necessary and that the trading entity should not be allowed to accept deposits. All other banking services and financial services should be allowed to be provided by the trading entity.

Activities that have to be provided by the ring-fenced bodies are thus payment services and e-money business, as well as the acceptance of retail deposits.

c. Summary

Summing up the findings, it can be stated that in banking groups that contain a CRR-credit institution and that exceed the thresholds, a distinction between entities within the ring-fence and a non-ring-fenced trading entity, a so-called financial trading institution, has to be made. This is illustrated according to *Britton et al.*,[1168] who form groups of key activities according to where they have to be provided. Due to significant uncertainties regarding the character of the trading entity outlined above,[1169] the following paragraphs cautiously strive to distribute activities that can with sufficient certainty be classified.

The first group consists of activities that have to be provided within the ring-fence. Due to the scope of the rules[1170] and the reflections on the character of the trading entity,[1171] it seems to be beyond controversy that the cumulative activity of providing deposit-taking and lending services falls

1168 See the illustration of *Britton et al.* (2016) Ring-fencing, 167.

1169 See Chapter III.IV.b.2: Other activity restrictions for the financial trading institution.

1170 See Chapter III.III.B: Germany.

1171 See Chapter III.IV.b.2: Other activity restrictions for the financial trading institution.

into this group; furthermore, payment services and e-money business. From an interpretation of the German Ring-fencing Act it can be concluded that the activity of deposit-taking (except of institutional investors) can also only be provided by the ring-fenced entities.

The second group comprises activities that have to be provided outside the ring-fence by the financial trading institution. These excluded activities are (i) proprietary business, (ii) high frequency trading except for market making and (iii) lending and guarantee business with hedge funds and AIFs.[1172]

The third group are activities that can be provided by both the entities within the ring-fence and the non-ring-fenced trading entity. Due to the unclear character of the trading entity, this group is the hardest to identify. The interpretation of the German Ring-fencing Act conducted above suggests that the third group contains all banking services within the meaning of Art. 1(1) German Banking Act, except for deposit-taking and all financial services within the meaning of Art. 1(1a) German Banking Act, with the exception of the excluded activities. It comprises *inter alia* underwriting, market making, fully collateralised lending and guarantee business with hedge funds and AIFs and the general loans business.

d. Affected banks

It is remarkable that there is very little information available on the implementation efforts of affected banks.[1173] This is particularly odd, as the provisions of § 3(2)-(3) and § 25f are applicable since July 2015.[1174] Even when taking into account the identification and implementation periods of § 3(3) German Banking Act and extensions granted by BaFin, such as the

---

1172 See Chapter III.B.a: non-ring-fenced body.

1173 Additionally to extensive research, the author contacted both BaFin and the Association of German Banks. BaFin was not able to answer the query due to its duty of confidentiality according to § 8 German Banking Act. The Association of German Banks did not have any information on its members activity concerning the establishment of financial trading entities available. Also in the BaFin Journal of February 2016 (*Stubbe* (2016) Trennbanken, 10) and in the response of the German Government to a parliamentary question (*Deutscher Bundestag* (2016) Antworten der Bundesregierung, 42–43) there is no information on the establishment of a financial trading institition.

1174 § 64s(2) German Banking Act. For a detailed discussion of the application timeline, see Chapter III.VI.B: Germany.

one granted for *Deutsche Bank*,[1175] it is noticeable that there is hardly any reporting of restructuring efforts. In the BaFin *Journal* of February 2016, there is also no information on the establishment of a financial trading institution.[1176] As far as the author is concerned, it can thus be concluded that no financial trading institution has been established so far.

C. Switzerland

a. Ring-fenced body

1. Ex ante Separation

The Swiss Banking Act stipulates in Art. 9(2)(d) that banks which are determined systemically important by the SNB must fulfil various special requirements. One of them is that they have to provide an emergency plan regarding structure, infrastructure, management and controls, as well as internal liquidity and capital flows. The emergency plan must be immediately realizable and must ensure that systemically important functions can be continued in case of an imminent insolvency.[1177]

In addition to the emergency plan, the Swiss Banking Ordinance sets down a framework for a resolvability assessment, which aims at incentivising banks with capital rebates to enhance their general resolvability exceeding the minimum requirements of the emergency plan.[1178] This chapter focuses on the emergency plan, as it sets down mandatory minimum requirements.

While, according to Art. 9(2)(d) Swiss Banking Act, a credible plan would suffice to fulfil the special requirement, there is strong evidence for the assumption that the parties involved had *"very concrete expectations"* on

1175 *Deutsche Bank* was granted an extension of the application of the German Ring-fencing Act until June 30, 2017. See *Deutsche Bank* (2017) 2016 SEC Form 20-F, 26.

1176 *Stubbe* (2016) Trennbanken, 10. See also the response of the German Government to a parliamentary question. *Deutscher Bundestag* (2016) Antworten der Bundesregierung, 42–43.

1177 See Art. 9 Swiss Banking Act.

1178 Art. 65, 66 Swiss Banking Ordinance. For a discussion of the relation between the emergency plan and measures to enhance general resolvability, see Chapter III.V.C.a: Legal sources.

certain concrete organisational measures that affected banks have to implement.[1179]

i. Caveat

In line with the research focus of the dissertation, the following review is focused on the organisational requirements for Switzerland's G-SIBs, *UBS* and *Credit Suisse.* As outlined above, a number of other banks have been considered systemically important by the SNB since 2013.[1180] Authorities differentiate quite prominently two groups of banks considered systemically important by the SNB: (i) globally active "big banks",[1181] and (ii) domestically oriented systemically important banks.[1182]

Domestically oriented systemically important banks are quite different to the globally active big banks. They are less complex and less interconnected with global markets. Furthermore, their investment banking activities are of less weight and their orientation is – as their name implies – mainly domestic.[1183] Therefore the Swiss organisational measures apply differently. It is likely that there is no need for an ex ante separation of systemically important activities, because these are to a large extent their core business.

This is also noted by the EFD, stating with regard to the implementation period for the emergency plan that *"based on today's state of knowledge"* domestically oriented systemically important banks, in contrast to the G-SIBs*"[...] do not plan larger organisational or structural changes"*.[1184] For do-

1179 See *Hofer* (2014) Structural Reforms, 325.

1180 See Chapter III.III.C.c: Affected banks.

1181 The term "big bank" corresponds to the SNB's category for banks it describes as *"economically important"*, active in all business areas, *"in particular [in] investment banking"*. *SNB*, Notes on the Banking Statistics, (September 28, 2017), https://data.snb.ch/en/topics/banken#!/doc/explanations_banken; see Chapter III.I.C.b: Number of banks and their nature.

1182 The distinction can already be found in the TBTF Review of 2015. See *Bundesrat* (2015) Bericht Too Big to Fail, 1929, 1942; see also the provision of Art. 60 Swiss Banking Ordinance (stipulating a different implementation period for domestically oriented banks). While globally active systemically important banks are primarily determined by the FSB, Finma determines other, domestically oriented systemically important banks. See Art. 124a ERV; see also *Bundesrat* (2017) Bericht systemrelevante Banken, 4850.

1183 See *EFD* (2016) Erläuterungsbericht, 6.

1184 Own translation from German original, see *EFD* (2016) Erläuterungsbericht, 6.

mestically oriented systemically important banks, the emergency plan is therefore likely to remain a plan.

ii. Mere planning?

The expert commission had already hinted that certain changes to the organisation of the affected institutes would possibly be necessary to ensure the credibility of the emergency plan.[1185] This understanding deepened in the course of the legislative process. While the Swiss Banking Act is rather vague regarding the emergency plan[1186] and does not explicitly mention measures exceeding mere planning, a different tone is set in particular by the Swiss Banking Ordinance and its legislative materials.

The Swiss Banking Ordinance concretises the emergency plan and organisational measures. It first stipulates in Art. 60(1) that a systemically important bank has to ensure that its systemically important functions can – independently from the rest of the bank – be continuously provided in the case of imminent insolvency; and that the bank has to take the necessary measures for that.[1187]

While this provision reminds of Art. 9(2)(d) Swiss Banking Act, it rephrases it – the word emergency plan is missing; it is first used in the subsequent section,[1188] which stipulates that the bank has to describe the necessary measures (that have already been taken according to Art. 60(1) Swiss Banking Ordinance) in an emergency plan, in which it proves that it

1185 The expert commission, for instance, noted that the "*emergency plan must be designed in such a way that it can be implemented within a very short space of time in the face of a crisis. The timing at which implementation would need to begin, as well as the question of what further organisational measures would need to be taken in addition to the emergency plan itself and even before its implementation, depend on the existing organisation of the bank, the specific emergency plan in question, and the remaining capital cover.*" *Expertenkommission* (2010) Final report, 39; see also *Expertenkommission* (2010) Schlussbericht, 40; The expert commission also noted that "*[a]t a contents level, the banks must be able to show that they have put in place the prerequisites for the continuation of systemically important functions through specific organisational measures that go beyond the mere planning stage*". *Expertenkommission* (2010) Final report, 39; *Hofer* (2014) Structural Reforms, 326.

1186 See Art. 9(2)(d), 10(2) Swiss Banking Act.

1187 Art. 60(1) Swiss Banking Ordinance.

1188 Art. 60(2) Swiss Banking Ordinance.

is capable to ensure the continuation of the systemically important activities.

This slight difference in the wording already reveals the understanding that mere planning does not suffice. Measures have to be taken in advance to ensure the survival of systemically important activities. Compared to Art. 9(2)(d), these measures are now in the focus of attention, not a comprehensive plan.

Art. 60(3) Swiss Banking Ordinance is more forthright, as it stipulates explicitly that measures of the emergency plan have to be implemented ex ante, as far as the uninterrupted continuation of systemically important functions requires.[1189] While this understanding, as demonstrated, already existed in the expert commission's report, it emerges in an unprecedented clarity in the Swiss Banking Ordinance and its legislative materials.

iii. Three options?

The legislative materials to the Swiss Banking Ordinance outline three different options for affected banks in the context of the emergency plan: two of the options require transferring systemically important functions in the case of imminent insolvency. They differ with regard to the the counterparty, which can either be (i) an independent legal entity with a banking license that has to be created beforehand, or (ii) a third party which has agreed to a bankruptcy remote arrangement.[1190] Both options constitute an ex post separation.

The third option is the ex ante separation of systemically important functions onto a legal entity within the framework of the bank's business model.[1191] A remarkable detail in this context is that the EFD claims this option matches UK ring-fencing.[1192] As pointed out by *Hofer*, the legis-

1189 Art. 60(3) Swiss Banking Ordinance.

1190 *EFD* (2012) Kommentar Bankenverordnung, 10.

1191 *EFD* (2012) Kommentar Bankenverordnung, 10.

1192 The EFD mentions this in a footnote (*EFD* (2012) Kommentar Bankenverordnung, 10 Fn 12; see also *Hofer* (2014) Structural Reforms, 329). While it is discussed in greater detail below (see Chapter III.IV.c: Ring-fencing method; Chapter III.V.D.b.2: Ring-fencing in Switzerland), the importance of this detail has to be underscored. It can be regarded as another hint for the suggestion that regulators had a clear concept in mind.

lative materials hardly conceal that this option is the regulator's favourite.[1193]

This can be gathered from the legislative materials in two ways. Firstly, they underscore that an ex ante separation has the advantage that through the provision of systemically important functions during daily business, it can be assumed that their continuation would work out in the case of an emergency.[1194] Secondly, they note that it is doubtful whether the first option (transferring systemically important functions in the case of imminent insolvency onto an independent legal entity that has to be created beforehand) can be effective without implementation of additional measures of an emergency plan.[1195]

The viability of a transfer of systemically important functions to a third party on the basis of a bankruptcy remote arrangement can also be questioned on reasonable grounds. *Hofer* notes that this *"basically means that UBS could sell to CS and vice versa in the Swiss banking environment"*. This would create an even bigger bank and would further contribute to too-big-to-fail. There could moreover be a scenario in which both banks are affected by a crisis. According to *Hofer*, a bank would only agree to acquiring systemically important functions in a bankruptcy remote arrangement under the condition of government support.[1196] *Bahar/Peyer* note that bankruptcy remote arrangements can be regarded realistic only in limited business segments characterised by intensive cooperation, e.g. in the form of a joint ventures.[1197]

It is furthermore hard to imagine that this option would not also require some form of ex ante separation. Otherwise, the transferral of systemically

1193 *Hofer* (2014) Structural Reforms, 329.

1194 *EFD* (2012) Kommentar Bankenverordnung, 10.

1195 See *EFD* (2012) Kommentar Bankenverordnung, 10; see also *Nobel* (2012) Bank- und Kapitalmarktrecht, 10 (noting that big banks are recommended to ex ante separate systemically important functions, as an ex post bridge bank solution cannot be considered reliable); *Hofer* (2014) Structural Reforms, 329. For a discussion of limits of a bridge bank, see *Binder* (2017) Systemkrisenbewältigung durch Bankenabwicklung?, 62–64.

1196 See *Hofer* (2014) Structural Reforms, 331–332. *Roth* (2012) Too-Big-to-Fail, 291–292 (*Roth* calls into question the ability of a purchaser to continue providing systemically important functions in case of an emergency). For a discussion of the sale to a purchaser that is not a bridge bank, see *Binder* (2017) Systemkrisenbewältigung durch Bankenabwicklung?, 62–64.

1197 See *Bahar/Peyer* (2013) Systemrelevante Banken, 411.

important activities in a short time frame (over a weekend)[1198] in a way that keeps them uninterrupted is hardly thinkable.

Of the options suggested by the legislative materials to the Swiss Banking Ordinance, therefore only the ex ante separation remains. In its 2015 report on the Swiss too-big-to-fail package, the Federal Council seems to confirm this noting that *"[i]n Switzerland, the ex post separation of systemically important parts [...] proved to be problematic"*.[1199] It then points out that both the Swiss G-SIBs decided for an ex ante separation.[1200]

It can thus be stated that while the authorities non-exhaustively mention three options of ex ante and ex post separation in the context of the emergency plan, affected big banks seem to have little choice than to implement an ex ante separation of systemically important functions.[1201]

2. Systemically important functions

Art. 8(1) Swiss Banking Act deems functions systemically important if they are indispensable for the Swiss economy and cannot be substituted in the short term. *Bahar/Peyer* point out that this definition derives from the FSB Guidance on identifying critical services.[1202] The FSB Guidance suggests that when determining the criticality of a service, it first has to be assessed whether a disruption of the service *"is likely to have a material negative impact on a significant number of third parties"*. In a second step, the market of the service has to be assessed. The lower the ability of the market to substitute a failing provider quickly, the more likely that a service is considered critical.[1203]

With regard to Art. 8(1) it can therefore be drawn that a specific function can be considered indispensable if its disruption would have a nega-

1198 The transferral has to be conducted in the course of a weekend. See *EFD* (2012) Kommentar Bankenverordnung, 10.

1199 *Bundesrat* (2015) Bericht Too Big to Fail, 1935 (Own translation from German original).

1200 *Bundesrat* (2015) Bericht Too Big to Fail, 1935; see also Chapter III.IV.C.c: Affected banks.

1201 While the assessment that the ex ante separation is more reliable than an ex post transfer of systemically important functions on bridge bank or third party is to be agreed to, the practice of listing potential options and simultaneously indicating that there is little choice to the ex ante separation is to be criticised.

1202 *FSB* (2013) Guidance Critical Functions; *Bahar/Peyer* (2013) Systemrelevante Banken, 381–382.

1203 See *FSB* (2013) Guidance Critical Functions, 8–9.

tive material impact on the Swiss economy; if it cannot be substituted in the short term, i.e. if other market participants cannot provide the function or a comparable service.[1204]

Art. 8(1) Swiss Banking Act emphasizes the domestic deposits and loans business and payment transactions, but is non-exhaustive.

The legislative materials to the Swiss Banking Act only slightly concretise these terms, mentioning in particular (i) all liabilities due to domestic customers, i.e. deposits, (ii) loans to businesses of the real economy and unused credit limits of businesses of the real economy, and (iii) domestic mortgage loans with a remaining term of under one year.[1205] They additionally identify operative services systemically important banks provide for other domestic banks as another potential systemically important function.[1206] The highlighted systemically important functions can be attributed to commercial banking.

A central requirement for the regulator to approve an emergency plan is furthermore that the entity is self-sufficient, i.e. that it constitutes a business unit that can survive on its own, independently from the rest of the bank.[1207] It can therefore be necessary to transfer other business units into the ring-fenced body, for example wealth management services.[1208] There are, however, no given requirements on how the bank has to ensure self-sufficiency.[1209]

b. Non-ring-fenced bodies

Bahar/Peyer note that the fact that the list of the systemically important functions in Art. 8(1) Swiss Banking Act is non-exhaustive implies that other activities than those specifically mentioned can be regarded systemically important. This is certainly true. However, they refer in this context to ac-

---

1204 See *Bahar/Peyer* (2013) Systemrelevante Banken, 381–382.

1205 See *Bundesrat* (2011) Botschaft TBTF, 4747.

1206 See *Bundesrat* (2011) Botschaft TBTF, 4747; *Bahar/Peyer* (2013) Systemrelevante Banken, 382.

1207 Expert Interview, Affected Bank, September 28, 2017; see also *FSB* (2014) Structural Banking Reforms, 10.

1208 Both *Credit Suisse* and *UBS* reinforced their national systemically important functions with wealth management functions. See Chapter III.IV.C.c: Affected banks.

1209 This can be regarded as a manifestation of the principle of subsidiarity. See Chapter III.II.C.b.2: Subsidiarity principle.

tivities attributed to investment banking. As an example, they give underwriting and market making, arguing that these services play an important role in the functioning of the capital market as alternative sources of finance for businesses of the real economy.[1210] This argumentation can be agreed to only with a major *caveat.*

According to the legislative materials to the Swiss Banking Ordinance, investment banking activities are explicitly not desired to be conducted within the entity that provides systemically important functions. The EFD indicates that the *"implementation of the emergency plan is to be granted considerably more weight if the systemically important functions are provided together with riskier operations such as investment banking under the roof of a universal bank"*.[1211] The EFD adds that *"[e]ven though no (full) separation of business segments can be demanded in the context of the emergency plan, it is an important element of the concept of systemically important functions that no contagion can be spread from the remaining bank"*.[1212]

Hofer rightly notes that this can be broken down to the message that even though no separation of retail banking and investment banking can be mandated, the regulator will make it considerably harder for banks to receive approval for their emergency plans if those business segments are kept together.[1213] *Bahar/Peyer* do not insinuate this, but simply derive that keeping systemically important functions within a universal bank would effect a more careful assessment of the emergency plan by Finma.[1214]

The aim of separating systemically important functions, which in themselves are largely attributable to commercial banking, from investment banking activities is also reflected in the EFD considering the ex ante separation (which, as established above, can be identified as the only viable option for affected banks) as matching *"the example"*[1215] of the UK Vickers Commission ring-fencing model.[1216] Similarly, Finma implies in its 2014

1210 See *Bahar/Peyer* (2013) Systemrelevante Banken, 384.

1211 Own translation from German original, see *EFD* (2012) Kommentar Bankenverordnung, 10–11; cf. *Hofer* (2014) Structural Reforms, 330.

1212 Own translation from German original, see *EFD* (2012) Kommentar Bankenverordnung, 11; cf. *Hofer* (2014) Structural Reforms, 330.

1213 See *Hofer* (2014) Structural Reforms, 330.

1214 See *Bahar/Peyer* (2013) Systemrelevante Banken, 425.

1215 Own translation from German original, see *EFD* (2012) Kommentar Bankenverordnung, 10 Fn 12.

1216 *EFD* (2012) Kommentar Bankenverordnung, 10 Fn 12; see also *Hofer* (2014) Structural Reforms, 329; While this is discussed in greater detail below (see

annual report that Swiss emergency planning leads to the functional separation of commercial banking and investment banking.[1217]

The intent to separate systemically important functions from investment banking and in particular proprietary trading is furthermore clearly articulated by the Federal Council in response to a parliamentary motion. The Federal Council noted that "*Finma will ensure with the emergency plan, which has to be constantly adjusted, that the continuation of systemically important functions is not endangered by other business segments in the event of a crisis. It is probable that these business segments that have to be delimited in the emergency plan will include investment banking as a whole or in parts and possibly proprietary trading*".[1218]

Time has shown that regulators in Switzerland indeed exerted pressure on affected banks to separate their retail banking activities considered systemically important from investment banking activities.[1219] This, however, is hardly surprising. It would indeed be counteracting against the key goal of ensuring the continuation of (domestic) systemically important functions if investment banking activities were allowed to be included. This particularly applies to high-risk trading activities and global investment banking activities. Only very limited investment banking activities can be thought to be conducted within the domestic entity, for instance domestic underwriting, M&A, or advisory services.

c. Affected banks

Because Swiss legislation only stipulates very few and rather vague provisions, special attention has to be paid to the implementation efforts of Swiss banks. In line with the research objective of the dissertation, the focus is set on G-SIBs, namely *UBS* and *Credit Suisse*. Both their Swiss entities that were established in the context of the ex ante separation of systemical-

---

Chapter III.IV.D.c: Ring-fencing method; Chapter III.V.D.b.2: Ring-fencing in Switzerland), the importance of this detail has to be underscored. The Vickers Report and the following Banking Reform Act 2013 put the spotlight on the separation of retail from investment banking. Referring to this model as being exemplary indicates clearly that there is a concrete expectation of banks for a separation of retail and investment banking.

1217 See *Finma* (2015) Jahresbericht 2014, 25.

1218 Own translation from German Original, see *Schweizerische Bundesversammlung* (2011) Motion Leutenegger Oberholzer; *Hofer* (2014) Structural Reforms, 331.

1219 See Chapter III.IV.C.c: Affected banks.

ly important functions shall be examined. The acquired investment banking activities are of particular interest, as they indicate potential limitations set by regulators.

1. UBS

UBS Switzerland AG was established in 2014 as a fully-owned subsidiary of *UBS AG*.[1220] It remained largely inactive[1221] until 2015, when it acquired from its parent company all assets and liabilities of the business divisions "Retail & Corporate" and "Wealth Management", as far as the latter is booked in Switzerland.[1222] Personal and corporate banking and wealth management booked outside of Switzerland remained in *UBS AG*. It furthermore acquired select back office functions, access to the financial market infrastructure for the respective business, including payment and custody infrastructure[1223], as well as certain business from the investment bank.[1224]

The acquired activities from the investment bank include (i) market making on the SIX Swiss Exchange,[1225] (ii) bank notes business[1226] and (iii) secured financing transactions.[1227] The remaining investment bank and as-

1220 See Commercial Register Entry, *UBS Switzerland AG*, (September 08, 2014), Public deed of the foundation of *UBS Epsilon AG*; Commercial Register Entry, *UBS Switzerland AG*, (October 29, 2014), Public deed regarding the resolutions of the extraordinary shareholders meeting of *UBS Epsilon AG*, (in which the company name was changed to *UBS Switzerland AG*).

1221 *UBS* (2016) Annual Report 2015, 766.

1222 See *UBS* (2016) Annual Report 2015, 766; see also Commercial Register Entry, *UBS Switzerland AG*, (May 28, 2015), Report on Share Capital Increase, 2.

1223 For a good explanation of custody services, see *TheClearingHouse* (2016) Custody Services of Banks, ii-iv.

1224 *UBS* (2016) Annual Report 2015, 766.

1225 For a description of market making, see Chapter I.II.B.b: Market making.

1226 Banknotes business refers to the business of trading in physical banknotes.

1227 Securities financing transactions are transactions in which *"securities are used to borrow cash (or other higher investment-grade securities), or vice versa – this includes repurchase transactions, securities lending and sell/buy-back transactions"*. *ESMA*, Securities Financing Transactions, https://www.esma.europa.eu/sections/securities-financing-transactions; see also *European Commission* (2017) Securities Financing Transactions, 2. For *UBS* transferred secured finance transactions include securities lending and borrowing, repo and reverse repo. Commercial Register Entry, *UBS AG*, (June 17, 2015), Public Deed of the Asset Transfer Agreement, 9.

set management functions were retained at *UBS AG.*[1228] Furthermore, *UBS* transferred the whole of its wealth management business, as far as it is booked in Switzerland, onto the Swiss entity. It is not limited to Swiss clients but also includes offshore clients.[1229] This is likely to strengthen the self-sufficiency of the bank containing the systemically important functions.[1230]

The asset transfer agreement specifically states that it was the intention of *UBS* to *"substantially improve the resolvability of the Group in response to Swiss 'too big to fail' requirements"* with the transfer.[1231] At the end of 2017, *UBS Switzerland AG* had assets of 290.3 billion CHF.[1232] This corresponds to 31.7% of the banking group's total assets.[1233]

2. Credit Suisse

Credit Suisse's Swiss entity, *Credit Suisse (Schweiz) AG* was established in 2015 as a fully-owned subsidiary of *Credit Suisse AG.*[1234] In November 2016, the bank acquired the universal bank business for Swiss customers from *Credit Suisse AG*, which includes a *"significant part of the Swiss Universal Bank Division and parts of the business area STS Trading"* and started its

1228 *UBS* (2016) Annual Report 2015, 766. However, according to *SIX Swiss Exchange*, market making services are provided by *UBS AG* (not *UBS Switzerland AG*) (see *SIX Swiss Exchange*, Liste der Market Maker, Passive ETFs, https://www.six-swiss-exchange.com/funds/etf/marketmaker_list_de.html; *SIX Swiss Exchange*, Liste der Market Maker, Aktive ETFs, https://www.six-swiss-exchange.com/funds/active_etf/marketmaker_list_de.html).

1229 This can be drawn from the scope of the transferred activities (see *UBS* (2016) Annual Report 2015, 766; Commercial Register Entry, *UBS AG*, (June 17, 2015), Public Deed of the Asset Transfer Agreement, 7); see also *Millischer/Heim*, Milliardenabflüsse bei der UBS Schweiz, Handelszeitung (March 31, 2016).

1230 See Chapter III.IV.C.a.2: Systemically important functions.

1231 Commercial Register Entry, *UBS AG*, (June 17, 2015), Public Deed of the Asset Transfer Agreement, 7.

1232 *UBS* (2018) Standalone financial statements UBS Switzerland AG, 2.

1233 Own calculation based on *UBS* (2018) Annual Report 2017, 317 (total assets of the banking group amounting to 915.6 billion CHF) and *UBS* (2018) Standalone financial statements UBS Switzerland AG, 2 (total assets of *UBS Switzerland AG* amounting to 290.3 billion CHF).

1234 See Commercial Register Entry, *Credit Suisse (Schweiz) AG*, (May 05, 2014), Public deed of the foundation of *Credit Suisse Switzerland AG.*

business operations. It was planned to conduct a partial IPO in late 2017.[1235] These plans, however, have been discarded so far.[1236]

Regarding the transfer of activities to *Credit Suisse (Schweiz) AG*, the Bulk Transfer Agreement of November 17, 2016, is of particular interest: It states that the transfer of the Swiss Universal Bank business intends to respond to the Swiss TBTF legislation, noting that *"with the transfer of the Swiss [Universal Bank] Business [...] and [its] continuation [...] substantial parts of the Swiss emergency plan of the group are implemented ex ante"*.[1237]

Concerning the transferred business two things in particular attract attention: firstly, the Swiss Universal Bank business includes, among other things, the business unit "Investment Banking Switzerland".[1238] It cannot be gathered from the annual report what activities it comprises in detail. From it being a part of the Swiss Universal bank business, one can, however, infer that it is limited to Swiss customers.[1239] Furthermore, some insights can be drawn from business that the bulk transfer agreement excludes from the transfer: among the excluded businesses is securities underwriting.[1240] The investment banking business transferred to the Swiss entity therefore is limited to Swiss clients and does not include securities underwriting.

Secondly, *Credit Suisse* not just transferred the Universal Bank business, but also parts of a trading business, so-called "STS Trading". It is divided in three groups: (i) STS Trading that is not transferred, but remains with *Credit Suisse AG*. It includes subareas of "Collateral Trading and Finance Solutions" and of trading with OTC derivatives; (ii) STS Trading, which was transferred and remains with the Swiss entity, among it is banknotes trading; and (iii) STS Trading that is transferred *"due to technical reasons for a transition period"*. *Credit Suisse "intends"* to transfer it back by the end of 2018. It includes, among other things, the subareas *"Fixed Income, Equity*

1235 *Credit Suisse (Schweiz) AG* (2017) Annual Report 2016, 9.

1236 See *Imwinkelried*, Doch kein Börsengang der Schweizer Einheit, NZZ (April 26, 2017).

1237 Commercial Register Entry, *Credit Suisse*, (November 23, 2016), Bulk Transfer Agreement, 5–7.

1238 Commercial Register Entry, *Credit Suisse*, (November 23, 2016), Bulk Transfer Agreement, 9.

1239 See Commercial Register Entry, *Credit Suisse*, (November 23, 2016), Bulk Transfer Agreement, 8–9.

1240 See Commercial Register Entry, *Credit Suisse*, (November 23, 2016), Bulk Transfer Agreement, 8–9; Commercial Register Entry, *Credit Suisse*, (November 23, 2016), Bulk Transfer Agreement, Annex 1, 1.

and Structured Products Trading, Investment Grade Capital Markets, […] Collateral Trading & Finance Solutions" and the business area *"STS Execution"* with corresponding accesses to the financial market infrastructure.[1241]

The fact that *Credit Suisse (Schweiz) AG* plans to transfer a considerable part of its trading business back to *Credit Suisse AG* until the end of 2018 is remarkable. It particularly appears unconventional to transfer an important business before the IPO intended at the time and transfer it back afterwards. Searching for an explanation, one finds that Finma seems to be responsible for this unusual arrangement: according to *Hässig*, *Credit Suisse* planned to raise the attractiveness of the Swiss entity for the intended IPO by adding the STS trading business. Finma, however, prevented such an organisation, allegedly to avoid burdening the Swiss entity with the risks of trading. *Credit Suisse* implied that Finma referenced the *UBS* ex ante separation, which also did not feature any trading business.[1242]

At the end of 2017, *Credit Suisse (Schweiz) AG* had assets of 246.3 billion CHF.[1243] This corresponds to 30.9% of the banking group's total assets.[1244]

3. Conclusio

Switzerland's G-SIBs both ex ante separated their systemically important functions. This occured to comply with the Swiss TBTF regime that requires (i) to ensure the continuity of systemically important functions with an emergency plan, (ii) if necessary, to implement measures for this goal ex ante, and (iii) to profit from capital rebates in case of *"reduc[ing] the resolvability risk beyond what is legally required"*.[1245]

Their systemically important functions seem to be in line with those explicitly mentioned in the Swiss Banking Act, namely the domestic deposits

1241 See Commercial Register Entry, *Credit Suisse*, (November 23, 2016), Bulk Transfer Agreement, 7–8; Commercial Register Entry, *Credit Suisse*, (November 23, 2016), Bulk Transfer Agreement, Annex 1, 1.

1242 See *Hässig*, Finma stellt sich gegen CS-Pläne, Tages Anzeiger (May 11, 2016); with a similar conclusion, *Padevit*, CS: Schweizer Tochter wird am 20. November geboren, Finanz und Wirtschaft (October 7, 2016).

1243 *Credit Suisse (Schweiz) AG* (2018) Annual Report 2018, 9.

1244 Own calculation based on *Credit Suisse* (2018) Annual Report 2017, 57 (total assets of the banking group amounting to 796.3 billion CHF) and *Credit Suisse (Schweiz) AG* (2018) Annual Report 2018, 9 (total assets of *Credit Suisse (Schweiz) AG* amounting to 246.3 billion CHF).

1245 Commercial Register Entry, *UBS AG*, (June 17, 2015), Public Deed of the Asset Transfer Agreement, 7.

and loans business and payment transactions.[1246] To ensure the self-sufficiency and potentially to diversify activities, *UBS* and *Credit Suisse* chose to transfer all wealth management business booked in Switzerland to the Swiss entities.[1247] However, in contrast to *UBS*, *Credit Suisse* only transferred its wealth management business for domestic clients.[1248] Both banks also transferred their banknotes business, which was previously part of their investment banks. One can assume that this is due to its critical importance for the Swiss economy.

It is furthermore striking that both banks only transferred limited parts of their investment banking business: in particular the securities underwriting business, and, more importantly, their trading businesses are not (or not permanently) transferred to the Swiss entity. The only exemption seems to be *UBS* transferring its market making activities on the SIX Swiss Exchange. In particular, the circumstances of the remarkable temporary transfer of parts of *Credit Suisse's* STS Trading business underscore that the Swiss regulator does not seem to allow for trading activities conducted in the Swiss entities and does not abstain from forceful interventions.

d. Summary

In summary, it can be found that globally active banks that are determined systemically important have to provide (i) an emergency plan, which sets out how the continuation of Swiss systemically important functions in a crisis scenario can be ensured, and take (ii) comprehensive organisational measures beforehand to ensure that the emergency plan is workable. These measures seem to necessarily include an ex ante separation of systemically

---

1246 Art. 8(1) Swiss Banking Act; see Chapter III.IV.C.a.2: Systemically important functions.

1247 Self-sufficiency of the ring-fenced entity, i.e. to create a self-sufficient business that can continue to work profitable on its own, is a key requirement of the emergency plan (Expert Interview, Affected Bank, September 28, 2017). It follows from the obligation to ensure the continuation of systemically important functions, set down in Art. 9 Swiss Banking Act and Art. 60 Swiss Banking Ordinance.

1248 This results from the scope of the transferred activities (see Commercial Register Entry, *Credit Suisse*, (November 23, 2016), Bulk Transfer Agreement, 8–9; see also the considerations regarding *UBS* in Chapter III.IV.C.c.1: UBS); The limited focus on Swiss clients is also stressed by *Credit Suisse*. See *Hässig*, Finma stellt sich gegen CS-Pläne, Tages Anzeiger (May 11, 2016) (emphasizing the motto "pure Swissness").

important activities into a separate legal entity and its operational and financial unbundling from the banking group. In addition, the entity has to be adequately equipped with capital and liquidity.[1249]

The emergency plan has thus undergone an evolution. At its start is the Swiss Banking Act, which stipulates that a plan has to describe the necessary measures to ensure the continuation of systemically important activities.[1250] The emergency plan then became the basis for the demand towards banks to put in place far reaching organisational requirements. Certain measures of the plan would have to be implemented ex ante, as without them the emergency plan would not work.[1251] In its last evolutionary step, the emergency plan becomes a plan again, describing measures to ensure the continuation of systemically important activities, which are now workable because considerable unbundling has already taken place.[1252]

The emergency plan is complemented by organisational measures to improve the general resolvability. While the former sets down mandatory minimum requirements, the latter incentivises further separation.[1253]

Illustrated according to *Britton et al.*,[1254] who form groups of key activities according to where they have to be provided, the emerging picture is clearer than the lack of clear publicly available requirements would allow to expect. This is particularly true once one reviews the factual separation that Switzerland's two G-SIBs have conducted and includes it in the consideration.

1249 See *Bundesrat* (2015) Bericht Too Big to Fail, 1935. The requirements regarding the independence of the Swiss entities (e.g. capital and liquidity requirements) will be discussed in Chapter III.V: Height of the Fence.

1250 See Art. 9(2)(d) Swiss Banking Act.

1251 See Chapter III.IV.C.a.1: Ex ante separation.

1252 This is reflected in the description of the Swiss organisational measures in the asset transfer agreement of *UBS*. It notes that *"Swiss 'too big to fail' requirements require systemically important banks [...] to put viable emergency plans in place to preserve the operation of systemically important functions despite the failure of the institution, to the extent that such activities are not sufficiently separated in advance [...]"*. See *UBS* (2015) Asset Transfer Agreement, 7. See e.g. governance requirements of the emergency plan, Chapter III.V.C.c: Governance.

1253 The exact attribution is sometimes hard to identify. From the above, it can nevertheless be concluded that there are considerable minimum requirements and that regulators do not refrain from intervening forcefully with regard to preventing the inclusion of trading activities into the separated entity. For a discussion of measures to enhance resolvability and their relation to the emergency plan, see Chapter III.V.C.a: Legal sources.

1254 See the illustration of *Britton et al.* (2016) Ring-fencing, 167.

The ring-fenced entity has to provide all functions that are considered systemically important. This includes the deposit-taking and loans business and payment transactions. It has to be emphasized that the requirements are limited to the Swiss domestic business.[1255] As the wording of Art. 8(1) Swiss Banking Act is non-exhaustive, other functions could be added. They would have to be identified by the SNB after consultation of Finma.[1256] Drawing from the ex ante separation of the two banks, banknotes trading seems to be a critical function that mandatorily is to be provided by the Swiss entities.

The second group comprises activities that have to be provided outside the ring-fenced entity, by entities of the remaining banking group. The Swiss TBTF package does not stipulate certain activities that must be excluded. It can, however, be derived from the legislative materials and other sources that certain activities attributed to investment banking are not to be included in the Swiss entity.[1257] As an assessment of the affected banks has shown, this particularly relates to investment banking and trading activities: securities underwriting as well as, for example, equities and structured products trading needs to be provided outside the ring-fence.

The third group consists of activities that can be provided by both the ring-fenced entity and the remaining banking group. Drawing from the purpose of the Swiss TBTF regime and the banks' changes to their structure, it can be established that the activities need to be comparatively low risk. As reflected by the organisational measures it includes, in particular, wealth management services, but is not limited to domestic clients.

D. Results

a. Activities within the ring-fence

Drawing from the focus of the Swiss Banking Act and from the organisational changes Swiss G-SIBs have conducted, one finds that Switzerland requires the most comprehensive activities to be provided within the Swiss entity. They include not just deposit-taking, but also part of the loans business and payment services. In addition, there are other activities important to the domestic economy, such as bank notes trading. Geographically,

1255 See Chapter III.IV.C.a.2: Systemically important functions.
1256 Art. 8(3) Swiss Banking Act.
1257 See Chapter III.IV.C.b: non-ring-fenced bodies.

however, the requirement is less comprehensive than the other jurisdictions, as it is limited to the domestic business.

Based on the scope of the German Ring-fencing Act, cumulative deposit-taking and loans business have to be provided by a ring-fenced entity. From the prohibition for the non-ring-fenced trading entity follows that also payment services and the e-money business can only be provided from inside the ring-fence. While a non-ring-fenced entity can also grant loans, the interpretation of the Act indicates that it should not be allowed to accept deposits (apart from institutional investors).[1258] Geographically, there are no limitations: once a banking group falls within the scope, all the activities have to be provided from within the fence (or to put differently, all of the trading activity has to be excluded).[1259]

In the UK, the focus is clearly set on core deposits. They have to be provided from within the ring-fence. It must be emphasised that not all deposits are core deposits, so that banks can accept large companies' or high net worth individuals' deposits with their non-ring-fenced entities. There is a geographic restriction: only deposits accepted in EEA account, i.e. an account opened at a branch in an EEA state, are core deposits.[1260] Regulators are obliged to protect core services of ring-fenced bodies, as they are connected to deposit-taking. They include overdraft facilities and payment services.[1261] With regard to other loans, no explicit legal requirements have been put down. It has, however, been concluded in the preparatory works that the loans business naturally follows deposit-taking.[1262]

In summary, it can be found that all jurisdictions, in one way or another, consider deposit-taking, parts of the loans business and payment services especially important and thus necessary to be protected from riskier activities in banking groups.

1258 See in detail Chapter III.IV.B.b.: Ring-fenced bodies.

1259 This is also highlighted by *Lehmann.* See *Lehmann* (2014) Extraterritorial Effects, 308.

1260 See Chapter III.III.A.a: Personal scope.

1261 See Chapter III.IV.A.a.2: Core services.

1262 This is discussed by the Vickers Commission and the UK Government, see Chapter III.IV.A.a.1: Core activities.

b. Excluded activities

1. Basis of the exclusion

In all three jurisdictions there are activities that are not allowed to be provided by the ring-fenced bank, but can be provided by non-ring-fenced banks. However, they strongly differ in how they articulate the exclusion.

Germany and the UK both clearly set out what activities are excluded for the then ring-fenced bodies: the German Ring-fencing Act strives to comprehensively define the excluded activities. However, in practice, a lot of weight is placed on BaFin's Interpretative Guidance, which clarifies the authority's views and in some aspects considerably modifies the provisions of the Act.[1263] The UK seems to acknowledge the difficulties in comprehensively defining excluded activities in primary law and thus only outlines them, stipulating that *"[t]he regulated activity of dealing in investments as principal (whether carried on in the United Kingdom or elsewhere) is an excluded activity unless it is carried on in circumstances specified by the Treasury by order"*. The Treasury is authorised under certain circumstances to add other excluded activities.[1264]

In Switzerland, in contrast, there are no general provisions on excluding certain activities from the Swiss entities. This is because there is not even a general requirement to establish such entities.[1265] The separation follows from Art. 60(1) Swiss Banking Ordinance, which stipulates that systemically important functions have to be continued *"independently from the rest of the bank"* in the case of imminent insolvency.[1266]

However, neither the Swiss Banking Act nor the Swiss Banking Ordinance comprehensively define the systemically important activities. While they indicate what activities are particularly worth considering, the final decision is made by the SNB.[1267] As argued by *Bahar/Peyer*, the wording would also allow for investment banking activities to be systemically important.[1268]

1263 See e.g. the exception for fully collateralised transactions with hedge funds and AIFs discussed in Chapter Chapter III.IV.B.a.1: Excluded activities.

1264 Art. 142D FSMA 2000; see Chater III.IV.A.b.1: Excluded activities.

1265 See Chapter III.IV.C.a.1: Ex ante separation.

1266 Own translation from German original, Art. 60(1) Swiss Banking Ordinance.

1267 See Chapter III.IV.C.a.2: Systemically important functions; Chapter III.III.B.c: Affected banks.

1268 As discussed, this is argued by *Bahar/Peyer* (2013) Systemrelevante Banken, 384. See Chapter III.IV.C.b: non-ring-fenced bodies.

The lack of a clear and general definition of systemically important functions leads to a lack of a clear and general definition of "the rest of the bank" and hence of a definition of excluded activities. As discussed above, the emergency plan sets down considerable minimum requirements and regulators do not hesitate to demonstrate the options available as well as their limits. This enforcement-based approach allows for a lot of flexibility and case-by-case decisions, but can be criticised for its lack of transparency[1269] and possibly from a constitutional perspective.[1270]

2. Activities

The three jurisdictions exclude activities from the ring-fenced bodies. They, however, differ with regard to the extent of excluded activities. This also reflects the method of ring-fencing chosen by the respective legislator.[1271]

In the UK, the exclusion is particularly comprehensive: It excludes proprietary trading using a considerably broad definition that includes not just the trading of financial instruments, in particular market making, but also underwriting them. Furthermore, the buying and selling of commodities is excluded.[1272] The comprehensive exclusion leads to a comparatively small ring-fenced body and a quite large non-ring-fenced body, with almost all investment banking, in particular proprietary trading, market making and underwriting in the latter.

As suggested by the legal separation conducted by the big banks and by events surrounding them, Switzerland's excluded activities are surprisingly similar to the UK's: they likely include all trading activity and also the underwriting of financial instruments, thus the main parts of investment banking. Only with regard to domestic market making does there seem to be a difference.[1273]

In contrast to the two jurisdictions above, the German Ring-fencing Act excludes only very few activities. They include proprietary business, i.e. proprietary trading that constitutes a bank's own short-term investment activity and is not a service for clients; high-frequency trading, i.e. the buying

1269 See Chapter III.II.D.b.3: Transparency.
1270 See Chapter III.II.D.b.2: Principle of legality.
1271 See Chapter III.IV.D.c: Ring-fencing method.
1272 See Chapter III.IV.A.b.1: Excluded activities.
1273 See Chapter III.IV.C: Switzerland.

and selling of financial instruments on own account via high-frequency algorithmic trading technique, with the exception of market making; and the lending and guarantee business with certain hedge funds and AIFs, with the important exception of fully collateralised transactions.[1274] The small scope of prohibited activities orientates less to the Liikanen Report than to the Volcker Rule. As it, however, entails only the ring-fencing of such activities and not the *activities ban* of full separation, it is referred to by *Vickers* as *"Volcker-lite"*.[1275]

3. Exceptions

There are considerable similarities regarding exceptions from excluded activities between Germany and the UK. As the Swiss TBTF package does not explicitly stipulate excluded activities, it thus also remains silent on exceptions. A legal comparative analysis of exceptions in Germany and the UK may therefore be of particular interest and result in findings that can also be applied in Switzerland. As the Swiss approach orientates towards the UK, it should be in the focus of the examination.

Among the UK's key exceptions to the excluded activities discussed above are the management of risk for ring-fenced bodies, such as interest rate changes or exchange rate changes and the management of liquidity risk. The German Ring-fencing Act, however, also allows ring-fenced bodies the management of interest rate, foreign exchange, liquidity, price, and credit risk for the whole banking group.[1276] From a legal comparison perspective, this suggests that such activities should also be excluded in Switzerland. Swiss banks that contain the systemically important functions also have the need to hedge risks stemming from the intermediation between savers and borrowers,[1277] as well as from other services they offer.

1274 See Chapter III.IV.B.a.1: Excluded activities.

1275 *Vickers* (2016) Banking Reform Presentation, 22. This is criticised, e.g. by *Schäfer* (2016) Trennbankengesetz (noting that the prohibition of proprietary trading is ineffective due to differences in differentiating it from market making). For this problem, see Chapter I.II.B: Proprietary trading and market making, and the criticism of the Volcker Rule, see Chapter I.IV.D: Ring-fencing and the activities ban.

1276 See *De Vogelaere* (2016) Bank Structure Reforms, 86; Chapter III.IV.A.b.1: Excluded activities; Chapter III.IV.B.a.2: Exceptions.

1277 See Chapter III.IV.A.b.1: Excluded activities.

In the UK, there is furthermore an exception for transactions with a central bank. Reason for the exception is that it ensures that a ring-fenced body can access central bank liquidity.[1278] Such transactions should also be allowed for the Swiss ring-fenced banks.

Another important exception that is stipulated in the UK is that ring-fenced bodies are allowed to provide their customers with simple derivative products to ensure they can hedge their own risk. A similar exception would make sense for Switzerland, as these needs are universal. It could be designed similarly to the UK with quantitative and qualitative limitations.[1279]

c. Ring-fencing method

1. Ring-fencing

In the chapters above, it was found that all of the three jurisdictions of interest differentiate between the value of certain activities attributed to commercial banking and certain activities attributed to investment banking. They all mandate the separation of certain activities attributed to commercial banking and certain activities attributed to investment banking, thereby constituting one of the core characteristics of ring-fencing.[1280]

Looking at the separation requirements for the affected banks it can, however, be established that none of the jurisdictions have decided for the *activities ban* of full separation as, for instance, the Volcker Rule and the EU Commission's draft regulation stipulate.[1281] This is remarkable, given the attention that the U.S. Volcker Rule and later the EU Commission's proposal has received. None of the jurisdictions have decided for full separation either.

In all three jurisdictions, it was considered better to allow for both groups of activities to be conducted under the same roof of a banking group. All three countries therefore allow universal banking, thereby constituting another core characteristic of ring-fencing.[1282] The third core

1278 See Chapter III.IV.A.b.1: Excluded activities.
1279 See Chapter III.IV.A.b.1: Excluded activities.
1280 See Chapter I.IV.B: Ring-fencing as a structural reform.
1281 See Chapter I.IV.D: Ring-fencing and the activities ban. For a review of the Volcker Rule, see Chapter I.IV.D.a: Digression: The Volcker Rule.
1282 See Chapter I.IV.B: Ring-fencing as a structural reform.

characterisation of ring-fencing, the fence, will be discussed in Chapter III.V.,[1283] and can for now be assumed.

2. Method of ring-fencing

The countries decided for different methods of ring-fencing. The UK's Banking Reform Act 2013 and the Swiss TBTF package in combination with the enforcement-based approach put into practice the *defensive method* of ring-fencing. This can be gathered from a number of indicators: first, they adopted provisions that are the basis for the separation of certain activities, namely of the desired activities as set out in Chapter I.VI.A,[1284] including deposit-taking, lending and payment services. Second, the separated entity may not provide the full spectrum of banking services, and is prohibited from engaging in activities considered risky, namely certain trading and investment banking activities.[1285]

For example, a banking group within the scope of the respective law faces in both countries the obligation to separate certain activities. In the UK, these activities are accepting core deposits and, in connection, core services, such as payment services and overdrafts. Retail and SME lending is expected to naturally follow the core deposits. In Switzerland, affected banks have to separate systemically important functions. As established in the chapters above, they include deposit-taking, parts of lending and payment services.[1286] In both countries, the desired activities are therefore separated from the rest of the banking group. In addition, the newly established entities face activities restrictions for certain trading and investment banking activities: in the UK, these restrictions comprise, in particular, proprietary trading, general trading activities, market making and underwriting. As established in the chapters above, similar restrictions apply in Switzerland, with the exception of domestic market making.

The German Ring-fencing Act, in contrast, puts into practice the *containment method* of ring-fencing. Again, this can be gathered from various indicators: first, the Act mandates the separation of certain activities. In contrast to the above, the activities to be separated are those considered particularly risky. Second, the separated entity may not provide the full

1283 See Chapter III.V: Height of the Fence.
1284 See Chapter I.VI.A: Underlying assumption.
1285 See Chapter I.VI.A: Underlying assumption.
1286 See Chapter III.IV.C.a.2: Systemically important functions.

spectrum of banking services – in contrast to the above, it is prohibited in some way or the other from engaging in the desired services.

For example, a banking group within the scope of the German Ring-fencing Act faces the obligation to separate certain activities. These are the activities considered high-risk by the German legislator, namely proprietary business, high-frequency algorithmic trading and the guarantee and loans business with hedge funds and AIFs. In Germany, the risky activities are therefore separated from the rest of the banking group. In addition, the newly established entity (the trading entity) faces activities restrictions for certain desired activities: in Germany, these restrictions comprise deposit-taking and payment services.

d. Flexibility

Another similarity between the jurisdictions is that the location of the ring-fence is not immovable. They all allow for a degree of flexibility. In Switzerland, this is achieved by the Swiss Banking Act, not conclusively stipulating which functions are systemically important. It mentions deposit-taking, loans and payment services only exemplarily. The SNB thus has some leeway in deciding what activities it finds systemically importtant.[1287] Even more flexibility is provided by the enforcement-based approach that delegates considerable power to Finma.[1288] In the UK, the FSMA 2000 empowers HM Treasury to provide for additional core activities and core services.[1289] The German Ring-fencing Act empowers BaFin to extend the prohibitions to additional activities (with the chance of being provided by the trading entity).[1290]

The adopted legislation does not strive to comprehensively stipulate the final rule. This can be traced back in particular to one reason: There seems to be a certain insecurity about the effects of ring-fencing. Far reaching structural requirements may entail consequences that are either not desired or unexpected. This is well reflected in the discussion on including

1287 See Explanatory Memorandum to FSMA 2014 Order No. 2080, Sec. 7.5; Chapter III.III.C.c: Affected banks.
1288 See Chapter III.II.C.c: Legal sources.
1289 See Art. 142B(5)-(6), Art. 142C(3)-(5) FSMA 2000. See Chapter III.III.A.a: Personal scope.
1290 See Chapter III.IV.B.b.1: Explicit activity restrictions for the financial trading institution.

retail credit as core activity in the UK. The Vickers Commission's *"expectations"* do not try to disguise that there is considerable uncertainty.[1291]

Another example is § 3(5) German Banking Act, which authorises BaFin to prohibit, *inter alia*, market making. This reflects that the legislator does not consider it risky enough to be separated in the first place, but does not rule out that it may be or become exactly that.[1292]

It can therefore be concluded that in a delicate matter such as ring-fencing, a degree of flexibility is considered appropriate by legislators internationally: they only outline the location of the fence and leave considerable leeway for specification to regulators. While this leeway differs between the examined jurisdictions, it can be generalised that regulators have considerable powers to shape the ring-fencing requirements for banks.

e. Relation to expert commission recommendations

There are some interesting observations when comparing the adopted legislation with the expert commissions' recommendations. While the UK Banking Reform Act 2013 and its secondary legislation stuck considerably close to the Vickers Report, in particuar Germany and Switzerland deviated considerably from the experts' recommendations.

In Germany, the key deviation from the recommendations of the Liikanen Report is that market making is allowed to be conducted within the ring fence (and does not have to be transferred to the trading entity).[1293] This, in combination with the far-reaching exceptions, considerably restricts the scope of activities that have to be transferred to the trading entity. However, it transposes the key problem of delimiting market making from proprietary trading,[1294] that *inter alia* the Volcker Rule faces,[1295] into

---

1291 *ICB* (2011) Vickers Report, 38 (*"If these expectations were not realised, and large portions of retail credit supply were provided by non-ring-fenced banks, this is an area which should be reviewed and activity restrictions tightened if appropriate"*); see also Chapter III.IV.A.a.1: Core activities.

1292 § 3(5) German Banking Act; *Deutscher Bundestag* (2013) Gesetzesentwurf Trennbankengesetz 27–28; see also Chapter III.IV.B.a.1: Excluded activities.

1293 See *HLEG* (2012) Liikanen Report, 101, 102; Chapter III.IV.B.a.1: Excluded activities.

1294 See Chapter I.II.B.a: Proprietary trading.

1295 See Chapter I.IV.D.a: Digression: The Volcker Rule.

German law. Because of this orientation towards the Volcker Rule, it can be referred to as *"Volcker-lite"*.[1296]

In Switzerland, the extent of the factual separation suggests that it exceeds the expectations of the expert commission. This is in particular because (i) mere planning was found not to suffice and because (ii) the ex ante separation of systemically important functions turned out to be the only viable option for globally active systemically important banks.[1297] In addition, (iii) the UK-oriented separation of commercial banking and investment banking[1298] presumably exceeds the expert commission's ideas.

V. Height of the Fence

This chapter addresses the height of the fence, i.e. the provisions that safeguard the legal, operational and economic independence of the separated entities. It takes on key measures with regard to capital and liquidity, governance, intragroup transactions and exposures, distributions and the continuity of services.

A. United Kingdom

The FSMA 2000 authorises the appropriate legislator, which is the PRA,[1299] to make general rules specifying the height of the fence. These rules (i) require a ring-fenced body to make arrangements to ensure that it can depend on services and facilities which it needs to carry out core activities,[1300] which currently only comprise deposit-taking.[1301] They also aim to (ii) ensure that the carrying on of deposit-taking is not negatively affected

---

1296 *Vickers* (2016) Banking Reform Presentation, 22.

1297 See Chapter III.IV.C.a.1: Ex ante separation.

1298 See Chapter III.IV.C.b: non-ring-fenced body.

1299 See *PRA* (2017) Ring-fenced Bodies, 5–6; Art. 142H(1)(a) in conjunction with 142H(8) FSMA 2000; The PRA is responsible for regulating banks, building societies credit unions, insurers and major investment firms. See *FCA*, About the FCA/PRA, https://register.fca.org.uk/; see also *PRA,* Which firms does the PRA regulate?, https://www.bankofengland.co.uk/prudential-regulation/authorisations/which-firms-does-the-pra-regulate. The legal basis for the PRA's duties is Part 1A Sec. 2B(5) FSMA 2000.

1300 Art. 142H(1)(a) FSMA 2000.

1301 See Chapter III.III.A.a: Personal scope.

by acts or omissions of other members of the banking group; that (iii) a ring-fenced body can take decisions independently and that (iii) it does not depend on resources of other members of the banking group, which could run dry in the case of their insolvency. They, in addition, aim to (iv) ensure that the ring-fenced body is able to carry on deposit-taking in the event of insolvency of other group members.[1302]

These rules therefore serve two important overall goals that are necessary for the stable provision of core activities: firstly, to ensure the independence of the ring-fenced body. Secondly, to protect it from insolvency of other members of the banking group. By putting up a fence, these rules distance the ring-fenced body from the rest of the bank. The FSMA 2000 roughly outlines some of them,[1303] but leaves considerable scope of action to the PRA. In the following sections, some of the particularly important rules are discussed.

a. Capital and liquidity

Ring-fenced bodies have to meet capital requirements of the CRR and related PRA rules on an individual basis. If a ring-fenced subgroup is formed, the ring-fenced body also needs to ensure that the requirements are met on the level of the subgroup.[1304]

Ring-fenced bodies have to put in place stress testing capabilities for themselves and, if applicable, the subgroup.[1305] They additionally have to conduct reverse stress testing that assesses the impact of a group entity's failure.[1306] Conducting SREP,[1307] the PRA considers exposures to other

---

1302 See Art. 142H(1)(b) in conjunction with Art. 142H(4) FSMA 2000.

1303 See Art. 142H(5) FSMA 2000.

1304 See *PRA* (2017) Ring-fenced Bodies, 13.

1305 See *PRA* (2017) Ring-fenced Bodies, 15.

1306 Reverse stress testing requires the ring-fenced entity to assess scenarios which would challenge its viability. By starting an assessment the other way around (namely with an unwanted scenario, such as the failure of the bank), hidden risks and overlooked interactions among risks can be identified (see *Basel Committee on Banking Supervision* (2009) Stress Testing, 14). In the reverse stress test the ring-fenced body has to include impacts on capital, liquidity funding, income, profitability and franchise value in the assessment. See *PRA* (2017) Ring-fenced Bodies, 16.

1307 SREP stands for Supervisory Review and Evaluation Process. It assesses credit institutions' risks, governance arrangements and their capital and liquidity situation. In addition to monitoring credit institutions' compliance with mini-

members of the banking group, which are not part of a subgroup, as if they were third parties. This may result in additional capital buffers in the context of Pillar 2A capital for concentration risk.[1308]

Ring-fenced bodies also have to meet liquidity requirements such as the Liquidity Coverage Ratio on an individual basis. If a ring-fenced subgroup is formed, the ring-fenced body also needs to ensure that the requirements are met on the level of the subgroup.[1309]

b. Governance

The independency of ring-fenced bodies is to be secured by a number of provisions that can be attributed to corporate governance. They can be divided into two groups: the first group includes general rules. They stipulate that ring-fenced bodies in managing their business have to make sure that they are able to take decisions independently from other banking group members. Furthermore, they have to take precautions to identify and manage conflicts of interest of their senior management. In addition, ring-fenced bodies have to identify and manage conflicts between their interests and those of other group members.[1310]

Specific rules form the second group. The PRA Rulebook stipulates, for example, how the board of a ring-fenced body has to be composed: at least half of its governing body's members have to be independent non-executive directors. The chairperson has to be an independent non- executive director. He additionally is not allowed to chair the governing body of any other member of the banking group, except a ring-fenced affiliate. Furthermore, a maximum of one-third of the members of the governing body can be employees or directors of other banking group members.[1311]

There are moreover specific requirements for important functions of the ring-fenced body, namely risk management, internal audit and human re-

---

mum capital requirements, the review may result in extra capital and liquidity buffers due to a credit institution's specific situation. See *European Central Bank* (2014) Banking Supervision, 23–25.

1308 See *PRA* (2017) Ring-fenced Bodies, 14.

1309 See *PRA* (2017) Ring-fenced Bodies, 17.

1310 *PRA* (2016) PRA Rulebook: Ring Fenced Bodies, Sec. 3(1)-(3).

1311 *PRA* (2016) PRA Rulebook: Ring Fenced Bodies, Sec. 4 in conjunction with Sec. 1(3).

sources, that strive to ensure that the person in charge is free of conflicts of interest.[1312]

c. Intragroup transactions and exposures

Also with regard to intragroup transactions and exposures, there are general rules and specific provisions. The general rule is that a ring-fenced body has to ensure, as far as reasonably practicable, that it applies the same standards to the management of its exposures and transactions to other banking group members (that are not ring-fenced affiliates) as it would to third parties.[1313] This rule should *"underpin a [ring-fenced body's] approach to all transactions arrangements and exposures with its wider group"*.[1314]

However, the PRA clarifies that the rule does not prohibit transactions solely because a ring-fenced body does not have identical transactions with a third party. It neither requires the ring-fenced body to *"apply precisely the same risk appetite, monitoring and oversight policies and procedures"*.[1315]

The general rule is reinforced by the specific requirement for ring-fenced bodies to enter into transactions with banking group members outside the fence *"only on arm's length terms"*. They have to put in place an effective policy and procedures to identify and assess intragroup transactions. The policy includes, for example, a description of how the pricing of a transaction is achieved, or mechanisms for dispute resolution between the parties. The procedures include, for instance, an at least annual assessment of the firm's policy and procedures by internal audit and the stipulation that the policy has to be approved and at least annually reviewed by the governing body.[1316]

The PRA, however, allows affected banks to use framework agreements for a number of transactions of similar character. Transactions with other entities within the ring-fence do not have to be on arm's length terms.[1317]

As already discussed in Chapter III.IV.A.b.2, prohibitions apply to certain transactions.[1318] The ring-fenced bank is only allowed to have expo-

---

1312 See *PRA* (2016) PRA Rulebook: Ring Fenced Bodies, Sec. 4 in conjunction with Sec. 5, 6, 7.
1313 See *PRA* (2016) PRA Rulebook: Ring Fenced Bodies, Sec. 3(5).
1314 *PRA* (2017) Ring-fenced Bodies, 24.
1315 *PRA* (2017) Ring-fenced Bodies, 24.
1316 See *PRA* (2016) PRA Rulebook: Ring Fenced Bodies, Sec. 12.
1317 *PRA* (2017) Ring-fenced Bodies, 27.
1318 See Chapter III.IV.A.b.2: Prohibitions.

sures to other (non-ring-fenced) members of its own group under the condition that transactions are conducted at arm's length.[1319] Large exposure limits of the CRR apply.[1320] The PRA clarified it will even consider further measures such as the lowering of the rate.[1321]

Similar requirements are in place for the handling of collateral. Ring-fenced bodies have to manage collateral from other members of the banking group that are outside the ring-fence as if they had received it from third parties.[1322]

Another provision aiming to ensure that a ring-fenced body remains independent and able to withstand the failure of another group entity mandates that ring-fenced bodies are, as far as reasonably practicable, not allowed to become dependent on income generated from transactions with group members outside the fence, or with customers where it is likely contingent on services by group members.[1323] After identifying such a business, the ring-fenced body has to either reduce it or prepare credible plans for the recovery from its loss.[1324]

d. Distributions

Ring-fenced bodies are not allowed to make distributions to entities not within the ring-fence unless they notify the PRA of their intention to do so.[1325] Distribution is to be understood within the meaning of the Companies Act 2006,[1326] which refers to *"every description of distribution of a company's assets to its members, whether in cash or otherwise"*[1327] except certain capital management techniques.[1328] This includes in particular the payment of dividends.[1329] The notice has to include *inter alia* information

---

1319 See Art. 14(4) in conjunction with Art. 2(1) in conjunction with Art. 1(4) FSMA 2014 Order No. 2080.

1320 Art. 395(1) CRR; *PRA* (2017) Ring-fenced Bodies, 24.

1321 See *PRA* (2017) Ring-fenced Bodies, 24.

1322 See *PRA* (2017) Ring-fenced Bodies, 25.

1323 See *PRA* (2016) PRA Rulebook: Ring Fenced Bodies, Sec. 13.

1324 See *PRA* (2017) Ring-fenced Bodies, 26.

1325 *PRA* (2016) PRA Rulebook: Ring Fenced Bodies, Sec. 11 in conjunction with Sec. 1(2).

1326 Companies Act 2006, c. 46.

1327 Sec. 829 Companies Act 2006.

1328 For example, capital increases or capital reductions. See Sec. 829 Companies Act 2006.

1329 See *PRA* (2017) Ring-fenced Bodies, 23.

on the ring-fenced bodies capital ratios and the amount of the intended distribution.[1330] The PRA is prone to prevent such distributions if they have *"a significant adverse effect on the capital position of [a ring-fenced body] that could adversely affect the continuity of the provision of core services"*.[1331]

The permission to make distributions to entities outside the ring-fence, e.g. trough dividends, was understood as a concession to banks subject to ring-fencing.[1332] It is definitely a major relief for affected banks, as it allows for trading business to be subsidised by the commercial banking profits.

e. Continuity of services

A ring-fenced body may make use of services by other entities, for example services supporting IT processing or treasury back office activities.[1333] A ring-fenced body, however, is only allowed to receive services it requires regularly from another entity within the ring-fence or from a group service entity. The agreement governing the provision of services has to be designed in a way that it remains valid in the case of a change in financial circumstances of another entity in the banking group of the ring-fenced body.[1334]

B. Germany

The key provision, setting out the German ring-fencing model is § 25f German Banking Act. As the concept of a financial trading institution is created by the German Ring-fencing Act,[1335] § 25f alone specifies its character and its relationship towards the rest of the banking group.

Assessing § 25f German Banking Act, one has to keep in mind that the German ring-fencing model separates certain trading activities from the rest of the banking group and thus follows the *containment method* of ring-

---

1330 See *PRA* (2016) PRA Rulebook: Ring Fenced Bodies, Sec. 11(2).

1331 See *PRA* (2017) Ring-fenced Bodies, 22.

1332 See e.g. *Binham/Dunkley*, Banks win fresh concession on ringfencing rules, Financial Times (October 15, 2015).

1333 *Britton et al.* (2016) Ring-fencing, 169.

1334 See *PRA* (2016) PRA Rulebook: Ring Fenced Bodies, Sec. 9 in conjunction with Sec. 1(2).

1335 *Auerbach/Schriever* (2016) CRR-Kreditinstitute, 848.

fencing.[1336] The ring-fence is circled around a particularly broad part of the business, a trading entity is located outside the fence.[1337]

The provision of § 25f German Banking Act has two parts: in its first part – section one – it aims to define the financial trading institution. It then explains that the other sections are to be understood as additional requirements to the general requirements for a proper business organisation that apply to all financial institutions.[1338] In its second part, sections two to six, these additional requirements are set out.[1339]

a. Financial trading institution

Based on the legal wording, the financial trading organisation can be defined as *economically, organisationally and legally independent undertaking that provides activities within the meaning of § 3(2) and § 3(4) German Banking Act and is subject to additional requirements for proper business organisation.*[1340]

Central characteristic for the financial trading institution is that it is *"economically, organisationally and legally independent"*.[1341] Because of the vague terminology, in particular the economic and organisational independence require further specification.[1342]

1. Proper business organisation

Based on the explanation of § 25f(1) that § 25f(2)-(6) are to be understood as *additional* requirements to the proper business organisation and based on the legislative materials to the German Ring-fencing Act, the financial

1336 See Chapter I.VI.B.b: The containment method.

1337 *Vickers* refers to the German Ring-fencing Act as *"Volcker-lite"*, due to the limited scope of activities that are excluded from the ring-fence, thus resembling the U.S. Volcker Rule (however, not applying the *activities ban* of full separation). See *Vickers* (2016) Banking Reform Presentation, 22; See also *Krahnen/ Kemmerer* (2013) Gesprächsreihe Strukturreformen, 16.

1338 § 25f(1) German Banking Act.

1339 § 25f(2)-(6) German Banking Act.

1340 See § 25(1) German Banking Act; see also *Deutsche Bundesbank* (2014) Banking Act, 123.

1341 *BaFin* (2016) Interpretative Guidance, 46; see § 25f(1) German Banking Act.

1342 See *Möslein* (2013) Spartentrennung, 404 (criticising the lack of detail concerning the organisation and independency of the financial trading institution).

trading institution has to adhere to § 25a, which sets out *general* requirements of proper business organisation.[1343]

The legislative materials note that, based on general and additional proper business organisation, both the trading entity and the ring-fenced rest of the banking group have to ensure the effective isolation of the risks of the former's speculative transactions.[1344]

This is important information, because it (i) identifies obligations the trading entity (general and additional requirements to proper business organisation) has to comply with, and specifies (ii) how to interpret them (with a view to ensuring the isolation of risks).

Examples for requirements that result from the obligation to comply with proper business organisation are ensuring appropriate staffing, an appropriate and effective risk management and a suitable and transparent remuneration system.[1345]

2. Regulatory requirements of the German Banking Act

According to the legislative materials to the German Ring-fencing Act, the financial trading institution has to comply with all regulatory requirements of the German Banking Act.[1346] While the legislative materials, as established in Chapter III.IV.B.b, mistakenly identify it as a financial service institution,[1347] it is certainly true that the trading entity requires its

1343 *Deutscher Bundestag* (2013) Gesetzesentwurf Trennbankengesetz, 42; *Braun* (2016) Geschäftsorganisation, para 6; *Auerbach/Schriever* (2016) CRR-Kreditinstitute, 848; for a detailed discussion of the general requirements of proper business organisation, see *Braun* (2016) Organisatorische Pflichten, para 15 et seqq.

1344 *Deutscher Bundestag* (2013) Gesetzesentwurf Trennbankengesetz 42; *Braun* (2016) Geschäftsorganisation, para 6.

1345 § 25a(1) German Banking Act; *Deutsche Bundesbank* (2014) Banking Act 108–109.

1346 *Deutscher Bundestag* (2013) Gesetzesentwurf Trennbankengesetz 42; see also *Auerbach/Schriever* (2016) CRR-Kreditinstitute, 849; *Braun* (2016) Geschäftsorganisation, para 4.

1347 See Chapter III.IV.B.b: Ring-fenced bodies.

own license and is subject to the full supervision of the German Banking Act.[1348] This is reiterated by BaFin.[1349]

The need to comply with all regulatory requirements of the German Banking Act is an important message, because it identifies obligations the financial trading institution has to comply with, for example requirements on advertising.[1350]

b. Capital and liquidity

The financial trading institution has to meet capital and liquidity requirements of the CRR on an individual basis. This is due to the additional requirement of proper business organisation of § 25f(2) German Banking Act, which stipulates that the exceptions for group companies set out in § 2a German Banking Act do not apply. Financial trading institutions thus have to comply in particular with CRR requirements concerning own funds, large exposures, liquidity and disclosure on an individual basis.[1351]

c. Governance

According § 25f(5), management and supervisory bodies of both the financial trading institution and the ring-fenced entities have to inform themselves regularly and as required of the transactions and related risks of the financial trading entity. They also have to ensure that the general and additional requirements to the proper business administration are complied with.[1352]

1348 See *Auerbach/Schriever* (2016) CRR-Kreditinstitute, 849; *Braun* (2016) Geschäftsorganisation, para 4.

1349 BaFin answers the question whether the trading entity requires a licence that it *"does not agree that it would be possible for the financial trading institution for an appropriate transitional period to continue to use the licences granted to the CRR credit institution for transferred business"*. (*BaFin* (2016) Interpretative Guidance, 50).

1350 § 23 German Banking Act.

1351 § 2a German Banking Act in conjuction with Art. 7, 8 CRR in conjunction with Parts 2–6, 8 CRR; see *Schäfer* (2016) § 2a Ausnahmen, para 2–3; see also *Möslein* (2013) Spartentrennung, 405; *Schelo/Steck* (2013) Trennbankengesetz, 241–242.

1352 § 25f(5) German Banking Act.

Other governance requirements for the financial trading institution derive from the general requirements of proper business organisation and from the requirement to comply with the German Banking Act. BaFin specifically lists a number of requirements that are based on the German Banking Act:[1353] A financial trading institution has to have appropriate staffing.[1354] It must comply with the provisions of the German Banking Act on the number of managers,[1355] and concerning the management bodies and supervisory bodies.[1356]

In addition to these general rules, BaFin stipulates that – to avoid conflicts of interest – managers of the banking group must not at the same time be managers of the financial trading institution.[1357]

The legislative materials to the German Ring-fencing Act emphasize that, based on the proper business organisation, both the financial trading institution and the ring-fenced rest of the banking group have to particularly focus in their risk management on the risks of speculative transactions of the financial trading institution. This could be the basis for a number of other specific governance requirements, which take into account the specific risks of the trading institution.[1358]

d. Intragroup transactions and exposures

The German Ring-fencing Act stipulates that transactions between the trading entity and entities within the ring-fence have to be treated like third party transactions.[1359] *Möslein* notes that the wording of the provision does not explicitly state that transactions have to meet third party conditions. It could therefore be interpreted in a way that allows for the transaction not being based on actual third-party conditions but being treated like a third-party transaction from the perspective of risk management and financial supervision.[1360]

1353 See *BaFin* (2016) Interpretative Guidance, 46–47.
1354 This requirement derives from § 25c(4a)(4) German Banking Act.
1355 This requirement derives from § 25c German Banking Act.
1356 This requirement derives from § 25d German Banking Act.
1357 See *BaFin* (2016) Interpretative Guidance, 47.
1358 *Deutscher Bundestag* (2013) Gesetzesentwurf Trennbankengesetz, 42; see also *Braun* (2016) Geschäftsorganisation, para 4.
1359 § 25f(3) sentence 2 German Banking Act.
1360 See *Möslein* (2013) Spartentrennung, 405.

The Interpretative Guidance seems to suggest that transactions have to meet concrete third party conditions.[1361] In the interest of a far reaching and effective separation, the provision should be understood as an obligation to enter transactions only on arm's length basis. This would also be in line with the stringent requirement on the financing of the trading entity, discussed below.

Exposures of the ring-fenced banking group to the trading entity have to meet market conditions and thus have to be arm's length. Furthermore, large exposure requirements apply.[1362]

e. Distributions

§ 25f(3) German Banking Act stipulates that trading entities have to ensure that they independently refinance themselves. As suggested by *Möslein*, that per se does not exclude every form of credit transaction.[1363] BaFin clarified in its Interpretative Guidance that the provision does not prohibit the supply of funds by entities within the ring-fence. However, this supply of funds has to be in line with the arm's length principle. For example, a loan to the financial trading institution has to satisfy a third-party comparison and therefore has to exhibit terms adequate for risk and market conditions.[1364] The legislative materials furthermore state that refinancing over a capital increase is permitted as long as the viability of other members of the banking group is not endangered.[1365]

From this follows that distributions of the ring-fenced entities to the trading entity, such as a plain cash distribution, are not allowed. The other way around there are no specific limitations, so that dividends or cash distributions from the trading entity to the ring-fenced entities are conceivable.

1361 This is indicated with regard to ring-fenced entities operating as clearing member or security trustee for the financial trading institution (*BaFin* (2016) Interpretative Guidance, 47) and with regard to the supply of funds to the financial trading institution (*BaFin* (2016) Interpretative Guidance, 48).

1362 See Chapter III.V.B.b: Capital and liquidity.

1363 *Möslein* (2013) Spartentrennung, 405.

1364 See *BaFin* (2016) Interpretative Guidance, 48; see also *Schelo/Steck* (2013) Trennbankengesetz, 242 (noting that intragroup financing on arm's length is in line with the recommendations of the Liikanen Report); Chapter II.I.B: Avenue 1.

1365 *Deutscher Bundestag* (2013) Gesetzesentwurf Trennbankengesetz, 43.

f. Continuity of services

A financial trading institution is generally allowed to make use of the infrastructure and services provided by the ring-fenced banking group.[1366] This is, however, only the case insofar as (i) there is no operative risk and no reputation risk for the ring-fenced banking group and (ii) the outsourcing is in line with the provisions of the German Banking Act.[1367] The relevant provision in this regard is § 25b German Banking Act, which sets out the limits of the outsourcing of activities.[1368]

Whether or not the ring-fenced group entities can make use of infrastructure and services provided by the financial trading institution is not answered by the German Ring-fencing Act. The legislative materials to the Act, however, underscore that a participation in the financial trading entity must not entail substantial risk to the rest of the banking group. In particular regarding resolvability, the participation must neither entail operative risk nor reputational risk.[1369] Taking this into account, an interpretation therefore suggests that this would neither be the idea of the legislator nor be compatible with the aim of the Act.

C. Switzerland

As already established, there is hardly an alternative option for Swiss G-SIBs beside separating systemically important functions ex ante onto a separate legal entity.[1370] According to the Federal Council, banks have to ensure the operational and financial unbundling from the remaining

---

1366 *Deutscher Bundestag* (2013) Gesetzesentwurf Trennbankengesetz, 42; *Braun* (2016) Geschäftsorganisation, para 7; *BaFin* (2016) Interpretative Guidance, 46.

1367 See *BaFin* (2016) Interpretative Guidance, 46.

1368 According to the provision, an institution should avoid excessive risks by making appropriate arrangements depending on the nature, scope, complexity and risk of an outsourcing of functions that are necessary for their business (see § 25b(1) German Banking Act; see also *Deutsche Bundesbank* (2014) Banking Act, 111). It further clarifies that outsourcing does not shift the responsibility from the management board to the external provider (see § 25b(2) German Banking Act; see also *Deutsche Bundesbank* (2014) Banking Act, 112). Specific requirements by BaFin complement § 25b German Banking Act. (see e.g. BaFin's Circular on supervisory requirements for IT in financial institutions. *BaFin* (2017) Anforderungen IT).

1369 See *Deutscher Bundestag* (2013) Gesetzesentwurf Trennbankengesetz, 43.

1370 See Chapter III.IV.C.a.1.: Ex ante separation.

banking group. They have to equip the separated entity with appropriate capital and liquidity[1371] and ensure that it is able to "go live" without the rest of the banking group over a weekend.[1372]

There are two means to this end: firstly, the emergency plan. It specifies what measures are necessary to ensure continuation of the systemically important functions. Many of these measures will have to be implemented ex ante[1373] (first and foremost the transfer of systemically important functions onto the separate legal entity). Others will be implemented after triggering the emergency plan, and ensure the full separation of the separate legal entity from the rest of the banking group will be possible.

Secondly, measures that enhance resolvability. They aim at simplifying and unbundling structural, financial and operative interdependencies.[1374] As will be discussed below, these measures often overlap with measures of the emergency plan. Since 2016, the resolvability is furthermore part of the emergency plan's review, insofar as it is crucial for its implementation.[1375]

The separate legal entity has to be designed in a way that allows it – after triggering the emergency plan – to operate fully independently und self-sufficiently.[1376] Measures that serve the goal of reaching independence, self-sufficiency, and enhanced resolvability set up a fence around the separated entity.[1377]

1371 See *Bundesrat* (2015) Bericht Too Big to Fail, 1935.

1372 The timeframe is the course of a weekend. See *EFD* (2012) Kommentar Bankenverordnung, 10; see also Chapter III.IV.C.a.1: Ex ante separation.

1373 See Art. 60(3) Swiss Banking Ordinance; Chapter III.IV.C.a.1: Ex ante separation.

1374 See below (Chapter III.V.C: Switzerland).

1375 Art. 61(2) Swiss Banking Ordinance. This is considered necessary because *"the successful implementation of the emergency plan is to a large extent dependent on the global resolvability (e.g. by the creation of an ex ante separated Swiss entity)"*. Own translation from German original, see *EFD* (2016) Erläuterungsbericht, 19.

1376 Expert Interview, Affected Bank, September 28, 2017; see also Chapter III.IV.C.a.2.: Systemically important functions.

1377 The intention to enclose the separated entity with a fence is already hinted in the legislative materials to the Swiss Banking Ordinance: The EFD considers the ex ante separation of systemically important functions as matching *"the example"* (own translation from German original, see *EFD* (2012) Kommentar Bankenverordnung, 10 Fn 12) of the UK Vickers Commission ring-fencing model. See *EFD* (2012) Kommentar Bankenverordnung, 10 Fn 12; see also *Hofer* (2014) Structural Reforms, 329.

a. Legal sources

1. Emergency plan assessment

The Swiss Banking Act provides only limited guidance with regard to independence and self-sufficiency.[1378] It is again the Swiss Banking Ordinance that sets out key aspects in its provisions on the emergency plan.[1379]

Central provision is Art. 61 Swiss Banking Ordinance, which stipulates that Finma reviews the measures of a bank's emergency plan regarding their effectiveness in case of imminent insolvency. Finma thereby takes into account how far in advance the measures have been implemented.[1380] The more measures are implemented in advance, the less measures have to be proven effective in the case of an emergency by the emergency plan. It follows that the more measures are implemented in advance, the less difficult it is to get Finma approval.[1381]

Finma reviews measures of the emergency plan with regard to a number of criteria, which should ensure the continuation of domestic systemically important functions:[1382] They outline areas which could impede this goal and establish desired results affected banks have to reach with their emergency planning. These criteria correspond well with key features of a ringfence. They are therefore discussed with regard to the respective feature.

In 2016, it was furthermore clarified that also the global resolvability is part of the review, insofar as it is crucial for the implementation of the emergency plan.[1383]

1378 See Art. 9(2)(d) Swiss Banking Act.

1379 Art. 60 et seqq. Swiss Banking Ordinance. These articles are inspired by the FSB Key Attributes, see *Schiltknecht* (2015) Internationale Standards, 606. In contrast to "living wills", emergency plans do not aim to enhance the resolvability of a bank, but to ensure the continuation of systemically important functions. *Von der Crone/Beeler* (2012) Systemrelevante Finanzinstitute, 15.

1380 See Art. 61(1) Swiss Banking Ordinance in conjunction with Art. 60(3) Swiss Banking Ordinance.

1381 See also *Bahar/Peyer* (2013) Systemrelevante Banken, 425; *Hofer* (2014) Structural Reforms, 330.

1382 See *EFD* (2012) Kommentar Bankenverordnung, 11.

1383 Art. 61(2) Swiss Banking Ordinance. This is considered necessary, because *"the successful implementation of the emergency plan is to a large extent dependent on the global resolvability (e.g. by the creation of an ex ante separated Swiss entity)"*. Own translation from German original, see *EFD* (2016) Erläuterungsbericht, 19.

2. Resolvability incentives

In addition to the measures of the emergency plan, systemically important banks can be awarded capital rebates by Finma, if they improve their resolvability beyond the minimum requirements of the emergency plan. Finma takes into account how far in advance such measures are implemented.[1384] Art. 66 of the Swiss Banking Ordinance stipulates such measures exemplarily.[1385] The list orientates towards the FSB's Key Attributes of Effective Resolution,[1386] but, as noted by the EFD,[1387] it is also inspired by the recommendations of the expert commission.[1388]

3. Relation between emergency plan and resolvability incentives

While according to the expert commission, the emergency plan sets down minimal requirements and the resolvability incentives reward measures that exceed them,[1389] the legal relation of the provisions of the Swiss Banking Ordinance on the emergency plan and on the resolvability incentives is not fully clear.[1390]

This is particularly because, on the one hand, according to Art. 61(2) Swiss Banking Ordinance, the global resolvability is part of Finma's emergency plan review.[1391] On the other hand, according to Art. 65(2) Swiss Banking Ordinance, no rebates are to be awarded for the emergency planning (the implementation of minimal requirements should not be rewarded, but is mandatory).[1392]

This results in odd inconsistencies: the ex ante separation of systemically important functions, for example, is discussed by the EFD as a measure of

---

1384 See Art. 65 Swiss Banking Ordinance.

1385 Art. 66 Swiss Banking Ordinance.

1386 *FSB* (2014) Key Attributes, 38–41; See *EFD* (2012) Kommentar Bankenverordnung, 16; *Schiltknecht* (2015) Internationale Standards, 603.

1387 *EFD* (2012) Kommentar Bankenverordnung, 16; Hofer (2014) Structural Reforms, 452.

1388 *Expertenkommission* (2010) Schlussbericht, 38–39.

1389 See *Expertenkommission* (2010) Schlussbericht, 38.

1390 The inconsistency between the two approaches is criticised by *Hofer*, see *Hofer* (2014) Structural Reforms, 452–453.

1391 Art. 61(2) Swiss Banking Ordinance.

1392 Art. 65(2) Swiss Banking Ordinance. See also *Hofer* (2014) Structural Reforms, 453.

the emergency plan.[1393] Being a measure of the emergency plan, Art. 65(2) Swiss Banking Ordinance would not allow for capital rebates. However, the EFD, at a different point, implies that it considers the ex ante separation a measure that improves the resolvability and that should thus be rewarded with capital rebates.[1394]

The unclear relation is also reflected in differences between explanations of the ex ante separation by the two G-SIBs: in its asset transfer agreement, *UBS* notes that the Swiss TBTF requirements *"require systemically important banks [...] to put viable emergency plans in place to preserve the operation of systemically important functions [...] to the extent that such activities are not sufficiently separated in advance"*[1395] and that it is the intention of *UBS* to *"substantially improve the resolvability of the Group in response to Swiss 'too big to fail' requirements"* with the transfer.[1396] This suggests the understanding that the ex ante separation in advance is based on resolvability incentives, which are complemented by an emergency plan.

Credit Suisse, in contrast, notes in its bulk transfer agreement that the Swiss TBTF requirements *"require systemically important banks to design an emergency plan. With the transfer of the [systemically important functions] to and the continuation of [their] operation, [...], substantial parts of the Swiss emergency plan of the group are implemented ex ante"*.[1397] This suggests the understanding that the ex ante separation is part of the emergency plan.

As argued by *Hofer*, the provision of Art. 65(2) Swiss Banking Ordinance *"puts a strong emphasis on creating a distinction between to issues, which are not very distinct at all"*.[1398] The provision could therefore be interpreted to mean that for mere planning, no capital rebates are awarded. This would, for instance, apply for domestically oriented systemically important banks that do not intend to implement far reaching structural changes[1399] but nevertheless have to prepare an emergency plan. The ex ante implementa-

---

1393 See *EFD* (2012) Kommentar Bankenverordnung, 10.

1394 *EFD* (2016) Erläuterungsbericht, 16–17. That the ex ante separation was thought as a measure to enhance resolvability was also noted by an interviewed expert. Expert Interview, Affected Bank, September 28, 2017.

1395 Commercial Register Entry, *UBS AG,* (June 17, 2015), Public Deed of the Asset Transfer Agreement, 7.

1396 Commercial Register Entry, *UBS AG,* (June 17, 2015), Public Deed of the Asset Transfer Agreement, 7.

1397 Commercial Register Entry, *Credit Suisse,* (November 23, 2016), Bulk Transfer Agreement, 7.

1398 *Hofer* (2014) Structural Reforms, 453.

1399 See Chapter III.IV.C.a.1: Ex ante separation.

tion of measures that enhance the resolvability, the self-sufficiency and the independence of the Swiss bank should, however, be rewarded with capital rebates. The inconsistent judgements of the EFD, discussed above, imply that it comes to a similar conclusion.

The relation between the emergency plan and the resolvability incentives can therefore be regarded as a "carrot-and-stick" approach: banks are incentivised to enhance their resolvability by simplifying and unbundling their structural, financial and operative interdependencies. The more the resolvability is improved, the more carrots in the form of capital rebates are awarded. The emergency plan constitutes the stick: it represents the minimum goals (that might, however, be quite far-reaching); if certain measures that obstruct the continuation of the systemically important functions are not implemented, Finma may reject the bank's emergency plan and may impose its own ideas on the bank.[1400]

b. Capital and liquidity

According to the Swiss Banking Ordinance, measures of the emergency plan have to ensure that there is sufficient capital and liquidity for the continuation of systemically important functions in the case of its triggering.[1401]

The legislative materials explain that there have to be sufficient own funds (i) to capitalise ex ante separated entities in charge of the systemically important functions. In addition, own funds must suffice (ii) to absorb the losses of the banking group during the implementation of the last stages of the emergency plan (after its triggering).[1402] When assessing the (iii) liquidity needs, it has to be taken into account that the ring-fenced bank and the remaining banking group are likely to experience a high outflow of funds and difficulties in refinancing.[1403]

1400 The Swiss Banking Ordinance stipulates that in case of a rejection of the emergency plan, Finma is empowered to take considerably invasive measures regarding the structure of the banking group. They include the separation of infrastructure and services necessary for the provision of systemically important functions, the modification of the legal and operative structure of the banking group. See Art. 62 Swiss Banking Ordinance.

1401 See Art. 61(1)(c) Swiss Banking Ordinance.

1402 See *EFD* (2012) Kommentar Bankenverordnung, 12.

1403 See *EFD* (2012) Kommentar Bankenverordnung, 12.

From these requirements it can be derived that the ex ante separated entity has to be equipped with considerable amounts of capital and liquidity.

The requirements of the Swiss Banking Ordinance are complemented by provisions of the Swiss Capital Adequacy Ordinance[1404] and the Swiss Liquidity Ordinance:[1405] (i) the Swiss Capital Adequacy Ordinance stipulates that capital requirements for systemically important banks are obligatory not just for the banking group, but also standalone for the ex ante separated entity, which contains the systemically important functions;[1406] (ii) the Swiss Liquidity Ordinance stipulates that liquidity requirements apply to systemically important banks both on group level and the level of the single institute.[1407]

Both *UBS Switzerland AG* and *Credit Suisse (Schweiz) AG* therefore have to comply with capital and liquidity requirements on a standalone basis.[1408]

c. Governance

Measures of the emergency plan have to ensure that there are sufficient personnel resources for the continuation of systemically important functions. Management and control functions are particularly emphasized.[1409] The legislative materials note that contracts should be prepared in a way that the triggering of the emergency plan cannot be used as grounds for termination.[1410]

1404 Verordnung über die Eigenmittel und Risikoverteilung für Banken und Effektenhändler, June 1, 2012, SR 952.03 (Swiss Capital Adequacy Ordinance). The respective provision was included by a revision of the Capital Adequacy Ordinance. The revision is based on the Federal Council's 2015 evaluation of the TBTF package. See Verordnung über die Eigenmittel und Risikoverteilung für Banken und Effektenhändler, Änderung vom 11. Mai 2016, AS 2016 1725.

1405 Verordnung über die Liquidität der Banken, November 30, 2012, SR 952.06 (Swiss Liquidity Ordinance).

1406 Art. 124(2) Swiss Capital Adequacity Ordinance; see also *EFD* (2016) Erläuterungsbericht, 4.

1407 See Art. 20 Swiss Liquidity Ordinance; *Bundesrat* (2012) Botschaft Liquiditätsverordnung, 9459; *Passardi/Jans* (2014) Neue Liquiditätsvorschriften, 296.

1408 See e.g. *UBS* (2017) Standalone financial statements UBS Switzerland AG, 20.

1409 See Art. 61(1)(e) Swiss Banking Ordinance.

1410 See *EFD* (2012) Kommentar Bankenverordnung, 12.

UBS and *Credit Suisse* ex ante transferred large numbers of personnel onto their separated entities.[1411] Important functions, for example the CFO or treasurer, are employed directly by the entity they are responsible for: the Swiss entity's treasurer thus needs to be employed by the Swiss entity.[1412]

This is arguably based on the awareness that the transfer of personnel and the related contractual changes cannot be conducted over a weekend. It is likely that these measures furthermore intend to ensure the independency of the Swiss entity and tackle conflicts of interest.

But it is not just important to adequately staff the ring-fenced bank, but also to address the question how it can be ensured that the management and control functions are ready for use in the case of the triggering of the emergency plan and do not face considerable conflicts of interest, in particular given their integration in the banking group during going concern.

This question is *inter alia* addressed by the implementation of so called "contingency organisations". They are organisational structures that change in the event of the triggering of the emergency plan.[1413] They can be understood as optional hierarchical structures that become effective in a certain a priori defined moment.

In the case of a crisis, for example, the Swiss entity's CFO would stop following the instructions of the banking group's CFO.[1414] This aims to ensure that conflicts of interest are avoided in case of the triggering of the emergency plan and management can act independently and in the sole interest of the separated entity.

In the example above, the Swiss entity's CFO would, however, continue to inform the banking group's CFO,[1415] which reflects that the contingency organisations are tailor made. They allow for flexible solutions in the interest of all affected parties.

1411 See e.g. *Millischer/Heim*, Milliardenabflüsse bei der UBS Schweiz, Handelszeitung (March 31, 2016), (noting that *UBS Switzerland's* personnel amounts to 11000 employees); *Padevit*, CS: Schweizer Tochter wird am 20. November geboren, Finanz und Wirtschaft (October 7, 2016), (noting that *Credit Suisse Schweiz*'s personnel amounts to 6600 employees).

1412 Expert Interview, Affected Bank, September 28, 2017.

1413 Expert Interview, Affected Bank, September 28, 2017.

1414 Expert Interview, Affected Bank, September 28, 2017.

1415 Expert Interview, Affected Bank, September 28, 2017.

There are comparable measures in place for the board of directors: Swiss entities have to demonstrate their autonomy with independent directors.[1416] Finma demands that at least a third of board members are independent.[1417] In case of the triggering of the emergency plan, independent directors would be able to constitute the majority in the board of directors. This would ensure that they make decisions in the favour of the entity, not the group.[1418]

Such measures are necessary in a global crisis scenario, in which group executives would possibly be incentivised to withdraw liquidity from the Swiss entity. The board of directors could prevent such actions.[1419]

While these findings are exemplary and do not allow for a comprehensive assessment of the Swiss governance requirements, they reflect that there are considerable efforts undertaken by the affected banks and Finma to address governance issues for the Swiss entity.

d. Intragroup transactions and exposures

Art. 61(1)(b) sets down that Finma reviews as part of the emergency plan, among other things, whether the legal and economic intragroup relations,

---

1416 This was underscored by *Markus Ronner,* who is responsible for *UBS's* implementation of the Swiss emergency plan, in an interview. *Schöchli,* "Wir werden bis Ende 2018 bereit sein", NZZ (June 20, 2015).

1417 General compliance rules that are applicable to all banks stipulate that at least a third of a bank's board of directors have to be independent. Independency is not given if a number of exclusion criteria are fulfilled. See *Finma* (2017) Corporate Governance – Banken, 5. Whether or not these rules sufficiently ensure the independence of the Swiss entity has been critically discussed in connection with the IPO of *Credit Suisse (Schweiz) AG* which was planned at the time. See *Hegglin,* Die CS Schweiz in Halbgefangenschaft, Finanz und Wirtschaft (September 6, 2016). See also *Credit Suisse (Schweiz) AG* (2018) Annual Report 2018, 13.

1418 Expert Interview, Affected Bank, September 28, 2017. The triggering of the emergency plan is defined in Art. 63 Swiss Banking Ordinance and refers to Art. 25(1) Swiss Banking Act. It is triggered when Finma decides, based on reasonable concern, that the bank is insolvent, or has not complied with capital or liquidity requirements for a certain time (Art. 25(1) Swiss Banking Act). With activation of the bank's recovery plan, an "emergency plan task-force" is activated that monitors events in the banking group. The emergency plan is fully triggered over the resolution-weekend. Expert Interview, Affected Bank, September 28, 2017.

1419 Expert Interview, Affected Bank, September 28, 2017.

in particular intragroup financing and guarantees, are designed in a way that does not obstruct the continuation of systemically important functions.

According to an interviewed expert, there are no financial dependencies on the banking group. There are limits set by Finma concerning intragroup arrangements[1420] and exposures.[1421] These are also mostly collateralised.[1422] There are furthermore requirements in place to transact with the group on an arm's length basis.[1423] *Ronner* also emphasizes the importance of financial unbundling.[1424]

Affected banking groups can be awarded capital rebates if they unbundle their financial interdependences exceeding minimal requirements, in particular through limitations of unsecured loans and guarantees and the establishment of incentives for a intragroup financing that corresponds as much as possible with market conditions.[1425]

e. Distributions

Neither the Swiss Banking Act nor the Swiss Banking Ordinance set down requirements on how distributions, e.g. dividends, from the ring-fenced bank to the remaining banking group are to be handled. Drawing from the standalone financial statements of *UBS Switzerland AG,* for example, one finds that dividends are paid to *UBS AG* exceeding the total net profit of the period.[1426] This indicates that there is no general restriction on the payment of dividends to other group members.[1427]

From the obligation of the Swiss entity to comply with capital and liquidity requirements on a standalone basis follows, however, that there

---

1420 Expert Interview, Affected Bank, September 28, 2017.

1421 Expert Interview, Affected Bank, March 6, 2018. The limitation of direct exposure of the Swiss entities to the rest of the banking groups are also recognized by rating agencies: For example, a limited exposure of *UBS Switzerland AG* to *UBS AG* was expected by *Fitch* already in 2015, see *Reuters,* Fitch Assigns UBS Switzerland AG 'A' IDR; Affirms UBS AG at 'A' (June 15, 2015).

1422 Expert Interview, Affected Bank, September 28, 2017.

1423 Expert Interview, Affected Bank, March 6, 2018.

1424 *Schöchli,* "Wir werden bis Ende 2018 bereit sein", NZZ (June 20, 2015).

1425 Art. 66(b) Swiss Banking Ordinance.

1426 *UBS* (2018) Standalone financial statements UBS Switzerland AG, 4.

1427 *Fitch*, for example, *"expect[s] that UBS Switzerland AG will make material dividend payments to UBS AG". Reuters,* Fitch Assigns UBS Switzerland AG 'A' IDR; Affirms UBS AG at 'A' (June 15, 2015).

must be certain limitations on distributions paid to the non-ring-fenced entities.[1428] As a minimum, the Swiss entity must not fall short of the capital and liquidity requirements.

There are furthermore limitations for distributions stemming from general corporate and criminal law: for non-ring-fenced entities (which are in the current setup the full owners of the ring-fenced entities)[1429] the limitations of Art. 680 Swiss Code of Obligations apply, which stipulate that shareholders may not be obliged to give more than the price of a share.[1430] Corresponding limitations for the ring-fenced entities are the fiduciary duties and relating thereto the liability of the executive board, as executives have to act in the interest of the company they represent.[1431]

f. Continuity of services

Art. 61(1)(d) stipulates that measures of the emergency plan have to safeguard that there are appropriate processes and the necessary infrastructure in place for the operability of systemically important functions. Necessary resources need to be accessible at any time and independently from the rest of the banking group.[1432] According to the EFD, in particular the establishment of group service entities has implications for the emergency plan.[1433]

1428 This seems to be acknowledged in *UBS Group*'s annual report, noting that *"[i]n particular, UBS Group AG's direct and indirect subsidiaries, including UBS AG, UBS Switzerland AG, UBS Limited and UBS Americas Holding LLC, are subject to laws and regulations that restrict dividend payments, authorize regulatory bodies to block or reduce the flow of funds from those subsidiaries to UBS Group AG, or could impact their ability to repay any loans made to, or other investments in, such subsidiary by UBS Group AG or another member of the Group"*. *UBS* (2018) Annual Report 2017, 55.

1429 See Chapter III.IV.C.c: Affected banks.

1430 See Art. 680 Bundesgesetz betreffend die Ergänzung des Schweizerischen Zivilgesetzbuches (Fünfter Teil: Obligationenrecht), March 30, 1911, SR 220 (Swiss Code of Obligations).

1431 See Art. 717(1) Swiss Code of Obligations; Art. 754(1) Swiss Code of Obligations. While fiduciary duties can be restricted to a large extent in the interest of the banking group in the articles of incorporation, there are limitations, namely when their acts constitute the criminal offense of disloyal management. See Art. 158 Schweizerisches Strafgesetzbuch, December 21, 1937, SR 311.0 (Swiss Criminal Code).

1432 See Art. 61(1)(d) Swiss Banking Ordinance.

1433 See *EFD* (2016) Erläuterungsbericht, 6.

Systemically important banks can furthermore be awarded capital rebates if they exceed minimum requirements and unbundle their operations in a way that ensures their access to infrastructure, data and services.[1434]

For *UBS*, a major step to reach this goal is the establishment of an independent legal entity that provides services to around 130 *UBS* entities worldwide.[1435] *UBS Business Solutions AG* improves the banking group's resolvability by maintaining the *"operational continuity of critical services should a recovery or resolution event occur"*.[1436] It provides internal services such as IT, payment transactions, risk management, human resources and marketing and legal services.[1437] Similar plans are pursued by *Credit Suisse,*[1438] which is in the process of establishing a service company for Switzerland.[1439]

D. Results

a. Elements of the fence

1. Capital and liquidity

In all three countries of interest, the ring-fenced banks have to independently comply with capital and liquidity requirements.[1440] The most detailed considerations are found in the UK, where the PRA outlines the obligation of the ring-fenced bank to put in place stress testing capabilities[1441] and articulates that it considers exposures to other members of the banking group as if they were third parties during SREP.[1442]

Similar requirements are likely to apply to the ring-fenced entities in Germany, because the separation of certain activities onto a trading entity

---

1434 See Art. 66(a)(2) Swiss Banking Ordinance.
1435 See *Schöchli,* Das Drehbuch für die nächste Krise, NZZ (June 6, 2017).
1436 *UBS* (2017) 2016 SEC Form 20-F, 13, 448.
1437 See *Schöchli,* Das Drehbuch für die nächste Krise, NZZ (June 6, 2017).
1438 *Schöchli,* Das Drehbuch für die nächste Krise, NZZ (June 6, 2017).
1439 *Credit Suisse* (2017) Annual Report 2016, 14.
1440 See the respective chapters on capital and liquidity above.
1441 See *PRA* (2017) Ring-fenced Bodies, 15; Chapter III.V.A.a: Capital and liquidity.
1442 See *PRA* (2017) Ring-fenced Bodies, 14; Chapter III.V.A.a: Capital and liquidity.

does not affect already existent stress testing capabilities of the rest of the banking group (which then becomes "ring-fenced"). In addition, exposures to the trading entity have to be at market conditions and risk-adequate and large exposure requirements of the CRR are applicable.[1443] During SREP, it can therefore be assumed that exposures to the trading entity will be considered as if they were third parties, which would result in additional capital buffers for the ring-fenced group. As the Swiss entities also have to independently comply with capital and liquidity requirements, it is to assume that they will have to put in place stress testing capabilities as well.[1444]

2. Governance

With regard to governance, all three jurisdictions also put in place specific requirements that constitute a fence. They aim (i) to ensure that the separated entities are adequately staffed; (ii) to avoid conflicts of interest of the management; and (iii) to avoid conflicts of interest between the ring-fenced and the non-ring-fenced bank.

The UK sets out the most detailed and elaborate rules. A good example are its specifications on the independence of a director: they include a complex set of reasons for exclusion, including, for instance, family ties or employments by other members of the banking group reaching back five years.[1445] The notion of the BaFin's Interpretative Guidance that managers of the banking group must not at the same time be managers of the financial trading institution appears blunt in comparison.[1446]

1443 See Chapter III.V.B.d: Intragroup transactions and exposures; Chapter III.V.B.e: Distributions.

1444 While there are limits for exposures between the ring-fenced bank and the non-ring-fenced bank (see Chapter III.V.C.d: Intragroup transactions and exposures), it could not be established whether exposures to the rest of the banking group have to be considered as if they were third parties as well in Switzerland. It is, however, likely, given the orientation towards the UK and could, for example, be mandated by Finma order. It could also, for Swiss ring-fenced bodies, result in additional capital buffers.

1445 See *PRA* (2016) PRA Rulebook: Ring Fenced Bodies, Sec. 1(3)(2).

1446 See *BaFin* (2016) Interpretative Guidance, 47; Chapter III.V.B.c: Governance. The general rules on the independence of board members, which are set down in § 25d(2) German Banking Act, are not very elaborate either.

In Switzerland, it seems that Finma is satisfied if at least a third of board members are independent.[1447] This indicates that the Swiss entities are less independent from their respective banking group during going concern than in the UK, where at least half of the members of the board of directors need to be independent.[1448] However, as discussed above, in a crisis situation, independent directors would be able to constitute the majority on the board of directors.[1449]

A particularly interesting feature of the Swiss approach are the contingency organisations.[1450] They also reflect the idea that the interests of the Swiss entities and the rest of the banking group are generally aligned during going concern. A reporting line from the group's management to the Swiss entity's management is found acceptable under normal business circumstances.

In the case of an emergency, however, the interests are likely to diverge. To avoid that actions are taken at the expense of the Swiss entity and to ensure the full independence, the reporting line is cut. The flow of information, however, remains ensured.[1451] The problematic questions of (i) who decides that the reporting line is cut; and (ii) when is the reporting line cut, are ex ante regulated by the automated entry into force by the triggering of the emergency plan.

The contingency organisations indicate that the Swiss entities are, for the moment, more integrated into their respective banking group than in the UK, where conflicts of interest have to be addressed already during going concern. They can also be considered a manifestation of the subsidiarity principle and the general tendency to avoid overly invasive requirements.[1452]

1447 See *Finma* (2017) Corporate Governance – Banken, 5. Whether or not these rules sufficiently ensure the independence of the Swiss entity has been critically discussed in connection with the IPO of *Credit Suisse (Schweiz) AG* which was planned at the time. See *Hegglin,* Die CS Schweiz in Halbgefangenschaft, Finanz und Wirtschaft (September 6, 2016).

1448 See Chapter III.V.A.b: Governance.

1449 Expert Interview, Affected Bank, September 28, 2017. See Chapter III.V.C.c: Governance.

1450 See Chapter III.V.C.c: Governance.

1451 See Chapter III.V.C.c: Governance.

1452 See Chapter III.II.C.b.2: Subsidiarity principle; Chapter III.II.D.e: Invasiveness.

3. Intragroup transactions and exposures

In all three jurisdictions requirements are in place that allow for intragroup transactions only to be conducted at arm's length.[1453] In Germany and the UK, intragroup exposures have to be at arm's length and large exposure limits of the CRR apply.[1454] In Switzerland there are limits set by Finma.[1455] Applying a legal comparative view, it can be assumed that also in Switzerland large exposure limits should apply between the ring-fenced entity and the non-ring-fenced entity.

The UK stipulation that the ring-fenced bank is not allowed to become dependent on income from transactions with group members outside the fence, or with customers where it is likely contingent on services by group members,[1456] finds its counterpart in the Swiss emphasis on the self-sufficiency of the entity:[1457] It also has to be structured in a way that allows for it to operate standing alone.

4. Distributions

Distributions include first and foremost dividends but can also include other contributions such as cash payments. All the jurisdictions have rules in place that regulate whether or not distributions can be made between the ring-fenced and non-ring-fenced entities.

In the UK, distributions between the entities are generally allowed. The PRA, however, established a regime to review distributions of the ring-fenced bank and to prevent them in case there is *"a significant adverse effect on the capital position of [the ring-fenced body] that could adversely affect the continuity of the provision of core services"*.[1458] There are no requirements for distributions, from the non-ring-fenced bodies to the ring-fenced bodies.

1453 See the respective chapters above.

1454 See the respective chapters above.

1455 Expert Interview, Affected Bank, March 6, 2018. The limitation of direct exposure of the Swiss entities to the rest of the banking groups are also recognized by rating agencies: For example, a limited exposure of *UBS Switzerland AG* to *UBS AG* was expected by *Fitch* already in 2015, see *Reuters,* Fitch Assigns UBS Switzerland AG 'A' IDR; Affirms UBS AG at 'A' (June 15, 2015).

1456 See *PRA* (2016) PRA Rulebook: Ring Fenced Bodies, Sec. 13; Chapter III.V.A.b: Governance.

1457 See Chapter III.IV.C.a.2: Systemically important functions.

1458 See *PRA* (2017) Ring-fenced Bodies, 22; Chapter III.V.A.d: Distributions.

In Switzerland the handling of distributions is likely to be similar: distributions from the Swiss entity to the rest of the banking group are limited by the obligation of the Swiss entities to adhere to capital requirements on their own. Furthermore, there are limitations due to general corporate and criminal law.[1459] In contrast to the UK, a regime of Finma to review and prevent distributions is not explicitly outlined.

For Germany, distributions from the ring-fenced entities to the trading entity are prohibited. This derives from the obligation of the latter to refinance itself independently from the ring-fenced group.[1460] Comparing the regulation of distribution, the German rule is thus the most stringent. Trading activities of the financial trading institution cannot be subsidised by the ring-fenced entities. A legal comparative view suggests that this requirement is potentially overshooting, as trading entities are likely unprofitable and hence unpopular.

5. Continuity of services

The continuity of services is addressed in all jurisdictions. In the UK, the ring-fenced bank may only receive regular services from another ring-fenced body or a group service company.[1461] In Switzerland, banks that provide systemically important functions need to ensure as part of the emergency plan there are appropriate processes and the necessary infrastructure in place to operate them. Furthermore, the necessary resources need to be accessible at any time and independently from the rest of the banking group. As such measures improve the resolvability of the group, capital rebates may be awarded. Both Swiss G-SIBs are in the process of establishing group service companies.[1462]

In contrast to the above, in Germany the trading entity is generally allowed to make use of the infrastructure and services provided by the ring-fenced banking group: however, only if there is no operative risk and no reputational risk for the ring-fenced banking group. The ring-fenced banking group, on the other hand, is not allowed to make use of the infrastruc-

1459 See Chapter III.V.C.e: Distributions.
1460 See Chapter III.V.B.e: Distributions.
1461 See Chapter III.V.A.e: Continuity of services.
1462 See Chapter III.V.C.f: Continuity of services.

ture or of services of the trading entity. This derives from an interpretation of the German Ring-fencing Act.[1463]

b. Other findings

1. Character

Again, the most detailed, forthright and clearest rules are found in the UK. This is because, as already discussed, it uses the traditional hierarchy of legal sources most consequently and the goals articulated by the Vickers Report are pursued forthright.[1464]

In particular with regard to the height of the fence, the German Ring-fencing Act requires a lot of interpretation, which is only to some extent provided by BaFin. Clearer rules, setting out what is meant by the "*economically, organisationally and legally independent*" trading entity, would thus be desirable.

The Swiss approach faces a similar problem regarding the height of the fence as it faces with regard to the ex ante separation of systemically important function: there is no clear obligation of banks to implement measures ex ante. Affected banks are, on the one hand, forced to do so with the prospect that the emergency plan review by Finma would turn out negatively and are, on the other hand, incentivised by capital rebates. The necessary (but not necessarily ex ante implemented) measures of the emergency plan to a large extent overlap with measures to improve resolvability. This can be criticised, in particular, from the perspective of transparency and the principle of legality.[1465]

2. Ring-fencing in Switzerland

All the jurisdictions of interest put in place specific requirements for affected banks that constitute a fence. While for Germany and the UK this is hardly surprising as the intention to ring-fence is emphasized prominent-

1463 See Chapter III.V.B.f: Continuity of services.
1464 See Chapter III.II.A: United Kingdom.
1465 For a discussion of transparency and the principle of legality, see Chapter III.II.D.b: Legal sources.

ly,[1466] for Switzerland it is an important finding. It is also surprising, as Swiss ring-fencing is mostly ignored in the international discourse. Based on the findings on the Swiss fence, the Swiss approach is therefore discussed in greater detail.

i. Generally unnoticed

Switzerland is generally not recognised for its adoption of structural reform rules. This becomes obvious when looking at the academic work exploring structural reform legislation comparatively:[1467] The Swiss organisational measures are seldom covered. The very few cases in which it is included or in which its relation to internationally recognized ring-fencing rules is underscored, are domestic sources.[1468] International recognition is scarce and mostly limited to a side note.[1469]

It seems odd that the second most important financial centre in Europe is not included in comparative analyses. This is likely due to a few special features of the Swiss approach that differ from the approach of other countries, notably Germany and the UK.

ii. Special features of the Swiss approach

The main difference is that there is no comprehensive act that sets down a requirement to ring-fence. The two main starting points are the emergency

1466 This is reflected, e.g. by the choice of name in Germany and by the title of the new Part 9B of the FSMA 2000 in the UK.

1467 E.g. *Lehmann* (2014) Ring-Fencing; *De Vogelaere* (2016) Bank Structure Reforms; *Krahnen/Noth/Schüwer* (2016) Structural Reforms; *Kumpan* (2014) Verbot von Eigengeschäften; *Masciandaro/Suardi* (2014) Public Interest and Lobbies; *Pflock* (2014) Europäische Bankenregulierung; *ZEW* (2013) Trennbanken.

1468 This is in particular *Hofer* (2014) Structural Reforms and to some extent *Bahar/Peyer* (2013) Systemrelevante Banken, 377–378; see also *Achermann* (2018) Organisation, 278–280.

1469 *"By the start of 2019, Britain's largest lenders will need to put their retail banking units inside a heavily capitalised subsidiary, protecting them in case the group fails. [...] Switzerland aside, no other country has introduced anything similar." Financial Times,* Ringfencing will help in the next banking crisis (January 10, 2017); *European Commission* (2014) Impact Assessment Part 2, 2; cf. *FSB* (2014) Structural Banking Reforms, 9–10.

plan and the improved resolvability.[1470] They are complemented by selective legislative measures, such as the requirement adopted in 2016 that stipulates that entities of globally active systemically important banks which contain the systemically important functions, have to comply with capital requirements on a standalone basis.[1471] The steering actions of the regulator furthermore play an important role in shaping factual requirements for affected banks.[1472]

Another special feature of the Swiss approach that potentially leads to less prominence in the international debate is that ring-fencing requirements apply only to a subset of large banks, namely the Swiss G-SIBs *UBS* and *Credit Suisse.* While other banks have also been designated systemically important status by the SNB, they are not expected to conduct "*larger organisational or structural changes*" due to differences in their business model and geographical orientation.[1473]

Another specialty is that, due to the difference in the approach, not all requirements become effective at the same time. It is to be understood rather as a process: a lot has changed since the expert commission's report was published in 2010, the requirements for the globally active systemically important banks have evolved.[1474] This is reflected in the structural changes that the two banks have implemented since then.

In addition, some parts of the Swiss ring-fence are on a contingent basis. This refers particularly to the governance measures, especially the contingency organisations. As changes in the reporting line are executed only in case of the triggering of the emergency plan, they are not noticeable during going concern.[1475] An important part of ring-fencing therefore lies dormant before the public.

iii. Considerable fence

Even if the Swiss approach is included in a comparison with the more prominent ring-fencing rules, the results are not convincing. *Hofer*, for in-

1470 See Chapter III.V.C.a: Legal sources.
1471 See Chapter III.V.C.b: Capital and liquidity.
1472 See Chapter III.II.C.c.2: Finma emergency plan assessment; Chapter III.IV.C: Switzerland.
1473 See Chapter III.IV.C.a: Systemically important functions.
1474 Steps in the evolutionary process are, e.g. the obligation to comply with capital requirements standalone. See Chapter III.V.C.b: Capital and liquidity.
1475 See Chapter III.V.C.c: Governance.

stance, comes to the conclusion that the creation of a fence *"is the most notable feature that completely lacks a match under Swiss law"*. While he is right in pointing out that a *"compelling ex ante separation protected by a (more or less) clear framework regulating legal, operational, and economic interdependencies"* is missing in the Swiss approach,[1476] the findings of the chapters above reveal that considerable efforts have been undertaken to establish a (i) compelling ex ante separation for Switzerland's globally active banks (ii) that is protected by a fence.

A comparison of key features of the fence suggests that the Swiss ring-fence may not be as transparent as the one of the UK, but that it is for itself of considerable height. As an example, one can refer to the obligation of the ring-fenced bank to comply with capital requirements standalone.[1477] But also other examples such as the governance measures or the continuity of services indicate that the fence is higher than one would expect.

The fact that parts of the ring-fence, in particular the contingency organisations, lie dormant during going concern and are thusly not noticeable to the public, should not conceal that there are measures in place to ensure the automated separation of the ring-fenced bank in case of an emergency.

The ex ante separation and the implemented governance measures may furthermore have the effect that decision-makers in the Swiss entities start to increasingly claim responsibility and independence from the rest of the banking group. This is in particular due to fiduciary duties and the corresponding liability.[1478] It is therefore thinkable that the fence is naturally heightened and is likely to assimilate to the UK's fence over time.

Furthermore, it should be noted that the most invasive step was the separation of the systemically important functions into a separate legal entity. Since that has been accomplished, the rest are minor changes that can be implemented over time.

3. Ring-fencing

In summary, it can be found that all three jurisdictions put in place requirements that govern the (i) legal, economic and operational indepen-

---

1476 *Hofer* (2014) Structural Reforms, 329–330.

1477 See Chapter III.V.C.b: Capital and liquidity; Chapter III.II.C.b.3: TBTF evaluation.

1478 See Chapter III.V.C.e: Distributions.

dence of the separated entities and thereby constitute a fence. In combination with the other core characteristics of ring-fencing, namely (ii) the separation of activities, and (iii) maintaining universal banking, all three core characteristics are fulfilled.

It can therefore be concluded that all three jurisdictions of interest put in place bank structural reforms that aim to shield deposits and services essential for the functioning of the real economy from services deemed riskier and less socially important by ensuring they are provided legally, financially and operationally separately from each other within a banking group, thereby preserving universal banking.[1479]

4. Practical relevance

In practice, however, there seem to be considerable differences in the relevance of the respective provisions in the three jurisdictions.

This is reflected in the news reporting and in affected banks' own publications: in the UK and Switzerland, there is a constant flow of information provided by both news outlets and affected banks. This is, among other reasons, because the costs of ring-fencing are enormous. For example, *Lloyd's Banking Group* alone, which is one of the less impacted banks, estimate 500 million £ implementation costs.[1480] The ex ante separation of systemically important functions for *UBS* alone was estimated at one billion CHF.[1481] Another reason is that numerous customers are affected by the changes in structure, e.g. by a change of their account details.[1482]

As already discussed in Chapter III.IV.B.d,[1483] no comparable information is available from Germany. To the knowledge of the author, no financial trading institution has been established so far.[1484] It is indeed conceiv-

1479 See Chapter I.IV.B: Ring-fencing as a structural reform.
1480 *Binham/Dunkley*, Regulators get ready to authorise 'ringfenced' UK banks, Financial Times (August 19, 2017).
1481 *Baches*, Pionierprojekt einer Grossbank, NZZ (June 26, 2015).
1482 See e.g. *Britton et al.* (2016) Ring-fencing, 171.
1483 See Chapter III.IV.B.d: Affected banks.
1484 Apart from extensive research, the author contacted both BaFin and the Association of German Banks. BaFin was not able to answer the query due to its duty of confidentiality according to § 8 German Banking Act. The Association of German Banks did not have any information on its members activity concerning the establishment of financial trading entities available. Also in the BaFin Journal of February 2016 (*Stubbe* (2016) Trennbanken, 10) and in the response of the German Government to a parliamentary question (*Deutscher*

able that the financial trading institution will remain a theoretical construct and that, in spite of the legal basis, ring-fencing is not going to be put in practice in Germany.

This may be because, in contrast to Switzerland and the UK, Germany decided to adopt the *containment method* of ring-fencing, excluding only very few activities from the ring-fenced entity, and set down far-reaching exemptions. This limited scope applies mainly to activities whose relevance has considerably decreased over the last decade.[1485] In addition, the stipulated fence is in some aspects more stringent than in the UK and Switzerland, in particular with regard to the requirement for trading entities to refinance themselves independently: while funds can be supplied by the ring-fenced entities, this supply has to comply with the arm's length principle. As such a supply at market conditions is costly, banks are strongly incentivized to avoid establishing a trading entity.[1486]

The view that the German Ring-fencing Act is not going to be of practical relevance is expressed frequently in the academic literature, however, typically regarding incoming EU structural reform legislation.[1487] With the withdrawal of the bank structural reform file, a comprehensive superses-

Bundestag (2016) Antworten der Bundesregierung, 42–43) there is no information on the establishment of a financial trading institution.

1485 The provision of proprietary trading – proprietary business to be in line with the German Banking Act's diction – has decreased considerably since the global economic crisis. Many banks claim that they do not engage in it at all anymore. (See *PwC* (2014) AFME: Bank Structural Reform Study, 7 (noting that *"[a]lmost 90% of banks studied announced reductions in proprietary trading activities since the financial crisis, with over half exiting these businesses"*)). For all banks that quit the provision of proprietary business, establishing a separate trading entity for this activity is therefore not necessary. In addition, the exception that allows for the loan and guarantee business with hedge funds and AIFs, if fully collateralised creates enough room for manoeuvre for affected banks, to make a trading entity dispensable. As market making is not prohibited, its provision does not require a ring-fence (see Chapter III.IV.B.a.1: Excluded activities). Long term investments are also covered by an exception, so that long-term speculation can be conducted by the banking groups (see Chapter III.IV.B.a.2: Exceptions).

1486 See Chapter III.V.B.e: Distributions.

1487 See e.g. *Schaffelhuber/Kunschke* (2015) Trennbankengesetz, 402 (expressing the opinion that the German Ring-fencing Act is not going to play an important role in practice due to its limited scope and less stringent legal consequences compared with European Union legislation); *Schäfer* (2016) § 3 Verbotene Geschäfte, para 3.

sion through European Union law has become considerably less probable.[1488]

If applied properly, it can be assumed that the provisions of the German Ring-fencing Act currently exert similar legal consequences as the *activities ban*, because no financial trading institution has been created yet in which excluded activities can be conducted. It will be interesting to see how the German Ring-fencing Act will evolve, in particular in a changing economic environment.

5. Switzerland as a role model for the EU?

As discussed in Chapter II.IV.C.c, provisions of the BRRD and the SRMR setting out far-reaching powers for regulators to address resolvability impediments are considered by some authors to be potential gateways for the introduction of an EU-wide ring-fencing regime.[1489]

Mandating ring-fencing via these provisions would resemble the Swiss approach to a certain extent. Before discussing the question whether Switzerland should be regarded as a role model for the EU, some similarities are pointed out.

In both cases (i) the legal basis would be within the setting of recovery and resolution and would be based (ii) on guidance of the FSB.[1490] In both cases the implementation of ring-fencing would be (iii) enforcement-based, i.e. to a great extent the responsibility of the respective regulators.[1491]

Switzerland's success in implementing ring-fencing for its largest banks can rightly be regarded as proof that an enforcement-based implementation of ring-fencing is possible. It demonstrates that it is not absolutely essential to adopt an act setting out every detail of ring-fencing, like the UK and Germany did. Such an approach has certain advantages: it allows, for example, for more flexibility, as a case by case assessment of banking

---

1488 See Chapter II.IV: Withdrawal of the File and Alternatives.

1489 See Chapter II.IV.C.c: Existing regimes.

1490 See, in particular, *FSB* (2014) Key Attributes, 37–43; see also *FSB* (2015) Obstacles to Resolvability, 12–18; *FSB* (2016) Operational Continuity, 9–15. For a summary of relevant *FSB* Guidances, see *Achermann* (2018) Organisation, 276–278. For a discussion of their legal character, see *Brändli* (2018) Internationale Standards, 47–50.

1491 See Chapter II.IV.C.c: Existing regimes; Chapter III.II.C.c: Legal sources.

groups is possible. It can furthermore be gradual, with not all requirements imposed at the same time.[1492]

However, in addition to the considerations on the EU's emphasis of proportionality set out in Chapter II.IV.C.c[1493] and concerns over transparency and the principle of legality, the factual differences of the banking sectors constitute, in the author's opinion, a major obstacle for a similar use of the resolvability assessment in the EU.

There are a number of factors that facilitate the success of an enforcement-based implementation of ring-fencing in Switzerland: (i) there are only two affected banks. It is easier to come to an agreement with two G-SIBs than to come to an agreement with 12 G-SIBs and all other banks affected by the rules.[1494] In Switzerland, (ii) affected banks have been included in the legislative process since the formation of the expert group.[1495] While there were select protests against measures demanded by Finma,[1496] generally it can be found that banks have been willing to implement the regulator's demands. Traditionally, there is an (iii) exceptionally close cooperation between regulators and banks that is likely not equalled in the European Union. In addition, (iv) a consistent and non-discriminatory application of the powers is facilitated by the limited number of affected banks in Switzerland. Furthermore, (v) Switzerland is particularly exposed to its G-SIBs, which is illustrated by the relation of size to the country's GDP,[1497] making necessary especially determined action by its regulators. The country's (vi) intervention on behalf of *UBS* moreover showed that the failure of large banks is a credible threat.

In the European Union the setting is naturally different: there is a large number of G-SIBs, there are interests of Member States to protect their na-

---

1492 See also in this regard the considerations of the Liikanen Report's HLEG concerning advantages of Avenue 1, Chapter II.I.B.b: Costs and benefits.

1493 See Chapter II.IV.C.c: Existing regimes.

1494 There are currently 12 EU banks considered global systemically important by the FSB. See *FSB* (2017) Global Systemically Important Banks, 3. The EBA considers 35 banks potentially systemically relevant. See *EBA*, Large Institutions with a leverage ratio exposure measure above 200bn EUR, http://www.eba.europa.eu/risk-analysis-and-data/global-systemically-important-institutions/2017.

1495 See Chapter III.II.D.a: Expert commissions.

1496 For example with regard to *Credit Suisse*'s re-transfer of STS Trading. See *Hässig*, Finma stellt sich gegen CS-Pläne, Tages Anzeiger (May 11, 2016).

1497 *UBS*'s balance sheet is 1.4 times the Swiss GDP, *CS*'s balance sheet 1.2 times. Together they account for 2.6 of Switzerland's GDP. See Chapter III.I.C.c: UBS and Credit Suisse.

tional champions. Regulators and banks can by their very nature not engage in a comparable informal dialogue that takes into account the specialties of the bank. The risk of a non-consistent and discriminatory application is higher, due to the large number of very diverse banks. Drawing from the larger number of affected banks, one can also assume that there would be less reluctance in taking legal action against decisions or pressure of authorities.

In summary, it can be argued that the Swiss success in implementing ring-fencing via an enforcement-based approach cannot be simply assumed to be reached similarly in the European Union: the differences between a (i) small country with a culture of cooperation between regulators and (only two) affected banks and a (ii) supranational body, with a large number of affected banks, are simply too big.

Adopting ring-fencing via an enforcement-based approach requires, in the author's opinion, either exactly the Swiss environment: a discrete, informal process in which banks and regulators over time move towards fully realized ring-fencing, complemented by specific legislative action (e.g. the requirement for ring-fenced banks to comply with capital and liquidity requirements stand-alone); or a solid legal basis that allows for far-reaching legal actions that are hard to contest.

For a supranational body like the European Union, clear-cut, transparent rules, either setting down legislative or an enforcement-based ring-fencing, are therefore recommended. There needs to be a solid legal basis that allows for far-reaching legal actions that are hard to contest. In the author's opinion, the provisions of the BRRD and SRMR do not completely exhibit these characteristics. While they may be a potential gateway for union-wide ring-fencing, they are definitely not an ideal one.

VI. Timeline and Full Implementation

A. United Kingdom

In the UK, banks within the scope of the ring-fencing regime will have to have concluded their structural changes until January 1, 2019.[1498] This

1498 *PRA* (2016) PRA Rulebook: Ring Fenced Bodies, 1.

deadline can rightly be considered tight.[1499] Particularly in combination with Brexit, it presents a considerable challenge for banks. While regulators acknowledge a *"resource issue"* due to the combination of ring-fencing and Brexit, they accept no delay in the implementation.[1500]

UK banks are currently in the process of implementing ring-fencing: The first step was setting up the new structure, including creating new UK banking entities which require banking licenses, and equipping them with sufficient capital and liquidity; reviewing and amending governance, such as the setting up of new boards and the modification of reporting lines; and reviewing and modifying interactions of the entities to ensure independence, e.g. IT or operational support.[1501]

The second step is moving assets and liabilities between different entities to ensure activities and clients are located where they supposed to be. For example, core deposit-taking is moved to ring-fenced bodies, and investment banking activities to non-ring-fenced bodies. The Banking Reform Act 2013 sets down a special process for transferring assets and liabilities, which is referred to as "ring-fencing transfer scheme".[1502]

The ring-fencing transfer scheme involves an application to court. The application has to be accompanied by a "scheme report" produced by a skilled person,[1503] an independent expert acting on behalf of the court,[1504] who answers the question (i) whether persons other than the transferor concerned are likely to be adversely affected by the scheme and (ii) if so, whether the adverse effect is likely to be greater than is reasonably necessary in order to achieve ring-fencing.[1505] In addition, the PRA's consent is necessary for a bank's application to the court. The court then decides

1499 See e.g. *Dunkley/Binham*, Banks risk missing 2019 ringfence deadline, Financial Times (January 8, 2017); *Martin*, Bank of England admits lenders face 'tight deadline' for ring-fencing, The Telegraph (June 16, 2017).

1500 *Binham/Dunkley*, Regulators get ready to authorise 'ringfenced' UK banks, Financial Times (August 19, 2017).

1501 *Britton et al.* (2016) Ring-fencing, 170.

1502 *Britton et al.* (2016) Ring-fencing, 171. This process is set down in Part 7 of the FSMA 2000 on business transfers, notably Sec. 106B and 109A FSMA 2000 and in Part 2B of Schedule 12 FSMA 2000.

1503 *PRA* (2016) Ring-Fencing Transfer Schemes, 7; See, for example, *Barclays's* scheme report, *Byers* (2017) Barclays Ring-fencing Transfer Scheme, 13–29.

1504 *Britton et al.* (2016) Ring-fencing, 171.

1505 *PRA* (2016) Ring-Fencing Transfer Schemes, 8; *Britton et al.* (2016) Ring-fencing, 171.

whether to sanction the ring-fencing transfer scheme and issue an order to effect it from a specified date.[1506]

Barclays was the first UK bank whose ring-fencing transfer scheme obtained High-Court approval, in spite of almost 100 pension scheme members expressing concerns in court hearings.[1507] Other banks are also in the process of having their ring-fencing transfer schemes examined by courts.[1508] The transfers are likely to be complete during 2018,[1509] ahead of the 2019 deadline.

B. Germany

The German Ring-fencing Act stipulates that its main provisions are applicable as of July 1, 2015.[1510] According to § 3(3) German Banking Act, banks that exceed the thresholds of the Act have 12 months to either stop providing excluded activities or to transfer them onto a trading entity. BaFin is authorised to extend this period on a case-by-case basis for 12 months.[1511] Such an extension was awarded to *Deutsche Bank*.[1512] Since July 1, 2017, however, the German Ring-fencing Act fully applies to the bank.[1513]

The German Ring-fencing Act does not provide for a special form of asset transfer.[1514] As discussed in Chapter III.V.D.b.4,[1515] no financial trading institution has been established thus far. Transferring assets and liabilities onto a trading entity, however, would in Germany entail a statutory joint

---

1506 *PRA* (2016) Ring-Fencing Transfer Schemes, 8–9.

1507 Concerns were raised about the responsability of the investment bank unit for the pension scheme. *Croff*, High Court approves Barclays ringfencing plan, Financial Times (March 9, 2018).

1508 *Croff*, High Court approves Barclays ringfencing plan, Financial Times (March 9, 2018).

1509 *Britton et al.* (2016) Ring-fencing, 171.

1510 § 64s(2) German Banking Act. An exemption exists for § 3(4), the authorisation of BaFin to exclude other activities than the ones excluded by the German Ring-fencing Act. The authorisation became applicable in July 1, 2016.

1511 § 3(3) German Banking Act.

1512 *Deutsche Bank* was granted an extension on the application of the German Ring-fencing Act until June 30, 2017. See *Deutsche Bank* (2017) 2016 SEC Form 20-F, 26.

1513 See *Deutsche Bank* (2018) 2017 SEC Form 20-F, 23.

1514 *Schelo/Steck* (2013) Trennbankengesetz, 242–243.

1515 Chapter III.V.D.b.4: Practical relevance.

and several liability of five years for both the transferor and the transferee.[1516] Depending on the individual case, a contractual joint and several liability exceeding the statutory five years may be necessary.

C. Switzerland

According to the Swiss Banking Ordinance, internationally oriented systemically important banks have to preparatively implement measures of the Swiss emergency plan until December 31, 2019.[1517] There is no final date for the implementation of measures to enhance the global resolvability, as it is considered a continuous process.[1518]

Domestically oriented systemically important banks are not expected to apply comparable changes to their structure and operations.[1519] Therefore, other deadlines apply to them: they have to complete their emergency planning three years after their determination as systemically important banks by the SNB.[1520]

There is no particular form of business transfer created for ring-fencing in Swiss law. The globally active systemically important banks, *UBS* and *Credit Suisse* therefore had to use general corporate law instruments to conduct their separation:

As discussed in Chapter III.IV.C.c,[1521] both banks first established entities with banking licenses and subsequently transferred assets and liabilities to them. For *UBS* this transfer took place in 2015, for *Credit Suisse* in 2016.[1522] Both banks transferred assets and liabilities through an asset transfer within the meaning of Art. 69 et seqq. Swiss Merger Act.[1523] Due

1516 See § 123(3), § 133 Umwandlungsgesetz, Oktober 28, 1994, Bundesgesetzblatt Part I, 3210 (German Transformation Act) (setting down a joint and several liability for both the transferor and the transferee for a period of 5 years). See e.g. *Schelo/Steck* (2013) Trennbankengesetz, 243; *Altvater/Von Schweinitz* (2013) Trennbankensystem, 630.

1517 Art. 69 Swiss Banking Ordinance.

1518 *EFD* (2016) Erläuterungsbericht, 6.

1519 See *EFD* (2016) Erläuterungsbericht, 6; see Chapter III.IV.C.1: Ex ante separation.

1520 Art. 60(3) Swiss Banking Ordinance.

1521 Chapter III.IV.C.c: Affected banks.

1522 *UBS* (2016) Annual Report 2015, 766; *Credit Suisse (Schweiz) AG* (2017) Annual Report 2016, 9; see further Chapter III.IV.C.c: Affected banks.

1523 Commercial Register Entry, *Credit Suisse*, (November 23, 2016), Bulk Transfer Agreement, 10–11; Commercial Register Entry, *UBS AG*, (June 17, 2015), Pub-

to Art. 75 Swiss Merger Act, the transferor is jointly and severally liable together with the transferee for a period of three years for all liabilities incurred before the transfer.[1524] Both banks also needed to address the problem that the asset transfer worsened the position of creditors of the transferor,[1525] which was dealt with by a contractual joint and several liability assumed by the transferees.[1526] In particular for *UBS*, the contractual joint and several liability of *UBS Switzerland AG* was of substantial size. However, since the asset transfer, the amount has been considerably reduced and is going to fade out over time: according to *UBS* the amount will be significantly lessened until 2020.[1527]

D. Results

The arguments stated above show that the UK will be the first of the countries of interest that, if all banks manage to implement the ring-fence in time, will have completed the separation of commercial banking activities from investment banking activities for large banks. With the ring-fencing

---

lic Deed of the Asset Transfer Agreement, 18; Art. 69 et seqq. Bundesgesetz über Fusion, Spaltung, Umwandlung und Vermögensübertragung, October 3, 2003, SR 221.301 (Swiss Merger Act).

1524 Art. 75 Swiss Merger Act; Commercial Register Entry, *Credit Suisse,* (November 23, 2016), Bulk Transfer Agreement, 23–24; Commercial Register Entry, *UBS AG,* (June 17, 2015), Public Deed of the Asset Transfer Agreement, 40–41.

1525 See e.g. *Watter/Kägi* (2015) Haftung des übernehmenden Rechtsträgers, 287–288. This problem was pointed out by the Swiss expert commission in 2014. See *Expertenkommission* (2014) Schlussbericht, 44 (noting that the financial independence of the ex ante separated banks may be obstructed by guarantees to avoid the option of creditors' rights to termination). See also *Bertschinger* (2015) Finanzmarktaufsichtsrecht, 635.

1526 See *UBS* (2016) Annual Report 2015, 767; *Credit Suisse (Schweiz) AG* (2017) Annual Report 2016, 7; Commercial Register Entry, *Credit Suisse,* (November 23, 2016), Bulk Transfer Agreement, 15, Annex 4; Commercial Register Entry, *UBS AG,* (June 17, 2015), Public Deed of the Asset Transfer Agreement, 41–43. For a discussion of contractual joint and several liabilities, see *Watter/Kägi* (2015) Haftung des übernehmenden Rechtsträgers, 280 et seqq.

1527 See *Millischer/Heim,* Milliardenabflüsse bei der UBS Schweiz, Handelszeitung (March 31, 2016); *UBS* (2016) Annual Report 2015, 767. *Reuters, Fitch Upgrades UBS Group to 'A+'; UBS AG and UBS Switzerland to 'AA-'* (September 28, 2017). The contractual joint and several liability has already been reduced from 325 billion CHF in 2015 (*UBS* (2016) Annual Report 2015, 767) to 61 billion CHF as of December 2017 (*UBS* (2018) Standalone financial statements UBS Switzerland AG, 3).

transfer scheme, a way of asset transfer was created that allows for a swift and reliable transfer of assets and liabilities. Joint and several liabilities can be avoided. This is a major advantage over the other jurisdictions.

Switzerland's G-SIBs, however, are catching up one year later, with the emergency plans needing to be preparatively implemented in December 2019. However, due to the joint and several liabilities it will, in practice, take a bit longer for ring-fenced banks to be free from all financial linkages.

In Germany, the prohibitions apply since July 2017 the latest (taking into account the potential 12-month extension of BaFin). As already discussed in Chapter III.IV.B.d[1528] and Chapter III.V.D.b.4,[1529] none of the affected banks has opted to establish a trading entity. It can thus be assumed that since July 2017, the excluded activities are therefore not conducted anymore in banks exceeding the thresholds of the German Ring-fencing Act. A separation of trading activities onto a trading entity would under the current legal basis be subject to a joint and several liability that would extend the length of the process of gaining independence of ring-fenced banks and the trading entity.

VII. Results and Outlook

The third part of the dissertation addressed the question what structural differences can be found in a legal comparative analysis of structural reform legislation in Europe's three financial capitals: the United Kingdom, Germany and Switzerland. An aspect-to-aspect analysis was conducted, taking the form of a micro-comparison as described by *Zweigert/Kötz*.[1530] It also examined whether legal requirements in the three jurisdictions fulfil or defer from the concept and the definition of ring-fencing established in the first part. The following paragraphs reiterate selected findings and provide a short outlook.

The UK, Germany and Switzerland are by far Europe's biggest and most important financial centres. They are home to a large share of Europe's G-SIBs. In particular, Switzerland (2.6 times) and the UK (2.3 times) are exposed to balance sheets of G-SIBs in relation to national GDP. With the

1528 See Chapter III.IV.B.d: Affected banks.

1529 Chapter III.V.D.b.4: Practical relevance.

1530 *Zweigert/Kötz (1996) Rechtsvergleichung*, 4, 42; See also *Zweigert/Kötz* (1998) Comparative Law, 5, 43–44.

balance sheet of *Deutsche Bank*, Germany's only G-SIB, at only at 0.5 times national GDP, Germany is the least exposed.

In contrast to Germany and the UK, it is a particularity of the Swiss approach is that it is largely enforcement-based: legislation only specifies the minimum goal that the continuation of systemically important activities has to be ensured. There is only limited legislative guidance regarding how this goal should be reached. This is a result of the principle of subsidiarity. It is, however, balanced by Finma's emergency plan assessment, which becomes a source of information of utmost importance for banks regarding the question how to design their new structure:[1531] Finma has wide discretion and a very powerful position in the shaping of the banks' structure. The assessment process therefore has to be considered a major source of information and regulation, complementing the scarce legislation.

While the Swiss emphasis on an approach that is as little invasive as possible via minimum goals and the principle of subsidiarity is in contrast with Germany and the UK and is to be appreciated, one has to point out that invasiveness is only mitigated as far as (i) there is more than one way of reaching the goal and (ii) there is transparency in reaching it. Both can be somewhat reasonably questioned.[1532] The Swiss approach may therefore be more invasive than originally thought. Taking into account that the other jurisdictions also allow for a degree of flexibility in the structure of affected banks, the minimum goal and principle of subsidiarity may be less of an advantage for affected banks than initially planned.

Exploring the question of what activities can and cannot be provided by the German financial trading institution, it was found that its characterisation in the legislative materials as financial service institution within the meaning of the German Banking Act is to be considered an editorial error. The trading entity is thus not limited to "financial services", but should also be allowed to provide "banking services". There is, however, also the need for limitations: it seems to be commonly agreed that a trading entity should at the very least be prohibited from accepting deposits (except of institutional investors).[1533]

1531 The *"critical importance"* of the discussions between Finma and banks is rightly indicated by *Schöchli*. *Schöchli*, Der lange Weg der Notfallplanung, NZZ (June 6, 2012); see also *Hofer* (2014) Structural Reforms, 332.

1532 See Chapter III.II.D.e: Invasiveness.

1533 *Schaffelhuber/Kunschke* come to a similar conclusion. They argue, in addition, that this should not apply to deposits of institutional investors (*Schaffelhuber/Kunschke* (2015) Trennbankengesetz, 400) thereby correctly underscoring that institutional investors are not included in the German Banking Act's under-

While it has been recognized by some authors that the Swiss approach approximates towards other structural reform initiatives, notably in the UK, Germany and the EU,[1534] this dissertation reviewed in detail what activities were shifted to the Swiss entities of *UBS* and *Credit Suisse* and what remained with the rest of the banking group. It compared this separation with the ones required in Germany and the UK. The emerging picture is indeed surprising, as not just trading businesses (with the exception of domestic market making), but also traditional investment banking services, such as underwriting, are excluded from the Swiss entities. The scope of Switzerland's separation is therefore surprisingly similar to the UK's.

All three examined jurisdictions put in place specific requirements that constitute a fence. While for Germany and the UK this is hardly surprising as the intention to ring-fence is emphasized prominently, for Switzerland this is an important finding: a comparison of key features of the fence also suggests that while not as transparent as in other jurisdictions, the Swiss fence is of considerable height. In particular with regard to independent governance, the Swiss approach is unique.

In summary, it can be found that all three jurisdictions fulfil the concept of ring-fencing established in the first part of the dissertation: they (i) separate commercial banking activities from investment banking activities, (ii) at the same time maintain universal banking, and (iii) ensure the separation of activities with a fence. They are also well within the scope of the definition of ring-fencing set up in the first part. The question whether they fulfil the concept and definition of ring-fencing established in the first part can thus be answered in the affirmative.

The countries, however, chose different methods of ring-fencing. The UK and Switzerland put into practice the *defensive method* of ring-fencing, separating activities that are important to the real economy and are thus to be protected. Germany, in contrast, chose the *containment method* of ring-fencing, separating activities considered particularly risky from the rest of the banking group. None of the jurisdictions found the need for more stringent structural reforms such as an *activities ban* of full separation.

Regarding the question of whether the Swiss approach could be a role model for the EU, in particular with regard to provisions allowing for in-

---

standing of deposits. (see *Schäfer* (2016) § 1 Begriffsbestimmungen, para 46; *BaFin* (2014) Merkblatt Einlagengeschäft, 2–3).

1534 See e.g. *Achermann* (2018) Organisation, 285; *Hofer* (2014) Structural Reforms, 5–6 (noting that there are many similarities between the UK's and Switzerland's structural reforms).

terferences with the structure of banks in the BRRD and SRMR, two conclusions can be drawn: (i) the Swiss approach can be regarded as an example for an enforcement-based implementation of ring-fencing. However, (ii) there are several factors that facilitate the success of the Swiss approach that are to be found in particularities of the Swiss banking market and that cannot be assumed to be the same for the EU. For a supranational body like the EU, clear-cut, transparent rules and a solid legal foundation, either setting down a legislative or an enforcement-based ring-fencing, are more suitable and are therefore to be recommended.

While in all three countries ring-fencing legislation is in place, there are considerable differences regarding its application in practice. Both in the UK and Switzerland, affected banks are currently taking on substantial efforts to restructure their business according to the ring-fencing requirements. In Germany, in contrast, it seems that no comparable efforts are being undertaken. There is no indication that *Deutsche Bank*, Germany's only G-SIB has established a financial trading institution yet. This leads to the situation that, if properly applied, the provisions of the German Ring-fencing Act exhibit similar legal consequences as an *activities ban*, as affected banks no longer provide excluded activities.

Regarding the implementation, the UK will likely be the first country to have completed the separation of commercial banking activities from investment banking activities for large banks with the deadline of January 1, 2019. In particular, the asset transfer via the ring-fencing-transfer-scheme can be considered a considerable advantage against the other jurisdictions. In Switzerland, the emergency plan must be preparatively implemented by globally active systemically important banks by December 31, 2019. While this will be a major step towards the independence of ring-fenced banks, it will be interesting to see whether the structure of the banking groups will further assimilate towards the UK's, based on the incentives to enhance resolvability and further updates of the emergency plan. It furthermore remains to be seen whether banks affected by the German Ring-fencing Act will establish trading entities.

Outlook

The three parts of the dissertation have discussed ring-fencing both theoretically and in practice. While the first part established a concept of ring-fencing as well as a definition, clearly delimiting it against other bank structural reforms, and identified its different methods, the second part addressed developments on a European Union level. It discussed the various legislative steps taken and the failure of the file. It then turned to discuss remaining options for the introduction of a union-wide ring-fencing requirement. The third part structurally compared bank structural reform legislation in the UK, Germany and Switzerland and assessed whether they match the concept and definition of ring-fencing established in the first part of the dissertation.

A number of interesting and valuable findings could be obtained. They are selectively reiterated at the end of each part of the dissertation. At this point, only a short outlook is considered beneficial. It shall flag up-to-date developments, which may have an effect on the ring-fencing rules discussed, and indicate developments one should keep an eye out for.

While UK banks are on track for fully implementing the separation of commercial banking from investment banking, attention should be paid to the banks' asset transfers via the ring-fencing transfer schemes, in particular the court decisions that will be made during 2018. An important and equally hard to foresee influence is Brexit: while regulators have not allowed for delay in the implementation of ring-fencing and claimed the combination of ring-fencing and Brexit to be *"perfectly manageable"*,[1535] a number of important implications are linked to the UK's exit from the EU.[1536] How they will be dealt with in detail is to be seen.

1535 *Binham/Dunkley*, Regulators get ready to authorise 'ringfenced' UK banks, Financial Times (August 19, 2017).

1536 These implications include questions regarding the scope of ring-fencing, as it applies to all banks incorporated in the UK that accept core retail deposits in any EEA state exceeding 25 billion £ in total. Currently, branches of EU based banks are exempted from the application of ring-fencing. Questions will thus arise regarding a potential loss of passporting rights. Ring-fenced banks are furthermore prohibited from having branches and subsidiaries outside the EEA. How these questions will be resolved remains to be seen.

In Switzerland, banks are currently in the process of preparatively implementing measures of the Swiss emergency plan. As established in Part III of the dissertation, the scope of Switzerland's separation is remarkably similar to the UK's. The Swiss fence is furthermore of considerable height. It will be interesting to see whether regulators will maintain their stringent approach, in particular regarding the separation of commercial banking and investment banking and with regard to an increasing independence of the ring-fenced banks.[1537] Furthermore, it will remain to be seen whether the Swiss ring-fence will develop towards the UK's or take its own direction.

In Germany, it will be interesting to see whether and how the provisions of the German Ring-fencing Act will evolve. The number of open questions regarding the financial trading institution make necessary a comprehensive Interpretative Guidance of BaFin, for which one should keep an eye out. In addition, modifications of the provisions of the Act may be necessary, to make the trading entity more appealing. It will furthermore remain to be seen to what extent Frankfurt, Germany's financial centre, will profit from Brexit and whether an increased significance in international finance may also have implications for the German ring-fencing provisions. Decision-makers in Germany are, in any case, well advised not to lose sight of the comprehensive ring-fencing that is currently being implemented in the UK and Switzerland.

While the three countries above already adopted ring-fencing legislation, the common European Union approach suffered a major setback with the withdrawal of the bank structural reform file by the European Commission. It will be interesting whether the discussed legislative options and already existing potential gateways will be used in the quest to establish a union-wide ring-fencing requirement. In such a case, the question of what form it would take, would arise: with the withdrawal, a new hand has been dealt, proposals could thus orientate towards the Liika-

1537 Drawing from recent publications, it can be assumed that Swiss regulators are in the foreseeable future not planning to ease pressure on banks to further enhance resolvability and implement viable emergency plans. See *SNB* (2018) Financial Stability Report 2017, 5 (noting that *"[f]urther progress must be made in drawing up robust resolution plans. […] In particular, by end-2019, the big banks will need to demonstrate that they would be able to maintain their systemically important functions in Switzerland in the event of impending insolvency"*); see also *Schiltknecht* (2018) Sanierungsmassnahmen, 310 (noting that it will require considerable efforts over the next years to allow for credible and feasible resolution and emergency plans for *UBS* and *Credit Suisse*).

nen Report, towards the Commission's draft regulation or in a completely different direction. They could also orientate towards the UK or Switzerland. Furthermore, several events lie ahead in the near future that have the potential to breathe new life into the EU's bank structural reform project: in 2019, elections for the European Parliament are held that may shift the distribution of votes towards proponents of structural reform. In addition, the European Commission's term ends in 2019, which may result in a new composition and potentially new initiatives.[1538]

In summary, it can be stated that the setback on a European Union level should not obscure the fact that bank structural reform will not be completely off the table for years to come. Ring-fencing is in the process of becoming an integral part of European banking regulation: Europe's most important financial centres are at the forefront of its implementation. It will be critical for decision makers around Europe and in the European Union to use a clear-cut concept of ring-fencing and its methods, and to comparatively keep an eye on already adopted legislation and established practices. With above the developments pending, ring-fencing will remain a highly controversial topic.

1538 Also a potential ECB presidency of *Erkki Liikanen* may have an effect on the European Union's current position on bank structural reform. See *Jones*, European Central Bank's marathon man moves to front of the pack, Financial Times (April 3, 2018).

List of Sources

I.Literature

Achermann (2018) Anforderungen an die Organisation und vorausschauende Abwicklungsplanung, in: *Sester et al.* (Eds.) St. Galler Handbuch zum Schweizer Finanzmarktrecht: Finanzmarktaufsicht und Finanzmarktinfrastrukturen, Dike, Zürich/St. Gallen (cited as: *Achermann* (2018) Organisation).

Akhigbe/Whyte (2004) The Gramm Leach-Bliley Act of 1999: Risk Implications for the Financial Services Industry, The Journal of Financial Research, 27:3, 435–446 (cited as: *Akhigbe/Whyte* (2004) Gramm Leach-Bliley Act).

Aldridge (2010) High-Frequency Trading: A Practical Guide to Algorithmic Strategies and Trading Systems, Wiley, New Jersey (cited as: *Aldridge* (2010) High-Frequency Trading).

Alexander (2015) Regulating the Universal Model Banking in Europe, in: *Busch/Ferrarini* (Ed.) European Banking Union, Oxford University Press, Oxford (cited as: *Alexander* (2015) Universal Model Banking).

Alexander/Lorez (2010) Universal Banks: The Risks and Alternatives, SZW, 459–468 (cited as: *Alexander/Lorez* (2010) Universal Banks).

Altvater/Von Schweinitz (2013) Trennbankensystem: Grundsatzfragen und alternative Regulierungsansätze, WM, 14:625–633 (cited as: *Altvater/Von Schweinitz* (2013) Trennbankensystem).

Armour et al. (2016) Principles of Financial Regulation, Oxford University Press, Oxford (cited as: *Armour et al.* (2016) Financial Regulation).

Asmundson et al. (2011) Trade and Trade Finance in the 2008–09 Financial Crisis, IMF Working Paper, No. 16 (cited as: *Asmundson et al.* (2011) Trade and Trade Finance).

Auerbach/Schriever (2016) Anforderungen an CRR-Kreditinstitute, in: *Schwennicke/Auerbach* (Ed.) Kreditwesengesetz (KWG) mit Zahlungsdiensteaufsichtsgesetz (ZAG) und Finanzkonglomerate-Aufsichtsgesetz (FKAG), 3rd Ed., C.H. Beck, München (cited as: *Auerbach/Schriever* (2016) CRR-Kreditinstitute).

Bahar/Peyer (2013) Abschnitt 5: Systemrelevante Banken, in: *Watter et al.* (Ed.) Basler Kommentar: Bankengesetz, 2nd Ed., Helbing Lichtenhahn Verlag, Basel (cited as: *Bahar/Peyer* (2013) Systemrelevante Banken).

Bahar/Stupp (2013) Abschnitt 1: Geltungsbereich des Gesetzes, in: *Watter et al.* (Ed.) Basler Kommentar: Bankengesetz, 2nd Ed., Helbing Lichtenhahn Verlag, Basel (cited as: *Bahar/Stupp* (2013) Geltungsbereich).

Baisch (2014) Risikogewichtete Aktiva (RWA) – Really Weird Accounting?, in: *Von der Crone/Rochet* (Eds.) Finanzstabilität: Status und Perspektiven, Schweizer Schriften zum Finanzmarktrecht, No. 112 (cited as: *Baisch* (2014) Risikogewichtete Aktiva).

Bao/O'Hara/Zhou (2016) The Volcker Rule and Market-Making in Times of Stress, https://ssrn.com/abstract=2836714 (cited as: *Bao/O'Hara/Zhou* (2016) Volcker Rule).

Barth/Brumbaugh/Wilcox (2000) Policy Watch: The Repeal of Glass-Steagall and the Advent of Broad Banking, The Journal of Economic Perspectives, 14:2, 191–204 (cited as: *Barth/Brumbaugh/Wilcox* (2000) Glass-Steagall).

Becalli/Anolli/Borello (2015) Are European Banks too Big? Evidence on Economies of Scale, Journal of Banking & Finance, 58:232–246 (cited as: *Becalli/Anolli/Borello* (2015) Are European Banks too Big?).

Behr/Schmidt (2015) The German Banking System: Characteristics and Challenges, SAFE White Paper, No. 32 (cited as: *Behr/Schmidt* (2015) German Banking System).

Benston (1994) Universal Banking, Journal of Economic Perspectives, 8:3, 121–143 (cited as: *Benston* (1994) Universal Banking).

Bertschinger (2015) Das Finanzmarktaufsichtsrecht Mitte 2014 bis ins vierte Quartal 2015, SZW, 630–650 (cited as: *Bertschinger* (2015) Finanzmarktaufsichtsrecht).

Binder (2017) Systemkrisenbewältigung durch Bankenabwicklung? Aktuelle Bemerkungen zu unrealistischen Erwartungen, ZBB, 2:57–128 (cited as: *Binder* (2017) Systemkrisenbewältigung durch Bankenabwicklung?).

Binder (2015) Ring-Fencing: An Integrated Approach with Many Unknowns, Eur Bus Org Law Rev, 16:97–119 (cited as: *Binder* (2015) Ring-Fencing).

Binder (2015) Gleichung mit (zu?) vielen Unbekannten: Nachhaltige Bankenstrukturen durch Sanierungs- und Abwicklungplanung?, ZBB, 3:153–212 (cited as: *Binder* (2015) Gleichung).

Binder (2014) To ring-fence or not, and how? Strategic questions for post-crisis banking reform in Europe, http://ssrn.com/abstract=2543860 (cited as: *Binder* (2014) To ring-fence or not, and how?).

Binder (2014) Resolution Planning and Structural Bank Reform within the Banking Union, SAFE Working Paper No 81 (cited as: *Binder* (2014) Resolution Planning).

Blundell-Wignall (2011) On the Necessity of Separating Investment and Commercial Banking, Intereconomics, 6:298–299 (cited as: *Blundell-Wignall* (2011) Necessity).

Blundell-Wignall/Atkinson (2012) Deleveraging, Traditional versus Capital Markets Banking and the Urgent Need to Separate and Recapitalise G-SIFI Banks, OECD Journal: Financial Market Trends, Vol 1 (cited as: *Blundell-Wignall/Atkinson* (2012) Capital Markets Banking).

Blundell-Wignall/Atkinson/Roulet (2013) Bank business models and the separation issue, OECD Journal: Financial Market Trends, Vol 2 (cited as: *Blundell-Wignall/Atkinson/Roulet* (2013) Bank Business Models).

Blundell-Wignall/Wehinger/Slovik (2010) The elephant in the room: The need to deal with what banks do, OECD Journal: Financial Market Trends, Vol 2 (cited as: *Blundell-Wignall/Wehinger/Slovik* (2010) The Elephant in the Room).

Bobek et al. (2011) Ökonomische Analyse europäischer Bankenregulierung: Verbriefung und Interbankenmarkt im Fokus, Bayreuther Arbeitspapiere zu Finanzierung, Rechnungslegung und Steuern, No. 2011–01 (cited as: *Bobek et al.* (2011) Ökonomische Analyse).

Boot (2014) Financial Sector in Flux, Journal of Money, Credit and Banking, Vol 46, No 1, 129–135 (cited as: *Boot* (2014) Financial Sector).

Boot (2011) Banking at the Crossroads: How to deal with Marketability and Complexity, Amsterdam Center for Law & Economics Working Paper No 2011–07 (cited as: *Boot* (2011) Banking). Part 2plex-to-fail" or "nt oft s still amount to aboutdit Suisse and UBS, amounted alled full separation, [US Chapter einfügen]

Boot/Ratnovski (2012) Banking and Trading, IMF Working Paper, No 238 (cited as: *Boot/Ratnovski* (2012) Banking and Trading).

Brandi/Gieseler (2013) Entwurf des Trennbankengesetzes: Sanierungs- und Abwicklungsplanung, Risikoabschirmung des Kundengeschäfts, Verschärfung von Geschäftsleiterpflichten, Der Betrieb, 14:741–747 (cited as: *Brandi/Gieseler* (2013) Entwurf des Trennbankengesetzes).

Brändli (2018) § 2 Internationale Standards, in: *Sester et al.* (Eds.) St. Galler Handbuch zum Schweizer Finanzmarktrecht: Finanzmarktaufsicht und Finanzmarktinfrastrukturen, Dike, Zürich/St. Gallen (cited as: *Brändli* (2018) Internationale Standards).

Brändli (2011) Die aufsichtsrechtliche Erfassung der Zentralen Gegenpartei im schweizerischen Kapitalmarkt – Eine Momentaufnahme des Status quo und eventueller Risikopotentiale, SZW, 2–19 (cited as: *Brändli* (2011) Zentrale Gegenpartei).

Brändli/Rieder (2009) Kapital- und personenbezogene Massnahmen zur Vertrauensbildung in Krisensituationen, in: *Haunreiter et al.* (Eds.) Auswirkungen von Krisen auf Wirtschaft, Recht und Gesellschaft, Stämpfli, Bern (cited as: *Brändli/Rieder* (2009) Vertrauensbildung).

Braun (2016) § 25a Besondere organisatorische Pflichten; Verordnungsermächtigung, in: *Boos/Fischer/Schulte-Matter* (Ed.) KWG, Crr-VO, 5th Ed., Beck, München (cited as: *Braun* (2016) Organisatorische Pflichten).

Braun (2016) § 25f Besondere Anforderungen an die ordnungsgemäße Geschäftsorganisation von CRR-Kreditinstituten sowie von Institutsgruppen, Finanzholding- Gruppen, gemischten Finanzholding-Gruppen und Finanzkonglomeraten, denen ein CRR-Kreditinstitut angehört; Verordnungsermächtigung, in: *Boos/Fischer/Schulte-Matter* (Ed.) KWG, Crr-VO, 5th Ed., Beck, München (cited as: *Braun* (2016) Geschäftsorganisation).

Britton et al. (2016) Ring-fencing: what is it and how will it affect banks and their customers, Bank of England Quarterly Bulletin, 4:164–172 (cited as: *Britton et al.* (2016) Ring-fencing).

Brown (2014) With this Ring, I Thee Fence: How Europe's Ringfencing Proposal Compares with U.S. Ringfencing Measures, Georgetown Journal of International Law, 45, 1030–1055 (cited as: *Brown* (2014) With this Ring, I Thee Fence).

Brunnermeier/Dong/Palia (2012) Banks' Non-Interest Income and Systemic Risk, AFA 2012 Chicago Meetings Paper (cited as: *Brunnermeier/Dong/Palia* (2012) Banks' Non-Interest Income).

Burghof (2016) Deutsche Bank: Deutsche Banken in der Krise? Wirtschaftsdienst, 96:11:784–785 (cited as: *Burghof* (2016) Deutsche Bank).

Byers (2017) Proposed Barclays Ring-fencing Transfer Scheme: Report of the Skilled Person under Section 109A of the Financial Services and Markets Act 2000, https://www.home.barclays/content/dam/barclayspublic/docs/AboutUs/ringfencing/REPORT%20-%20Barclays%20Ring-Fencing%20Transfer%20Scheme.pdf (cited as: *Byers* (2017) Barclays Ring-fencing Transfer Scheme).

Canals (1997) Universal Banking: International Comparisons and Theoretical Perspectives, Clarendon Press, Oxford (cited as: *Canals* (1997) Universal Banking).

Carnell/Macey/Miller (2017) The Law of Financial Institutions, 6th Ed., Wolters Kluwer (cited as: *Carnell/Macey/Miller* (2017) Financial Institutions).

Carney (2017) The High Road to a Responsible, Open Financial System, Speech by Mark Carney, Governor of the Bank of England, April 7, 2017 (cited as: *Carney* (2017) High Road).

Carpenter/Murphy (2010) Permissible Securities Activities of Commercial Banks Under the Glass-Steagall Act (GSA) and the Gramm-Leach-Bliley Act (GLBA), Congressional Research Service (cited as: *Carpenter/Murphy* (2010) Permissible Securities Activities).

Casu/Gall (2016) Building Societies in the Financial Services Industry, Macmillan Publishers, London (cited as: *Casu/Gall* (2016) Building Societies).

Cerrutti/Schmieder (2014) Ring fencing and consolidated banks' stress tests, Journal of Financial Stability, 11, 1–12 (cited as: *Cerrutti/Schmieder* (2014) Ring Fencing).

Chambers-Jones (2011) The Vickers Report, Business Law Review, 32:11, 280–284 (cited as: *Chambers-Jones* (2011) Vickers Report).

Chapuis (2013) Abschnitt 1: Geltungsbereich des Gesetzes, in: *Watter et al.* (Ed.) Basler Kommentar: Bankengesetz, 2nd Ed., Helbing Lichtenhahn Verlag, Basel (cited as: *Chapuis* (2013) Geltungsbereich).

Chow/Surti (2011) Making Banks Safer: Can Volcker and Vickers Do it?, IMF Working Paper Monetary and Capital Markets Department, No 236 (cited as: *Chow/Surti* (2011) Making Banks Safer).

Claessens/Van Horen (2015) The Impact of the Global Financial Crisis on Banking Globalization, IMF Economic Review, 63:868–918 (cited as: *Claessens/Van Horen* (2015) Global Financial Crisis).

Coates (2015) The Volcker Rule as Structural Law: Implications for Cost-Benefit Analysis and Administrative Law, ecgi Law Working Paper, No 299 (cited as: *Coates* (2015) Volcker Rule).

Crawford (2017) A Better Way to Revive Glass-Steagall, Stan. L. Rev. Online, Vol. 70 (cited as: *Crawford* (2017) Glass-Steagall).

D'Hulster (2014) Ring-fencing cross border banks: How is it done and why is it important?, http://papers.ssrn.com/abstract=2384905 (cited as: *D'Hulster* (2014) Ring-Fencing).

D'Hulster/Oetker-Robe (2014) Ring-Fencing Cross Border Banks: An Effective Supervisory Response?, Journal of Banking Regulation, Vol. 16(3), 169–187 (cited as: *D'Hulster/Oetker-Robe* (2014) Ring-Fencing).

De Vogelaere (2016) Implementing Volcker, Vickers and Liikanen: Comparative Analysis of Bank Structure Reforms, https://lib.ugent.be/fulltxt/RUG01/002/272/106/RUG01-002272106_2016_0001_AC.pdf (cited as: *De Vogelaere* (2016) Bank Structure Reforms).

Detzer et al. (2017) The German Financial System and the Financial and Economic Crisis, Financial and Monetary Policy Studies Vol. 45, Springer, Cham (cited as: *Detzer et al.* (2017) German Financial System).

Diamond/Dybvig (1983) Bank Runs, Deposit Insurance, and Liquidity, Journal of Political Economy, 91:3:401–419 (cited as: *Diamond/Dybvig* (1983) Bank Runs).

Djankov (2017) The City of London after Brexit, Financial Markets Group Discussion Paper Series, No 762 (cited as: *Djankov* (2017) City of London).

Dobler et al. (2016) The Lender of Last Resort Function After the Global Financial Crisis, IMF Working Paper, No 10 (cited as: *Dobler et al.* (2016) Lender of Last Resort).

Dombalagian (2015) The Volcker Rule and regulatory complementarity, Capital Markets Law Journal, 10:4, 469–487 (cited as: *Dombalagian* (2015) Volcker Rule).

Dombalagian (2013) Proprietary Trading: Of Scourges, Scapegoats, and Scofflaws, University of Cincinatti Law Review, 81:387–420 (cited as: *Dombalagian* (2012) Proprietary Trading).

Dombret/Liebig/Stein (2014) Trennbankensystem – ein Weg zu mehr Finanzstabilität in Deutschland, Perspektiven der Wirtschaftspolitik, 15:1:41–55 (cited as: *Dombret/Liebig/Stein* (2014) Trennbankensystem).

Doyle et al. (2010) New "Volcker Rule" to Impose Significant Restrictions on Banking Entities, Other Significant Financial Service Companies, Banking Law Journal, 127:686–694 (cited as: *Doyle et al.* (2010) Volcker Rule).

Duffie (2012) Market Making Under the Proposed Volcker Rule, Stanford University Graduate School of Business, Working Paper, No 3118 (cited as: *Duffie* (2012) Market Making).

Elliott/Litan (2011) Identifying and Regulating Systemically Important Financial Institutions: The Risks of Under and Over Identification and Regulation, Brookings Institution Policy Brief, Washington DC (cited as: *Elliott/Litan* (2011) Systemically Important Financial Institutions).

Elliott/Rauch (2014) Lessons from the Implementation of the Volcker Rule for Banking Structural Reform in the European Union, SAFE White Paper Series, No 13 (cited as: *Elliott/Rauch* (2014) Volcker Rule).

Elmore (1995) Structural Reform and Educational Practice, Educational Researcher, Vol. 24, No. 9:23–26 (cited as: *Elmore* (1995) Structural Reform and Educational Practice).

Eucken (1990) Grundsätze der Wirtschaftspolitik, 6th Ed, Mohr, Tübingen (cited as: *Eucken* (1990) Wirtschaftspolitik).

Felsenfeld/Glass (2011) Banking Regulation in the United States, 3rd Ed, Juris Publishing, New York (cited as: *Felsenfeld/Glass* (2011) Banking Regulation).

Frame/White (2014) Technological Change, Financial Innovation, and Diffusion in Banking, in: *Berger/Molyneux/Wilson* (Ed.) The Oxford Handbook of Banking, 2nd Ed (cited as: *Frame/White* (2014) Technological Change).

Gambacorta/Van Rixtel (2013) Structural bank regulation initiatives: approaches and implications, BIS Working Papers, No 412 (cited as: *Gambacorta/Van Rixtel* (2013) Structural Bank Regulation Initiatives).

Gary (2012) Creating a Future Economic Crisis: Political Failure and the Loopholes of the Volcker Rule, Oregon Law Review, Vol 90, 1339–1388 (cited as: *Gary* (2012) Economic Crisis).

Gilles (2000) Reinventing Structural Reform Litigation: Deputizing Private Citizens in the Enforcement of Civil Rights, Columbia Law Review, 100:1384–1454 (cited as: *Gilles* (2000) Reinventing Structural Reform Litigation).

Goldstein/Veron (2011) Too Big To Fail: The transatlantic debate, Working Paper Series, 11–2 (cited as: *Goldstein/Veron* (2011) Too Big To Fail).

Gordon/Ringe (2015) Bank Resolution in Europe: the Unfinished Agenda of Structural Reform, ecgi Law Working Paper, No 282 (cited as: *Gordon/Ringe* (2015) Bank Resolution).

Götz/Krahnen/Tröger (2017) Fünf Jahre nach dem Liikanen-Bericht: Was haben wir gelernt?, Perspektiven der Wirtschaftspolitik, 18:3, 205–225 (cited as: *Götz/Krahnen/Tröger* (2017) Liikanen-Bericht).

Grundmann (2016) Band 10: Bankvertragsrecht Teil 1, in: *Canaris/Habersack/Schäfer* (Ed.) Handelsgesetzbuch, 5th Ed, De Gruyter, Berlin (cited as: *Grundmann* (2016) Bankvertragsrecht).

Grundy (2017) Summary of the Report of the Skilled Person on the Proposed Ring-Fencing Scheme to Transfer Business from The Royal Bank of Scotland ("RBS plc") to Adam & Company ("Adam & Company") and to National Westminster Bank Plc ("NatWest Plc"), https://www.rbs.com/content/dam/rbs_com/rbs/PDFs/ring-fencing/Summary%20of%20the%20Report%20of%20the%20Skilled%20Person%20-%20171117%20-%20Final.pdf (cited as: *Grundy* (2017) Ring-Fencing Scheme Royal Bank of Scotland).

Guynn/Kenadjian (2015) Structural Solutions: Blinded by Volcker, Vickers, Liikanen, Glass Steagall and Narrow Banking, in: Dombret/Kenadjian (Eds.) Too Big to Fail III: Structural Reform Proposals, Institute for Law and Finance Series 25, De Gruyter, Berlin, Boston (cited as: *Guynn/Kenadjian (2015)* Structural Solutions).

Hackethal (2004) German Banks and Banking Structure, in: *Krahnen/Schmidt* (Ed.) The German Financial System, Oxford University Press, Oxford (cited as: *Hackethal* (2004) German Banks).

Haldane (2012) On being the right size, Speech by Mr Andrew G Haldane, Executive Director, Financial Stability, Bank of England, at the Institute of Economic Affairs' 22nd Annual Series, The 2012 Beesley Lectures, at the Institute of Directors, London, 25 October 2012 (cited as: *Haldane* (2012) On Being the Right Size).

Hardie/Howarth (2013) Framing Market-Based Banking and the Financial Crisis, in: *Hardie/Howarth* (Eds.) Market-Based Banking and the International Financial Crisis, Oxford University Press, Oxford (cited as: *Hardie/Howarth* (2013) Market-Based Banking).

Hardie/Macartney (2016) EU ring-fencing and the defence of too-big-to-fail banks, West European Politics, 39:3, 503–525 (cited as: *Hardie/Macartney* (2016) EU Ring-Fencing).

Haynes (2015) Banking Reform Struggles On, Statute Law Rev 36:2, 123–133 (cited as: *Haynes* (2015) Banking Reform).

Herring/Carmassi (2014), Complexity and Systemic Risk: What's Changed Since the Crisis, in: *Berger/Molyneux/Wilson* (Ed.) The Oxford Handbook of Banking, 2nd Ed (cited as: *Herring/Carmassi* (2014), Complexity).

Hoeck (2018) § 10 Schattenbanken als Regulierungsfrage, in: *Sester et al.* (Eds.) St. Galler Handbuch zum Schweizer Finanzmarktrecht: Finanzmarktaufsicht und Finanzmarktinfrastrukturen, Dike, Zürich/St. Gallen (cited as: *Hoeck* (2018) Schattenbanken).

Hofer (2014) Too Big to Fail and Structural Reforms, Schulthess, Zürich (cited as: *Hofer* (2014) Structural Reforms).

Huertas (2018) Scheme Report: HSBC Bank plc and HSBC UK Bank plc, https://investments.hsbc.co.uk/pdf/Skilled_Persons_Report.pdf (cited as: *Huertas* (2018) Scheme Report: HSBC).

Jordan (2010) SNB-Stabfund – Aufbau und Betrieb einer Bad Bank: Positive Zwischenbilanz für den komplexen Rettungsanker, Der Schweizer Treuhänder, 11:823–829 (cited as: *Jordan* (2010) SNB-Stabfund).

Koch (2016) The United Kingdom as a Hub for International Banking, BIS Quarterly Review, September 2016, 30–31 (cited as: *Koch* (2016) United Kingdom).

Korotana (2016) The Financial Services (Banking Reform) Act 2013: Smart Regulatory Regime?, Statute Law Review, 37:3, 195–211 (cited as: *Korotana* (2016) Banking Reform Act).

Krahnen (2014) On the European Commission's Proposal for a Structural Reform of Banking, SAFE Press Article, http://safe-frankfurt.de/uploads/media/Krahnen_Banking_Separation_Opinion_Piece.pdf (cited as: *Krahnen* (2014) Structural Reform).

Krahnen (2013) Rettung durch Regulierung? Eckpunkte des Liikanen-Berichts, Perspektiven der Wirtschaftspolitik, 14(3–4), 167–185 (cited as: *Krahnen* (2013) Rettung durch Regulierung?).

Krahnen/Kemmerer (2013) Gesprächsreihe zu Strukturreformen im europäischen Bankensektor: Zukunft der Universalbanken, SAFE Policy Letter, No 9 (cited as: *Krahnen/Kemmerer* (2013) Gesprächsreihe Strukturreformen).

Krahnen/Noth/Schüwer (2016) Structural Reforms in Banking: the role of trading, SAFE Whitepaper, No 33 (cited as: *Krahnen/Noth/Schüwer* (2016) Structural Reforms).

Krawiec (2013) Don't "Screw Joe the Plummer": The Sausage-Making of Financial Reform, Arizona Law Review, 55:53–84 (cited as: *Krawiec* (2013) Joe the Plummer).

Krawiec/Liu (2015) The Volcker rule: a brief political history, Capital Markets Law Journal, 10:4, 507–522 (cited as: *Krawiec/Liu* (2015) Volcker Rule).

Kroszner/Rajan (1994) Is the Glass-Steagall Act Justified? A Study of the U.S. Experience with Universal Banking Before 1933, The American Economic Review, 84:4, 810–832 (cited as: *Kroszner/Rajan* (1994) Glass-Steagall Act).

Kuck (2017) Top 100 der deutschen Kreditwirtschaft, die bank, No 8 (cited as: *Kuck* (2017) Deutsche Kreditwirtschaft).

Kumpan (2014) Das Verbot von Eigengeschäften für Banken – eine rechtsvergleichende Analyse, ZBB/JBB, 4:14, 201–211 (cited as: *Kumpan* (2014) Verbot von Eigengeschäften).

Laeven/Ratnovski/Tong (2014) Bank Size and Systemic Risk, IMF Staff Discussion Note, SDN14/04 (cited as: *Laeven/Ratnovski/Tong* (2014) Systemic Risk).

Lambert/Noth/Schüwer (2013) How Do Insured Deposits Affect Bank Risk? Evidence from the 2008 Emergency Economic Stabilization Act, DIW Berlin Discussion Papers, No 1347 (cited as: *Lambert/Noth/Schüwer* (2013) Insured Deposits.

Langfield/Pagano (2015) Bank bias in Europe: effects on systemic risk and growth, ECB Working Paper Series, No 1797 (cited as: *Langfield/Pagano* (2015) Bank Bias).

Lehmann (2014) Extraterritorial Effects of Legislative Acts on the Separation of Banking Activities, Int'l Bus. L. J., 305–316 (cited as: *Lehmann* (2014) Extraterritorial Effects).

Lehmann (2014) Volcker Rule, Ring Fencing or Separation of Bank Activities: Comparison of Structural Reform Acts Around the World, LSE Working Papers, No 25 (cited as: *Lehmann* (2014) Ring-Fencing).

Lindo/Przewoska (2015) Separating Universal Banks from Too-Big-to-Fail Banks (TBTF), Finance Watch Policy Brief, http://www.finance-watch.org/ifile/Publications/Reports/Finance-Watch-Policy-Brief-March-2015.pdf (cited as: *Lindo/Przewoska* (2015) Universal Banks).

Manasfi (2013) Systemic Risk and Dodd-Frank's Volcker Rule, Wm. & Mary Bus. L. Rev. 4:181 (cited as: *Manasfi* (2013) Systemic Risk).

Martel/Van Rixtel/Mota (2012) Business Models of International Banks in the Wake of the 2007–2009 Global Financial Crisis, Bank of Spain, Revista de Estabilidad Financiera, 22:99–121 (cited as: *Martel/Van Rixtel/Mota* (2012) Business Models of International Banks).

Masciandaro/Suardi (2014) Public interest and lobbies in reforming banking regulation: three tales of ring fencing, Int Rev Econ 61:305–328 (cited as: *Masciandaro/Suardi* (2014) Public Interest and Lobbies).

Maurenbrecher/Kramer (2013) Abschnitt 2: Bewilligung zum Geschäftsbetrieb, in: *Watter et al.* (Ed.) Basler Kommentar: Bankengesetz, 2nd Ed., Helbing Lichtenhahn Verlag, Basel (cited as: *Maurenbrecher/Kramer* (2013) Geschäftsbetrieb).

Merkley/Levin (2011) The Dodd-Frank Act Restrictions On Proprietary Trading and Conflicts of Interest: New Tools to Address Evolving Threats, Harvard Journal on Legislation, Vol 48, 515–553 (cited as: *Merkley/Levin* (2011) Dodd-Frank Act).

Mersch (2016) Current developments in the German banking market, Speech by Yves Mersch, Member of the Executive Board of the ECB, at an event organised by the Bayerischer Sparkassenverband, Munich, 27 January 2016, https://www.bis.org/review/r160128b.pdf (cited as: *Mersch* (2016) German Banking Market).

Moenninghoff/Ongena/Wieandt (2015) The perennial challenge to counter Too-Big-To-Fail in banking: Empirical evidence from the new international regulation dealing with Global Systemically Important Banks, Journal of Banking and Finance, 61, 221–236 (cited as: *Moenninghoff/Ongena/Wieandt* (2015) Too-Big-to-Fail).

Molyneux (2016) Banking in the UK, in: *Beck/Casu* (Ed.) The Palgrave Handbook of European Banking, Macmillan Publishers Ltd., London (cited as: *Molyneux* (2016) Banking in the UK).

Morrison (2011) Systemic Risks and the 'Too-Big-to-Fail' Problem, Oxford Review of Economic Policy, 27:3, 498–516 (cited as: *Morrison* (2011) Systemic Risks).

Möslein (2013) Die Trennung von Wertpapier- und sonstigem Bankgeschäft: Trennbankensystem, ring-fencing und Volcker-Rule als Mittel zur Eindämmung systemischer Gefahren für das Finanzsystem, ORDO: Jahrbuch für die Ordnung von Wirtschaft und Gesellschaft, Vol. 64, 349–376 (cited as: *Möslein* (2013) Trennung).

Möslein (2013) Grundsatz- und Anwendungsfragen zur Spartentrennung nach dem sog. Trennbankengesetz, BKR 2013, 397 (cited as: *Möslein* (2013) Spartentrennung).

Nahmias (2016) UK Banks Facing Tighter Regulatory Rules, BNP PARIBAS Economic Research, http://economic-research.bnpparibas.com/Views/DisplayPublication.aspx?type=document&IdPdf=28915 (cited as: *Nahmias* (2016) UK Banks).

Nemeczek/Pitz (2016) Intermediate EU Parent Undertaking Requirement for non-EU G-SIBs, Oxford Business Law Blog, https://www.law.ox.ac.uk/business-law-blog/blog/2016/12/intermediate-eu-parent-undertaking-requirement-non-eu-g-sibs (cited as: *Nemeczek/Pitz* (2016) Intermediate EU Parent Undertaking).

Nobel (2012) Entwicklungen im Bank- und Kapitalmarktrecht, SJZ, 108:10–15 (cited as: *Nobel* (2012) Bank- und Kapitalmarktrecht).

Nobel/Brändli (2017) Can Banks Still Keep a Secret? Switzerland. In: *Booysen/Neo* (Ed.) Can Banks Still Keep a Secret? Bank Secrecy in Financial Centres Around the World. Cambridge University Press, Cambridge (cited as: *Nobel/Brändli* (2017) Can Banks Still Keep a Secret?).

O'Hara/Oldfield (1986) The Microeconomics of Market Making, The Journal of Financial and Quantitative Analysis, 21:4, 361–376 (cited as: *O'Hara/Oldfield* (1986) Market Making).

Pace (2012) Limitations on the Business of Banking: An Analysis of Expanded Securities, Insurance and Real Estate Activities, 25th ed., Routledge, New York (cited as: *Pace* (2012) Business of Banking).

Pagano et al. (2014) Is Europe Overbanked?, European Systemic Risk Board Reports of the Advisory Scientific Committee, No 4 (cited as: *Pagano et al.* (2014) Is Europe Overbanked?).

Passardi/Jans (2014) Die neuen Liquiditätsvorschriften für Schweizer Banken, Finanz- und Rechnungswesen: Jahrbuch, 275–302 (cited as: *Passardi/Jans* (2014) Neue Liquiditätsvorschriften).

Pflock (2014) Europäische Bankenregulierung und das "Too big to fail-Dilemma", BWV, Berlin (cited as: *Pflock* (2014) Europäische Bankenregulierung).

Proctor (2014) The Law and Practice of International Banking, 2nd Ed., Oxford University Press, Oxford (cited as: *Proctor* (2014) International Banking).

Proudman (2017) Putting Up a Fence, Speech by James Proudman, Excecutive Director, UK Deposit Takers Supervision, Prudential Regulation Authority, Bank of England (cited as: *Proudman* (2017) Putting Up a Fence).

Richardson (2012) Why the Volcker Rule Is a Useful Tool for Managing Systemic Risk, NYU White Paper https://www.sec.gov/comments/s7-41-11/s74111-316.pdf (cited as: *Richardson* (2012) Volcker Rule).

Richardson/Smith/Walter (2011) Large Banks and the Volcker Rule, in: *Acharya et al.* (Eds.) Regulating Wall Street: The Dodd-Frank Act and the New Architecture of Global Finance, Wiley, New York (cited as: *Richardson/Smith/Walter* (2011) Large Banks).

Rime/Stiroh (2003) The performance of universal banks: Evidence from Switzerland, Journal of Banking & Finance 27, 2121–2150 (cited as: *Rime/Stiroh* (2003) Universal Banks).

Roth (2012) „Too big to fail" – Stärkung der Stabilität im Finanzsektor, SJZ, 108:285–293 (cited as: *Roth* (2012) Too-Big-to-Fail).

Sants et al. (2016) The Impact of the UK's Exit from the EU on the UK-Based Financial Services Sector, Oliver Wyman Report, http://www.oliverwyman.com/content/dam/oliver-wyman/global/en/2016/oct/Brexit_POV.PDF (cited as: *Sants et al.* (2016) Impact of the UK's Exit from the EU).

Saunders/Walter (1994) Universal Banking in the United States: What Could We Win What Could We Lose?, New York, Oxford University Press (cited as: *Saunders/Walter* (1994) Universal Banking).

Schäfer (2016) § 1 Begriffsbestimmungen, in: *Boos/Fischer/Schulte-Mattler* (Ed.) KWG, CRR-VO: Kommentar zu Kreditwesengesetz, VO (EU) Nr. 575/2013 (CRR) und Ausführungsvorschriften, 5th Ed., Beck, München (cited as: *Schäfer* (2016) § 1 Begriffsbestimmungen).

Schäfer (2016) § 2a Ausnahmen für gruppenangehörige Institute und Institute, die institutsbezogenen Sicherungssystemen angehören, in: *Boos/Fischer/Schulte-Mattler* (Ed.) KWG, CRR-VO: Kommentar zu Kreditwesengesetz, VO (EU) Nr. 575/2013 (CRR) und Ausführungsvorschriften, 5th Ed., Beck, München (cited as: *Schäfer* (2016) § 2a Ausnahmen).

Schäfer (2016) § 3 Verbotene Geschäfte, in: *Boos/Fischer/Schulte-Mattler* (Ed.) KWG, CRR-VO: Kommentar zu Kreditwesengesetz, VO (EU) Nr. 575/2013 (CRR) und Ausführungsvorschriften, 5th Ed., Beck, München (cited as: *Schäfer* (2016) § 3 Verbotene Geschäfte).

Schäfer (2016) Trennbankengesetz: Keine Schuld an Börsenturbulenzen, DIW Wochenbericht, Vol 5 (cited as: *Schäfer* (2016) Trennbankengesetz).

Schaffelhuber/Kunschke (2015) Das sogenannte Trennbankengesetz – Zwang zur Verlagerung bestimmter Handelsaktivitäten und Geschäfte mit stark gehebelten Investmentvehikeln auf ein gruppenangehöriges Finanzhandelsinstitut, in: *Everling/Goedeckemeyer* (Ed.) Bankenrating: Normative Bankenordnung in der Finanzmarktkrise, 2nd Ed., Springer, Wiesbaden (cited as: *Schaffelhuber/Kunschke* (2015) Trennbankengesetz).

Schelo/Steck (2013) Das Trennbankengesetz: Prävention durch Bankentestamente und Risikoabschirmung, ZBB/JBB 4/13, 227–244 (cited as: *Schelo/Steck* (2013) Trennbankengesetz).

Schich/Aydin (2014) Measurement and analysis of implicit guarantees for bank debt: OECD survey results, OECD Journal: Financial Market Trends, Vol. 2014/1 (cited as: *Schich/Aydin* (2014) OECD Survey Results).

Schildbach (2010) Direct fiscal cost of the financial crisis: Probably much lower than feared, Deutsche Bank Research, https://www.dbresearch.com/PROD/RPS_EN-PROD/PROD0000000000454766/Research_Briefing%3A_Direct_fiscal_cost_of_the_finan.pdf (cited as: *Schildbach* (2010) Financial Crisis).

Schiltknecht (2018) Besondere Anforderungen an systemrelevante Banken, in: *Sester et al.* (Eds.) St. Galler Handbuch zum Schweizer Finanzmarktrecht: Finanzmarktaufsicht und Finanzmarktinfrastrukturen, Dike, Zürich/St. Gallen (cited as: *Schiltknecht* (2018) Sanierungsmassnahmen).

Schiltknecht (2015) Internationale Standards in den Vorlagen zur neuen Finanzmarktarchitektur, SZW, 598–606 (cited as: *Schiltknecht* (2015) Internationale Standards).

Schiltknecht (2013) Stabilität und Instabilität des schweizerischen Bankensystems, SZW 2013, 461–471 (cited as: *Schiltknecht* (2013) Stabilität und Instabilität).

Schiltknecht (2013) Das neue schweizerische Bankeninsolvenzrecht, in: *Sprecher* (Ed.) Sanierung und Insolvenz von Unternehmen III, Europa Institut Zürich, Vol. 138, Schultheiss, Zürich (cited as: *Schiltknecht* (2013) Schweizerisches Bankeninsolvenzrecht).

Schiltknecht (2010) Die "Too big to fail"-Problematik: Neueste Entwicklungen in der Schweiz, SZW 2010, 435–445 (cited as: *Schiltknecht* (2010) "Too Big to Fail").

Schoenmaker (2016) The Impact of the Legal and Operational Structures of Euro-Area Banks on their Resolvability, Bruegel Policy Contribution, No. 23 (cited as: *Schoenmaker* (2016) Euro-Area Banks).

Schultz (2013) Conclusions, in: *Schultz* (Ed.) Perspectives on Dodd-Frank and Finance, MIT Press, Cambridge (cited as: *Schultz* (2013) Conclusions).

Schwarcz (2016) Perspectives on Regulating Systemic Risk, in: *Anand* (Ed.) Systemic Risk, Institutional Design, and the Regulation of Financial Markets, Oxford University Press, Oxford (cited as: *Schwarcz* (2016) Systemic Risk).

Schwarcz (2013) Ring-Fencing, Southern California Law Review, 87:69–110 (cited as: *Schwarcz* (2013) Ring-Fencing).

Schwarcz (2011) The Conundrum of Covered Bonds, The Business Lawyer, 66:561–586 (cited as: *Schwarcz* (2011) Covered Bonds).

Schwennicke (2016) Begriffsbestimmungen, in: *Schwennicke/Auerbach* (Ed.) Kreditwesengesetz (KWG) mit Zahlungsdiensteaufsichtsgesetz (ZAG) und Finanzkonglomerate-Aufsichtsgesetz (FKAG), 3rd Ed., C.H. Beck, München (cited as: *Schwennicke* (2016) Begriffsbestimmungen).

Schwennicke (2016) Verbotene Geschäfte von CRR-Kreditinstituten und mit diesen verbundenen Unternehmen (Abs. 2–4), in: *Schwennicke/Auerbach* (Ed.) Kreditwesengesetz (KWG) mit Zahlungsdiensteaufsichtsgesetz (ZAG) und Finanzkonglomerate-Aufsichtsgesetz (FKAG), 3rd Ed., C.H. Beck, München (cited as: *Schwennicke* (2016) Verbotene Geschäfte).

Sester (2018) § 3 Verhältnis zum EU-Finanzmarktrecht, in: *Sester et al.* (Eds.) St. Galler Handbuch zum Schweizer Finanzmarktrecht: Finanzmarktaufsicht und Finanzmarktinfrastrukturen, Dike, Zürich/St. Gallen (cited as: *Sester* (2018) EU-Finanzmarktrecht).

Sester (2015) Die neue Generation des EU-Finanzmarktrechts und der autonome Nachvollzug in der Schweiz, in: *Waldburger et al.* (Eds.) Law & Economics Festschrift für Peter Nobel zum 70. Geburtstag, Stämpfli, Bern (cited as: *Sester* (2015) Neue Generation).

Sester (2010) Towards a transnational bank restructuring law? The attempt of the G20 to initiatie and monitor regulatory responses to the "too big to fail" problem, ECFR, 4:512–549 (cited as: *Sester* (2010) Bank Restructuring Law).

Sethe (2011) Ein Indianer kennt keinen Schmerz: Reaktion der Schweiz auf Finanzmarktkrise und Steuerstreit, ZBB 2/11, 106–129 (cited as: *Sethe* (2011) Finanzmarktkrise und Steuerstreit).

Shughart (1988) A Public Choice Perspective of the Banking Act of 1933, in: *England/Huertas* (Eds.) The Financial Services Revolution: Policy Directions for the Future, Walter Kluwer, Boston/Dordrecht/Lancaster (cited as: *Shughart* (1988) Public Choice Perspective).

Siegert/Willison (2015), Estimating the extent of the "too big to fail" problem – a review of existing approaches, Bank of England Financial Stability Paper, No 32 (cited as: *Siegert/Willison* (2015), The "Too Big to Fail" Problem).

Smith (1904) An Inquiry into the Nature and Causes of the Wealth of Nations, 5th Ed, Methuen & Co., London, http://www.econlib.org/library/Smith/smWNCover.html (cited as: *Smith* (2007) Wealth of Nations).

Stubbe (2016) Trennbanken: Auslegungshilfe zum Abschirmungsgesetz, Bafin Journal, No 2 (cited as: *Stubbe* (2016) Trennbanken).

Tyler (2017) Financial Services: Contribution to the UK Economy, House of Commons Library Briefing Paper, No 6193 (cited as: *Tyler* (2017) Financial Services).

Van Kann/Rosak (2013) Der Regierungsentwurf des Trennbankengesetzes, Betriebsberater, 25, 1475–1483 (cited as: *Van Kann/Rosak* (2013) Regierungsentwurf des Trennbankengesetzes).

Vickers (2016) Banking Reform in the UK, Presentation at Griswold Center for Economic Policy Studies and Julis-Rabinowitz Center for Public Policy and Finance, Princeton University, September 22, 2016 (cited as: *Vickers* (2016) Banking Reform Presentation).

Vickers (2012) Some Economics of Banking Reform, University of Oxford Department of Economics Discussion Paper Series, No 632 (cited as: *Vickers* (2012) Banking Reform).

Von der Crone/Beeler (2012) Die Regulierung von systemrelevanten Finanzinstituten nach schweizerischem Recht, ZBB, 1:12–20 (cited as: *Von der Crone/Beeler* (2012) Systemrelevante Finanzinstitute).

Waibel (2011) Bank Insolvency and Sovereign Insolvency, in: *Lastra* (Ed.) Cross-border Bank Insolvency, Oxford University Press, Oxford (cited as: *Waibel* (2011) Bank Insolvency).

Watter/Kägi (2015) Haftung des übernehmenden Rechtsträgers für „zurückbleibende" Verbindlichkeiten bei Vermögensübertragung/Ausgliederung? – Zulässigkeit einer reziproken Ausgestaltung von Art. 75 FusG auf vertraglicher Basis, in: *Waldburger/Sester/Peter/Baer* (Eds.) Law & Economics Festschrift für Peter Nobel zum 70. Geburtstag (cited as: *Watter/Kägi* (2015) Haftung des übernehmenden Rechtsträgers).

White (1986) Before the Glass-Steagall Act: An Analysis of the Investment Banking Activities of National Banks, Explorations in Economic History, 23:33–55 (cited as: *White* (1986) Glass-Steagall Act).

White (2013) The Basics of Too-Big-to-Fail, in: *Schultz* (Ed.) Perspectives on Dodd-Frank and Finance, MIT Press, Cambridge (cited as: *White* (2013) Too-Big-to-Fail).

White/Mehmood (2017) 10 years on, world's biggest banks keep getting bigger, S&P Global: Market Intelligence, http://www.bankingexchange.com/images/Dev_SNL/112917BigBanks1.pdf (cited as: *White/Mehmood* (2017) 10 years on).

Whitehead (2011) The Volcker Rule and Evolving Financial Markets, Harvard Bus. L. Rev., Vol. 1:39–73 (cited as: *Whitehead* (2011) Volcker Rule).

Wilmarth (2017) The Road to Repeal of the Glass-Steagall Act, GW Law School Public Law and Legal Theory Paper No. 2017-61 (cited as: *Wilmarth* (2017) Glass-Steagall Repeal).

Wilmarth (2016) Prelude to Glass-Steagall: Abusive Securities Practices by National City Bank and Chase National Bank During the "Roaring Twenties", Tulane Law Review, Vol 90, 1285–1329 (cited as: *Wilmarth* (2016) Glass-Steagall).

Wilmarth (2014) Narrow Banking as a Structural Remedy for the Problem of Systemic Risk: A Comment on Professor Schwarcz's Ring-Fencing, Southern Californa Law Review Postscript, 88:PS1, 1–10 (cited as: *Wilmarth* (2014) Narrow Banking).

Wilmarth (2011) The Dodd-Frank Act: A Flawed and Inadequate Response to the Too-Big-To-Fail Problem, Or. L. Rev. 89:951–1058 (cited as: *Wilmarth* (2011) Dodd-Frank Act).

Wilmarth (2005) Did Universal Banks Play a Significant Role in the U.S. Economy's Boom-and-Bust-Cycle of 1921–33? A Preliminary Assessment, Current Dev. in Monetary & Fin. L. 4:559–645 (cited as: *Wilmarth* (2005) Universal Banks).

Wilmarth (2002) The transformation of the U.S. financial services industry, 1975–2000: Competition, Consolidation and Increased Risk, University of Illinois Law Review, 2:215–476 (cited as: *Wilmarth* (2002) U.S. Financial Services Industry).

Winzeler (2013) Abschnitt 13: Einlagensicherung, in: *Watter et al.* (Ed.) Basler Kommentar: Bankengesetz, 2nd Ed., Helbing Lichtenhahn Verlag, Basel (cited as: *Winzeler* (2013) Einlagensicherung).

Wyss (2014) Finanzmarktenforcement der FINMA: die Instrumente und ihr Einsatz in der Praxis, in: *Emmenegger* (Ed.) Schweizerische Bankrechtstagung 2014: Banken zwischen Strafrecht und Aufsichtsrecht, Helbing Lichtenhahn, Basel (cited as: *Wyss* (2014) Finanzmarktenforcement).

Zaring (2014) Ring-Fencing and It's Alternatives, Southern California Law Review Postscript, 88:PS11, 11–15 (cited as: *Zaring* (2014) Ring-Fencing).

Zweigert/Kötz (1998) Introduction to Comparative Law, 3rd Ed., Clarendon Press, Oxford (cited as: *Zweigert/Kötz* (1998) Comparative Law).

Zweigert/Kötz (1996) Einführung in die Rechtsvergleichung auf dem Gebiet des Privatrechts, 3rd Ed., Mohr, Tübingen (cited as: *Zweigert/Kötz* (1996) Rechtsvergleichung).

II.Materials

AFME (2016) AFME Post Trade Division: Client Asset Protection Task Force: AFME Principles on Asset Segregation Due Diligence and Collateral Management, https://www.afme.eu/globalassets/downloads/publications/afme-position-and-proposed-principles-on-asset-segregation-07.09.16.pdf (cited as: *AFME* (2016) Client Asset Protection).

AGV Banken (2017) Bericht 2016, http://www.agvbanken.de/AGVBanken/Publikationen/_Jahresberichte/Jahresbericht_AGV-Banken_2016-2017.pdf (cited as: *AGV Banken* (2017) Bericht 2016).

BaFin (2018) Hinweise zu den Tatbeständen des Eigenhandels und des Eigengeschäfts, Merkblatt, Stand Januar 2018, https://www.bafin.de/SharedDocs/Veroeffentlichungen/DE/Merkblatt/mb_110322_eigenhandel_eigengeschaeft_neu.html (cited as: *BaFin* (2018) Merkblatt Eigenhandel und Eigengeschäft).

BaFin (2017) Bankaufsichtliche Anforderungen an die IT (BAIT), Rundschreiben 10/2017 (BA) vom 03.11.2017 (cited as: *BaFin* (2017) Anforderungen IT).

BaFin (2016) Interpretative Guidance on Article 2 of the German Act on Ring-Fencing Risk and the Recovery and Resolution Planning for Credit Institutions and Financial Groups dated 7 August 2013, Official Journal I p. 3090 (Bank Separation Act (Abschirmungsgesetz)), https://www.bafin.de/SharedDocs/Downloads/EN/Auslegungsentscheidung/dl_ae_161214_abschirmungsgesetz_en.pdf?__blob=publicationFile&v=5 (cited as: *BaFin* (2016) Interpretative Guidance).

BaFin (2016) Auslegungshilfe zum Artikel 2 des Gesetzes zur Abschirmung von Risiken und zur Planung der Sanierung und Abwicklung von Kreditinstituten und Finanzgruppen vom 7.8.2013, BGBL. I S. 3090 (Abschirmungsgesetz), https://www.bafin.de/SharedDocs/Downloads/DE/Auslegungsentscheidung/dl_ae_161214_abschirmungsgesetz.pdf;jsessionid=D586C950260790369D918863BF996CA1.1_cid290?__blob=publicationFile&v=3 (cited as: *BaFin* (2016) Auslegungshilfe).

BaFin (2015) Konsultation 11/2015 – Entwurf der Auslegungshilfe zum Risikoabschirmungsgesetz, R 1-FR 2311–2015/0011, https://www.bafin.de/SharedDocs/Veroeffentlichungen/DE/Konsultation/2015/kon_1115_risikoabschirmungsgesetz.html;jsessionid=49B73F3351BDB066E6A1D47E44BAEC1C.1_cid381?nn=9450992 (cited as: *BaFin* (2015) Begleitschreiben Konsultation Auslegungshilfe).

BaFin (2014) Merkblatt Einlagengeschäft, https://www.bafin.de/SharedDocs/Veroeffentlichungen/DE/Merkblatt/mb_140311_tatbestand_einlagengeschaeft.html (cited as: *BaFin* (2014) Merkblatt Einlagengeschäft).

BaFin (2009) Merkblatt Garantiegeschäft, https://www.bafin.de/SharedDocs/Veroeffentlichungen/DE/Merkblatt/mb_090108_tatbestand_garantiegeschaeft.html (cited as: *BaFin* (2009) Merkblatt Garantiegeschäft).

BAKBASEL (2016) Die volkswirtschaftliche Bedeutung des Schweizer Finanzsektors: Studie im Auftrag der Schweizerischen Bankiervereinigung SBVg und des Schweizerischen Versicherungsverbands SVV, https://www.bak-economics.com/fileadmin/user_upload/BAKBASEL_Die_volkswirtschaftliche_Bedeutung_Finanzsektor_Schweiz__2016.pdf (cited as: *BAKBASEL* (2016) Schweizer Finanzsektor).

Bank of England (2017) List of Building Societies As Compiled by the Bank of England as at 30 November 2017, https://www.bankofengland.co.uk/-/media/boe/files/prudential-regulation/authorisations/which-firms-does-the-pra-regulate/list-of-building-societies-november-2017-excel.xls?la=en&hash=58B204B050030E375F04A2E28A4D694193CBFC8C (cited as: *Bank of England* (2017) List of Building Societies: November).

Bank of England (2017) Stress testing the UK banking system: 2017 results, https://www.bankofengland.co.uk/-/media/boe/files/stress-testing/2017/stress-testing-the-uk-banking-system-2017-results.pdf?la=en&hash=ACE1E2FB54482F5DC3412864C6907928B622044A (cited as: *Bank of England* (2017) Stress Testing).

Bank of England (2017) The Bank of England's approach to the authorisation and supervision of international banks, insurers and central counterparties, News Release December 20 (cited as: *Bank of England* (2017) Authorisation and Supervision of International Banks).

Bank of England (2017) The financial crisis 10 years on: what's been done to make the system safer?, Fact Sheet, https://www.bankofengland.co.uk/-/media/boe/files/news/2017/september/the-financial-crisis-10-years-on-fact-sheet.pdf?la=en&hash=011B5436AEF0E971766958FC6CE20F9619F2D2B8 (cited as: *Bank of England* (2017) Financial Crisis 10 Years On).

Bank of Finland (2012) Members appointed to Expert Group on reforming the structure of the EU banking sector, News Release February 22 (cited as: *Bank of Finland* (2012) Expert Group).

Bankenverband (2017) Zahlen, Daten, Fakten der Kreditwirtschaft, https://bankenverband.de/media/publikationen/16112017_Zahlen_und_Fakten_web.pdf (cited as: *Bankenverband* (2017) Kreditwirtschaft).

Barclays (2017) Annual Report 2016, https://www.home.barclays/content/dam/barclayspublic/docs/InvestorRelations/AnnualReports/AR2016/Barclays%20PLC%20Annual%20Report%202016.pdf (cited as: *Barclays* (2017) Annual Report 2016).

Basel Committee on Banking Supervision (2013) Global systemically important banks: updated assessment methodology and the higher loss absorbency requirement (cited as: *Basel Committee on Banking Supervision* (2013) Global Systemically Important Banks).

Basel Committee on Banking Supervision (2012) A framework for dealing with domestic systemically important banks (cited as: *Basel Committee on Banking Supervision* (2012) Domestic Systemically Important Banks).

Basel Committee on Banking Supervision (2009) Principles for sound stress testing practices and supervision, https://www.bis.org/publ/bcbs155.pdf (cited as: *Basel Committee on Banking Supervision* (2009) Stress Testing).

BBVA Research (2015) Financial Regulation Outlook: June 2015 Financial Systems and Regulation Area (cited as: *BBVA Research* (2015) Financial Regulation Outlook).

Committee on the Global Financial System (2014) Market-making and proprietary trading: industry trends, drivers and policy implications, CGFS Papers, No 52 (cited as: *Committee on the Global Financial System* (2014) Market-making).

Council of the EU (2015) Outcome of the Council Meeting: 3399th Council Meeting, Economic and Financial Affairs, Presse 44, 10089/15 (cited as: *Council of the EU* (2015) ECOFIN Council Meeting).

Council of the EU (2015) Proposal for a Regulation of the European Parliament and of the Council on structural measures improving the resilience of EU credit institutions, 10150/15 (cited as: *Council of the EU* (2015) Negotiating Stance).

Council of the EU (2015) Restructuring risky banks: Council agrees its negotiating stance, Press Release 474/15 (cited as: *Council of the EU* (2015) Restructuring Risky Banks Press Release).

Credit Suisse (2017) Annual Report 2016, https://www.credit-suisse.com/media/asset s/corporate/docs/about-us/investor-relations/financial-disclosures/financial-repor ts/csg-ar-2016-en.pdf (cited as: *Credit Suisse* (2017) Annual Report 2016).

Credit Suisse (Schweiz) AG (2018) Annual Report 2018, https://www.credit-suisse.co m/media/assets/corporate/docs/about-us/investor-relations/financial-disclosures/f inancial-reports/csch-ar-2017-en.pdf (cited as: *Credit Suisse (Schweiz) AG* (2018) Annual Report 2018).

Credit Suisse (Schweiz) AG (2017) Annual Report 2016, https://www.credit-suisse.co m/media/assets/corporate/docs/about-us/investor-relations/financial-disclosures/f inancial-reports/csch-ar-2016-en.pdf (cited as: *Credit Suisse (Schweiz) AG* (2017) Annual Report 2016).

DESTATIS (2018) Deutsche Wirtschaft 2017, https://www.destatis.de/DE/Publikati onen/Thematisch/VolkswirtschaftlicheGesamtrechnungen/DeutschWirtschaft.p df?__blob=publicationFile (cited as: *DESTATIS* (2018) Deutsche Wirtschaft 2017).

DESTATIS (2017) Bruttoinlandsprodukt 2016 für Deutschland: Begleitmaterial zur Pressekonferenz am 12. Januar 2017 in Berlin, https://www.destatis.de/DE/Press eService/Presse/Pressekonferenzen/2017/BIP2016/Pressebroschuere_BIP2016.pdf ?__blob=publicationFile (cited as: *DESTATIS* (2017) Bruttoinlandsprodukt).

DESTATIS (2017) VGR des Bundes – Bruttowertschöpfung, Tabelle Nr. 81000–0103, ("VGR des Bundes – Bruttowertschöpfung (nominal/preisbereinigt): Deutschland, Jahre, Wirtschaftsbereiche"), https://www-genesis.destatis.de/genes is/online/data;jsessionid=E14BDBACA3CD6C605E3DDF996B17B9D1.tomcat_ GO_2_2?operation=abruftabelleBearbeiten&levelindex=1&levelid=15173927379 69&auswahloperation=abruftabelleAuspraegungAuswaehlen&auswahlverzeich nis=ordnungsstruktur&auswahlziel=werteabruf&selectionname=81000-0103&a uswahltext=&werteabruf=starten (cited as: *DESTATIS* (2017) Bruttowertschöpfung).DESTAalculation based on to witzerland'so Chapters 909, 912–913.t becomes clear that the UK and Germany are almost equal. adjust

Deutsche Bank (2018) Annual Report 2017 SEC Form 20-F, https://www.db.com/ir/ en/download/Deutsche_Bank_20_F_2017.pdf (cited as: *Deutsche Bank* (2018) 2017 SEC Form 20-F).

Deutsche Bank (2017) Annual Report 2016 SEC Form 20-F, https://www.db.com/ir/ en/download/Deutsche_Bank_20_F_2016.pdf (cited as: *Deutsche Bank* (2017) 2016 SEC Form 20-F).

Deutsche Bank (2017) Annual Report 2016, https://www.db.com/ir/en/download/D eutsche_Bank_Annual_Report_2016.pdf (cited as: *Deutsche Bank* (2017) Annual Report 2016).

Deutsche Bundesbank (2017) Monthly Report February 2017, 69:2 (cited as: *Deutsche Bundesbank* (2017) Monthly Report February).

Deutsche Bundesbank (2017) Monatsbericht November 2017, 69:11 (cited as: *Deutsche Bundesbank* (2017) Monatsbericht November).

Deutsche Bundesbank (2016) Merkblatt über die Erteilung einer Erlaubnis zum Erbringen von Finanzdienstleistungen gemäß § 32 Absatz 1 KWG, https://www.bafin.de/SharedDocs/Downloads/DE/Merkblatt/WA/dl_fidierlaubnis_buba.pdf?__blob=publicationFile&v=2 (cited as: *Deutsche Bundesbank* (2016) Merkblatt Finanzdienstleistungen).

Deutsche Bundesbank (2015) Monatsbericht April 2015, 47:4 (cited as: *Deutsche Bundesbank* (2015) Monatsbericht April).

Deutsche Bundesbank (2014) Banking Act (Gesetz über das Kreditwesen), https://www.bafin.de/SharedDocs/Downloads/EN/Aufsichtsrecht/dl_kwg_en.pdf;jsessionid=339CA3DE4773B9B6C6580AD4CE651A73.2_cid290?__blob=publicationFile&v=3 (cited as: *Deutsche Bundesbank* (2014) Banking Act).

Deutscher Bundestag (2016) Schriftliche Fragen mit den in der Woche vom 1. Februar 2016 eingegangenen Antworten der Bundesregierung, Drucksache 18/7473, http://dipbt.bundestag.de/dip21/btd/18/074/1807473.pdf (cited as: *Deutscher Bundestag* (2016) Antworten der Bundesregierung).

Deutscher Bundestag (2013) Stenografischer Bericht 229. Sitzung Berlin, Freitag, den 15. März 2013, http://dipbt.bundestag.de/dip21/btp/17/17229.pdf#P.28613 (cited as: *Deutscher Bundestag* (2013) Stenografischer Bericht).

Deutscher Bundestag (2013) Gesetzesentwurf der Bundesregierung: Entwurf eines Gesetzes zur Abschirmung von Risiken und zur Planung der Sanierung und Abwicklung von Kreditinstituten und Finanzgruppen, Drucksache 17/12601 (cited as: *Deutscher Bundestag* (2013) Gesetzesentwurf Trennbankengesetz).

Deutscher Bundestag (2013) Bericht des Finanzausschusses (7. Ausschuss), Drucksache 17/13539 (cited as: *Deutscher Bundestag* (2013) Bericht Finanzausschuss).

Deutsches Bundesministerium für Finanzen (2013) Bundesregierung beschließt Trennbankengesetz und neue Strafrechtsregelungen im Finanzsektor, Pressemitteilung, No. 12 (cited as: *Deutsches Bundesministerium für Finanzen* (2013) Trennbankengesetz).

DZ Bank (2017) Annual Report 2016, https://www.annualreport.dzbank.com/gb2016/static/export/docs/DZBANK_Group_AR2016.pdf (cited as: *DZ Bank* (2017) Annual Report 2016).

EBA (2014) Guidelines on the specification of measures to reduce or remove impediments to resolvability and the circumstances in which each measure may be applied under Directive 2014/59/EU, https://www.eba.europa.eu/documents/10180/933988/EBA-GL-2014-11+%28Guidelines+on+Impediments+to+Resolvability%29.pdf (cited as: *EBA* (2014) Guidelines Impediments Resolvability).

Economist Intelligence Unit (2017) Industry Report Financial Services: Switzerland, 2nd Quarter 2017 (cited as: *EIU* (2017) Financial Services: Switzerland).

Economist Intelligence Unit (2017) Industry Report Financial Services: Germany, 3rd Quarter 2017 (cited as: *EIU* (2017) Financial Services: Germany).

Economist Intelligence Unit (2017) Industry Report Financial Services: United Kingdom, 3rd Quarter 2017 (cited as: *EIU* (2017) Financial Services: United Kingdom).

EFD (2016) Erläuterungsbericht zu Änderungen der Eigenmittelverordnung und der Bankenverordnung (Eigenmit-telanforderungen Banken – Rekalibrierung TBTF und Kategorisierung), https://www.newsd.admin.ch/newsd/message/attachments/43961.pdf (cited as: *EFD* (2016) Erläuterungsbericht).

EFD (2012) Kommentar zur Änderung der Bankenverordnung und der Eigenmittelverordnung: Umsetzung der Änderung des Bankengesetzes vom 30. September 2011 (Stärkung der Stabilität im Finanzsektor; „too big to fail"). https://www.newsd.admin.ch/newsd/message/attachments/43074.pdf (cited as: *EFD* (2012) Kommentar Bankenverordnung).

EFD (2009) Bundesrat setzt Expertenkommission zum Thema "too-big-to-fail" ein, Medienmitteilung 4. November, http://www.news-service.admin.ch/NSBSubscriber/message/attachments/17309.pdf (cited as: *EFD* (2009) Expertenkommission Medienmitteilung).

Esisuisse (2017) Jahresbericht 2016, https://www.esisuisse.ch/de/publikationen/jahresberichte (cited as: *Esisuisse* (2017) Jahresbericht 2016).

European Central Bank (2017) Report on Financial Structures: October 2017, https://www.ecb.europa.eu/pub/pdf/other/reportonfinancialstructures201710.en.pdf (cited as: *European Central Bank* (2017) Financial Structures).

European Central Bank (2017) List of supervised entities, https://www.bankingsupervision.europa.eu/ecb/pub/pdf/list_of_supervised_entities_201704.en.pdf?cf307b8bc923b7869e40e0effffeb712 (cited as: *European Central Bank* (2017) List of supervised entities).

European Central Bank (2016) Financial Stability Review: November 2016, https://www.ecb.europa.eu/pub/pdf/other/financialstabilityreview201611.en.pdf (cited as: *European Central Bank* (2016) Financial Stability Review).

European Central Bank (2014) Guide to Banking Supervision, https://www.bankingsupervision.europa.eu/ecb/pub/pdf/ssmguidebankingsupervision201411.en.pdf (cited as: *European Central Bank* (2014) Banking Supervision).

European Commission (2017) Report from the Commission to the European Parliament and the Council under Article 29(3) of Regulation (EU) 2015/2365 of 25 November 2015 on transparency of securities financing transactions and of reuse and amending Regulation (EU) No 648/2012, COM(2017) 604 final, http://eur-lex.europa.eu/legal-content/EN/TXT/PDF/?uri=CELEX:52017DC0604&from=EN (cited as: *European Commission* (2017) Securities Financing Transactions).

European Commission (2017) Commission Work Programme 2018: Annex to the Communication from the Commission to the European Parliament, the Council, the European Economic and Social Committee and the Committee of the Regions, COM(2017) 650 final ANNEX 4 (cited as: *European Commission* (2017) Commission Work Programme 2018: Annex 4).

European Commission (2015) Updated version of first memo published on 15/04/2014 – Banking Union: restoring financial stability in the Eurozone, MEMO/15/6164 (cited as: *European Commission* (2015) Banking Union).

European Commission (2015) Speaking notes of Commissioner Jonathan Hill on Bank Structural Reform at ECOFIN meeting, STATEMENT/15/5237 (cited as: *European Commission* (2015) Speaking Notes of Commissioner Hill).

European Commission (2015) Single Resolution Mechanism to come into effect for the Banking Union, IP/15/6397 (cited as: *European Commission* (2015) Single Resolution Mechanism).

European Commission (2014), Structural Reform of the EU banking sector, Press Release, IP/14/85 (cited as: *European Commission* (2014), Structural Reform Press Release).

European Commission (2014) Proposal for a Regulation of the European Parliament and of the Council on structural measures improving the resilience of EU credit institutions, COM(2014) 43 final (cited as: *European Commission* (2014) Proposal for a Regulation).

European Commission (2014) Commission Staff Working Document: Impact Assessment Part 3, http://eur-lex.europa.eu/resource.html?uri=cellar:e186dd0b-89b3-11e3-87da-01aa75ed71a1.0001.01/DOC_3&format=PDF (cited as: *European Commission* (2014) Impact Assessment Part 3).

European Commission (2014) Commission Staff Working Document: Impact Assessment Part 2, https://eur-lex.europa.eu/resource.html?uri=cellar:e186dd0b-89b3-11e3-87da-01aa75ed71a1.0001.01/DOC_2&format=PDF (cited as: *European Commission* (2014) Impact Assessment Part 2).

European Commission (2014) Commission Staff Working Document: Impact Assessment Part 1, https://eur-lex.europa.eu/resource.html?uri=cellar:e186dd0b-89b3-11e3-87da-01aa75ed71a1.0001.05/DOC_1&format=PDF (cited as: *European Commission* (2014) Impact Assessment Part 1).

European Commission (2013) Minutes of the 2037th meeting of the Commission held in Brussels (Berlaymont) on Wednesday 6 March 2013 (morning), PV(2013) 2037 final (cited as: *European Commission* (2013) Meeting of the Commission).

European Commission (2012) Summary of the Replies to the Consultation of the Internal Market and Services Directorate General on the Recommendations of the High-Level Expert Group on Reforming the Structure of the EU Banking Sector, http://ec.europa.eu/finance/consultations/2012/hleg-banking/docs/replies-summary_en.pdf (cited as: *European Commission* (2012) Replies to the Consultation).

European Commission (2011) Mandate of the High Level Expert Group, http://ec.europa.eu/finance/bank/docs/high-level_expert_group/mandate_en.pdf (cited as: *European Commission* (2011) Mandate of the HLEG).

European Commission (2009) Commission staff working document accompanying the proposal for a Directive of the European Parliament and of the Council on Alternative Investment Fund Managers and amending Directives 2004/39/EC and 2009/.../EC: Executive summary of the impact assessment, SEC(2009) 577 (cited as: *European Commission* (2009) Alternative Investment Fund Managers).

European Covered Bond Council (2009) European Covered Bond Factbook, http://www.housingfinance.org/uploads/Publicationsmanager/ECBC%20Fact%20Book%202008.pdf (cited as: *European Covered Bond Council* (2009) European Covered Bond Factbook).

European Parliament (2016) Briefing on Brexit: the United-Kingdom and EU financial services, http://www.europarl.europa.eu/RegData/etudes/BRIE/2016/587384/IPOL_BRI%282016%29587384_EN.pdf (cited as: *European Parliament* (2016) Brexit).

European Parliament Committee on Economic and Monetary Affairs (2018) Amendments 310–427, 2016/0364(COD) (cited as: *European Parliament Committee on Economic and Monetary Affairs* (2018) Amendments CRDV).

European Parliament Committee on Economic and Monetary Affairs (2015) Minutes: Meeting of 26 May 2015, 15.00 – 18.30 Brussels, ECON_PV(2015)0526_1, http://www.europarl.europa.eu/sides/getDoc.do?type=COMPARL&reference=PE-560.570&format=PDF&language=EN&secondRef=02 (cited as: *European Parliament Committee on Economic and Monetary Affairs* (2015) Minutes: Meeting of 26 May 2015).

European Parliament Committee on Economic and Monetary Affairs (2013) Draft Report on the proposal for a regulation of the European Parliament and of the Council on structural measures improving the resilience of EU credit institutions, http://www.europarl.europa.eu/sides/getDoc.do?pubRef=-//EP//NONSGML+COMPARL+PE-546.551+02+DOC+PDF+V0//EN&language=EN (cited as: *European Parliament Committee on Economic and Monetary Affairs* (2013) Draft Report).

European Parliament Committee on Economic and Monetary Affairs (2013) Report on reforming the structure of the EU banking sector, A7–0231/2013, http://www.europarl.europa.eu/sides/getDoc.do?pubRef=-//EP//NONSGML+REPORT+A7-2013-0231+0+DOC+PDF+V0//EN (cited as: *European Parliament* (2013) Report on Structural Reform).

Expertenkommission zur Limitierung der volkswirtschaftlichen Risiken durch Grossunternehmen (2010) Schlussbericht, https://www.sif.admin.ch/dam/sif/de/dokumente/FinWeb/101004-SB-TBTF-DE-FINAL.pdf.download.pdf/101004-SB-TBTF-DE-FINAL.pdf (cited as: *Expertenkommission* (2010) Schlussbericht).

Expertenkommission zur Limitierung der volkswirtschaftlichen Risiken durch Grossunternehmen (2010) Final Report (English Translation), https://www.sif.admin.ch/dam/sif/en/dokumente/TBTF/101004-SB-TBTF-EN-FINAL.pdf.download.pdf/101004-SB-TBTF-EN-FINAL.pdf (cited as: *Expertenkommission* (2010) Final Report).

Expertenkommission zur Weiterentwicklung der Finanzmarktstrategie (2014) Schlussbericht, http://www.news.admin.ch/NSBSubscriber/message/attachments/37585.pdf (cited as: *Expertenkommission* (2014) Schlussbericht).

Financial Crisis Inquiry Commission (2011) The Financial Crisis Inquiry Report: Final Report of the National Commission on the Causes of the Financial and Economic Crisis in the United States, https://www.gpo.gov/fdsys/pkg/GPO-FCIC/pdf/GPO-FCIC.pdf (cited as: *Financial Crisis Inquiry Commission* (2011) Financial Crisis).

Financial Stability Oversight Council (2011) Study and Recommendations on Prohibitions on Proprietary Trading & Certain Relationships with Hedge Funds & Private Equity Funds, https://www.treasury.gov/initiatives/Documents/Volcker%20sec%20%20619%20study%20final%201%2018%2011%20rg.pdf (cited as: *Financial Stability Oversight Council* (2011) Proprietary Trading).

Finma (2017) Jahresbericht 2016, https://www.finma.ch/de/~/media/finma/dokumente/dokumentencenter/myfinma/finma-publikationen/geschaeftsbericht/20170404_fin_jb16.pdf?la=de&hash=D46CA6E3E20D37BFFCCA9A8E0CC1BD33E0751A56 (cited as: *Finma* (2017) Jahresbericht 2016).

Finma (2017) Corporate Governance – Banken, Rundschreiben 2017/1, https://www.finma.ch/de/news/2016/11/20161101-mm-rs-corporate-governance-bei-banken/ (cited as: *Finma* (2017) Corporate Governance – Banken).

Finma (2017) Annual Report 2016, https://www.finma.ch/en/~/media/finma/dokumente/dokumentencenter/myfinma/finma-publikationen/geschaeftsbericht/20170404_fin_jb16.pdf?la=en&hash=0D16237F6210737F3EB8014FEA872EF486778F1E (cited as: *Finma* (2017) Annual Report 2016).

Finma (2015) Jahresbericht 2014, https://www.finma.ch/FinmaArchiv/gb2014/download/2014/de/Downloads/Finma_JB14_De.pdf (cited as: *Finma* (2015) Jahresbericht 2014).

FSB (2017) 2017 list of global systemically important banks (G-SIBs), http://www.fsb.org/wp-content/uploads/P211117-1.pdf (cited as: *FSB* (2017) Global Systemically Important Banks).

FSB (2016) Guidance on Arrangements to Support Operational Continuity in Resolution, http://www.fsb.org/wp-content/uploads/Guidance-on-Arrangements-to-Support-Operational-Continuity-in-Resolution1.pdf (cited as: *FSB* (2016) Operational Continuity).

FSB (2015) Removing Remaining Obstacles to Resolvability: Report to the G20 on progress in resolution, http://www.fsb.org/wp-content/uploads/Report-to-the-G20-on-Progress-in-Resolution-for-publication-final.pdf (cited as: *FSB* (2015) Obstacles to Resolvability).

FSB (2014) Structural Banking Reforms: Cross-border consistencies and global financial stability implications, Report to G20 Leaders for the November 2014 Summit, http://www.fsb.org/wp-content/uploads/r_141027.pdf (cited as: *FSB* (2014) Structural Banking Reforms).

FSB (2014) Key Attributes of Effective Resolution Regimes for Financial Institutions, http://www.fsb.org/wp-content/uploads/r_141015.pdf (cited as: *FSB* (2014) Key Attributes).

FSB (2013) Recovery and Resolution Planning for Systemically Important Financial Institutions: Guidance on Identification of Critical Functions and Critical Shared Services, http://www.fsb.org/wp-content/uploads/r_130716a.pdf (cited as: *FSB* (2013) Guidance Critical Functions).

FSB (2011) Policy Measures to Address Systemically Important Financial Institutions, http://www.fsb.org/wp-content/uploads/Policy-Measures-to-Address-Systemically-Important-Financial-Institutions.pdf (cited as: *FSB* (2011) Systemically Important Financial Institutions).

FSO (2017) Gross domestic product: production approach, https://www.bfs.admin.ch/bfs/en/home/statistics/national-economy/national-accounts/gross-domestic-product.assetdetail.3322024.html (cited as: *FSO* (2017) Gross domestic product).

FSO (2017) Industries production account (aggregated by sections), https://www.bfs.admin.ch/bfsstatic/dam/assets/3322005/master (cited as: *FSO* (2017) Industries production account).

Group of Thirty (2009) Financial Reform: A Framework for Financial Stability, http://group30.org/images/uploads/publications/G30_FinancialReformFrameworkFinStability.pdf (cited as: *Group of Thirty* (2009) Financial Reform).

High Level Expert Group on reforming the structure of the EU banking sector (2012) Final report, http://ec.europa.eu/internal_market/bank/docs/high-level_expert_group/report_en.pdf (cited as: *HLEG* (2012) Liikanen Report).

HM Revenue & Customs (2016) Pay-As-You-Earn and Corporate Tax Receipts from the Banking Sector: An Official Statistics release, https://www.gov.uk/government/uploads/system/uploads/attachment_data/file/548384/PAYE__Corporate_Tax_Receipts_from_the_Banking_Sector_2016_FINAL.pdf (cited as: *HM Revenue & Customs* (2016) Tax Receipts Banking Sector).

HM Treasury (2013) Impact Assessment Financial Services (Banking Reform) Bill, https://www.parliament.uk/documents/impact-assessments/IA13-21.pdf (cited as: *HM Treasury* (2013) Impact Assessment).

HM Treasury (2012) Sound Banking: delivering reform. https://www.gov.uk/government/uploads/system/uploads/attachment_data/file/211866/icb_banking_reform_bill.pdf (cited as: *HM Treasury* (2012) Sound Banking).

HM Treasury (2012) Banking reform: delivering stability and supporting a sustainable economy, https://assets.publishing.service.gov.uk/government/uploads/system/uploads/attachment_data/file/32556/whitepaper_banking_reform_140512.pdf (cited as: *HM Treasury* (2012) Banking Reform).

HM Treasury (2010) Maintaining the financial stability of UK banks: update on the support schemes, Report by the Comptroller and Auditor General, HC 676 Session 2010–2011, https://www.nao.org.uk/wp-content/uploads/2010/12/1011676es.pdf (cited as: *HM Treasury* (2010) Maintaining the Financial Stability of UK Banks).

HSBC (2017) Annual Report 2016, http://www.hsbc.com/-/media/hsbc-com/investorrelationsassets/hsbc-results/2016/annual-results/hsbc-holdings-plc/170221-annual-report-and-accounts-2016.pdf (cited as: *HSBC* (2017) Annual Report 2016).

IMF (2017) Global Financial Stability Report, World Economic and Financial Surveys (cited as: *IMF* (2017) Global Financial Stability Report).

IMF (2016) Financial Sector Assessment Program: United Kingdom, Financial Stability Assessment, IMF Country Report, No 16/167 (cited as: *IMF* (2016) Financial Stability Assessment: United Kingdom).

IMF (2016) Financial Sector Assessment Program: Germany: Stress Testing the Banking and Securities Sector: Technical Note, IMF Country Report, No 16/191 (cited as: *IMF* (2016) Stress Testing).

IMF (2016) Financial Sector Assessment Program: Germany, IMF Country Report, No 16/195 (cited as: *IMF* (2016) Germany).

IMF (2014) Switzerland: Financial Stability Assessment, IMF Country Report, No 14/143 (cited as: *IMF* (2014) Switzerland).

IMF (2011) Financial Sector Stability Assessment: Germany, IMF Country Report, No 11/169 (cited as: *IMF* (2011) Germany).

IMF (2011) Technical Note on Banking Sector Structure: Germany, IMF Country Report, No 11/370 (cited as: *IMF* (2011) Banking Sector Structure: Germany).

IMF (1998) Towards a Framework for Financial Stability, World Economic and Financial Surveys (cited as: *IMF* (1998) Financial Stability).

Independent Commission on Banking (2011) Final Report: Recommendations, http://webarchive.nationalarchives.gov.uk/20131003105424/https:/hmt-sanctions.s3.amazonaws.com/icb%20final%20report/icb%2520final%2520report%5B1%5D.pdf (cited as: *ICB* (2011) Vickers Report).

Independent Commission on Banking (2011) Interim Report: Consultation on Reform Options, https://s3-eu-west-1.amazonaws.com/htcdn/Interim-Report-110411.pdf (cited as: *ICB* (2011) Interim Report).

JP Morgan Chase & Co (2017) Corporate & Investment Bank, https://www.jpmorganchase.com/corporate/investor-relations/document/cib_investor_day_2017.pdf (cited as: *JP Morgan Chase & Co* (2017) Corporate & Investment Bank).

KPMG (2016) A New Landscape: Challenger banking annual results, https://home.kpmg.com/content/dam/kpmg/pdf/2016/05/challenger-banking-report-2016.PDF (cited as: *KPMG* (2016) New Landscape).

Norton Rose Fulbright/Association of Foreign Banks (2017) Brexit survey: The impact on the foreign banking sector, http://www.foreignbanks.org.uk/uploads/content/newsletter/afb-nrf-brexit-survey-the-impact-on-the-foreign-banking-sector-2017.pdf?1511877909 (cited as: *Norton Rose Fulbright/Association of Foreign Banks* (2017) Brexit survey).

OECD (2015) Structural Reforms in Europe: Achievements and Homework, Better Policies Series, https://www.oecd.org/eu/structural-reforms-in-europe-achievements-and-homework.pdf (cited as: *OECD* (2015) Structural Reforms in Europe).

Office for National Statistics (2017) Dataset: Nominal and real regional gross value added (balanced) by industry, https://www.ons.gov.uk/economy/grossvalueaddedgva/datasets/nominalandrealregionalgrossvalueaddedbalancedbyindustry (cited as: *Office for National Statistics* (2017) Gross Value Added).

Office for National Statistics (2017) Time series: Gross Domestic Product at market prices: Current price: Seasonally adjusted £m, https://www.ons.gov.uk/generator?format=xls&uri=/economy/grossdomesticproductgdp/timeseries/ybha/qna (cited as: *Office for National Statistics* (2017) Gross Domestic Product).

Office of the Comptroller of the Currency/Board of Governors of the Federal Reserve/ Federal Deposit Insurance Corporation/Securities and Exchange Commission/ Commodity Futures Trading Commission (2014) Prohibitions and Restrictions on Proprietary Trading and Certain Interests in, and in Relationships With, Hedge Funds and Private Equity Funds, Federal Register, 79:21, 5536 (cited as: *U.S. Agencies* (2014) Final Rule).

PRA (2017) Ring-fenced Bodies (RFBs), Supervisory Statement, SS8/16 (cited as: *PRA* (2017) Ring-fenced Bodies).

PRA (2016) PRA Rulebook: CRR Firms and Non-authorised Persons: Ring Fenced Bodies Instrument 2016, PRA 2016/26 (cited as: *PRA* (2016) PRA Rulebook: Ring Fenced Bodies).

PRA (2016) The Implementation of Ring-Fencing: the PRA's approach to ring-fencing transfer schemes, Statement of Policy, https://www.bankofengland.co.uk/-/media/boe/files/prudential-regulation/statement-of-policy/2016/the-implementation-of-ring-fencing-the-pras-approach-to-ring-fencing-transfer-schemes-sop.pdf?la=en&hash=733EEB4079CB43212D449C0B066BAB87FCCDB18B (cited as: *PRA* (2016) Ring-Fencing Transfer Schemes).

PwC (2016) City of London Corporation Research Report: Total Tax Contribution of UK Financial Services Ninth Edition, https://www.cityoflondon.gov.uk/business/economic-research-and-information/research-publications/Documents/research%202016/total-tax-report-2016.pdf (cited as: *PwC* (2016) Tax Contribution of UK Financial Services).

PwC (2014) AFME: Bank Structural Reform Study, https://www.afme.eu/globalassets/downloads/briefing-calls/bank-structural-reform-study-summary-afme.pdf (cited as: *PwC* (2014) AFME: Bank Structural Reform Study).

PwC (2014) Impact of bank structural reforms in Europe, Report for AFME, https://www.pwc.com/il/he/bankim/assets/pwc-study-impact-of-bank-structural-reform.pdf (cited as: *PwC* (2014) Bank Structural Reforms).

Royal Bank of Scotland (2017) Annual Report 2016, https://investors.rbs.com/~/media/Files/R/RBS-IR/results-center/annual-report-2016.pdf (cited as: *Royal Bank of Scotland* (2017) Annual Report 2016).

Schweizerische Bundesversammlung (2012) Bundesbeschluss über die Genehmigung der Änderungen der Bankenverordnung und der Eigenmittelverordnung (too big to fail) vom 18. September 2012, Bundesblatt 2012, 8395–8396 (cited as: *Bundesversammlung* (2012) Genehmigung Bankenverordnung).

Schweizerische Bundesversammlung (2011) Bundesgesetz über die Banken und Sparkassen (Bankengesetz, BankG) (Stärkung der Stabilität im Finanzsektor; too big to fail), Änderung vom 30. September 2011. https://www.parlament.ch/centers/eparl/curia/2011/20110028/Schlussabstimmungstext%20NS%20D.pdf (cited as: *Bundesversammlung* (2011) Änderung BankG).

Schweizerische Bundesversammlung (2011) Motion Leutenegger Oberholzer: Grossbanken ohne Investment-Banking-Risiko, 11.3895, https://www.parlament.ch/de/ratsbetrieb/suche-curia-vista/geschaeft?AffairId=20113895 (cited as: *Schweizerische Bundesversammlung* (2011) Motion Leutenegger Oberholzer).

Schweizerischer Bundesrat (2017) Bericht des Bundesrates zu den systemrelevanten Banken (Evaluation gemäss Artikel 52 Bankengesetz) vom 28. Juni 2017, Bundesblatt 2017, 4847–4864, https://www.admin.ch/opc/de/federal-gazette/2017/4847.pdf (cited as: *Bundesrat* (2017) Bericht systemrelevante Banken).

Schweizerischer Bundesrat (2016) Verordnung über die Eigenmittel und Risikoverteilung für Banken und Effektenhändler (Eigenmittelverordnung, ERV) Änderung vom 11. Mai 2016, Bundesblatt 2016, 1725–1742 (cited as: *Bundesrat* (2016) Änderung Bankenverordnung).

Schweizerischer Bundesrat (2015) Bericht des Bundesrates „Too big to fail": Evaluation gemäss Artikel 52 Bankengesetz und in Beantwortung der Postulate 11.4185 und 14.3002 vom 18. Februar 2015, Bundesblatt 2015, 1927–1944, https://www.admin.ch/opc/de/federal-gazette/2015/1927.pdf (cited as: *Bundesrat* (2015) Bericht Too Big to Fail).

Schweizerischer Bundesrat (2015) Gesetzesentwurf Fidleg, https://www.newsd.admin.ch/newsd/message/attachments/41567.pdf (cited as *Bundesrat* (2015) Gesetzesentwurf Fidleg).

Schweizerischer Bundesrat (2014) Botschaft zum Finanzmarktinfrastrukturgesetz (FinfraG) vom 3. September 2014, Bundesblatt 2014, 7483–7646 (cited as: *Bundesrat* (2014) Botschaft Finanzmarktinfrastrukturgesetz).

Schweizerischer Bundesrat (2012) Bundesrat setzt Bestimmungen zu „Too big to fail" in Kraft, Press Release, https://www.admin.ch/gov/de/start/dokumentation/medienmitteilungen.msg-id-43419.html (cited as: *Bundesrat* (2012) TBTF Press Release).

Schweizerischer Bundesrat (2012) Botschaft zum Bundesbeschluss über die Genehmigung der Änderungen der Bankenverordnung und der Eigenmittelverordnung (too big to fail) vom 1. Juni 2012, Bundesblatt 2012, 6670–6687 (cited as: *Bundesrat* (2012) Botschaft Bankenverordnung).

Schweizerischer Bundesrat (2012) Botschaft zum Bundesbeschluss über die Genehmigung des 4. Kapitels der Verordnung über die Liquidität der Banken (too big to fail) vom 30. November 2012, Bundesblatt 2012, 9455–9460 (cited as: *Schweizerischer Bundesrat* (2012) Botschaft Liquiditätsverordnung).

Schweizerischer Bundesrat (2011) Entwurf zur Änderung des Bundesgesetz über die Banken und Sparkassen (Bankengesetz, BankG) (Stärkung der Stabilität im Finanzsektor; too big to fail), Bundesgesetzblatt 2011, 4807–4816, https://www.admin.ch/opc/de/federal-gazette/2011/4807.pdf (cited as: *Bundesrat* (2011) Entwurf Bankengesetz).

Schweizerischer Bundesrat (2011) Botschaft zur Änderung des Bankengesetzes (Stärkung der Stabilität im Finanzsektor; too big to fail), Bundesblatt 2011, 4717–4806, https://www.admin.ch/opc/de/federal-gazette/2011/4717.pdf (cited as: *Bundesrat* (2011) Botschaft TBTF).

Schweizerischer Bundesrat (2008) Botschaft zu einem Massnahmenpaket zur Stärkung des schweizerischen Finanzsystems, Bundesblatt 2008, 8943–9002 (cited as: *Bundesrat* (2008) Botschaft Massnahmenpaket schweizerisches Finanzsystem).

Schweizerischer Bundesrat (2002) Botschaft zur Änderung des Bundesgesetzes über die Banken und Sparkassen vom 20. November 2002, Bundesblatt 2002, 8060–8116 (cited as: *Bundesrat* (2002) Botschaft Bankengesetz).

SIF (2017) Swiss financial Centre: Key figures October 2017, https://www.sif.admin.ch/dam/sif/en/dokumente/Zahlen-Fakten/Kennzahlen%20Finanzstandort%20April%202017.pdf.download.pdf/Key%20figures%20Swiss%20financial%20centre%20(october%202017).pdf (cited as: *SIF* (2017) Swiss financial Centre: Key figures).

SNB (2018) Financial Stability Report 2017, https://www.snb.ch/en/mmr/reference/stabrep_2017/source/stabrep_2017.en.pdf (cited as: *SNB* (2018) Financial Stability Report 2017).

SNB (2017) Banks in Switzerland 2016, https://www.snb.ch/en/mmr/reference/banks_2016/source/banks_2016.en.pdf (cited as: *SNB* (2017) Banks in Switzerland).

SNB (2015) Verfügung der Schweizerischen Nationalbank betreffend Systemrelevanz, Medienmitteilung vom 1. September 2015) (cited as: *SNB* (2015) Verfügung Systemrelevanz).

SNB (2014) Verfügung der Schweizerischen Nationalbank betreffend Systemrelevanz, Medienmitteilung vom 13. August 2014) (cited as: *SNB* (2014) Verfügung Systemrelevanz).

SNB (2013) Verfügung der Schweizerischen Nationalbank betreffend Systemrelevanz, Medienmitteilung vom 11. November 2013) (cited as: *SNB* (2013) Verfügung Systemrelevanz).

SNB (2012) Verfügungen der Schweizerischen Nationalbank betreffend Systemrelevanz, Medienmitteilung vom 20. Dezember 2012) (cited as: *SNB* (2012) Verfügungen Systemrelevanz).

TheCityUK (2016) Key Facts about the UK as an International Financial Centre, https://www.thecityuk.com/assets/2016/Reports-PDF/Key-Facts-about-the-uk-as-an-international-financial-centre-2016.pdf (cited as: *TheCityUK* (2016) International Financial Centre).

TheClearingHouse (2016) The Custody Services of Banks, https://www.davispolk.com/files/20160728_tch_white_paper_the_custody_services_of_banks.pdf (cited as: *TheClearingHouse* (2016) Custody Services of Banks).

U.S. Department of the Treasury (2017) A Financial System That Creates Economic Opportunities: Banks and Credit Unions, Report to President Donald J. Trump, Executive Order 13772 on Core Principles for Regulating the United States Financial System, https://www.treasury.gov/press-center/press-releases/Documents/A%20Financial%20System.pdf (cited as: *U.S. Department of the Treasury* (2017) Treasury Report).

U.S. Department of the Treasury (2012) The Financial Crisis Response: In Charts, https://www.treasury.gov/resource-center/data-chart-center/Documents/20120413_FinancialCrisisResponse.pdf (cited as: *U.S. Department of the Treasury* (2012) Financial Crisis Response).

UBS (2018) UBS Switzerland AG: Standalone financial statements and regulatory information for the year ended 31 December 2017. https://www.static-ubs.com/global/en/about_ubs/investor_relations/disclosure-legal-entities/_jcr_content/par/accordionbox_3ac5/linklist_d49c/link_ee9d.1360992460.file/bGluay9wYXRoPS9jb250ZW50L2RhbS9zdGF0aWMvZ2xvYmFsL2ludmVzdG9yX3JlbGF0aW9ucy9hbm51YWwtcmVwb3J0LzIwMTcvdWJzLXN3aXR6ZXJsYW5kLWFnLXN0YW5kYWxvbmUtMzEtMTItMTcucGRm/ubs-switzerland-ag-standalone-31-12-17.pdf (cited as: *UBS* (2018) Standalone financial statements UBS Switzerland AG).

UBS (2018) Annual Report 2017, https://www.ubs.com/global/de/about_ubs/investor_relations/annualreporting/2017/_jcr_content/par/teaserbox_1087569181/teaser/linklist/link.0515972108.file/bGluay9wYXRoPS9jb250ZW50L2RhbS9zdGF0aWMvZ2xvYmFsL2ludmVzdG9yX3JlbGF0aW9ucy9hbm51YWwtcmVwb3J0LzIwMTcvZnVsbC1yZXBvcnQtdWJzLWdyb3VwLWFnLWNvbnNvbGlkYXRlZC0yMDE3LWVuLnBkZg==/full-report-ubs-group-ag-consolidated-2017-en.pdf (cited as: *UBS* (2018) Annual Report 2017).

UBS (2017) UBS Switzerland AG: Standalone financial statements and regulatory information for the year ended 31 December 2016, https://www.ubs.com/global/en/about_ubs/investor_relations/disclosure-legal-entities/_jcr_content/par/accordionbox_3ac5/linklist_a858/link.1875997655.file/bGluay9wYXRoPS9jb250ZW50L2RhbS9zdGF0aWMvZ2xvYmFsL2ludmVzdG9yX3JlbGF0aW9ucy9hbm51YWwtcmVwb3J0LzIwMTYvdWJzLXN3aXR6ZXJsYW5kLWFnLTIwMTYtZW4ucGRm/ubs-switzerland-ag-2016-en.pdf (cited as: *UBS* (2017) Standalone financial statements UBS Switzerland AG).

UBS (2017) Switzerland and UBS: Strong Partners 2017/2018, http://www.ubs.com/content/dam/static/epaper/index.html?id=253a09e3 (cited as: *UBS* (2017) Switzerland and UBS).

UBS (2017) Annual Report 2016, https://www.ubs.com/global/en/about_ubs/investor_relations/annualreporting/2016/_jcr_content/par/teaserbox_f1a7/teaser/linklist/link_a6d4.0036442955.file/bGluay9wYXRoPS9jb250ZW50L2RhbS9zdGF0aWMvZ2xvYmFsL2ludmVzdG9yX3JlbGF0aW9ucy9hbm51YWwtcmVwb3J0LzIwMTYvdWJzLWdyb3VwLTIwMTYtZW4ucGRm/ubs-group-2016-en.pdf (cited as: *UBS* (2017) Annual Report 2016).

UBS (2017) Annual Report 2016 SEC Form 20-F, https://www.static-ubs.com/global/de/about_ubs/investor_relations/annualreporting/2016/_jcr_content/par/columncontrol/col1/linklist/link.0890637089.file/bGluay9wYXRoPS9jb250ZW50L2RhbS9zdGF0aWMvZ2xvYmFsL2ludmVzdG9yX3JlbGF0aW9ucy9hbm51YWwtcmVwb3J0LzIwMTYvc2VjLWZvcm0tMjAtZi0yMDE2LnBkZg==/sec-form-20-f-2016.pdf (cited as: *UBS* (2017) 2016 SEC Form 20-F).

UBS (2016) Annual Report 2015, https://www.ubs.com/global/de/about_ubs/investor_relations/annualreporting/2015/_jcr_content/par/columncontrol/col1/linklist/link_0.1939044028.file/bGluay9wYXRoPS9jb250ZW50L2RhbS9zdGF0aWMvZ2xvYmFsL2ludmVzdG9yX3JlbGF0aW9ucy9hbm51YWwtcmVwb3J0LzIwMTUvdWJzLWdyb3VwLWFuZC11YnMtYWctMjAxNS1lbi5wZGY=/ubs-group-and-ubs-ag-2015-en.pdf (cited as: *UBS* (2016) Annual Report 2015).

Worldbank (2018) Global Financial Developments Report: Bankers without borders, https://openknowledge.worldbank.org/bitstream/handle/10986/28482/9781464811487.pdf?sequence=11&isAllowed=y (cited as: *Worldbank* (2018) Global Financial Developments Report).

Worldbank (2017) Global Financial Development Database, http://www.worldbank.org/en/publication/gfdr/data/global-financial-development-database (cited as: *Worldbank* (2017) Global Financial Development Database).

Z/Yen Group/China Development Institute (2017) The Global Financial Centres Index 22, http://www.longfinance.net/images/GFCI22_Report.pdf (cited as: *Z/Yen Group/China Development Institute* (2017) GFCI Nr. 22).

Z/Yen Group/China Development Institute (2014) The Global Financial Centres Index 16, http://www.longfinance.net/images/GFCI16_22September2014.pdf (cited as: *Z/Yen Group/China Development Institute* (2014) GFCI Nr. 16).

Z/Yen Group/China Development Institute (2010) The Global Financial Centres Index 8, http://www.zyen.com/GFCI/GFCI%208.pdf (cited as: *Z/Yen Group/China Development Institute* (2010) GFCI Nr. 8).

ZEW (2013) Trennbanken: Eine analytische Bewertung von Trennbankenelementen und Trennbankensystemen im Hinblick auf Finanzmarkstabilität, Abschlussbericht für den Bundesverband Öffentlicher Banken, https://www.voeb.de/download/zew-studie-gesamt.pdf (cited as: *ZEW* (2013) Trennbanken).

III.Press Articles

Baches, Pionierprojekt einer Grossbank, NZZ (June 26, 2015).

Barker, Banking groups push Brussels to ditch overhaul of big lenders, Financial Times (November 23, 2014).

Barker, EU bank reforms set out to reduce complexity and curb speculation, Financial Times (January 29, 2014).

Barker, EU finance ministers back drive to tackle 'too big to fail' banks, Financial Times (June 19, 2015).

Barker, EU's Hill considers shelving bank structural reforms, Financial Times (December 4, 2014).

Barker, Europe set to ease reform on bank splits, Financial Times (January 5, 2014).

Binham/Dunkley, Banks win fresh concession on ringfencing rules, Financial Times (October 15, 2015).

Binham/Dunkley, Regulators get ready to authorise 'ringfenced' UK banks, Financial Times (August 19, 2017).

Brush/Glover, Banks Win as EU Scraps Proposal to Split Off Trading Units, Bloomberg (October 25, 2017).

Buhayar, Trump May Ax Volcker Rule, Ease Banks' Burden First, Whalen Says, Bloomberg, (November 10, 2016).

Cassidy, The Volcker Rule: Obama's economic adviser and his battles over the financial-reform bill, The New Yorker (July 26, 2010).

Cooper, Obama Signs Overhaul of Financial System, New York Times, (July 21, 2010).

Croff, High Court approves Barclays ringfencing plan, Financial Times (March 9, 2018).

Dexheimer, Volcker Rule Change Backed in House Panel's Dodd-Frank Remedy, Bloomberg (March 21, 2018).

Dunkley/Binham, Banks risk missing 2019 ringfence deadline, Financial Times (January 8, 2017).

Financial Times, Deutsche Bank and Credit Suisse pay billions to settle US probe (December 23, 2016).

Financial Times, EU sets out vision for safer banking: Liikanen report on structural reforms is a promising start (October 3, 2012).

Financial Times, Ringfencing will help in the next banking crisis (January 10, 2017).

Fontevecchia, Dimon's Volcker Rule Contradiction: On Hedging, Prop Trading, And The London Whale, Forbes (June 13, 2012).

Gribben, 'Wonderkid' and old girl form part of Sir John Vickers' Banking Commission team, The Telegraph (April 11, 2011).

Hamilton, Trump Watchdog Tells Banks He Really, Really Likes Them, Bloomberg (April 9, 2018).

Hässig, Finma stellt sich gegen CS-Pläne, Tages Anzeiger (May 11, 2016).

Hegglin, Die CS Schweiz in Halbgefangenschaft, Finanz und Wirtschaft (September 6, 2016).

Imwinkelried, Doch kein Börsengang der Schweizer Einheit, NZZ (April 26, 2017).

Jenkins, Ringfencing will make it harder to wind up failing banks, The Financial Times (January 29, 2014).

Jenkins/Barker, Big banks face hardest hit from ringfencing, Financial Times (October 2, 2012).

Johnson, Resurrecting Glass-Steagall, Project Syndicate: The World's Opinion Page (October 25, 2015).

Jones, European Central Bank's marathon man moves to front of the pack, Financial Times (April 3, 2018).

Jones, Stand-off traps EU's 'too big to fail' bank reform in limbo, Reuters (October 26, 2016).

Lallemand, Bank Reforms will help lift Europe's struggling economy, Financial Times (November 26, 2014).

Macalister, Revealed: Goldman Sachs 'made fortune betting against clients', The Guardian (April 25, 2010).

Martin, Bank of England admits lenders face 'tight deadline' for ring-fencing, The Telegraph (June 16, 2017).

Millischer/Heim, Milliardenabflüsse bei der UBS Schweiz, Handelszeitung (March 31, 2016).

Mont, Push for Volcker rule reforms gains momentum, Compliance Week (April 16, 2018).

Moshinski, EU Bank-Structure Rules Falter with Parliament Divided, Bloomberg (May 26, 2015).

Nijdam, Need for sustainable prosperity comes first, Financial Times (October 15, 2015).

Oudéa, Europe needs homegrown bulge bracket banks, Financial Times (October 11, 2015).

Padevit, CS: Schweizer Tochter wird am 20. November geboren, Finanz und Wirtschaft (October 7, 2016).

Rankin, UK's European Commissioner quits in wake of Brexit vote, The Guardian (June 25, 2016).

Reid, We were wrong about universal banking, Financial Times (November 11, 2015).

Reuters, Fitch Assigns UBS Switzerland AG 'A' IDR; Affirms UBS AG at 'A' (June 15, 2015).

Reuters, Fitch Upgrades UBS Group to 'A+'; UBS AG and UBS Switzerland to 'AA-' (September 28, 2017).

Reuters, Highlights – Bank of England's Carney speaks on UK banking risks (November 30, 2016).

Reuters, Trump calls for '21st century' Glass-Steagall banking law (October 26, 2016).

Schöchli, "Wir werden bis Ende 2018 bereit sein", NZZ (June 20, 2015).

Schöchli, Das Drehbuch für die nächste Krise, NZZ (June 6, 2017).

Schöchli, Der lange Weg der Notfallplanung, NZZ (June 6, 2012).

Schultz, US Regierung gegen Deutsche Bank: Der 14 Milliarden-Schock, Der Spiegel (September 16, 2016).

The Economist, Bernie Sanders's obsession with Glass-Steagall is misplaced (February 18, 2016).

The Economist, The Liikanen Review: Into the ring (October 6, 2012).

The Economist, What structural reform is and why it is important (December 9, 2014).

Tracy/Carney, How to Kill the Volcker Rule? Don't Enforce It, Wall Street Journal (November 28, 2016).

Volcker, How to Reform Our Financial System, The New York Times (January 30, 2010).

Weber, EU Bank-Breakup Push Still 'Locked' After Dombrovskis Effort, Bloomberg (October 25, 2016).

Wolf, Liikanen is at least a step forward for EU banks, Financial Times (October 4, 2012).

IV. Internet Sources

BaFin, Supervision of financial conglomerates and groups, (January 01, 2016), https://www.bafin.de/EN/Aufsicht/VersichererPensionsfonds/FinanzkonglomerateGruppen/gruppenaufsicht_artikel_en.html

British Bankers' Association/Federation Bancaire Francaise, Letter to Frans Timmermans, First Vice President Better Regulation, Interinstitutional Relations, the Rule of Law and Charter of Fundamental Rights, (November 13, 2014) http://www.fbf.fr/fr/files/9R6M5Q/Letter-EU-Structural-Reform-Better-Regulation.pdf

Council of the EU, Structural reform of EU banking sector: improving the resilience of credit institutions, http://www.consilium.europa.eu/en/policies/banking-structural-reform/

Deutscher Bundestag, Gesetz zur Abschirmung von Risiken und zur Planung der Sanierung und Abwicklung von Kreditinstituten und Finanzgruppen, http://dipbt.bundestag.de/extrakt/ba/WP17/508/50871.html

EBA, Large exposures and structural measures, https://www.eba.europa.eu/regulation-and-policy/large-exposures

EBA, Large Institutions with a leverage ratio exposure measure above 200bn EUR, http://www.eba.europa.eu/risk-analysis-and-data/global-systemically-important-institutions/2017

ECB, Number of monetary financial institutions (MFIs) in the non-participating Member States: December 2016, https://www.ecb.europa.eu/stats/ecb_statistics/escb/html/table.en.html?id=JDF_MFI_MFI_LIST_NEA&period=2016-12

ECB, Number of monetary financial institutions (MFIs) in the non-participating Member States: December 2015, https://www.ecb.europa.eu/stats/ecb_statistics/escb/html/table.en.html?id=JDF_MFI_MFI_LIST_NEA&period=2015-12.

Escow, 5 Reasons Glass-Steagall Matters, (November 16, 2015) https://berniesanders.com/yes-glass-steagall-matters-here-are-5-reasons-why/

ESMA, Securities Financing Transactions, https://www.esma.europa.eu/sections/securities-financing-transactions

EUR-Lex, Procedure 2014/0020/COD, http://eur-lex.europa.eu/procedure/DE/2014_20

European Banking Authority, Large exposures and structural measures, https://www.eba.europa.eu/regulation-and-policy/large-exposures

European Commission, Jonathan Hill, http://ec.europa.eu/commission/2014-2019/hill_en

European Commission, State Aid Scoreboard 2017, http://ec.europa.eu/competition/state_aid/scoreboard/index_en.html

European Parliament, 2014/0020(COD), http://www.europarl.europa.eu/oeil/popups/ficheprocedure.do?lang=en&reference=2014/0020(OLP)

European Parliament, 2017/2072(INI), http://www.europarl.europa.eu/sides/getDoc.do?pubRef=-//EP//TEXT+CRE+20180301+ITEM-002+DOC+XML+V0//EN&language=EN

European Parliament, Banking Structural Reform, (February 20, 2018), http://www.europarl.europa.eu/legislative-train/theme-deeper-and-fairer-internal-market-with-a-strengthened-industrial-base-financial-services/file-banking-structural-reform

European Parliament, Seats by Political Group, http://www.europarl.europa.eu/meps/en/hemicycle.html

Eurostat, Employment by A*10 industry breakdowns, (January 31, 2018), http://appsso.eurostat.ec.europa.eu/nui/show.do?query=BOOKMARK_DS-406759_QID_-48796ABF_UID_-3F171EB0&layout=NACE_R2,B,X,0;TIME,C,X,1;GEO,L,Y,0;UNIT,L,Z,0;NA_ITEM,L,Z,1;INDICATORS,C,Z,2;&zSelection=DS-406759NA_ITEM,EMP_DC;DS-406759UNIT,PC_TOT_PER;DS-406759INDICATORS,OBS_FLAG;&rankName1=UNIT_1_2_-1_2&rankName2=INDICATORS_1_2_-1_2&rankName3=NA-ITEM_1_2_-1_2&rankName4=NACE-R2_1_2_0_0&rankName5=TIME_1_0_1_0&rankName6=GEO_1_2_0_1&rStp=&cStp=&rDCh=&cDCh=&rDM=true&cDM=true&footnes=false&empty=false&wai=false&time_mode=NONE&time_most_recent=false&lang=EN&cfo=%23%23%23%2C%23%23%23.%23%23%23

Eurostat, Gross value added and income by A*10 industry breakdowns, (January 31, 2018), http://appsso.eurostat.ec.europa.eu/nui/show.do?query=BOOKMARK_DS-406765_QID_-4FCE2BB0_UID_-3F171EB0&layout=NACE_R2,B,X,0;TIME,C,X,1;GEO,L,Y,0;UNIT,L,Z,0;NA_ITEM,L,Z,1;INDICATORS,C,Z,2;&zSelection=DS-406765NA_ITEM,B1G;DS-406765UNIT,PC_TOT;DS-406765INDICATORS,OBS_FLAG;&rankName1=UNIT_1_2_-1_2&rankName2=INDICATORS_1_2_-1_2&rankName3=NA-ITEM_1_2_-1_2&rankName4=NACE-R2_1_2_0_0&rankName5=TIME_1_0_1_0&rankName6=GEO_1_2_0_1&rStp=&cStp=&rDCh=&cDCh=&rDM=true&cDM=true&footnes=false&empty=false&wai=false&time_mode=NONE&time_most_recent=false&lang=EN&cfo=%23%23%23%2C%23%23%23.%23%23%23

FCA, About the FCA/PRA, https://register.fca.org.uk/

Finance Watch, Too-big-to-regulate: The EU's bank structural reform proposal failed, (October 25, 2017), http://www.finance-watch.org/press/press-releases/1468

Finma, Enforcement division, https://www.finma.ch/en/finma/organisation/finma-s-divisions/enforcement-division/

Finma, Branches of Foreign Banks, https://www.finma.ch/en/authorisation/banks-and-securities-dealers/getting-licensed/branches-of-foreign-banks/

Finma, Recovery and resolution planning for systemically important banks, https://www.finma.ch/en/supervision/banks-and-securities-dealers/supervisory-instruments/recovery-and-resolution-planning/

Helin-Villes, The withdrawal of the Bank Structural Reform file marks an unfortunate turning point in the European agenda on regulating large banks, say S&Ds, (October 25, 2017), http://www.socialistsanddemocrats.eu/newsroom/withdrawal-bank-structural-reform-file-marks-unfortunate-turning-point-european-agenda

Hill, Letter to Frans Timmermans, (November 18, 2014) http://www.eunews.it/wp-content/uploads/2014/12/Letter-to-VP-Timmermans_Hill.pdf

Hill, Speech at Chatham House, the Royal Institute of International Affairs, Speech by Commissioner Hill, (June 9, 2016) https://ec.europa.eu/commission/commissioners/2014-2019/hill/announcements/commissioner-hills-speech-chatham-house-royal-institute-international-affairs_en

HM Treasury, EU referendum: 6 reasons why the EU is good for financial services jobs (Archived), (May 12, 2016), https://www.gov.uk/government/news/eu-referendum-6-reasons-why-the-eu-is-good-for-financial-services-jobs

Hogan, Bank Ring Fencing Edges Closer in Europe, KPMG Insights, (June 28, 2015), https://home.kpmg.com/xx/en/home/insights/2015/06/bank-ring-fencing-edges-closer.html.

Hökmark, Commission withdraws proposal on Banking Structural Reform (BSR), (October 24, 2017), http://hokmark.eu/commission-withdraws-proposal-on-banking-structural-reform-bsr/

PRA, Enforcement, (March 21, 2018) https://www.fca.org.uk/about/enforcement

PRA, Which firms does the PRA regulate?, https://www.bankofengland.co.uk/prudential-regulation/authorisations/which-firms-does-the-pra-regulate

Reich, Hillary Clinton's Glass-Steagall, (July 14, 2015) http://robertreich.org/post/124114229225

SIX Swiss Exchange, Liste der Market Maker, Aktive ETFs, https://www.six-swiss-exchange.com/funds/active_etf/marketmaker_list_de.html

SIX Swiss Exchange, Liste der Market Maker, Passive ETFs, https://www.six-swiss-exchange.com/funds/etf/marketmaker_list_de.html

SNB, Chronicle of monetary events 1848–2017, https://www.snb.ch/en/iabout/snb/hist/id/hist_wpc#t14

SNB, Dataportal, https://data.snb.ch/en/topics/banken#!/doc/

SNB, Notes on the Banking Statistics, (September 28, 2017), https://data.snb.ch/en/topics/banken#!/doc/explanations_banken

Thomson Reuters Practical Law, PRA Rulebook, supervisory statements and other supervisory material, https://uk.practicallaw.thomsonreuters.com/5-573-3805?__lrTS=20171230004551129&transitionType=Default&contextData=(sc.Default)&firstPage=true&bhcp=1.

UBS, Switzerland and UBS: Strong Partners 2017/2018, http://www.ubs.com/content/dam/static/epaper/index.html?id=253a09e3

Worldbank, GDP (current US$), https://data.worldbank.org/indicator/NY.GDP.MKTP.CD